Beethoven

ALSO BY JOHN CLUBBE

BOOKS

Victorian Forerunner: The Later Career of Thomas Hood
English Romanticism: The Grounds of Belief (with Ernest J. Lovell, Jr.)
Byron et la Suisse: deux études (with Ernest Giddey)
Cincinnati Observed: Architecture and History
Byron, Sully, and the Power of Portraiture

EDITED VOLUMES

Selected Poems of Thomas Hood
Two Reminiscences of Thomas Carlyle
Carlyle and His Contemporaries
Froude's Life of Carlyle

COEDITED WORKS

The Collected Letters of Thomas and Jane Welsh Carlyle, volumes 1–9
Victorian Perspectives (with Jerome Meckier)

Beethoven

THE RELENTLESS REVOLUTIONARY

JOHN CLUBBE

W. W. NORTON & COMPANY

Independent Publishers Since 1923

New York | London

For information about permission to reproduce selections from this book, write to
Permissions, W. W. Norton & Company, Inc., 500 Fifth Avenue, New York, NY 10110

For information about special discounts for bulk purchases, please contact
W. W. Norton Special Sales at specialsales@wwnorton.com or 800-233-4830

Manufacturing by LSC Harrisonburg
Book design by Chris Welch Design
Production manager: Julia Druskin

Library of Congress Cataloging-in-Publication Data

Names: Clubbe, John, author.
Title: Beethoven : the relentless revolutionary / John Clubbe.
Description: First edition. | New York : W. W. Norton & Company, [2019] | Includes
bibliographical references and index.
Identifiers: LCCN 2018061106 | ISBN 9780393242553 (hardcover)
Subjects: LCSH: Beethoven, Ludwig van, 1770–1827—Criticism and interpretation.
| Music—Political aspects—History—18th century. | Music—Political aspects—
History—19th century.
Classification: LCC ML410.B42 C55 2019 | DDC 780.92—dc23
LC record available at https://lccn.loc.gov/2018061106

W. W. Norton & Company, Inc., 500 Fifth Avenue, New York, N.Y. 10110
www.wwnorton.com

W. W. Norton & Company Ltd., 15 Carlisle Street, London W1D 3BS

1 2 3 4 5 6 7 8 9 0

For Joan

CONTENTS

OVERTURE

To us Beethoven *is* the Revolution.
HUGH OTTAWAY[1]

Beethoven revolutionized the world of music—taking what music was in his time, and revealing what it could become. He was also, importantly, a *political* revolutionary—in his unique way, a true heir of the French Revolution. This study presents Beethoven within the context of the revolutionary era that followed, through which he lived and during which he composed his astonishing and overwhelming music. It also places Beethoven alongside contemporary literary and artistic figures. It offers a new approach to the composer's heroic striving, his equally heroic despair, and his messianic mission to improve through music the world both of his own time and of times to come.

Beethoven's music thus reflects both the turmoil of the age in which he lived and no less the turmoil within himself. As he matured, he affirmed ever more passionately the ideals in which he believed. By focusing on the revolutionary origins of his music, itself a response to the revolutionary age in which he lived, we enter into the heart of his genius. For listeners, past and present, who have yearned for political and social change, Beethoven's music has been and remains an inspiration. Placing Beethoven in the foreground of his era brings us closer, I believe, to a true evaluation of the man and his creativity. Though roughly chronological, my chapters can be regarded as a series of studies taking up interrelated ideas and themes. This method, as much an interpretation of Beethoven as biography, allows me to explore aspects of Beethoven's genius hitherto neglected.

We may never fully fathom the mystery of Beethoven's phenomenal range of creativity, but attempts at understanding it happily continue. Nor can we fully determine the role of the French Revolution in shaping him politically and creatively. Beyond doubt it exerted far greater stimuli than has been recognized. Through his compositions of the 1790s Beethoven took part, admittedly from afar, in the ongoing revolution that had begun in France in 1789 and whose ideals soon crossed European borders. The Revolution exerted a lifelong influence upon Beethoven's thinking—and his creativity. It offered no less than a new path for humankind to follow. In 1792 Beethoven moved from Bonn to Vienna, the music capital of the largest absolutist and repressive state within Europe. Usually but not always he had to remain verbally silent on political issues. Yet through his revolutionary music he began to serve as a leader in the German-speaking world.

Is regarding Beethoven as a revolutionary such a radical claim? If we contemplate past composers within the context of the musical world of their day, was not Bach a revolutionary? Gluck? Haydn? Mozart? And, subsequent to Beethoven, weren't Wagner, Mahler, Schoenberg, Ives, and Cage revolutionaries? Can we not also say the same of creative geniuses in fields other than music? Were not Jefferson, Wordsworth, Byron, Goya, Joyce, Cézanne, Marie Curie, Mies van der Rohe, Einstein, along with others in their respective fields, also revolutionaries? Did they not change the way their contemporaries and those who came after them perceived the world? It seems necessary to explore Beethoven's genius within the profound effect the French Revolution had on him, first in Bonn, then in Vienna.

Beethoven's spectrum of compositions, from the early cantatas for Joseph II and Leopold II to the late Ninth Symphony, teems with revolutionary sentiment. Works of astounding dimensions in between— the *Eroica* Symphony, *Fidelio*, the Fourth and Fifth Piano Concertos, the music for Goethe's drama *Egmont*—incarnate his revolutionary approach. In the structure of their composition, in their sonorities, their rhythms, their treatment of the rules of harmony, in his conception of them as a body, Beethoven wanted his music to help bring about a world renewed. He composed his startling works fully aware he faced in Vienna a government vigorously hostile to revolutionary ideas. Still, by imposing upon Viennese music lovers his new appreciation of how to listen to music, he did not hesitate to challenge the status quo. The emerging political climate helped shape Beethoven's vision of an ideal republic and its social relationships.

Western music reached a high point in the half century from 1779 to 1828. The period begins with the mature works of Mozart and Haydn and closes with the death of Beethoven in 1827 and of Schubert a year later. As well, Beethoven lived in a formative period of European history, one marked by huge societal and intellectual changes fueled by the Revolution. From the first the composer responded vigorously to the new currents stirring around him. Admittedly, the wealth of his ideas could create disturbing music. Lenin a century later would fear the power of this music. Over the past two hundred years Beethoven's genius has elicited far more positive than negative political responses. To elucidate Beethoven's life and creativity within the context of the times, I bring in a number of leading contemporaries, among them Goethe and Schiller, Hegel and Fichte, Chateaubriand and Byron, Goya and Kleist, as well as a host of others whose achievements shed light upon Beethoven's. Asked why he put aside his work on other composers to focus exclusively on Beethoven, Romain Rolland, the French Nobel Prize–winning author and Beethoven biographer, replied that the more he thought about Beethoven, the more he "remains unfathomable to

me."[2] That many still find the composer unfathomable gives evidence
of a complex greatness.

ঽ

No less than the Revolution did Beethoven ponder the equally unfathomable figure of Napoleon Bonaparte. Scholars have trod lightly on the
composer's absorption in the career and exploits of this genius. Napoleon, born a year before Beethoven, serves as a key to understanding
his life. Both were geniuses, though of different kinds. Both embodied
a new concept of greatness. When inspired, they moved with relentless speed, Napoleon in his campaigns, Beethoven in his compositions.
General Bonaparte made a dramatic arrival upon the European scene in
1796, when he blazoned forth with a string of dazzling victories in Italy.
His initial successes inspired in Beethoven a fertile emulation: he envisaged his career in music equivalent to Napoleon's on the battlefield. He
would match Napoleon's military, strategic, and political triumphs with
equally resonant triumphs in music.

Napoleon helped shape Beethoven's subsequent development. Works
influenced by him are not limited to one or two time periods in the
composer's career but stretch over several decades. Beethoven regarded
Napoleon as the inheritor and embodiment of the French Revolution,
even as a forerunner of still greater figures and revolutions to come. A
new Prometheus forging a society of republics, Napoleon incarnated an
ancient ideal of freedom, an ideal that animated those seeking to throw
off the yoke of absolutism. In Napoleon, Beethoven perceived a promise
of liberty for Europe. Later, as political repression in Austria increased
and Napoleon failed to hold Europe together, Beethoven had to shackle
his dreams.

ঽ

This study is not a full-scale life-and-times of Beethoven, of which there
are no lack, but an attempt to set the composer within the context of

the political events and human energy swirling around him during the decades of his maturity, from 1790 to 1827. Prometheus Unbound, alias Beethoven, intended his music not only for his contemporaries but also for future generations, for us. Instead of detailed interpretations of Beethoven's considerable oeuvre I have restricted myself to discussing a few of the compositions that embody Beethoven's revolutionary thinking. I focus on historical context, expression, style, and meaning. Much as I respect the work of musicologists, my own approach to Beethoven is through cultural history. Though I hope this book will interest professional students of music, I focus on Beethoven within the social and political life of his time. I intend its argument to appeal to the many who love his music.

Born in 1770, the same year as the poet William Wordsworth and the philosopher Hegel, and a year after the explorer and naturalist Alexander von Humboldt and Napoleon, Beethoven responded early on to the fresh new winds from France. For someone not yet nineteen when the Revolution exploded in Paris, the event opened up a larger European world for him and his contemporaries, as they witnessed a monarchy topple in France, though not elsewhere.

For the thesis of this book—that Beethoven was a "revolutionary"— I cannot claim originality. It was the Austrian emperor Franz I, Beethoven's almost exact contemporary, who coined for posterity that most accurate one-word definition of the composer and the music he created. Franz did not intend it as a compliment. No more damning word could he find for either Beethoven or his creations. He never met the man and cannot have known much about his music, for he avoided concerts in which it was played. But he sensed, rightly, that both man and music embodied a passion for revolutionary ideas. Richard Wagner, himself a revolutionary and one who would man the barricades (in Dresden in 1848), also referred to Beethoven as a revolutionary. But whereas Emperor Franz intended denigration, Wagner meant high praise. "Progress and freedom" became Beethoven's watchwords. But the Hapsburgs responded to neither. They sought the opposite: stagnation and repression. Life in an absolutist state, we must never forget, differs from life elsewhere.

That was brought home to me long ago when I spent time in such an absolutist state—two actually. I visited Russia in 1961, where a person at a desk on each floor of my hotels in Leningrad (now St. Petersburg) and Moscow kept track of my comings and goings. Five years later, having research in Weimar to do, I drove my little Austin Cooper through what was then East Germany, meandering along pocked roads from Checkpoint Charlie in Berlin down to the Czech border. In this somewhat tense journey the police must have stopped me at least thirty times to ask to see my papers. Both experiences were for weeks only, not, as was Beethoven's, for most of his adult years. But those weeks left me aware how greatly an absolutist state differs from a democratic one. Under a totalitarian system it is easier to impose or increase tyranny than it is to achieve freedom, for the simple reason that the forces of tyranny are usually better organized than those of freedom. Though Beethoven found that out soon enough after he moved to Vienna, the knowledge never dissuaded him from subsequently advocating freedom wherever he was and in whatever ways he could. My experience also brought home to me that political systems can determine the orientation of books. During the more than four decades of the Berlin Wall, East German writings on Beethoven often differed greatly in social and political orientation from those in West Germany. Whereas West German scholars focused more on the works than on the life and times, their East German counterparts often interpreted Beethoven within a socialist or Marxist context. Presumably they had to.

With Beethoven it is, some will say, primarily the music, less so the life, that commands attention. I do not disagree, but as overwhelming as is that music, it emerged from a living human being, someone who constantly dealt with complex professional, personal, social, and political issues. I find understanding the man as challenging as under-

standing the music. Though not a believer in human or societal per-
fectibility, Beethoven had a strong utopian strain. The ultimate utopia,
he believed, exists within the mind or spirit. Beethoven's interior life
must have been truly extraordinary. Full of puzzles and mysteries, it
demands continued exploration. To do this I examine in detail three of
his portraits for what they tell us about his thinking at different times
in his life. I also introduce several figures who have rarely appeared
in studies of Beethoven, but who left a lasting impact upon his being:
among them, the Roman hero Lucius Junius Brutus, founder of the
long-lived Roman Republic, and Beethoven's near contemporary, the
Saxon writer Johann Gottfried Seume, for what he can tell us about
Beethoven's response to the revolutionary world in which Seume and
the composer lived. This attempt to comprehend Beethoven within the
larger European scene in which he found himself has constituted a
chief pleasure in writing *Beethoven: The Relentless Revolutionary*. I hope
readers will discover in it an afterglow of that pleasure.

The book interprets Beethoven as a revolutionary not only in his
music but also, and not least, in his social and political thinking. I place
the composer within a larger European context. Focusing on societal
and political issues, on what Beethoven read or saw or heard (as long as
he could hear), I leave out with regret much in regard to his personal life
and to his creativity in order to focus on a few key works, among them
the early cantatas, the *Death of Joseph II* and the *Accession of Leopold II*;
the song "The Free Man" (Der freie Mann); Beethoven's variations on
Handel's "See the conqu'ring hero comes"; the *Eroica* and *Fidelio;* the
Fifth Symphony and Fifth Piano Concerto; the music for *Egmont*; public
compositions for the Congress of Vienna (1814–15); and later, the *Missa
solemnis* and the Ninth Symphony. More than any other composer then
alive, Beethoven's music reflects the spirit and substance of the new,
radically altered world that came into being with the French Revolution
and, subsequent to that event, the rise of Napoleon and the Europe that
evolved under his aegis and in his wake.

ᕯ

Most post–World War II biographies of Beethoven in English, and to a
lesser degree in other languages, have been written by musicologists
for other musicologists. Beethoven scholarship in America today is
very much an in-house enterprise controlled by university academics.
Yet musicologists comprise only a small percentage of those who love
Beethoven's music and desire to learn more about it and the man who
wrote it. From the mid-nineteenth century on, nonspecialists as well as
specialists have found it fascinating to learn about the richness of his
genius and the trials of his life. Earlier studies of Beethoven written for
the general public can in this regard be more pleasurable to read than
later ones.

Beethoven's music continues to enthrall many. Should it not challenge those who wish to understand it in ways they can grasp? Though
I hope this study will be of interest to music professionals, I have presented my perspective on Beethoven so as to be accessible to lay readers.
What this strategy offers is a way for those who are interested to enjoy
his music within the context of the composer's times, as well as to ponder how it relates to (and enhances) their own.

This book presupposes that prospective readers have an interest in
Beethoven's life, the world in which he came to maturity, as well as
an awareness of his music. I hope for readers willing to approach that
music with an inquisitive mind, to think through for themselves what
they like about it, what it might mean. They can do this even for the
works they don't enjoy as much. As must surely be evident by now, I am
not a musicologist. Trained chiefly in history and literature, with excursions into art and European languages, I think of myself as a cultural
historian. Exploring the era in which Beethoven lived from the perspective of cultural history—especially Enlightenment and revolutionary
history, literature, and art—I found myself repeatedly amazed by the
energy of the man and the vastness of his genius. The political and

societal events that took place during Beethoven's lifetime stagger the imagination. In this book I have probed his responses to key moments, explored his social and political perspectives, and interpreted the music he wrote to present it as inseparable from his interaction with the currents of life swirling about him.

Beethoven

1

Beethoven in Bonn

What can I know? What should I do? What may I hope?

IMMANUEL KANT

Early Years

Apart from his mother, young Beethoven valued most his Flemish grandfather and namesake, who became, at least in memory, his closest friend and protector, who he remembered watched over him as a child. The elder Beethoven's death, shortly after Ludwig's third birthday, affected him deeply. Years after he had moved to Vienna he asked a friend in Bonn, Franz Wegeler, to send him the portrait of his grandfather most likely done by Leopold Radoux in 1770.[1] It had great meaning for him and remained a treasured possession until his death. The Flemish "van" in Beethoven's name is not the equivalent of the German "von," which requires a patent of nobility (as Beethoven in Vienna later learned to his regret), but a simple preposition, "of," indicating place of origin. Grandfather Beethoven had been born in Malines, now Belgium, but then part of the Austrian Netherlands, an integral unit of the far-flung and loosely federated Hapsburg empire. In 1740 the musically gifted Ludwig emigrated to the small city of Bonn on the Rhine to join the lively musical scene at the court of Maximillian Friedrich, elector of Cologne, which actually was based in nearby Bonn. Eventually he rose to the position of Kapellmeister, leader of the court orchestra. Ludwig married and had one son, Johann, born three years after his move. In 1767 this son married Maria Magdalena Keverich of Ehrenbreitstein, a village upriver from Bonn. A son born to the couple in 1769, Ludwig Maria, died shortly thereafter. A second son, named after his deceased older brother, likely came into the world on December 16, 1770. No record of his birth exists, but infants then usually underwent baptism the day after they were born. The parents, and in later years Beethoven himself, sometimes confused his own birth year with his brother's. Of the five other children born subsequently, only the next two, both boys, Kaspar Karl and Nikolaus Johann, survived to maturity.

Germany at this time was a linguistic unit, not a nation. It embraced a multiplicity of states and political systems and even, unlike Italy on the other side of the Alps, a religious schism. Bonn, with approximately ten thousand inhabitants inside the city walls, was mostly Catholic. Despite its relatively small size it was a lively cosmopolitan center, progressive-minded and culturally vibrant. Located on the middle Rhine at a crossroads of the new ideas circulating throughout Europe, it had a flourishing Flemish community as well as a number of Italian residents. "Niederländer" was the usual term used for families like the Beethovens. Apparently some contemporaries looked upon the grandfather as a Dutchman of sorts. Like most people of his generation, Beethoven little realized that in a few years the old order in which he spent his youth would soon be changed utterly.

Bonn lay at the center of a variegated landscape of scenic beauty, cultural depth, and considerable economic vitality. It had (and has) in places some of the most lovely riverine scenery in Europe. With the Rhine serving as a major transportation corridor, cities along its edge are closer together than elsewhere in Germany. Across the Rhine, south of Bonn and visible on clear days, are the Seven Hills (*Siebengebirge*), a picturesque region crowned with ruined castles and full of folk and medieval legends. Further to the south, at the confluence of the Rhine and the Moselle, lies Coblenz, which after 1789 would become a major base for nobles fleeing the Revolution in France. Downriver, within easy reach of Bonn, is Cologne, originally the Roman empire's most easterly outpost and one of Germany's oldest cities, in medieval times its largest. It served as the great entrepôt of the Rhine, where goods left the river for transport overland to Holland and Flanders.

Encircled by ramparts in Beethoven's day, Bonn crowded its inhabitants into an area only a few streets wide. To cross from one side to the other on foot took less than fifteen minutes. Beethoven was born in a house (now the city's Beethoven Museum) on the Bonngasse, but grew up on the Rheingasse, no longer in existence, in a dwelling whose back faced the river. Today's swiftly flowing stream, now in large part canalized, was then more meandering and slower moving. Outside the front door of the Rheingasse house a lively street life greeted the growing boy, with neighbors scrubbing the cobblestones clean and chatting with each other as horses and coaches clattered by.

There were seven electors throughout the vast Austrian realm who were allowed to choose the emperor, four of them ecclesiastics. Persons of considerable importance, the electors exercised complete secular power over their realms. They were in fact princes, and they behaved like princes. The French monarchs had numerous imitators in the German lands, and some of them built palaces almost as ambitious as that of Versailles.

In culture as well as in politics Bonn took its lead less from nearby Cologne than from Vienna, the distant Hapsburg capital. At that time, in musical matters the elector's regime could be fairly said to rival, though on a much smaller scale, Vienna's imperial court, for it sponsored a repertory of Catholic church music, contemporary operas (including those of Mozart), and instrumental music of all kinds. Of the instruments then favored, the harpsichord was yielding to the piano; the symphony was slowly becoming central to the repertoire. As a fledgling composer in Bonn, young Beethoven would write several sets of variations and leave incomplete sketches for two symphonies.

By the beginning of the 1780s a group of self-made men from different professions lived in Bonn. The Order of the Illuminati, founded in

Bavaria by Adam Weishaupt, had quickly spread into the Rhineland. It attracted individuals who wished to influence the monarchy and the Church to implement Enlightenment ideals. It led to the Bonner Illuminati, the lodge of the local branch of the Masonic Illuminati, which held similar beliefs. Influential for young Beethoven were the pioneering translations of Homer's epics by Johann Heinrich Voss; the *Odyssey* appeared in 1781, the *Iliad* a dozen years later. Both epics, the *Odyssey* especially, proved crucial in Beethoven's subsequent career.

Understandably, the powers in control often viewed Masonic lodges with unease, even suspicion. The Bonn lodge of the Illuminati, accused of subversive political activities, dissolved itself of its own accord in 1785. In 1787 the Society of the Friends of Literature, or Reading Society (*Lesegesellschaft*), in effect took the place of the Illuminati. It devoted itself to the dissemination of Enlightenment thought and literature. Members often held meetings in the Zehrgarten, an inn just off the marketplace where they would drink, dine, and talk in its garden. Owned by the Koch family, it contained one of Bonn's five bookshops, that run by Frau Koch, and sold the latest editions of classics old and new, Plato and Plutarch, Rousseau and Montesquieu. Husband and wife had three pretty daughters, of which Babette, the most spirited and popular, was admired by young Beethoven among others. The Zehrgarten, a rallying point for liberal ideas, enlivened for several decades the city's cultural scene.[2] Its social and musical activities, and the friendships formed there, constituted a main reason why Beethoven in distant Vienna later looked back so fondly upon his early years.

ঙ্

Mentors

Beethoven's father, Johann, the court tenor, had early sensed his son's musical potential. Aware of Leopold Mozart's success with his talented son Wolfgang, Johann wished to make young Ludwig into another child prodigy. Of Ludwig's several teachers, he was the first and worst.

His pedagogy was unremarkable, his method cruel, his behavior—influenced by a growing addiction to alcohol—abominable. He often beat his son. Eventually realizing that young Beethoven needed better instruction than he could provide, Johann turned him over to several other teachers with varying results. In 1779 Christian Gottlob Neefe, having accepted an appointment as music director of Bonn's National Theater, arrived in the city. A many-sided musician and occasional composer himself, particularly of lieder (art songs), Neefe later became the court organist and orchestra leader. As one of the city's chief intellectual figures, an editor and a poet influenced by Christian Fürchtegott Gellert and especially Friedrich Gottlob Klopstock (whose *Odes* he set to music), as well as a "prince" of the Bonn Reading Society, Neefe was above all a philosopher of music. Every composition he believed must have a philosophical basis. For a career as composer, a student must study works of philosophy even more than the information in professional music manuals. In effect, music for Neefe "was the language of the soul."[3] Fortunately for ten-year-old Beethoven, in 1781 this talented individual became his teacher.

Though himself lacking in compositional skills, Neefe quickly recognized the boy's talent and took him under his wing. A man of generous ideals, he proved an excellent role model. Once under the direction of this remarkable individual, Beethoven made great progress in his musical studies. Neefe, a Lutheran who had previously lived in Saxony, introduced young Beethoven to the *Well-Tempered Clavier* of Johann Sebastian Bach. He also admired the work of Carl Philipp Emanuel Bach, then far better known than his father. Beethoven thus grew up playing the keyboard music of at least two Bachs.

After Neefe became court organist in 1783, Beethoven served as his assistant. He played at the Minoriten Church. Beethoven would only write three pieces for organ, but to create such grand sounds as a youth must have given him a sense of power. His musical style announced itself early. Though he also learned from senior members of the court orchestra, Neefe remained his primary teacher and expressed great confidence in his young prodigy if he would work hard and persevere. From these experiences young Beethoven must have formed early his ideas about the possibilities of life as a musician. Several of his early works—for example, the "Dressler" Variations and the incomplete piano concerto (WoO, or works without opus number, 63 and 64) imply huge promise.

୶

Max Franz

Little of this early success could have happened without Maximilian Franz, archbishop-elector of Cologne beginning in 1784. He succeeded, first as adjutant, then as elector, his predecessor Maximilian Friedrich, a merry prince who during his long tenure (1761–84) had often indulged in his fondness for female company. The last male child of the Empress Maria Theresa, Max Franz was thus the youngest brother of the current Hapsburg emperor, Joseph II. Max Franz strongly believed in the liberal practices adopted and put into practice by Joseph. He transformed the Electorate of Cologne into one of the truly enlightened states of Europe. An amiable, decent man, Max Franz did much to improve the economy and administration.[4] "I have no nephews or family whom I ought to help," he claimed, "no mistresses or bastards to make nest eggs for." Dressed in a shabby gray overcoat, he walked about Bonn unattended and had an easy, unforced relationship with the townspeople. "It shall be my lifelong endeavor," he said in a private letter, "to protect the weak and oppressed; and I shall be guided solely by the justice of their cause, not by my personal advantage." His words curiously anticipate several of Beethoven's later statements. Max Franz cared equally about education and the arts, and he carried on the tradition of liberal thinking already being fostered in Bonn.[5] After making fundamental reforms in elementary education and in the training of schoolteachers, he set about furthering plans for a reform of the empire and for a new league of princes.[6] In 1786 he established a university that quickly became known as a bulwark of liberal ideas, in marked contrast to conservative Cologne. No less than had Frederick the Great of Prussia, Max Franz believed the duty of a prince was to form the best possible administration.[7] In short, he wished to make Bonn into a miniature Athens.

Max Franz served as a model for all the German princes who still soldiered on during the Holy Roman Empire's last decades, observes Friedrich Heer, a leading Austrian historian. These leaders did much fruitful work as reformers and enlighteners: "they established schools and universities, founded laboratories for medical and scientific research, and encouraged industry, agriculture, and the craft trades."[8] An influential personage in the secular as well as the spiritual world of late Enlightenment Europe, Max Franz at the time of his accession was only twenty-eight, Beethoven not yet fourteen. The talented youngster looked up to him as an enlightened leader. In significant ways the elector exerted a determining influence upon young Beethoven. He learned much from Max Franz's modesty, his generous acts, and his thoughtful regard for the welfare of his subjects.

Many eighteenth-century German rulers, like their counterparts throughout Europe, had long looked to Louis XIV of France, the *Roi Soleil* (Sun King), as their model of what a monarch should look like and how he should live.[9] In addition to the impressive palace in Bonn, the elector had a smaller summer palace in Poppels, then just south of the city, and another in nearby Bad Godesberg called Le Redouten, which Max Franz had built as the spa assembly rooms, and which even today serves as a center for privileged social life. Max Friedrich's predecessor as elector, Clemens August, had constructed a magnificent establishment in nearby Bruhl, northwest of Bonn. Built during the close of the Rococo era, this grandiose structure reflected an aristocracy given over to the pleasures of life. During Max Friedrich and Max Franz's time the court continued to pass summer sojourns there. Through his duties as a court musician Beethoven would have known these establishments well and imbibed the aristocracy's French influence and devotion to the arts, especially music. In Bruhl Beethoven heard Haydn's newest symphonies and by playing them made himself to an extent familiar with them. When he came to write his own symphonies a decade later, this experience lay in the back of his mind.

For nearly ten years as a pianist, violist, organist, orchestra member, and fledgling composer, Beethoven led an active musical life in Bonn. At the Hofkapelle in the castle he often had to play the organ at the six a.m. service. The first image made of him, a silhouette at age sixteen, presents him as a junior member of the court establishment, in uniform, his shirt with a jabot and his powdered wig in place, above a dark-skinned face that often led contemporaries to think of him as having Spanish blood.

Max Franz introduced into Bonn the latest music of Haydn and Mozart, both of whom he had known well in Vienna. He served as Beethoven's principal patron, continuing his employment as assistant organist and as violist in the court orchestra. Max Franz's connection with Mozart had begun in 1775 when Mozart wrote his opera *Il re pastore* (*The Shepherd King*, i.e., Prince of Peace). First performed at Salzburg on April 23 of that year, the opera had saluted eighteen-year-old Max Franz.

Under the elector's benign reign Beethoven came to musical maturity. At the court theater, tucked into another part of Bonn's castle complex, Shakespeare's *Hamlet* and *Macbeth* vied with Schiller's *The Robbers* and *Fiesco* as well as Lessing's *Miss Sara Sampson*. Although the National Theater had closed in 1784, it reopened, thanks to the new elector, in 1789 in the former Hôtel de Ville. It offered operas by Grétry (*Zémir et Azor*), Dittersdorf, Piccinini, Salieri, Gluck, Benda, and, not least, Mozart, including *The Abduction from the Seraglio* and *The Marriage of Figaro*.

و

Beethoven Visits Vienna

In 1787 Max Franz provided funds for young Beethoven to travel to Vienna to study under Mozart, whom the elector had earlier known well. Then as later, Beethoven admired Mozart's phenomenal talent tremendously. If legend be trustworthy, Beethoven did meet Mozart, who upon hearing him improvise judged his talent favorably. Mozart, so the story goes, could not believe such impromptu playing unpremeditated until Beethoven had proven his ability by performing one of Mozart's own compositions. No eyewitness reports exist to substantiate this much-repeated account, but even so, longstanding anecdotes can be reliable. During the composer's sojourn, two persons impressed themselves deeply on this youth of sixteen: Mozart and Joseph II.[10] In Vienna Beethoven may well have seen the Austrian emperor, an unpretentious if imperfect man who, like Max Franz, often walked about the city unescorted. Henceforth Joseph reigned in Beethoven's imagination as the ideal of an enlightened monarch.

Recent scholarship has suggested that Beethoven remained in the Hapsburg capital not for the previously thought two weeks—roughly May 7–20, 1787—but for several months, from May to July.[11] Early in July he received news that his mother was gravely ill. Though he had had troubles with his father, he had always remained close to his mother. He returned to Bonn just in time to tend to her during what turned out to be her last illness. She died on July 17 of that year. Her death further destabilized his father, whose alcoholism worsened. Given this situation, Beethoven took charge of his two younger brothers and a baby sister who soon died. Virtually an orphan in his mid-teens, he became the de facto head of the family, largely responsible for what was now a disintegrating household.

But he had experienced life in Vienna, the multinational capital of the German-speaking music world, a city twenty times the size of Bonn. The compact Austrian city was encircled by ramparts, with suburbs across the Glacis, the open area surrounding much of the inner city. Even then it was a cosmopolitan marketplace, full of peoples from all parts of the vast Hapsburg empire that stretched across half of Europe, from Belgium to the border of the Turkish empire and that, among much else, encompassed modern Hungary and the former Czechoslovakia, as well as parts of northern Italy. Its diverse population spoke their native languages and often dressed in native garb. Time spent in such a cosmopolitan center must have left a powerful impression upon the young Beethoven. Even with his visit cut short, he must have sensed the possibilities the great world offered to a young man of talent. Although the Bonn to which he returned was an enlightened community, to an enterprising sixteen-year-old Vienna represented an arena of far greater magnitude, one he probably already dreamed to conquer.

ੴ

The Education of a Musician

Given the difficulties of life in his shattered household, such happiness as came Beethoven's way lay elsewhere than at home. He became almost a part of the progressive von Breuning family. The father, who had died during the fire that devastated Bonn's castle in 1778, left behind a widow and their four children, two daughters and two sons. Cultivated, well read, musically inclined, the family favored Enlightenment ideas and republican ideals. Beethoven was ostensibly hired to teach piano to the younger son Lorenz (or "Lenz") and daughter Eleonore (or "Lorchen"). To the sometimes morose Beethoven, the von Breunings were invariably kind and understanding. He was spending more time with high society than with the Bonn court. Among the von Breunings Beethoven relished having a second home, a peaceful refuge from his own fraught household.

A family of readers, the von Breunings fostered Beethoven's interest in books and learning. Frau von Breuning exposed him to classical writers and thought.[12] Literature and philosophy now occupied him: Schiller, Goethe, Klopstock, Kant, the poems of Friedrich von Matthisson. The writings and poems of Eulogius Schneider, to whom we shall return, also caught his attention. The older son, Stephan, became a good friend, as did Lenz. For a while he developed a romantic attachment to Eleonore. Later, long after Beethoven had left Bonn for Vienna,

Eleonore would marry Franz Wegeler, a man who also became a long-time friend and supporter. The young composer's creative gifts blossomed during these years. He flourished in his relationships within this family. Moments in which he had a "raptus"—Frau von Breuning's word to describe his sudden bursts of inspiration or absorption in his musical dreams—became more frequent.

Except for a varied and occasionally rigorous training in music, Beethoven had only a limited formal education. Yet the intellectual currents and ideas swirling about the German states fascinated him. New ideas from elsewhere circulated in Bonn, and Beethoven during these years learned much about the larger world. He read a lot and did so all his life. No subject, he once said, was beyond his interest. Enlightenment philosophers "spouted 'reason' but expressed their passion for life, for justice, for humanity. . . . What they expressed was sheer *vitality*."[13] Beethoven's years in Bonn proved a fertile ground for maturing and developing his openness to a wider world. Without this activity, the composition of music would have been for him far less fruitful.

᠍ᢌ

Influences from France

French influence in the realm of ideas easily and frequently crossed into the Rhineland. Of Enlightenment thinkers—the *philosophes* who helped shape the French Revolution—Jean Jacques Rousseau stands preeminent. Through his travels and the frequent translations of his writings, he became from the late 1760s onwards an international figure well known in intellectual circles in the German states. Contemporaries ideologically as far apart as Kant and Robespierre acknowledged a debt to his writings. For Herder, Goethe, Fichte, Schelling, and Hegel, he became the single most important philosopher. In asserting the supremacy of "feeling" and "nature," he released tremendous hidden energies in the minds of many contemporary thinkers. Both

the Revolution and the Romanticism that came in its wake were part
of his legacy.

Beethoven would have encountered advanced thinking among
enlightened circles in Bonn. He, too, felt the revolutionary impact of
Rousseau's thought. Like Rousseau, Beethoven sometimes seems to
evince little liking for or interest in specific humans. Yet the ideal and
the potentiality of Man—especially of Man in society—must already
have enthralled him. As well as being a writer and philosopher, Rousseau also composed music and theorized about music's nature. His
short opera *Le Devin du village* (*The Village Soothsayer*, 1752) enjoyed in
its day considerable popularity. In his bestselling novel *Julie, ou la nou-
velle Héloïse* (*Julie, or the New Héloïse*, 1761) he speaks of the energy of
music with more passion than in the dry words he accorded the subject
in his article for the *Encyclopédie*. But class prejudice does not allow the
noble-born Julie in the novel to wed her beloved Saint-Preux, who was
not noble-born. Beethoven, who would have little success in pursuing
well-born or aristocratic young women, would have sympathized with
Saint-Preux's plight.

Rousseau, even as he blamed the whole of society for corrupting
him, was not one to doubt his own inner integrity. Contemporaries,
not knowing how deep Rousseau's paranoia went, saw him chiefly as
a great genius hounded and persecuted by the Philistines.[14] Actually, if
Beethoven had known of Rousseau's persecutions, real or imagined,
they might have intensified the philosopher's appeal for him. Rousseau's message, bluntly stated at the beginning of his influential *Social
Contract* (1762), was that man was born free, but everywhere found himself in chains. In it and in *Émile*, also of 1762, he placed more stress on
citizenship than on equality. Schiller, for one, felt with the keenness of
his own experience the truth of that message. Both he and Rousseau
believed in freedom, in which man attempts to spread his wings and fly,
to be the arbiter of his own destiny, even to change the world in accor-
dance with his own designs.

With the outbreak of the French Revolution in 1789, *The Social Con-*

tract became Rousseau's best-known work. In effect it inspired the course of the Revolution. Robespierre, Marat, and others regarded it almost as a bible.[15] Rousseau's main question in this work was, "if there is no such thing as morality in man's heart, what is the source of his rapturous admiration of noble deeds, his passionate devotion to great men?"[16] In Germany *The Social Contract* exerted a major influence, ranking in popularity second only to *Émile*. The young Hegel treasured the latter, as did Herder, Goethe, and Kant. The stress shifted to human dignity and moral participation. Even freedom, the most important promise to the individual in England, America, and France, would become in Germany a property not of the individual but of society as a whole. There was and is no specific German word for "liberty."

ঽ

Sturm und Drang

Whereas the *Aufklärung* (Enlightment), with its focus on reason and progress, had developed in reaction to late Baroque emotionalism, the movement known as *Sturm und Drang* derives its name from a 1776 play by Friedrich Maximilian Klinger, *Der Wirwarr, oder Sturm und Drang*. *Wirwarr*, or "disorder," meant to contemporaries what "irrational" or "eccentric" might imply today. *Sturm und Drang* (storm and stress) represented "a violent explosion of undisciplined creative energy—violent is the key word—unlike anything elsewhere in the eighteenth century."[17] This mode of thinking had analogies in the literary and musical worlds. The eccentric or irrational in works by young writers of the epoch like Klinger, Jacob Michael Reinhold Lenz, and the early Friedrich von Schiller have their counterpart in works of music by Haydn, Mozart, and C. P. E. Bach. While Haydn's Symphony No. 45 ("The Farewell") may well be the greatest single symphonic work of the period, *Sturm und Drang* also affected his Symphonies No. 46 and, especially, No. 49, "*La Passione*."[18] C. P. E. Bach's works also show signs of *Sturm und Drang*.[19] If Klinger's *Wirwarr* announced the magnificent dawn of the *Sturm und Drang* in 1766, Schiller's *The Robbers* of 1782 provided its sunset triumph.[20]

The *Sturm und Drang* literature of the late 1770s left its mark upon Beethoven. Though other thinkers also played significant roles in his intellectual development, he felt closer to the writers of *Sturm und Drang* and a few years later Schiller, more in communion with their thoughts than he would subsequently feel with the Romantic authors of his own generation, of whom his knowledge would remain scanty and fragmentary.[21] With Schiller he encountered tense dramatic situations: Karl Moor, a Romantic hero gone astray in *The Robbers*; aristocratic injustice in *Intrigue and Love*; the tension between treachery and love in *Don Carlos*; and, a decade later, a selfless hero combating tyranny in *William Tell*.

ی

Kant and Herder

To those receptive to Enlightenment ways of thinking, the philosopher Immanuel Kant became the great beacon. During the decade preceding the French Revolution his fame as a thinker spread throughout Germany. Even before the Revolution began in 1789, Kant had hoped to extend his notions of moral freedom to the political world. He served as a guide for Schiller. What the seventeenth-century philosopher Spinoza was to Goethe, Kant's credo—that an authentic freedom is manifest only in art—was to Schiller. In 1789, Kant greeted the Revolution with open arms and high expectations. So unflagging an enthusiast was he regarding the dramatic events unfolding in France that the German poet Heinrich Heine would later compare him, mockingly, to the French revolutionary Robespierre.

Though sixty-nine in 1789, Kant believed the Revolution heralded exciting and undreamed-of possibilities for human thought and freedom. He viewed it, however, more as a mental construct than as a government in which people might participate. He thought he could provide it with intellectual leadership.[22] His treatise "Perpetual Peace" advocated a world federation of free republics. Every effort to suppress free reasoning he termed "a crime against human nature." Historians of ideas believe that Rousseau's conception of human nature and morality had greatly altered Kant's thinking. His ideas in turn greatly influenced post-Kantian philosophy and thought. "One cannot understand spiritual matters," Kant claimed; "one can only bear witness with moral behavior."[23]

Neither Kant, nor Hegel later, ever ranked music as the ultimate art. Kant had even gone so far as to dismiss instrumental music—music without voices, without words—as simple pleasure, a form of "wallpaper," certainly not culture.[24] But his was a minority view. By contrast, during Beethoven's lifetime many—notably the writer-musician E. T. A. Hoffmann—considered music the purest expression of the sublime. Subsequently Arthur Schopenhauer, no doubt influenced by Beethoven's ongoing career and achievement, would in *The World as Will and Idea* (1819–20) hail music as the greatest of the arts. In pursuing a career in music decades earlier young Beethoven had chosen a discipline whose present significance and future renown seemed limitless.

Beethoven apparently never made a systematic study of Kant or familiarized himself with his major works. But however limited his actual knowledge, Kant's thinking turns up everywhere in the writings of the age. It seems likely that, through intermediaries like Schiller, Beethoven engaged early with Kant's philosophical ideas, which at this time were widely discussed. Whatever he actually read of Kant, Beethoven would have valued him for his insistence on what the philosopher termed "the moral law within and the starry heavens above."[25] This maxim, though cited by Beethoven at a later time, seems to have accompanied him through life. By it he meant that he recognized the potential within God's universe, but no less did it indicate the need for man to show responsible, enlightened behavior during his earthly journey. In effect, Beethoven implies that man is an ethical being and that

God watches over humans. *His* chosen path would be through music, and Kant's words would be his guide.

Another figure who helped shape the young Beethoven was Johann Gottfried Herder, who, like Kant, believed that a "new and different age" was coming, one that "without doubt [would be] the most important and brilliant time in the whole history of culture."[26] Herder's ideas about primitive genius, and about *Humanität*, that is, about human nature and ways, reinforced Beethoven's own thinking about the glorious future possibilities available to mankind.

2

Key Influences

SCHILLER AND SCHNEIDER

Freedom is his breath
But death lurks in the air of vaults and caverns.
FRIEDRICH SCHILLER, *WILLIAM TELL*

Friedrich Schiller

Greater than the impact of either Kant or Herder upon Beethoven was that of Schiller. Having quickly outgrown his *Sturm und Drang* phase, Schiller became the representative figure of German Enlightenment thinking. Young Schiller's literary harmonies, like the musical harmonies of the young Beethoven, Schiller's junior by eleven years, were eruptive. Was either made for a quiet life? Intensely political, Schiller, especially in *The Robbers* and *Don Carlos*, depicted in bold strokes good and evil, horrific deeds and psychological sensationalism, with virtue and vice as presented in antithetical biographies by Plutarch. Schiller, growing up in Württemberg during the early 1780s, would have little dreamed that down the Rhine, in Bonn, lived another young German artist who, along with the leading figures of the French Revolution—Robespierre, Mirabeau, Saint-Just, and Desmoulins— would become "the purest embodiment of the revolutionary ideal."[1] In 1794 France's National Assembly, admiring his radical thinking and virtuous character, would make Schiller an honorary citizen.

By the time Beethoven began to imbibe liberal ideas in the von

Breuning household and at the revived university, he had already read much of Schiller, seen several of his plays, and taken them to heart. He valued Schiller's courage and independent stance: "I write as a citizen of the world, who serves no prince," Schiller claimed.[2] Beethoven adopted a similar view in regard to his music. He sought to compose as a citizen of the world, unbeholden to those above him socially. If in time Beethoven came to think Shakespeare a greater poet than Schiller, the German writer may have had a more profound impact upon him. Schiller's moral probity, his passion for the truth, the high seriousness of his beliefs helped focus the vision of life that Beethoven began to form in Bonn. As Schiller's powerful dramatic language influenced his hearers' visceral responses, so Beethoven's emotionally charged music sought to move the hearts and minds of those who heard it. As Schiller intended his poems, plays, and histories both to instruct the German people and to prepare them for an era of greater freedom, so Beethoven sought through his compositions to enlighten and restore humanity, to give it a vision of a better future.

In the eighteenth century the theater exerted a vast influence on people's education. Württemberg, the German state in which Schiller grew up, suffered under the repressive authority of its absolutist ruler, Duke Karl Eugen, who governed with an often restless coalition of princely and bureaucratic authority. Whereas Beethoven benefited from the benevolent reign of the liberal electors Max Friedrich and Max Franz, Schiller experienced under Karl Eugen the full power of state tyranny.[3] Moreover, Max Franz held a Schillerian vision of the possibilities of mankind's improvement. His enlightened policies created a cultural environment for Beethoven totally different from the repressive regime in Württemberg under which Schiller had suffered. Beethoven underwent a less structured, more haphazard education than did Schiller. With its intense focus on music, it left him little time to acquire Schiller's humanistic breadth. Yet in his way he acquired an impressive breadth of his own.

Schiller became the champion of liberty for all the young intellectuals of Hegel's and Beethoven's generation. His revolutionary ideas, his idealistic vision of humanity, and the dramatic power with which he projected that vision early riveted Beethoven. In many ways Schiller was a revolutionary before the Revolution. Yet he never became a revolutionary in the French sense, implying active or total commitment. Though Schiller hated despotism and aimed his best plays against tyrants, his sense of liberty would have seemed to the embattled philosophers behind the barricades in Paris downright conservative, if not reactionary.

Schiller's works accompanied Beethoven throughout his career. For Paul Bekker, one of the composer's wisest and least fashionable early twentieth-century German interpreters, Beethoven's true relationship with Schiller lies in their both being men who stood for ideas.[4] *The Robbers*, written when Schiller was twenty-one, was strongly, even painfully, autobiographical. Duke Karl Eugen of Württemberg had sent Schiller early to a military school against both his and his parents' will. There he underwent rigid military discipline with all its pomp and circumstance—and unpleasantness. Outside the school doors circulated the revolutionary literature of the *Sturm und Drang*.[5] Such literature did not please his liege lord, the duke. According to the shrewd assessment of the English scholar E. M. Butler, all the tyrants in Schiller's plays were "one way or another . . . dramatisations or sublimations" of this ruler, "the tyranny emanating from him, and the servants who performed his commands."[6]

❧

The Robbers

The Robbers (1782) is the first as well as the most sensational of Schiller's plays. Its chief protagonist, a young noble named Karl Moor, is a good, potentially great man who suffocates in the soulless, wicked world around him. When he reads about great men in Plutarch, he states, the present age of scribblers disgusts him. Not knowing that his evil brother Franz has told lies about him to their father, he departs from the family home and forms a band that attracts outcasts who become robbers. Many people in absolutist Europe at this time, especially in Spain, Italy, Serbia, and Russia, regarded bandits as romantic figures and held them in high esteem. The young Johann Kaspar Lavater in the 1760s, later the author of the vastly influential *Essays on Physiognomy*, dreamed of joining such a band. Karl Moor, disillusioned by hard experience in a world he believes alien, is driven to commit frightful crimes. Once manifesting greatness of soul, his gradually becomes a tarnished glory. His decline and fall are inevitable.

Paradoxically, Karl Moor in doing evil works for the good. Although he fails to convert his dreams to reality, Schiller's portrayal of a man striving to change the world retains its power. While the play was being typeset, Schiller toned down the revolutionary preface and a few passages in the text. And at the request of the Mannheim impresario, he transposed the action, originally set in the present, to the close of the Middle Ages. The young Beethoven's enthusiasm for Schiller developed early. He may not have seen many of the plays, but he would certainly have read or heard talk about them.

"Plutarch" is almost the first word Karl Moor utters. And Plutarch stands behind Karl Moor. Contemporaries of Schiller's heroes valued them for the inexhaustible courage with which, single-minded in their integrity, they pursued justice and determined to right wrongs. That Moor loved music more than words further cemented the young Beethoven's adulation. *The Robbers* established Schiller's notoriety in the Germanic world. By the intensity of his language, and no less the dramatic confrontations that occur between Moor's band and civic society, the play astounded a generation. To Beethoven's development as a rebel and as an artist it proved crucial.

ᢤ

Intrigue and Love

Schiller described his next play, *Intrigue and Love* (1784), as "a bourgeois drama." Variations spun on the theme of the noble lover courting a simple girl below his station appear frequently in German literary works of this era, among them Lessing's *Emilia Galotti*, a bourgeois tragedy famous for its reprimand to royalty and court life, as well as Goethe's *Sorrows of Young Werther* and *Urfaust* (the original version of *Faust*). In a sequence of intense agons, highly emotional and tragic in their consequences, *Intrigue and Love* pits Luise, the straightforward and simple bourgeois heroine, and her aristocratic lover Ferdinand, against the "President," Count von Walther, and his chief secretary, the aptly named Wurm, "dragon" or "snake" in German. The protagonists engage in violent confrontations, mental theater at its most dramatic. Unlike her noble oppressors, von Walther and Wurm, Luise does not sprinkle her speeches with French words characteristically employed by aristocrats. Against Luise's love, her sensibility in relation to others, Schiller sets the rigid, uncompromising antagonism of von Walther and Wurm; against the emotional freedom for which Luise and her lover fight, he posits authority, unbending and unyielding.

Schiller offers a critical perspective on aristocratic court life. The father–son conflict pits young Ferdinand against his old father, the Count; the new generation, fluid and generous, faces the uncomprehending old. Count von Walther misrules his fiefdom. That the humble Miller, Luise's father, had served as a soldier, was even a hero, does not exempt him from abuse or even from being murdered. Though the sensitive Ferdinand occasionally stands up to his own father, he comes across as weak.

In *Intrigue and Love* Schiller criticized the times intensely. Considered by the scholar Erich Auerbach "a dagger-thrust to the heart of absolutism," this work, like *The Robbers*, examines the nature of liberty and how absolutism suppresses liberty. It presents a world in which "subjects have no rights whatsoever."[7] Schiller's point is that, under absolutism, characters cannot become full human beings. He savagely attacks the practice in the German states of selling soldiers to other nations, most often to Britain, to engage in action elsewhere, chiefly

America.[8] Even before the Revolution in France broke out, revolutionary ideas had begun to take root in the German lands. Egon Friedell believes these ideas uncannily anticipate "the chaotic but secretly logical atmosphere" of the French Revolution.[9] Inevitably, the Revolution soon crossed the Rhine. It stunned absolutist princes in the German states and elsewhere in Europe, who, in response, often attempted severe repression.

Along with Beaumarchais' *Marriage of Figaro* (1784), Schiller's early plays exerted a powerful effect on contemporaries. Convinced of the solidarity of mankind and its destiny toward progress, happiness, even perfection, he attempted in *The Robbers* and *Intrigue and Love* to present human nature and fate in great and ideal dimensions.[10] Designing his plays as intellectual constructs, Schiller did not always veil successfully his chief didactic purpose: namely, to educate a future generation of free men, a purpose that soon became paramount in Beethoven's music.

These early dramas constituted a passionate indictment of tyranny. The first productions in Germany caused an uproar. The author's fame spread rapidly, if unevenly, since many regimes did not want such heretical ideas as freedom and liberty to migrate to their kingdoms. Consequently, the plays often fell victim to the censor or were banned. In Vienna, a bastion of conservative thinking, the censor's office, after initially allowing performances of both plays, cited *The Robbers* as "immoral" and "dangerous" and banned both it and *Intrigue and Love* from 1793 until 1808.[11] From the perspective of an absolutist monarchy, it had good reason to do so. Traditionally, theater audiences had been solidly middle-class and conservative; performances were often mediocre. But the fire of Schiller's plays sometimes threw these stodgy audiences into a kind of revolutionary frenzy. They became Schiller fanatics, dangerous indeed.[12] After all, was not Schiller himself, like Lucifer, a son of the morning, glorying in his power? It was a time when, as Wordsworth said regarding the early days of the Revolution, there was "bliss in that dawn to be alive, but to be young was very heaven!"[13] The young Beethoven would have responded positively to such thoughts.

꙳

Don Carlos

Don Carlos (1787) marks Schiller's first attempt to write a drama in verse. Like *Intrigue and Love*, the play, set in the sixteenth century, also involves six main figures. Their interactions in each other's lives make *Don Carlos* a complex work. The plot revolves around Philip II, the emperor of Spain, Austria, and Flanders, and his weak-willed son Carlos, the infante (a figure foreshadowed by Ferdinand in *Intrigue and Love*). Carlos had previously been betrothed to Philip's young queen and is still in love with her, and she with him, leaving the prince distraught. The other male leads are Rodrigo, the Marquis of Posa, idealistic friend of Carlos; and the ancient, immensely powerful Grand Inquisitor before whom all, the king not least, cringe. The female characters are the Queen, previously betrothed to Carlos, then taken from him and married to his father, the emperor; and the Countess of Eboli, a force of evil who works to undermine Carlos and Posa. The play takes place in the Escorial, the royal palace outside of Madrid.

The idealistic Posa, metaphorically bearing freedom's banner, enrolls Carlos in the cause of liberating the Protestant Netherlands from Catholic Spain. Carlos, despondent at having lost his betrothed to his father, utters a moving plea for freedom of thought. Personally frustrated, he cries out: "Twenty-three and nothing done for immortality."[14] Posa pleads with Philip to allow the Netherlands their independence. Schiller's passion for liberty turns the words to fire on his lips. Though the play takes place in the sixteenth century, its message regarding present-day politics was clear. At this later time, advanced thinking posited an enlightened absolute ruler philosophically promoting the welfare of his subjects, even giving up some of his power to endow them with political rights. No longer subjects, they would become citizens. But in Schiller's play that could not yet be. Although Posa's actions led to his and Carlos's deaths, Posa's passionately declared belief in freedom may well have stirred Beethoven's own developing awareness of its importance. Thomas Carlyle, in his otherwise admiring biography of Schiller, criticized him because the poet's heart, like that of Posa, beat not for oppressed individuals but "for all mankind, for the world and all coming generations."[15] Carlyle assumes it is easier to imagine the sufferings of generic mankind than of an oppressed individual. He has a point, and, we shall discover, it applies to Beethoven no less than it does to Schiller.

In *Don Carlos* both the women protagonists, Queen Elizabeth and Princess Eboli, are powerful figures, intelligent, psychologically sensitive, perceptive, taking charge of their destinies against historical and social odds. The queen's nobility of manner and strength of will would have stirred Beethoven's imagination. And they would leave their mark on the depiction of his own heroine Leonore in his opera of that name that became *Fidelio*.

Beethoven may even have sympathized with King Philip II, unloved and unable to love. Cold, introverted, without frankness or charm, deeply suspicious and trusting neither himself nor others, Philip gradually reveals himself perplexed by his having caused a tragedy of his own making. For reasons of state Philip had married the woman destined for his son. Later he asks the Inquisition to murder Posa for his rebellious thoughts and deeds. Before he dies Posa persuades a heartbroken Carlos to support the cause of liberty in the Netherlands. He does, but Philip, after hearing Carlos's pleas for justice, hands him over to the Inquisition as well—in effect, sentencing him to death. Such extremes characterize all of Philip's actions. Schiller may have wished to show that weakness undergirds tyranny as much as strength. Although Philip possesses raw political power, he lacks strength of character. He remains lonely, jealous, and miserable. One of Beethoven's heroes, the

Roman consul Lucius Junius Brutus (whose impact upon Beethoven we shall examine subsequently), similarly abandons his sons to justice and thus to death.

Magnificent drama that it is, *Don Carlos* is historically misleading. Facts mattered less for Schiller than motivation. He actually based his plot, not on history, but on a contemporary novel. However, Schiller saw the late sixteenth century during which *Don Carlos* takes place as a time significant for Europe's future, particularly its political future. He felt that the Europe of his day had a chance for freedom. He was right about the period's sensibility. Wherever the authorities allowed performances, *Don Carlos* exerted an enormous impact across Germany. Unsurprisingly, its tone and subject matter offended Duke Karl Eugen in Württemberg. Its successful premiere had to take place once again in Mannheim, the capital of Baden, a state more liberal than Württemberg. For slipping across the frontier into Baden to attend performances, the duke forbade Schiller to publish anything further. His creative focus usefully sharpened by the unwelcome attention of the duke's spies, the young dramatist defied the ban by leaving Württemberg for good.

Of Schiller's early dramas, *Don Carlos* may well have resonated longest in Beethoven's imagination. Its power and purpose impressed him. He also understood its relevance to the contemporary situation. Posa's idealism influenced, as we shall see, Beethoven's intensely moving *Cantata on the Death of Joseph II* (1790), his homage to the Austrian emperor of the 1780s. Admittedly, autocratic tyrants did not affect Beethoven's life as directly as they had Schiller's. Beethoven's world had in it no Franz Moor, no Philip II or Grand Inquisitor. Though petty tyrants ruled with near-absolute sway over many of the other German states, Max Franz was no Karl Eugen, no Wurm. Well-intentioned, liberally inclined, and favoring the arts, he was an exception to contemporary rulers. Beethoven, aware of his liberality and openness, recognized his good fortune in residing in the Electorate of Cologne.

Beethoven was just nine when Joseph's mother, Maria Theresa, died in 1780. During her forty-year reign, she had maintained an autocratic

regime in the rigorous and exacting Spanish tradition, leavened somewhat after the death of her husband in 1765, when Joseph, her eldest
son, became co-regent. Almost all Europeans then alive grew up under
monarchs. Sometimes they regarded their rulers with affection. Maria
Theresa never lost her popularity among the Viennese. Ironically, her
son Joseph II, full of well-intended if somewhat utopian projects during
his reign, never quite won the hearts of his subjects.

ঙ্গ

Eulogius Schneider

In Bonn's liberal community new ideas from abroad circulated freely.
Although Beethoven had deficiencies in his formal education, he sought
to engage keenly with the intellectual currents swirling about him. In
1789, he enrolled in courses at the university that Max Franz had recently
reestablished in Bonn. There, listening to lectures, chatting with his fellow students, and engaging with the professors, he hoped to learn much.
That year Max Franz had appointed to the faculty Johann Georg Schneider, better known as Eulogius Schneider, as professor of belles lettres.
Though he had begun as a Franciscan monk, the charismatic Schneider, an admirer of Voltaire and Rousseau, had become an adherent of
Enlightenment values and ideas. The outbreak of revolution in France
galvanized his thinking even more. Of the democratically inclined
figures active in the Rhineland, Schneider, along with Georg Forster
in Mainz, ranks among the most notable. One of the truly important
German Jacobins, he was perhaps the best known and the most fully
engaged. Outspoken, radical in word and deed, Schneider delivered ser-
mons and lectures in Bonn that placed him squarely within the context
of Enlightenment and revolutionary thinking. Contemporaries often
attacked him for his extreme views, his teachings and writings.

Schneider's *Poems* included panegyrics on contemporaries whom he
valued, among them an ode to Frederick II ("the Great"), who had died
in 1786, and on "the immortal Joseph II," who died in 1790. The lat-

ter begins: "Oh! so were these walls from the [feared] enemy of death, TOLERANT JOSEPH." After learning more about Joseph's illness and unexpected death, Schneider published a revised version entitled "Elegy on the Dying Emperor Joseph II." Other poems focus on revolutionary subjects. His *Discourse, on the Present State, and the Difficulties of Belles Lettres in Catholic Germany* evinces support for new ways of thinking. Difficult as it is to re-create his character from the writings he left behind, what is certain is that Schneider exuded charisma in his person as well as in his writings.

Poems fervently proclaims Schneider's democratic beliefs. After the Revolution broke out, he quickly became one of its main supporters in Germany. The day after the news reached Bonn that a mob had captured the Bastille on July 14, 1789, Schneider, overjoyed, interrupted his lecture to read a poem he had written the night before, "On the Destruction of the Bastille." That symbol of oppression he terms "the horror of a nation." Two years before the French king would be removed from his throne, the last stanzas celebrate French independence:

> The chains of despotism are fallen away,
> Fortunate people! from your hand:
> From the throne of princes to your place of freedom
> From the realm of kings to the Fatherland.
> No royal edict, no: This is our will,
> Henceforth it shall shape the burgher's destiny.
> There lies, in ruins, the Bastille,
> A free Man is the French man![16]

The poem's last line—"A free Man is the French man!"—celebrates the disappearance of royal edicts and of the monarch who promulgated them. Political freedom would become a lifelong passion for young Beethoven, a subject he returned to again and again. Schneider's poem almost certainly influenced that by Gottlieb Konrad Pfeffel, "The Free Man," which Beethoven would soon set to music. Other poems reflect Enlightenment ideas, moral and religious themes, and a belief in comradeship, as in "The Friendship." Humor makes occasional appearances. A sarcastic poem "To Reason" begins, "Reason, you are a naughty woman." Although many of Schneider's poems lack poetic merit, most of them—even from the perspective of more than two hundred years—radiate energy of some kind. Occasional poems, deliberately lighthearted, celebrating *Namenstage* (name days) are intended for *Stammbücher*, friendship albums then popular. "Farewell to Theology" begins, "Farewell Theology! Long have you tormented me!" It closes with "Good night, Theology!" Needless to say, despite a certain technical expertise, such a poem and such a volume in the Catholic Rhineland would have offended many.

Besides a certain local éclat, Schneider's *Poems* achieved a much wider circulation than we might expect. Individuals excited by the promise of the French Revolution and Schneider's teachings set up a subscription list. The professor had a good sense of marketing, for his list of subscribers constitutes a Who's Who of German liberals active in the Rhineland and south Germany. A substantial number lived in Augsburg, where Schneider had studied. Fifty or sixty subscribers lived either in Bonn or in nearby Cologne. Local subscribers included Max Franz, the elector, along with nine other members of the local nobility, several of whom took multiple copies. Beethoven's friends, the von Breunings, subscribed, as did the nineteen-year-old Beethoven himself.[17] Beethoven attended lectures by the dynamic Schneider, the faculty member who would have the most influence on him. His impact upon Beethoven proved lifelong. At the heart of Beethoven's being roiled a radical cauldron that on occasion could (and did) erupt. The intensity with which the mature Beethoven pursued his goals suggests that within his political core simmered a truly determined individual.

But even for relatively liberal-minded Bonn Schneider soon proved too radical. Little antimonarchical feeling then existed in much of the Rhineland. Though the populace expressed curiosity about the Revolution in France, it lacked any overwhelming sympathy for the events taking place there.[18] Schneider's radical politics, his expressions of support for the most advanced ideas of the French Revolution, eventually strained even the patience of the liberal elector, Max Franz. While Schneider was giving a speech at Wetzlar, the authorities in Bonn and Cologne banned the circulation of his poems, as he discovered upon his return.[19] In 1791 Max Franz dismissed him from his professorship at the university, though he did so generously, with a year's salary.

Schneider's later career provided further drama. After leaving Bonn, he went to Strasbourg, where he joined the Jacobin Club. In his *Avowal of Political Beliefs* (1792), he states his revolutionary credo. It was he who first translated the "Marseillaise" into German shortly afterwards, and in July 1792 he founded the radical newspaper *Argos*.[20] Appointed public prosecutor to the Revolutionary Tribunal in Strasbourg, he fulfilled his duties with exemplary ruthlessness. Using the guillotine he had received from Paris to detach the heads of those opposing Jacobin control, he won, apparently happily, the name of the "Marat of Strasburg." The guillotine prompted what is surely his most unusual poem. It begins, "O dear Guillotine! How welcome thou art!" Even Saint-Just and Robespierre found his righteous zeal and extreme views excessive. In 1794 Robespierre ordered Schneider to come to Paris, where he had him guillotined on April 1, just months before his own guillotining.[21] But by then Beethoven was in Vienna.

3

Two Cantatas

Naturally the cantata on the death of Joseph II
interests us chiefly. For such a historical event one
doesn't write merely a *pièce d'occasion*. Were we to
commemorate the unforgettable, irreplaceable man
today, we would be as impassioned about it [Joseph's
rule] as Beethoven and everyone else at that time. . . .
The young Beethoven also understood that he had
something important to say and, as was right, said it
forcefully right at the start in the powerful Overture.

—JOHANNES BRAHMS[1]

Emperor Joseph II

Folklore has long since canonized Joseph II as "the people's
emperor." His mother Maria Theresa made Joseph, her eldest
son, co-regent after the death of her husband in 1765. A difficult boy
from the nursery onwards, Joseph now became a more difficult man.
Mother and son formed an awkward alliance, for his progressive stances
clashed sharply with her more conservative positions. Often forced to
yield to his mother's wishes, he expressed his frustration in letters to
his nearest brother in age, Leopold. Nonetheless, he and his mother
formed a successful team. They initiated and implemented legislation
more substantial than any previously attempted in a single historical
period. Along with the reforms instituted in Prussia by their contemporary, Frederick the Great, those they put through represented the climax

of reforming absolutism in Europe. Upon his mother's death in 1780 Joseph became emperor in his own right.

The headstrong son, full of Enlightenment ideas, wanted to turn the feudal world upside down. Joseph's edicts, seemingly good, often had a negative effect on his subjects. He had an obstinacy of character that prevented him from successfully implementing his thoughtful but overly ambitious plans. His single-minded determination to have things his way, along with his unwillingness to take advice from others, often doomed his proposed reforms. An enlightened despot he proved to be, but a despot all the same. "The emperor is very talented, capable and energetic," Leopold wrote in a balanced assessment of his elder brother:

> he has a quick understanding, a good memory and a command
> of languages, so that he can talk well and on paper is even better.
> He is a hard, forceful and ambitious man, whose every word and
> deed is calculated to attract praise and enhance his reputation in
> the world. He does not tolerate contradiction, his principles are
> arbitrary, violent and vehemently held, and he is imbued with the
> harshest and most extreme form of despotism. Anything he has
> not thought of himself he dismisses with contempt.[2]

Opinionated and willful, reckless and highhanded, Joseph learned little from experience. Some regarded him as an unthinking tyrant. To others, he was spiritual kin to the enlightened Roman monarch Marcus Aurelius, who, coincidentally, had died in Vienna (then a Roman outpost, Vindabona) in 180 C.E.

All the same, eager to become a *Volkskaiser*, or people's emperor, Joseph was approachable and responsive to his subjects. Conscious that in an age of Enlightenment an absolute monarch who stubbornly defended illusory and outdated privileges was an anachronism, he presented himself (despite his brother Leopold's skepticism) as readily accessible to new ideas. In a way unthinkable in Paris or London, the people looked up to him, their "benevolent despot," for solutions. Joseph's cultural reforms pleased many. For Ernst Wangermann, a leading Austrian historian, "the emergence of [a] critical body of public opinion" turned out to be "Joseph's most glorious achievement."[3] Of all the eighteenth-century rulers, he was the most revolutionary reformer. Montesquieu's *Spirit of the Laws* guided him in his decisions. The splendid dual portrait (1769) of Joseph and Leopold in Vienna's Kunsthistorisches Museum prominently displays that instrumental book.[4] In his efforts to centralize the government, his attempts at leveling class differences and in reducing religious influence in governmental affairs, Joseph carried enlightened absolutism one stage further than had his rival, Frederick the Great. That he could speak French, German, Italian, Hungarian, Czech, and Latin, the main languages of the lands he ruled, indicates not only the multinational character of his dynasty but the breadth of his own study. In 1766, only a year after becoming co-regent with his mother, he had opened the Prater, the vast garden and deer park along the Danube, long a royal preserve, to all of Vienna's citizens. Once it had become a public domain, it proved an enormously popular meeting ground. Joseph also opened the Augarten, another nearby royal park, to the public.

In 1780 Goethe, after attending the coronation ceremony of Joseph II in Frankfurt, felt moved in his play *Torquato Tasso* to include the lines:

> There is no fairer sight in all the world
> Than a prince who rules his subjects with intelligence
> Or a realm where men take pride in their obedience,
> Believing that they only serve themselves
> Because it is only the law that is enjoined on them.[5]

In a major governmental reform Joseph proclaimed the Edict of 1782. It not only freed the peasants from serfdom but, with keen foresight, prohibited aristocrats from buying up their lands. In addition, Joseph created the civil service, which helped quicken Austria's rate of commercial development. Furthermore, he limited the Roman Catholic Church's influence upon Austrian society. His radical and comprehensive program of Church reforms met with an angry clerical response, however. On October 13, 1781, he signed an Edict, or Patent, of Tolerance. It accorded Protestants and other Christian denominations full freedom of worship and civic equality, thus ending the period in which the monarchy was completely identified with the Church. Nor did Joseph share his mother's hatred and contempt for the Jews. The 1782 Edict of Tolerance broadened their rights to choose where they lived and how they earned a living. Though the edict made a few concessions to popular prejudice, it realized most of Joseph's intentions. One of its results was that the Jewish community of Prague, a city then within the Hapsburg empire, paid homage to Joseph by officially naming its ghetto after him, the Josefov, a name it still bears.

Joseph's reign, from 1780 to 1790, encompassed the years between nine and nineteen for Beethoven. Growing up under Joseph's distant wing, he admired him as a symbol and even more as an enlightened ruler who cared for his subjects. We do not know which of the measures that Joseph promulgated pleased him especially, only that he greatly valued the man's progressive ideas. That his edicts were all imperial decrees, for which he consulted no one, would probably not have overly bothered young Beethoven. Here was a progressive ruler, a stunning contrast to rulers elsewhere, whose vast realm included the Rhineland and extended as far west as the Austrian Netherlands, now mostly Belgium. Like the electors of Cologne, Max Friedrich and his successor Max Franz, Joseph strove to improve life for his subjects. Beethoven, even as a relative youth, served an informal apprenticeship under all three leaders.

Unlike his mother, Joseph was fond of music, and during his reign Vienna's musical life prospered. Even more than before, the salons of Vienna became the musical heart of Austria. In 1781 Mozart settled in the capital, where Joseph became his patron, and where a decade later he would die, less than two years after Joseph. It was not a good time for Mozart, however. Upon hearing *The Abduction from the Seraglio*, Joseph told the composer, "Too many notes"[6]—to which Mozart wisely replied that he had put in only as many as were needed. Yet Mozart viewed Joseph more positively than he had Joseph's mother, Maria The-resa, who had been a declared enemy of Freemasonry. Some believe that he portrayed her in *The Magic Flute* as the Queen of the Night. Likewise, others attribute features of Joseph II to the wise Sarastro in the same work. Critics have long associated Mozart's last opera, *The Clemency of Titus*, with the life and deeds of both Joseph and Leopold: Joseph, because he made sincere, if often ill-advised, efforts to improve the lives of his subjects; Leopold, because during his reign of less than two years—the same length as that of the Roman emperor Titus—he, like that emperor, became known for his good intentions. Whereas Joseph generally responded favorably to Mozart's music, he disliked and derided the humor he found in Haydn's. The Austrian musical public clearly held other opinions. In 1790 Haydn took up residence in Vienna, where in a superlative late flowering, which included two extended and productive stays in London, he composed a number of his greatest works, including the twelve "London" Symphonies, six masses, and two oratorios, *The Creation* and *The Seasons*.

During Joseph's decade of rule he revealed weaknesses equal to his strengths. After the death of his first wife, Isabella of Parma, his dis-trust of people increased. His plans were too well made, his being was too inflexible. In his domestic policies Joseph attempted too much too quickly. Often, when in Vienna, Joseph spent the whole day granting audiences to all sorts of people. Yet, while accessible to the populace, he made no effort to empower them and never became truly liked by them.

Joseph also made an absolute fetish of secrecy. His fear that his edicts, numbering some six thousand in ten years, might not be prop-erly executed by his officials or followed by the population led him to develop an elaborate police system.[7] Ominous for the future was his appointment in 1789 of Count Pergen as minister of police, a man of harsh measures who developed an insidious surveillance network and would continue in that office long after Joseph's death. In significant ways, then, we can judge Joseph's reign a failure. Madame de Staël wrote of him that he "brought all manner of Enlightenment [ideas] to a state that wasn't prepared for either the good or the evil that they might do."[8] As early as 1781 the Hapsburg monarchy had faced political upheavals in the Austrian Netherlands and also in Hungary, where Joseph II's ambitious land reforms had provoked passionate protests from peasants who resented the loss of their plots as estates were consolidated. Toward the close of his reign Joseph lost control of the Austrian Netherlands. He also failed to win a crucial war against the Turks. Military defeats at their hands alienated him from the army as well as from the civilian population. Opposition groups on several fronts forced him to revise or rescind many of his progressive decrees. Few citizens disputed that any attempt at sharing power with the people would have been wildly impractical. The problems Joseph II faced explain why the *philosophes* generally put their faith in reform from above, in government for rather than by the people, or why Rousseau believed democracy feasible only in a small city-state.

When Joseph succumbed to tuberculosis on February 20, 1790, he died with most of his dreams unfulfilled. Many Viennese lamented the loss. Others felt relief. As he lay dying, rebellion spread throughout his lands. When his death was announced some offered prayers of thanksgiving for their deliverance from his rule.[9] Others regretted he had by no means finished his efforts at enforced tolerance and reform. Yet Joseph's revolution from above had failed—in great things, rather than small. He had made no changes in the structure of society. This was one reconstruction that he had no wish to see. Like many other public benefactors, Joseph was by nature an autocrat. To what extent his high-minded, visionary spirit is to be admired, or his lack of prudence and foresight to be contemned, posterity has not yet decided. Joseph wanted to impose a revolution from above because he feared the backward Hapsburg lands would be left still further behind. In the end his attempts at reform chiefly brought him numerous enemies.

Though full of good ideas, Joseph chose an imperfect strategy to achieve them. His heart burned to serve mankind, but he was so sure he was right that his societal gains were few. He lacked his mother's warm humanity. Although he always had enlightened educational goals in mind, he tried too hard and too often to impose them. On his deathbed he realized that he had failed in his attempts at reform. Even his burial ordinances caused dismay. They would no longer allow citizens wooden coffins but only a cotton wrapping. Many people were shocked. The overly showy Viennese liked extravagant tombs. To his credit, Joseph practiced what he preached: he had himself buried in one of the simple coffins of the kind that he had recommended. Hapsburg royalty are buried in Vienna's *Kapuchinergrüfte*, the crypt in the Church of the Capuchins. Joseph ordered the epitaph for his grave to read: "Here lies the man who, with the best intentions, never succeeded in anything."[10] Tourists visiting the crypt today, goggle-eyed before the baroque drama of the nearby monument in which Maria Theresa looks longingly at her husband, may easily miss Joseph's simple and understated coffin.

Historians have often considered Joseph "a precursor of liberalism." In the long and tangled history of the Hapsburg dynasty Joseph does indeed stand out as its most liberal monarch. Committed by nature and education to Enlightenment values, he of all the Hapsburgs had perhaps the most lasting impact upon the minds of his subjects. Once the most disliked man in Europe, Joseph in the nineteenth century stood as the symbolic figure of the upright ruler, the emperor who was the servant of his people. "Josephinism," as his legacy became known, struck deep roots. As a wise contemporary, the Prince de Ligne, put it, Joseph II, "forceful and unscrupulous, . . . has been more successful in capturing the imagination of posterity than the hearts of contemporaries."[11] Though liberal for his time, he also possessed a strong despotic streak, insisting his subjects do his bidding. Many of Joseph II's well-intentioned policies failed to appeal to the Austrian populace— but they appealed to the young Beethoven, at least in memory. Part of

Joseph's attraction for Beethoven was that in contrast to his successors as emperors—the brief reign of his brother Leopold and the long reign of Leopold's son, Franz—he seemed open to the possibilities of change.

◈

Cantata on the Death of Joseph II

Four days after Joseph died in Vienna on February 20, 1790, the news reached Bonn, where Beethoven still resided. Soon afterwards, the liberal-minded Bonn Reading Society asked or commissioned young Beethoven to write a piece commemorating the departed emperor. He had considered Joseph II an ideal prince. On the basis of the cantata he wrote in his memory, he seems to have revered him almost without qualification, placing upon Joseph his hopes for a better life for mankind. Beethoven had thus entered maturity as a "Josephinist," an enlightened reformer—and he remained one. When the French Revolution erupted on July 14, 1789, Beethoven was eighteen. He must have been well aware that in the Austrian Netherlands, the homeland of his paternal ancestors and long under Hapsburg rule, a "Sovereign Congress of Belgium" had deposed Joseph in January 1790 and issued a revolutionary constitution modeled upon those of France and the United States.[12] When Joseph died unexpectedly, a month later, with the matter unresolved, Beethoven, greatly agitated, was two months past his nineteenth birthday.

Joseph's death stands out as a landmark in Beethoven's young life. His *Cantata on the Death of Joseph II* (WoO 87) and the subsequent *Cantata on the Accession of Leopold II* are his first major contributions to the literature of revolution. It was an exciting time for his generation all over Europe. The heartfelt and genuinely moving composition that is the Joseph cantata reveals not only Beethoven's admiration for the deceased emperor and his enlightened policies but also his hopes that the Revolution in France had truly announced a new era for humanity. Idealized as Beethoven's vision of the future appears in retrospect, it seemed at the time to be within reach of humankind—humankind, that is, on its best behavior.

The radical Bonn professor Eulogius Schneider wrote an "Elegy on the Dying Emperor Joseph II," as well as two other poems Beethoven would likely have known. Active in the Reading Society, to which the composer had close ties, Schneider may even have helped shape Beethoven's emotional response to Joseph's death. He surely had a major share in inspiring Beethoven's cantata. Severin Anton Averdonk, a friend of Schneider's, adapted the poem that served as the text for the cantata.

> Dead! Dead! a moaning is heard in the desolate night,
> Cliffs echo the cries!
> And the waves of the sea cry out from their depths: Joseph the
>   Great is dead!
> Joseph, the father of immortal deeds,
> Is dead, yes dead!

Like Schneider, Averdonk praises Joseph for fostering freedom and for having curbed *Fanatismus*, the Church's omnipresence and unchecked power in Austrian society. The emperor's death is the world's loss; its irrevocability haunts the cantata. The aria supported by the chorus praises Joseph's achievement in curbing the powers of the "Monster"— that is, the priests of the Catholic Church.

> Yet there remains hope.
> Thus rose the people toward the light,
> Thus turned the joyful earth around the sun.
> And the sun warmed God's creation with heavenly rays.[13]

Beethoven sympathized with those who opposed the Church's religious absolutism. In the overwhelmingly Catholic Rhineland the Church worked hand in hand with the aristocratic leadership. Though raised a Catholic, Beethoven does not appear to have responded to the

Church's precepts during his youth or, for that matter, at any other time in his life. He believed, it seems, that in matters of faith people did not need intermediaries. Already a deeply spiritual young man, he felt he could form his own relationship with God.

Bonn had dissolved the Jesuit order in 1778. The city actively supported Freemasonry and, until 1785, maintained a chapter of the liberal Order of the Illuminati, which Max Franz would restart after Beethoven's departure for Vienna. By using Averdonk's poem Beethoven bitterly attacks *Fanatismus*. He intended the cantata to strike a blow against excessive religiosity—and, by extension, any doctrinaire monarch who supported religious or political excess. The churning intensity of Beethoven's music resonates powerfully to the insistent beat of Averdonk's mainly monosyllabic language; to the grim reality of the words the music offers powerful credence: "Thus rose the people toward the light" (Da stiegen die Menschen an's Licht). The Masons had charted a passage through darkness to an illuminated state of being. We see that happening in *The Magic Flute* (1791), but well before then Enlightenment thinking had stressed the movement from darkness to light. Beethoven, deeply spiritual but not formally religious, insists upon the universality of personal religious experience. If he says, in effect, "Keep the faith," that faith is not a blind fanaticism but a belief in reason and in what Herder, and through him other thinkers, had denominated as *Humanität,* or *humanitas.* Beethoven's cantata, in the wise words of the French Beethoven biographer and statesman Édouard Herriot, "is at once a tribute to the Elector, a farewell to the dead, and without wishing to exaggerate the similarity, the first suggestion of the themes of benevolence, fraternity, and peace that later, very much later, were developed in the Ninth symphony."[14]

To Averdonk's straightforward if homely verses Beethoven wrote music of deep feeling and impressive power. Repeating the word "death" five times in the first strophe numbs listeners into silence and awe. The last strophe repeats the first. It is a withering and sustained attack on priests who preach fanaticism or religious obscurantism. Through reason, the *Cantata on the Death of Joseph II* advocates, mankind can experience salvation. The Joseph II whom Beethoven mourns is not the Joseph familiar to the Viennese of his time. It is a Joseph created by an idealistic youth in a provincial Hapsburg city far distant from Vienna, where the most benevolent of Joseph's younger brothers now ruled. Presumably Beethoven did not wish to offend him.

Schiller's writings also loom large behind the Joseph cantata. It was a theatrical age, and "the stage," Schiller wrote, brought together "all classes and estates in itself." No less did the stage, in a period of frequent censorship of the written word, provide "the best-paved way to the mind and to the heart."[15] Beethoven wished to create for the cantata's hearers an effect similar to that which Schiller achieved through his plays. But that did not happen. The cantata was not performed in Beethoven's lifetime. The father of Beethoven's friend Norbert Burgmüller tried but failed to arrange a performance. We can only speculate why he did not succeed. The time for it might already have passed, or the circumstances surrounding Joseph's death were deemed unpropitious, or possibly the musicians he knew found the score too difficult. Perhaps, as happened occasionally with later Beethoven commissions, the composer did not complete his cantata in time. Whatever the reason, for almost a century we hear no more about it.

Despite not being performed, the music remained vibrant in Beethoven's memory. Full of ideas and themes that will recur again, and often in C-sharp minor, one of Beethoven's favorite keys, the work foreshadows numerous passages in his mature compositions. Twenty years later, echoes of the cantata will find their way into Beethoven's music for Goethe's play *Egmont.* The grim dungeon scene that opens Act 2 of the 1814 *Fidelio* re-creates the cantata's opening. Rather than reusing a single musical idea, Beethoven re-creates the music of four bars. What has become known as the *Humanitätsmelodie,* or Song of Humanity, in the cantata accompanies the words sung by the Seraphim. Moving and impressive wherever it appears, this song will reoccur in *Fidelio*'s Finale, sung by an enraptured Leonore. Later still, Beethoven will expand and elaborate themes first broached in the *Humanitätsmel-odie*. The cantata stands behind lines in the choral movement of the Ninth Symphony, with its presentiment of a dream of happiness.

Beethoven as a child had mourned the death of his cherished grand-father. In 1800, already in Vienna for eight years, he requested his close friend Franz Wegeler in Bonn to send him his grandfather's portrait by Radoux. Grandfather Ludwig, along with Joseph, had served Beethoven as a surrogate for the paternal affection he rarely received from his own father. The portrait occupied a prominent place in his various abodes to his dying day. With the death of Joseph—who may well have reminded him of that grandfather—he felt a major loss. Beethoven's anger at the *Fanatismus* he excoriated in the Joseph cantata remained fresh. In later life he continued to remember Joseph positively, and after 1815 he joined a Josephinist circle in Vienna.

The Joseph cantata waited nearly a hundred years for its first hear-ing. In the spring of 1884, Brahms, long resident in Vienna, heard a private performance that was followed by a public one. He spoke of it as an overwhelmingly powerful work. Himself a "Josephinist," Brahms acknowledged in a letter to a friend, the famous if opinionated Vien-nese critic Eduard Hanslick, the greatness of the emperor's reformist vision and the lasting impact the memory of his reign had had upon Hapsburg Austria: "I cannot help thinking back on that time when—as his vehement words demonstrate—the entire world understood what it had lost in Joseph."[16]

One of the ways to gauge Beethoven's opinion of certain individuals is to evaluate the music he composed or dedicated in their honor. The words regarding Joseph that he drew upon, and the music he composed to accompany them, indicate a deep involvement with the deceased emperor. Aside from a few instrumental compositions, of which the best known remains the *Eroica* Symphony, Beethoven rarely expressed through music his opinion of anyone. That he had done so in the Joseph cantata indicates his high opinion of the reformist emperor. In his subsequent oeuvre few individuals ranked higher. Though largely unknown even today (and with rare performances in concert halls), the *Cantata on the Death of Joseph II* has not yet gained its due place in the canon of Beethoven's major compositions. Yet it is a key work, foundational for Beethoven's subsequent political as well as musical development.[17] An imposing achievement, the cantata ranks as Beethoven's first masterpiece.

At the beginning of September 1791 Max Franz chose Beethoven along with eighteen other musicians to go to Mergentheim, where was based the headquarters of the Teutonic Order. As the elector of Cologne, he served as the order's grand master. To reach this city in southern Germany they went up the Rhine in two vessels, then up the Main. Along the way they stopped at Aschaffenburg, where Beethoven heard the pianist Johann Franz Xaver Sterkel play Beethoven's own Variations on a Theme by Righini. The young composer then played them himself, as well as several of his other works, to the amazement and pleasure of all. Once the party had arrived in Mergentheim, where they stayed several months, Beethoven performed with equal success. Widening his musical horizons amid other trained musicians, he impressed them by his virtuosity and improvisational skills. Before this venture he had only made, as a boy of twelve with his mother in 1783, a trip from Bonn to the Austrian Netherlands. There he met relatives and demonstrated his burgeoning musical talent. Little is known about either trip, though it seems likely that the earlier one lasted several months instead of two weeks, considerably longer than previously thought, and that he saw the North Sea, an experience perhaps recalled later in his cantata Calm Sea and Prosperous Voyage.[18]

٭

Cantata on the Accession of Leopold II

Joseph II had died childless. His closest brother in age, Leopold, succeeded him as Emperor Leopold II on September 30, 1790. His mother had long before appointed him grand duke of Tuscany, with Florence as his capital, and Leopold had provided the duchy with impeccably enlightened rule. Early in his tenure he had carried through notable reforms for his subjects and advanced progressive measures. Not an absolutist like his brother, he governed with moderation. He believed in the people's right to have taxation limited and to be protected against arbitrary rule. Contemporaries considered his administration of his Tuscan dominions successful and forward-looking. He also gained the reputation of getting along with the local power structure. "One of the ablest rulers of the eighteenth century," the Prince de Ligne termed him. Leopold, thought the prince, "had turned Tuscany into a model state of the Enlightenment."[19]

Never as progressive-minded as Joseph, Leopold had a more stable personality, one willing to compromise and listen to others. He opted to rule in a liberal spirit. Following the lead of Cesare Beccaria, the foremost prison reformer of the era, Leopold abolished torture and the death penalty and made criminal procedures uniform for all classes. Some hoped that as emperor Leopold would continue his older brother's enlightened policies; others hoped he would not. He chose to adopt measures less liberal or illusionary than those of Joseph; he also reversed several of Joseph's acts. Leopold suppressed the unproductive and unpopular taxation that Joseph had somewhat chimerically adopted. Still, he is now seen more as a continuer of Joseph's reforms than as someone who attempted to redirect them. Unlike his brother, Leopold dedicated his realm to peace. Although distrustful of the aristocratic emigrés from France who had settled in towns along the Rhine as well as in Vienna, he had no desire to lead a crusade against the French revolutionaries in Paris.

Even though for a quarter of a century Leopold had ruled—and ruled well—the archduchy of Tuscany, in the vast Hapsburg realm of 1790 north of the Alps he was relatively unknown. Few in Vienna knew much about him, and what little they knew was contradictory. Clouding the picture was that in his long reign in Tuscany Leopold had built up a police force that easily matched in efficiency that of Joseph in Vienna, and by many accounts surpassed it. Once emperor, Leopold maintained his surveillance of individuals he considered potentially dangerous, a practice that he, no less than Joseph, regarded as essential to maintain the security of the state.[20] Long critical of Joseph's enlightened but absolutist measures, Leopold began to defuse the anger building throughout the realm as a result. But on March 1, 1792, Leopold died, two years after Joseph. He had desired to establish a constitutional monarchy, but the brevity of his reign did not allow him sufficient time to attain that goal, nor to put his stamp on the empire.

Shortly after finishing his cantata for Joseph in the spring of 1790, a still hopeful Beethoven decided to compose a *Cantata on the Accession of Leopold II*. With words again by Averdonk, it examines the qualities needed for a ruler. It focuses as much on Joseph's death as upon the accession of his successor, about whom, like the Viennese themselves, he would have known little.

The Leopold cantata continues the lament expressed in the Joseph cantata but lacks that work's resonance, nor does it equal its emotional power. How could it? Leopold had reigned for such a short time. Although Beethoven no doubt hoped Leopold would continue Joseph's enlightened policies, in that hope he seems to have had only an uncertain confidence. Almost as if to justify his forebodings, the less vigorous music he wrote to Averdonk's words implies a lack of belief, even doubt. Yet he ended the Leopold cantata with a rousing chorus, which he drew upon in later works, notably in the Credo of the *Missa solemnis* nearly three decades later. Beethoven did not dislike Leopold, but he may have felt instinctively, and rightly, that in boldness of vision no one could replace Joseph. Besides, knowing Joseph's but not Leopold's policies, Beethoven may also have believed that the vision of what an enlightened state could be, or become, had died with Joseph.

Unlike the Joseph cantata, which was composed out of love and admiration and probably did not need a commission (though the Bonn Reading Society may have given Beethoven one), the Leopold cantata was more likely commissioned. As an achievement the Joseph cantata rises above that for Leopold, but both reveal Beethoven at the ripe age of nineteen thinking intensely about how to improve the world into which he had been born. Already he was occupied with trying to fathom the nature of society. Complementing the Joseph and Leopold cantatas is an incomplete sketch entitled "The Good Prince" (Der gute Furst). Beethoven in these years apparently gave much thought to understanding what qualities characterized a "good prince."

In 1792 Leopold's son succeeded him to the throne as Franz I. Whether Beethoven hoped for a performance of either the Joseph or the Leopold cantatas, we shall never know for certain. If he did, he would have suffered disappointment. Franz's rapprochement with the Catholic Church, as well as his overall distancing of himself from Joseph's and Leopold's policies, made that unlikely. Beethoven continued to feel distaste for the stranglehold that Catholicism in conjunction with the aristocracy exerted upon civic life.

❧

"The Free Man"

Events in France had resulted in hundreds of revolutionary songs not only in that country but elsewhere. In 1790 Beethoven wrote one for questioning choir and responding soloist entitled "The Free Man" (Der freie Mann), WoO 117. Adapted from a popular Jacobin work by Gottlieb Konrad Pfeffel, the Colmar poet of the Revolution, the words express egalitarian and fraternal sentiments similar to those in Schiller's "Ode to Joy."[21] Only the man who obeys laws of his own choice, Pfeffel insists, not ones made by those in power, is truly free. Beethoven's music to Pfeffel's words, likely set down in Bonn in 1792, constitutes a manifesto. He regarded himself as a free man, and anyone who thought otherwise had a surprise coming. Beethoven's music for "The Free Man" may have drawn inspiration from the unexpected French victory at Valmy on September 20, 1792, where untrained French conscripts, free citizens, defeated a combined Austrian-Prussian force of regulars. The outcome astounded many Europeans. The praxis of C major, as so often in Beethoven's compositions, implies triumph. Later, at the beginning of his Fifth Symphony, he would take up the first bars of the song, again in C major.

The poem repeatedly asks, "Who is a free man?"

Who is a free man?
He who from neither birth nor title,
Neither velvet jacket nor smock
Can conceal the brother,
He is a free man![22]

The question was often posed during the Revolution's tumultuous early years. Each of the succeeding eight stanzas poses a variant of the same question. Pfeffel provides answers. In each stanza he gives a further reason why man should be free, always concluding, "He is a free man." Neither birth, nor rank, nor attire can define the truly free man. Beethoven's music supports Pfeffel's conception of a free man as an individual of independent thought who does not submit to rule by aristocrats or clerics.

The second stanza again asks, "Who is a free man?" The answer is the person who does not hold a cleric as his master. A free man need not obey the dogmas of organized religion or submit to coercion by priests. The fourth stanza, repeating the first, again takes up a subject dear to the composer's heart: that true nobility has nothing to do with dress, title, or inheritance. It is not a matter of birth or rank but resides within the individual who recognizes the brotherhood of mankind. That it resided in character became a lifelong belief of Beethoven's. The ninth stanza takes up the need of free men to maintain freedom. Freedom is of more worth than mere "possessions" or even life itself. Being a free man means that nothing truly of value can "be lost." These stanzas are, in effect, Beethoven's credo. Both words and music suggest his determination, even as a young man, to live as independently as he could. His vigorous music for these stanzas testifies that he intended to devote his energies as a composer to realizing in them the importance of Pfeffel's words.

"The Free Man" accords with Beethoven's growing awareness that he lived in a constricted world, a world lacking basic freedoms. Had not the American Revolution, followed by the French, invented the modern "citizen"? Beethoven regarded himself not as a subject, but as a citizen: a citizen was free, a subject was not. The concept was so new that Thomas Jefferson initially wrote "subject" in a draft of the Declaration of Independence, then rubbed it out and replaced it with "citizen."

Beethoven was a pathfinder in what was a new mode of thinking, a new way of viewing the world. He distinguishes between liberty and freedom. Liberty comes first, freedom after. "Though liberty is certainly a precondition for freedom," Hannah Arendt reminds us, "it by no means guarantees that revolutionary freedom will follow. . . . The very idea of equality as we understand it, namely that every person is born as an equal by the very fact of being born and that equality is a birthright, was utterly unknown prior to the modern age."[23] Beethoven believed in liberty and, even more, in brotherhood, but he did not believe in equality among individuals. Yet he gave credence, at least on most occasions, to a civic equality that respected the rights of everyone.

~

A *Stammbuch* for Beethoven

On Christmas Day 1790, Joseph Haydn, then rising to the peak of his European reputation, passed through Bonn. Admirers of Beethoven's talent brought the young composer to the attention of the famed older man on Haydn's way to London and probably again upon his return journey in July 1792. Shown several of Beethoven's compositions— presumably the Joseph cantata among them—an impressed Haydn invited the young Rhinelander to study with him in Vienna.

Thrilled by Haydn's belief in his creative gift and the support of his friends, Beethoven prepared to leave for Vienna. About a week before his departure, a number of his friends and well-wishers put together for him, as was the German custom, a *Stammbuch*. No English word or phrase quite captures the meaning of *Stammbuch*, which is both a farewell album and a friendship album. Beethoven's *Stammbuch* is an extraordinary document. Impressed by his talent as a pianist, a string player, an organist, and, not least, as a composer over the past decade, the contributors felt confident that in the Hapsburg capital, the city of Gluck, Mozart, and Haydn, he would achieve the greatness in music that they felt lay within him.[24] It was a collaborative effort in which Beethoven's close friends in the Reading Society set down their appreciation of the young composer, either by citing favorite passages from mutually cherished literary works, or by expressing in their own words the immense respect and affection they felt for him. This slender tome, which has survived, gives us a sense of the admiration and fellowship of Beethoven's friends on the eve of his departure to the music capital of German-speaking Europe. Most moving of all were the words of rare eloquence that young Count Waldstein, among Beethoven's most ardent supporters in Bonn, wrote: once in Vienna he wished him to "receive Mozart's spirit from Haydn's hands."[25]

Within Beethoven's circle Schiller's *Don Carlos* must have been required reading, for three of his Bonn friends cited passages from the play.[26] No other work was cited more than once. The play runs through Beethoven's early life like a musical leitmotif. Presumably he valued Schiller's noble sentiments and shared the high opinion his friends expressed of the play. They cherished its themes of political idealism, of personal integrity, of commitment to freedom even at the risk of death, and they knew that Beethoven also espoused them. During his early years in the Hapsburg capital Beethoven would attempt to justify the wishes and hopes that his faithful Bonn circle had expressed in the *Stammbuch* they had created for him.

How deeply *Don Carlos* resonated within Beethoven's soul we can discover by quotations from the play that he inscribed in a 1793 *Stammbuch* for a new acquaintance made in Vienna. Beethoven quotes the outcry of the vacillating Carlos, distressed at having lost his beloved, who has instead become the bride of his father: "I am not wicked—hot blood is my fault—my crime is that I am young. I am not wicked, truly not wicked. Even though wildly surging emotions may betray my heart, yet my heart is good."[27] Although the Marquis of Posa's idealistic declarations of freedom in the play thrilled Beethoven (and would later find reflection in Leonore's impassioned words in *Fidelio*), Beethoven also clearly felt deep sympathy for the lovesick, ineffectual Don Carlos. Though Carlos found only frustration in love, he had truly loved. In Beethoven's scale of values true love ranked high. Although Count Stadion, the Austrian secretary of state, had banned *Don Carlos* from the stage in 1792, Beethoven quoted from it in his friend's *Stammbuch*. He must have trusted him and his friends to disagree with the banning of the play, which lasted until 1808. He knew, however, that he must practice greater discretion for he no longer lived in Bonn but in the heart of the absolutist Hapsburg empire.

To underscore the words of Carlos and Posa, Beethoven appends to his chosen quotation four "precepts" of desirable qualities. These are his own words:

> To do good whenever one can,
> To love liberty above all else,
> Never to deny the truth,
> Even though it be before the throne.[28]

The words encapsulate Beethoven's deepest beliefs. Similar sentiments would later appear in *Fidelio*, *Egmont*, and the Ninth Symphony. Even though Jean-François Bouilly, Goethe, and Schiller had written the words that inspired Beethoven to express such sentiments, it is Beethoven's music that amplifies them and makes them resonate.

4

The French Revolution

The French Revolution is a landmark in all countries. . . .
[It] thus remains *the* revolution.

ERIC HOBSBAWM[1]

It's true that one cannot fully understand [Beethoven] in
humanitarian and social terms if one knows nothing of
the impulses that went to make the French Revolution; it's
equally true that one cannot fully understand the French
Revolution if one has no awareness of Beethoven's music.

WILFRID MELLERS[2]

The death in 1790 of Joseph II, followed two years later by that of
Leopold II, did not diminish Beethoven's enthusiasm for change
in society. In Vienna, where he arrived after a week's journey by coach
in mid-November 1792, he retained his youthful hopes and beliefs.
But Franz I, who succeeded Leopold early that year, had quickly—and
with a vengeance—reimposed repressive rule upon Austrian domains.
With each passing year censorship became more severe. If Beethoven
wished to have a successful career in Vienna as a pianist-composer he
had to mute his words, keep his political beliefs to himself, or share
them only with trusted friends. Of necessity he became discreet. He
says enough, however, or contemporaries who knew him recalled
enough, that we can fill in a few of the gaps regarding his response
to the French Revolution and, later, to Napoleon. Beethoven's ideal for
Austrian society would have been a republic, but he would accept a

progressive political leader or aristocratic redeemer, even a monarch, who had the public's interests at heart.

ঌ

The French Revolution Erupts

The two or three decades after dissatisfied French citizens stormed the Bastille on July 14, 1789, marked a key stage in European history and culture. Beethoven was then five months short of his nineteenth birthday. Revolutions are unpredictable. Of the seven prisoners liberated from the Bastille, two were madmen, four were counterfeiters, and the last the Marquis de Sade. It hardly mattered who they were. As a symbol of tyranny and absolutism the Bastille far outweighed any legal importance it had. Along with the dreaded *lettres de cachet*, letters sealed by the king that could lead to imprisonment without trial, it stood for repression of civil liberties. The destruction of this ancient prison-fortress sent successive shock waves across France, then across Europe, where they soon became a catalyst for change.

Although the young Beethoven would have heard of political stirrings during the 1780s in the German states and elsewhere in Europe, it was the Revolution of '89 and its reverberations that roiled Europe in the decades following and significantly molded the mature man. From its first dramatic outburst, the Revolution affected Beethoven both in how he faced the future and in the music he wrote. An appalling catastrophe to some, to others—Beethoven among them—an event suggesting possibilities of change, the Revolution appeared to mark the funeral of despotism. Whereas most historians claim it began with the fall of the Bastille, few agree when it ended. I find convincing Jonathan Israel's dating of the Revolution's close (in his major study *Revolutionary Ideas* of 2014) to the accession of Napoleon Bonaparte as First Consul of France on November 18–19, 1799.

Europeans during this decade keenly followed the latest develop-

ments in France. News might travel slowly, but all the same it traveled. Newspapers in many cities carried extensive foreign reports and
reprinted articles from correspondents across Europe. Politically savvy
contemporaries, however lacking in perspective, may have known more
about events that occurred during the revolutionary epoch than all but
the most assiduous historians of today. Bonn was closer to revolutionary Paris than was Vienna, but even the Viennese press, despite close
governmental censorship, reported tactfully if briefly on day-to-day happenings in Paris and elsewhere.

A young generation in Europe now came face to face with newly
founded hopes. Ideas of liberty, equality, and fraternity filled the air,
and discussions of popular sovereignty, representative democracy, civil
rights, and even civic happiness become commonplace. Revolutionary
thinkers soon became aware that poetry and politics, writing and freedom, went hand in hand. The poets and musicians of many nations
with their songs of freedom formed, whether they knew it or not, a kind
of Holy Alliance, a vanguard in the cause of humanity. Enthusiasm for
the new political developments in France was for many almost as exciting in Britain and in the German-speaking states along the Rhine as
in Paris.

᠙

The Idea of a Republic

Enlightenment thinkers had refused to accept truths based on revelation and miracles. To them the word "republic" meant something
quite different than it does to those living in the twenty-first century.
Influenced by Montesquieu and Rousseau, most educated Europeans
thought republics feasible only in small city-states like Athens or Venice. Though they regarded the evolution of the new United States with
fascination, the future of so large and new a republic as America—and
now France—constituted a huge question mark. A republic, as James
Fenimore Cooper described it in *The American Democrat* (1838), can be

either democratic or aristocratic. It "can have a large or a small base"; it can be both the United States or eighteenth-century Venice. For Cooper, "the only quality that distinguishes [a republic] from a monarchy is that in the one the rights of the monarch [prevail], in the other the rights of the community."[3] Admittedly, he wrote these words almost fifty years after the Revolution in France. In 1789 the future of the French Republic had seemed far from certain. Fifty years later, with absolutism again triumphant across Europe, the uncertainty had returned.

Rousseau had given the name "republic" to every state governed by laws, no matter what the form of its administration. A republic could thus be, in the thinking of the time, a constitutional monarchy. After all, the idea of representative democracy in Europe was still new and unformulated. Autocratic if not absolutist rulers controlled most of the Continent's older political entities. The Greek and Roman history that students learned at school largely formed their notions of republics. The heroes most valued were Lycurgus, Brutus the Elder, and Pericles. But hoisting the republican flag over the capitals of Europe formed no part of the philosophical program of the eighteenth-century thinkers who wished to regenerate humanity. To many then alive, the idea of founding a republic looked like venturing upon an unknown sea.

Oddly, it was the Batavian Republic (roughly the present-day Netherlands), not the French, that first put together the official motto "Liberty, Equality, Fraternity." In the First French Republic of 1792 only "Liberté" and "Égalité" appeared together in official documents. Fraternity was in the air, though not till later did people use "Salut et fraternité" as a complimentary close to letters and other documents.[4] Even when kept apart, *liberté, égalité,* and *fraternité* became humanity's new watchwords. It was one thing to respond intellectually to these words; it was an altogether different one to experience them directly as an emotional reality, as did the generation of '89.

Despite not appearing together in France during the revolutionary era, the words "liberté, égalité, fraternité" became a rallying cry not only in enlightened urban circles across Europe but also among ordinary citizens everywhere. The far-away American colonies had made a beginning; great, seemingly rich France had followed, and what the French did—so people thought, given their leadership and linguistic dominance over the past two centuries—many in the other European nations also felt compelled to do. By the late summer of 1790 they considered the Revolution over, with people joyfully anticipating the future as never before and never afterward.

Only months after the Bastille fell, Louis XVI, the monarch held to be plotting against his people in July 1789, had been officially decreed the "Restorer of French Liberty." After Louis, intending to incite a counter-revolution, attempted to flee the country in June 1791, the tide turned against him. All the same, the National Assembly allowed him to cling to his throne until August 10, 1792. For much of this time the people continued to see him, with blind optimism, as the potential savior of his people, one who stood up against aristocratic reactionaries. This first French Revolution, regardless of its failure, incoherence, and reliance on terrorism, remains to this day in France a source of immense patriotic pride.[5]

ა

War

The revolutionaries attempted to revitalize French society by creating a secular state in which every aspect of the daily life of their citizens underwent change. In 1792 supporters of the "second" French Revolution decreed the Catholic Church in France out of existence. They closed (and often desecrated) its places of worship. In view of the new questioning of religion, the Church proper found itself replaced by the opera, the concert hall, and the theater. The new revolutionary calendar, replacing the long-established Julian calendar, was intended to mark the end of the Christian era. Ten-day units, *décades* in the new calendar, replaced the seven days of the week. In November 1792 the French Republic went even further and offered aid and fraternity to all people wishing to recover their liberty. The Republic's leaders did not yet, how-ever, show much interest in revolutionaries from other countries. The Mainz radical Georg Forster, who had come to Paris in search of sup-port for activities in his homeland, soon learned that grim truth.

In the autumn of 1792 momentous events took place in France. Two months after the failed flight of Louis XVI in June of that year the National Assembly abolished the Bourbon monarchy. On September 2, in what became known as the September massacres, riots against the revolutionaries broke out in the streets of Paris, leaving at least fourteen hundred people dead. With the rising tide of violence under Jacobin rule and with a joint Austrian-Prussian invasion looming, it seemed that the French Revolution, like the British Civil War the century before, might bring about mob rule instead of a new Eden.

France's ongoing internal revolution led, inevitably, to a conflict between the country's republican government and monarchic Europe. Austria made the first move in what would become an on-and-off military campaign that lasted more than two decades. Intending to avenge the misdeeds of the Revolution and curb those who had perpe-trated them, perhaps even to rescue the imprisoned Louis XVI and his Austrian-born queen, Marie Antoinette, it declared war against France on April 20, 1792. Upon hearing the news, the constitutional monarchy then in power in Paris reciprocated by declaring war on Austria. Aus-tria persuaded Prussia to be its ally, for the Prussian army still enjoyed the fine reputation it had had under Frederick the Great. Along with observers from most other European countries, the invading Austrian and Prussian armies expected a short and successful campaign. The campaign was indeed short, but it was not successful—at least for Aus-tria and Prussia.

At Valmy, in eastern France, on September 20, 1792, French revolu-tionary forces faced off against crack Austrian and Prussian regiments, the latter led by Prussia's Duke of Brunswick, widely regarded as the finest soldier of the day. Their destination was Paris. The duke had threatened to destroy the city if the republican government touched a hair on the head of Louis XVI or his wife. The revolutionaries, led by Generals Dumouriez and Kellermann, he despised as "rabble." But they fought under officers they had chosen themselves. When the battle began, the untrained French forces stood firm against the enemy's blistering cannonades. It turned out they could use weapons as effectively as troops led by the old warrior caste. Their determined resistance led the Austrian and Prussian troops to cede the ground. The do-or-die attitude of the French republicans proved decisive and resulted in a stunning victory. It indicated that in the test of war the new order in France, with its *levée en masse* (mass conscription), its citizen army full of patriotic enthusiasm, had proved stronger than the paid and conscripted troops of the old regimes that opposed it. Valmy was thus a key French victory. It ended the invasion. On September 22, two days after the victory, the National Assembly proclaimed the First French Republic.

Even outside France, many hailed the success of a makeshift army of citizens against the mercenary ranks of dynastic Europe. Goethe, who accompanied the Prussian forces and observed at first hand their ignominious retreat, seems to have grasped almost immediately the significance of Valmy. Recollecting the event in his *Campaign in France, 1792* (1822), he remembered telling Prussian officers at the campfire that evening: "From this time and place a new epoch is beginning, and you will be able to say that you were there."[6] He was right. In the face of the novel forces engendered by the French Revolution, old Europe had proved its helplessness. Kant, Herder, Klopstock, Lavater, and Hegel—all regarded Valmy as marking the beginning of a new stage in history. It was there that the Revolution became an uncontrollable force. Many regarded the victory of the revolutionary armies as an extension of a revolution that had already begun in philosophy, literature, and the arts.

Upon learning of the success at Valmy, the French composer François-Joseph Gossec, in the pay of royalty before 1789, adopted the revolutionary cause. Known as "the Tyrtaeus of the French Revolution"—the allusion is to the Spartan poet who incited his compatriots to victory—Gossec through his impassioned words and music helped redefine the new era. His stirring oratorio *The Triumph of the Republic, or the Camp on the Great Meadow* (1794) depicts French troops on the day before the battle. A chorus chants: "Down with despotism; and let the whole of Europe— / The blood of the oppressors enriching its fields— / Be a vast sanctuary for our Goddess [of Liberty]."[7] The oratorio's concluding outburst calls forth the virtues of a personified Liberty: "Essential birthright of mankind / O most cherished Liberty." To which the Goddess of Liberty replies: "France is henceforth the temple / Wherein I would wish to dwell."[8] Each of the nine dances that close *The Triumph of the Republic* characterizes a country identified with the Revolution. In putting aside their national differences, participants become "citizens of the world."

Until the autumn of 1792 the monarchs of absolutist Europe, those of Prussia and Austria excepted, did not believe the French example affected their own thrones. That belief soon changed. Catherine the Great, empress of Russia, felt that the victory at Valmy threatened her native Germany with a plethora of incalculable woes. In truth, this initial campaign did inaugurate more than two decades of fighting. For Beethoven's generation, Europe after Valmy would never again be quite the same.

❧

The Terror

In 1789 virtually all members of France's National Assembly were convinced that the country must remain a monarchy. Such thinking lasted about three years. For a time Louis XVI appeared willing to accept becoming a constitutional ruler, although he had his own conception of what that meant. But when the insurrection of August 10, 1792, overthrew the monarchy, all pretence of grafting a new regime onto the old came to an end. On September 22, two days after the battle of Valmy, the Assembly declared France a republic. Montesquieu had taught people that republics were viable only if the public actions of their citizens were based on *vertu,* or disinterested civic spirit. Not until French armies continued to win victories over the monarchies of Europe in the autumn of 1792 did republicanism become an unequivocal identifying principle of the Revolution. Only when the French declared that they intended to export the principles of their Revolution to whatever peoples asked for their fraternity and help did the other monarchs of Europe begin to feel threatened on their thrones.

With the Terror of 1793–94, fear escalated. For many months the guillotine claimed waves of victims. It seemed that to maintain itself the Reign of Terror had to keep on repeating the initial act of violence, the storming of the Bastille. This spectacle of violence directed against itself proved a shock to many and led to a coalition of groups rising up against the Jacobin revolutionaries. Most of the public welcomed the overthrow of Robespierre in 1794. Hope still gleamed among the enlightened. While under friendly house arrest to escape prosecution during the Terror, Condorcet composed his *Historical Picture of the Progress of the Human Mind* (1795), one of the most dazzling, if somewhat wrongheaded, utopias ever set down on paper. Friedrich Nietzsche, the radical philosopher of a century later, referred to the Revolution as "the prime event of the last millennium."[9] Not only had it fatally eroded the ancien régime, it had torn France in two. Yet the country needed—and found—the means to defend itself. Without the external and internal tumult, the departure of many royalists into exile, and the army's need for new officers to replace those who had left, the meteoric rise of young Napoleone Buonaparte through the ranks during these years is inconceivable.

The two decades from 1790 to 1810 appeared to mark the beginning of a new stage in the history of mankind. New and strange ideas, cheering to many but highly upsetting to others, infiltrated Europe. This creative spirit, as later historians have observed, produced a tremendous flowering in science, technology, literature, art, and music, and reforms of all kinds. Poets and musicians differentiated and refined the language of the inner life. Presumably they saw more deeply because they had felt and suffered more.

᠊ᢒ

The French Revolution in Germany

Had not Edmund Burke, the eighteenth-century English sage, prophesied that the gravest and, for the rest of the world, the most dangerous consequences of the French Revolution, the real French Revolution, would occur not in France, but in Germany?[10] Burke was not alone in such thoughts. Mirabeau, before his death in 1791, had predicted that the French Revolution would affect the German states more than it would France.

The tocsin announcing the Revolution that rang out in 1789 echoed across the German states. Germans watched with fascination, and often with trepidation, the ongoing revolutionary activity. Friedrich von Schlegel, the brilliant German critic and contemporary of Beethoven, once held up Goethe's novel of self-education, *Wilhelm Meister's Apprenticeship*, as "the German counterpart of the French Revolution."[11] No real political revolution in the multitudinous German states, he implied, was possible or likely. His was a minority view. "The three decades between 1785 and 1815," recalled the German memoirist Varnhagen von Ense, "were moved by political and spiritual powers as in seldom a time before and after." Varnhagen lived through the tumult. He knew whereof he spoke.

"It seems to me," wrote Johann Gottlieb Fichte in 1793, "that the French Revolution affects the whole human race."[12] Later he advocated an alternative solution for human progress in Germany: better education along with German unity. The reasons why so many German Enlightenment thinkers responded so favorably to the events of 1789 was that they believed, along with the Mainz revolutionary Georg Forster, that it is glorious to see realized in the state what philosophy has ripened in the brain. After Mainz capitulated to the French on October

21, 1792, there developed, under Forster's direction and with the support of radical German sympathizers, a Jacobin republic. Like most liberals, Forster, who had traveled widely (as a teenager he had accompanied Captain James Cook on his second voyage around the world), felt that improvement in Germany could only come from above. He placed his faith in enlightened princes who would provide for the happiness of their subjects and grant them, sooner or later, the equivalent of the liberties that he imagined Englishmen already had. In Mainz and in the German territories west of the Rhine, republican sympathies grew. Mainz was the first such republic founded outside of France. Forster put through, with French support, an election for a National Convention of Free Germans on the west side of the upper Rhine. French influence also extended into the southern German states of Baden, Württemberg, and Bavaria, where plans were devised and uprisings instigated to institute a south German republic.

In March 1793 the Convention in Paris, called to determine the future of postrevolutionary France, proclaimed Mainz a free state. Its territory ranged between the Rhine towns of Landau and Bingen. This new Mainz Republic belonged to France, according to the ideas of the Convention, and the French were at first well received throughout the Rhineland. The Mainz Jacobins now found hundreds of like-minded persons in the neighboring cities and principalities. Partisans of the Revolution planted Trees of Liberty, symbolic of a new era. This new era did not last long. While Forster was trying to carry out negotiations in Paris, Hessian troops overran the area around Mainz in April and the city fell in July.

Germans along the Rhine, from Alsace up to the Dutch border, recognized that the Revolution represented a principle of change on a scale never before deemed possible. Throughout the 1790s many left-bank Germans—no doubt influenced by the colonies of disillusioned French emigrés in their midst, aristocrats mainly, once wealthy but now increasingly impoverished—also engaged in persistent passive resistance to their new French masters. In his last anguished letters to his wife, written from Paris in the course of 1793, Forster revealed that although a committed revolutionary in principle, he was essentially at odds with the Revolution as it now manifested itself in France. The Terror had begun. Forster died in Paris, ill and disappointed, in January 1794. Ironically, the French soon returned to the Rhineland, and under French occupation it again began to prosper economically.

The Terror effectively quashed the optimism that many in the German states still held. Although ideas about liberty and fraternity were still bandied about, in the north of Germany as well as along the Rhine, progress toward a new society was no longer seen as inevitable. German intellectuals had greeted the ideals of the Revolution not because the ideals were French but because they were human and believed to be universal. The Revolution itself now evoked sighs of regret. Forster's disillusionment foreshadowed that of many German intellectuals. The thoughts of Schiller, Wieland, and Klopstock, all of whom had once viewed the Revolution as a new dawn, underwent a sea change. They now reacted strongly against it. Though still adhering to the enlightened principles of their youth, some Germans—Friedrich von Gentz, Heinrich von Kleist, August Wilhelm von Schlegel, even Schiller eventually—ended up in the conservative camp.

A decade after the acute crisis in France, the Revolution's main effects began to manifest themselves elsewhere in Germany. But not until Napoleonic armies had twice defeated Prussian forces, in separate battles at Jena and Auerstädt, on October 14, 1806, did nationalistic agitation in the German states come to a boil. For Hegel "the world historical significance" of the Revolution lay in the principles it passed on to other nations, particularly the German states. Observing Napoleon riding through the streets of Jena in 1806, Hegel envisioned him as the "world-spirit" or "world-soul." Like Kant (and later Karl Marx), he considered the Revolution a fateful turning point in modernity, one to which philosophical thinking needed urgently to respond.

Writers, painters, sculptors, artists, philosophers, and musicians increasingly grappled with the possibilities of the new order. For the

older German writers—Klopstock, Jean Paul, Wieland, Herder—the
Revolution had initially seemed to promise a world transformed. For
Kant and Fichte, it heralded exciting and undreamed-of possibilities
for human thought and freedom. Everywhere the outbreak of the Revolution aroused hopes that in the offing lay a better society. Change
would not happen all at once. Although the Revolution's active phase
had petered out by the mid-1790s, creative spirits continued to hold a
half-ironic, half-serious hope for a spiritual rebirth, a transformation of
the world through art. Creative endeavor, much of it inspired by revolutionary energy, reached a peak around 1800.

In this renewal of the arts, literature played a leading role. Although
ignited by the French Revolution, German works also drew strength
from the writings of Friedrich Klopstock, especially his Miltonic epic
poem *Messiah*. It rang out, in the poetic prose of Bernt von Heiseler,
"flowing like rays of light or waves of the sea." In it "the genius of the
German language spoke anew."[13] Klopstock, beloved of Goethe, Schiller, Hölderlin, Jean Paul, and, not least, the young Beethoven, inspired a
generation to rethink the power of words. Reading Klopstock was a convention of the age. *Messiah*, as well as Klopstock's *Odes*, won admiration
for the intensity of passion expressed in creative language and form.
The flowing hexameters of his lyric poetry became a voice for the new
self-confidence of the Third Estate, or commoners: if God is present in
everything, distinctions no longer exist, and everyone is of equal rank.

The extraordinary impression Klopstock made upon contemporaries
in the 1790s lay in his capacity for setting a person in relation to the
infinite through the exaltation of individual sentiments untrammeled
by reason. With help from Klopstock's example, German poets revital-
ized the German language. Klopstock had welcomed the French Revolution enthusiastically and called upon the German people to rise up
against their princes. When war broke out between the French Republic and Prussia and Austria in 1792, he penned an "Ode to the French
Revolution."[14] So active were Klopstock and (for a time) Schiller in initially propagating the ideas of the Revolution that the French National

Assembly conferred on them the title of *citoyen français*, French citizen. Both, it hardly needs saying, admired Plutarch intensely. Klopstock's poems had as much influence upon music as upon literature. One of Beethoven's favored poets, Klopstock left his mark on him early. His poems may well have inspired the young composer to think about revitalizing German music.

Johann Wolfgang von Goethe, by contrast, never showed the slightest enthusiasm for the Revolution. The only word for a world catastrophe on this scale was, for him, tragedy. Neither inevitable nor great, the Revolution was to be deprecated. Goethe's antirevolutionary writings include his *Venetian Epigrams* of 1790 and his pastoral idyll *Hermann und Dorothea* (1796–97). Both attempt victory over the daimonic element he believed inherent in the Revolution. Goethe's writings about the Revolution are on the whole undistinguished. Gradually, under Herder's influence, he freed himself from French influence and the dry, pedantic manifestations of the Enlightenment.[15] In his *Faust*, the first part published in 1808, he mocked pedantry in the figure of Faust's servant, Wagner.

For years to come in "Germany," fragmented as it was into several hundred separate entities, a "patriot" meant exclusively a French revolutionary. Only gradually did the word become more generally adopted and acquire its present meaning. For mass movements Goethe had no sympathy. The Revolution seemed to him a wild confusion, a clamor of many voices, all fighting among themselves. Given the internecine rivalries taking place in France, Goethe had a point. We cannot understand his attitude simply by labeling him "conservative." Later he became an enthusiastic admirer of Napoleon because he saw in him "the great creator of order." He viewed him too, with the eye of an artist, as the clearly defined figure of a daimon, a living *Ur-Pflanze* (primitive plant) of the will for power, as it were. Napoleon "developed superbly before his very eyes and flowered unimaginably, until once more," as he later underwent defeat and exile, "it had to wither and die," an eventuality Goethe accepted calmly as "a matter of destiny."

No less intently did a slightly later figure, Friedrich Hölderlin, known for his unequaled poems on classical subjects, watch the Revolution unfolding. Falling in his response somewhere between Klopstock and Goethe, Hölderlin became one of the few exceptions to the German tradition of political noninvolvement. His "To Freedom," circa 1791, eulogizes revolutionaries in France.[16] In his later ode "Buonaparte" (1798) he praised the genius of the young French general's victories over Austrian armies in northern Italy during 1796–97. He sensed that the Revolution and the achievement of Napoleon would foster a widespread surge in creative endeavor. Hölderlin was not alone in his Napoleonic sympathies. In German lands, works regarding Napoleon positively included the Schlegels' aphorisms and critiques in the Athenäum as well as Schiller's epic dramas, among them Wallenstein and The Maid of Orleans. During these years Napoleon gradually became associated in German lands with the Revolution. Joseph von Görres in 1799 and 1800, and Ernst Moritz Arndt as late as 1803, also expressed a favorable response to, even enthusiasm for, Napoleon. Hölderlin admired not only his military successes but also his founding of new Italian republics in which the ideals of the French Revolution would be put into practice. In Italy Ugo Foscolo, inspired by the dazzling victories against Austrian armies in his Italian campaign of 1796–97, eulogized the young general in an early poem, as would Vincenzo Monti in his Prometeo.

Thomas Jefferson's aim in the American Revolution had been to pursue happiness. When the Declaration of Independence speaks of the pursuit of happiness, it really means the pursuit of joy. Much has been made of Jefferson's yearnings for the realization of the aims of the French Revolution, but these yearnings, accompanied by a Romantic tinge, have only been half understood. Most idealists who desired change in the German states were either silenced or became mere utopians.

⌇

Beethoven Responds to the French Revolution

And Beethoven? His goal, inspired in part by Schiller's poems and plays, was to achieve both freedom and joy. The development of his creative genius took place over an extended time span. He was indeed an idealist, but his development, so unlike Wordsworth's early enthusiasm, was cautious, if essentially positive. Every energetic impulse he had either found expression in some dimension of his creativity or, if necessary, turned inward until the day arrived when it could find expression.

Born the same year as Wordsworth and Hegel and only a year later than Napoleon, Beethoven came of age with the Revolution. He believed that the events in France heralded a new era. News of the "Declaration of the Rights of Man and the Citizen," approved by the National Assembly in Versailles on August 26, 1789, would have reached Bonn quickly. Though silent regarding women and slaves, its language, echoing that of the American Declaration of Independence, promised freedom and equality to all French males. On May 22, 1793, Beethoven in Vienna wrote Theodora Johanna Vocke in Nuremberg: "Love liberty above all else" (Freiheit über alles lieben).[17] Liberation can make people happy, but often enough, let us admit, it seems liberated people are happy about their liberation for only a limited period of time. Then they begin to find fault with the new system. But that is to anticipate. For those who had long yearned for change, the excitement they felt during the early years of the Revolution must have brought much joy.

Riding the crest of a wave, Beethoven, along with the rising generation of writers and intellectuals in Europe, yearned through his music to play an active role in society. He imagined the years to come as potentially glorious years. He had a message to impart. In his chosen field of music he must have believed himself a revolutionary. Even at this early stage in his career he was speaking to audiences of friends interested in his music, yes, but he was also speaking to the world. He announces a theme, one often of revolutionary import. Then he comes back to it, again and again, revising it, altering it, until it sinks deep into people's consciousness.[18]

Beethoven had a quite rare and extraordinary sense of values. Though he did not express the slightest interest in political theory, he followed the public life of the times closely. But he never became a doctrinaire revolutionary. He was more an idealistic rebel, or rather, often a rebel, sometimes a revolutionary, more usually somewhere in between. Beethoven judged the laws and conventions of the society of his day by a wholly subjective standard, that of his own nature.

Could a sensitive youth such as he was live through the tempestuous events of 1789 and the years subsequent and remain the same? The answer, for Beethoven at least, was no. Before the Revolution, reform had always come from above. Where else would it come from? Not from a populace disenfranchised and powerless. No wonder Beethoven associated ideas of reform not with revolutionaries, whether active in France or more or less inactive in Bonn, but with progressive leaders like Joseph II and, he hoped, his successor Leopold II. Having the fever of revolution did not preclude acknowledgment that France had intended to make itself into a constitutional monarchy. Why could not the German states do the same? It was possible, even if unlikely. Given his inherently orderly mind, Beethoven valued control, discipline, organization. He realized that for societal reform to succeed new approaches were needed. "A man of the New Age," Beethoven had to live, not with hopes of utopia or for some kind of future republic, but with a strong belief in his own impressive gift to create music of lasting resonance, not only for his own day but for eras to come. About that gift he seems to have had no doubt.

Admittedly, Beethoven did regard republics as the best solution. Such a belief reflects a historic change in the way people looked upon the world. In 1789 absolute monarchies were, outside of England, which had a parliament, almost universal in Europe. When eighteenth-century writers had discussed republics their models had usually been classical city-states, small enough for the entire citizen body to make its own decisions. Beethoven nourished the idea of revolution in an ideal conception of ancient Greek republics and Roman virtue. Bonn, with perhaps ten thousand inhabitants within the city walls and two thousand more beyond them, may have put him in mind of earlier republics. The ideals of classical antiquity, whether represented by the Greek city-states or by the Roman Republic, were there for Beethoven to draw upon. Already he knew his Plutarch well. Many alive in 1789 also drew upon more recent examples of republics: the Italian principalities of the Renaissance, the Swiss cantons, Venice (though increasingly more an oligarchy than a republic), even the very new United States. Willingness to trust a king or leader to keep the people's interest at heart in guiding a republic was not at this time an unusual position to hold. A number of Napoleon's marshals were republicans and would have preferred that France be a republic, yet they learned to work with Napoleon. Beethoven wished to have as a leader for a future society nothing more, or better, than a second, somewhat more successful, Joseph II.

It was not just the young Beethoven who responded to the challenges possible through revolution. Comparing Beethoven to Byron may prove useful here. Byron, the literary critic Tony Tanner once observed, was "always oppositional, you might say insurrectionary, but never truly revolutionary." He finds Byron "a strong republican," one who "knew what royalties and courts were."[19] He doubts, however, that Byron would have admired the American republic. That is debatable, for Byron at various times expressed interest in visiting both North and South America. Why visit them, we may ask, unless he wished to see how the new countries worked? But Tanner's thoughts on Byron have relevance for Beethoven. Past republics had been small, few in number, of questionable efficacy. The United States struck many as an untested experiment, which in 1789, as a society very much in process, it was. Could so unusual a form of government, one so seemingly volatile and unwieldy, broken up in semi-independent states and spread over a large area, provide the stable, hierarchical society that many deemed necessary to nurture a rich cultural life? Even today it remains to some degree an open question.

In France the Directory of 1795–99 followed the Terror of 1793–94. Both became failed experiments. Neither boded well for the success of republics elsewhere. Beethoven's "favorite theme," in the view of his biographer W. J. Turner, "was not politics of the politician intriguing for party, place and power to aggrandize self and friends," but " 'politics' as the art of creating society, a society that will express a richer and fuller life."[20] Enlightenment thinkers, from Kant through the Romantics, had developed a more benevolent view of society. Its purpose was to improve the morals of its citizens, to encourage them in benign fashion to become better. Instead of the state being a "necessary evil," checking baser instincts, it should act as a force for good by giving meaning to the lives of its citizens.

Enlightenment philosophers valued liberty. "I have always preferred liberty above all else," said Voltaire.[21] A full-size sculpture of him by Jean Antoine Houdon shows the philosopher sitting in a chair quietly reading a book. The sculpture bears an unusual title: *Écrasez l'infâme* (Crush the infamy), that is, the tyranny of state, class distinctions, and the Church. By the simple act of reading, the statue and its title imply, we can educate ourselves and thus undermine oppression. Most revolutionaries felt as Voltaire did. Like anyone else who has wrestled with the concept of *liberté*, Beethoven valued and understood it in his own way. Liberty for him consisted chiefly in living in a political entity, whether monarchy or republic or other, that allowed its citizens the freedom to lead a fulfilling existence within a framework of just laws. One year of liberty (*Freiheit*), his Bonn professor, Eulogius Schneider, had claimed, "is more useful to humanity than a century of despotism." Beethoven may not have gone that far, but he believed in *liberté* both as a practical principle in his own life, then increasingly as its spiritual apex.[22]

Fraternité, however, Beethoven held more as an ideal than as a reality. As an ideal, it provided him the emotional satisfaction that he often lacked in personal terms. He was not close to his brothers by blood, nor with individuals of lesser social rank than himself. He had experienced fraternity in Bonn's Reading Society, however, and amid the von Breuning family. As an ideal, *fraternité* resonates in his Joseph cantata and in his music for the poem "Der freie Mann." Subsequently he embodied *fraternité* in *Fidelio* and the Ninth Symphony. In the latter the chorus sings its determination not to yield for less. His emphasis on *fraternité* was as much German as French, deriving as it does from the ideal of *Bruderschaft* (brotherhood) that formed one of Schiller's hopes for the future of mankind.

Only at *égalité* did Beethoven balk. *Égalité* was the odd man out, not because Beethoven did not respond to the concept in terms of equal legal rights but because for him it clashed with *Freiheit* ("liberty" in English). Though *Freiheit* remained his mantra, *liberté* does not have to imply *égalité*. Though civic *égalité* he more or less accepted, this staunch individualist found repugnant the idea of full social *égalité*. Beethoven's own egalitarianism did not extend very far beyond his fellow artists and his dearest friends like the von Breunings and Ferdinand Ries, as well as the nobles who helped him. All the same, Beethoven often expressed a wish that his music have meaning and resonance for all of humanity, not least the poor.

᛭

Schiller's "Ode to Joy"

Well before the Revolution broke out, Schiller had published in 1785 his lighthearted poem "Ode to Joy" (*An die Freude*), with its soon to become famous lines "Seid umschlungen, Millionen / Dieser Küss der ganzen Welt" (Be embraced, ye millions / This kiss [is for] the whole world). The poem came about, like others of Schiller's works, because he enthusiastically believed in humanity's common nature and in its capacity for moral progress. Oddly enough, Schiller subsequently never much favored his creation. Fifteen years later he expressed embarrassment before it.[23] "My Freude is a bad poem," he wrote his friend Christian Gottfried Körner, "and marks a stage in my development, which I had to put completely behind me, in order to produce something decent."[24] The poem proved instantly popular, however. In essence a drinking song, it became in the 1790s a favorite of German republicans. Choruses across Germany sang its stirring words with enthusiasm. Others embraced it as well. Liberal circles in Beethoven's Bonn would certainly have heard of Schiller's poem. Beethoven may even have encountered the "Ode to Joy" in the year of its publication. The poem acquired special import for him, for he responded to its warmth toward humanity. For nearly four decades the "Ode to Joy" reverberated powerfully in his imagination, an abiding work in his pantheon, a fundamental ground tone (*Grundton*) within his musical memory.

Beethoven had the poem in mind when composing his Joseph cantata in 1790. Later, close to the time of his move to Vienna, he pondered the meaning of freedom not only in Schiller's words but in the music he wrote for Gottfried Conrad Pfeffel's poem, "The Free Man." Though Schiller's ethical influence comes out most palpably in the Ninth Symphony, it pervades more or less subtly almost all of Beethoven's work. In addition to the Joseph cantata and "The Free Man," the "Ode to Joy" subsequently made its presence felt, literarily or musically or both, in the *Eroica*, in *Leonore/Fidelio*, in the Choral Fantasy, in the Fifth Piano Concerto, and in the incidental music for Goethe's *Egmont*. It reappears, most powerfully and fully, in the Finale of the Ninth Symphony. In it Beethoven once again restated his belief in *Freude* as the noblest creed of mankind, active not only in brotherhood but in the way we choose to live. Uwe Martin has rightly termed the "Ode to Joy" an "outspoken song of revolution."[25]

ᔡ

Music of the French Revolution

Music in the revolutionary France of the early 1790s raced ahead of the other arts. Innumerable songs, marches, operas, and cantatas both inspired and rendered the age's visionary fervor. As a partial replacement for the civic institutions that the Revolution had eliminated or reduced, organizations devoted to new music came into being. Parisians followed with interest, sometimes with enthusiasm, the careers of contemporary composers who praised the Revolution and wrote about liberty.

Beethoven closely followed these developments. The works of the mostly Paris-based composers, several of them of Flemish or Italian origin—Gossec, Grétry, Méhul, Cherubini, Paisiello, Le Sueur, and others—influenced his own compositions. Marches and marchlike themes that recall French revolutionary music later found their way into several of his major works, especially his oratorio *Christ on the Mount of Olives (Christus am Ölberge)*, the variations in the last movement of the *Eroica* Symphony, the C-major martial tune in the second movement of the Fifth, the Turkish march in the last movement of the Ninth, and, briefly but dramatically, in the Finale of the *Missa solemnis.*

During the last decade of the eighteenth century the place of music among the humanistic arts evolved rapidly in Germany. Geniuses like Goethe and Schiller—and, in time, Beethoven—represented the quasidivine apogee of human perfection around whom cults grew. Exposure to art, literature, and music as a means for cultivation of the self, as well as moral and spiritual improvement, became a vocation.[26] Once audiences came to regard a concert hall less as a secular establishment and more as a church, they increasingly expected a kind of transcendence.

꙼

The "Marseillaise"

Among the thousands of songs to emerge from the Revolution, the "Marseillaise" quickly became the best known. It was birthed in Strasbourg soon after absolutist Austria had declared war on the French Republic.[27] Republican France had reciprocated on April 24, 1792. That night a twenty-year-old lieutenant in the French army, Claude-Joseph Rouget de Lisle, a largely unsuccessful poet and occasional composer, became inspired and wrote down both words and music. Initially known as the "Battle Hymn for the Army of the Rhine," Rouget's effort met with an immediate and enthusiastic response, not least because of its rousing tune.

Rouget had initially intended the "Marseillaise" to raise the spirits of revolutionary partisans and troops as they marched off to battle. Of the groups of patriots who responded, among the most enthusiastic were troops from the Mediterranean port of Marseilles. Starting on July 11 and pulling their cannon behind them, they marched all the way to Paris singing Rouget's song as their battle cry. They arrived in the capital on July 30. On August 10 the monarchy fell. Now, as Parisians soon adopted it, the song received the name by which it is known. In the process they turned it into a musical symbol of the French Revolution and subsequently of all revolutions.

Within a month words and music had spread like wildfire across France and well beyond. Its words inspired hearers to believe in *liberté* and *fraternité* and to hope for *égalité*. "Allons enfants de la patrie," it begins, "Le jour de gloire est arrivé" (Forward, children of the beloved country, / The day of glory has come). But to usher into being a new age, to bring about a "day of glory," required sacrifice, a willingness to fight and die for the ideals the song expresses. The "Marseillaise" possesses an irresistible propulsive movement, with each stanza closing with the refrain "Aux armes, citoyens, formez vos bataillons / Marchons, marchons! / Qu'un sang impur abreuve nos sillons" (Gather your weapons, citizens, form yourselves into battalions / Forward, forward! / That an impure blood may water our furrows).[28]

Few could resist the impetuous energy of the "Marseillaise." The "initial cry of alarm" ("Marchons, marchons!") may even have found an echo in the *Eroica*'s opening chords. Equally, the song's energy and propulsive force announce the symphony's irresistible forward movement. Later Beethoven through that mighty creation would implement the message of the "Marseillaise" on a scale infinitely larger and deeper. One reason why he would have valued the "Marseillaise" is that it is more than a song about marching off to battle: it is a hymn to human brotherhood.

The song expresses in plain language the aspirations for freedom of people everywhere. It became popular in German as well as in French armies. Even Goethe, never a partisan of the Revolution, found the "Marseillaise" "compelling and terrible" when in 1795 he first heard it sung in Weimar. For him it was a "revolutionary Te Deum."[29] Though its lyrics changed as circumstances changed, the tune retained its subversive power and became throughout Europe and well beyond a symbol of progress, of liberty, even of civilization. Virtually disappearing during Napoleon's hegemony, it began to be sung again late in 1813, when France found itself again threatened. A century after it emerged from a Strasbourg drawing room as a battle song intended for the Rhine army, the "Marseillaise" became France's national anthem. It was, said Stefan Zweig, one of the "Guiding Stars of Humanity."[30] It embodied the hatred of tyranny, the love of freedom, a belief in victory. It embodied no less the voices of mothers trembling for their sons off to war and of farmers fearful of their lands becoming fields of blood.

ہ

The "Marseillaise" along the Rhine

The importance of the "Marseillaise" for Beethoven has been insufficiently appreciated.

Bonn is a leisurely two or three days' trip downriver from Strasbourg, where the "Marseillaise" originated. Although Beethoven does not mention the song in the few writings by him from this period that have survived, the distinguished French Beethoven scholars Jean and Brigitte Massin conjecture that during the late summer or early fall of 1792 he, while still in Bonn, likely heard its strains.[31] As they point out, Schiller's "Ode to Joy" and the "Marseillaise"—the first written a few years before the outbreak of the Revolution, the second a few years after—date from about the same time. And people sang both songs, they believe, in the same manner.[32] Over a hundred German texts were set to the music of the "Marseillaise" alone, a number comparable only to the hymns disseminated in Luther's Reformation. Understandably, most of these German versions, their authors fearing reprisals of one kind or another, were anonymous.[33]

Between Schiller's "Ode to Joy" and Rouget de Lisle's "Marseillaise" there exists an important link. In Cologne, Michael Venedey, born the same year as Beethoven, recalled hearing his father, Jacob, sing the "Marseillaise" to the tune of the first two stanzas of the "Ode to Joy." Jacob, drawing upon the latter's melody, alternated the couplets of the "Ode to Joy" with those of the "Marseillaise."[34] As had Michael Venedey, young Beethoven may well have heard the "Marseillaise" sung, presumably in German, in Bonn in 1792 to the tune of Schiller's "Ode." An original or early version of the "Marseillaise" contains the words "And that the thrones of tyrants would collapse at the sound of our glory." This message validates the belief that Beethoven had expressed in his *Cantata on the Death of Joseph II*: that upon hearing his music people would be inspired to lead heroic lives, and that as a consequence monarchic Europe would collapse into states, republics presumably, in which citizens would enjoy personal freedom and a full range of civic liberties. The moment of his likely hearing the song was propitious, and its results far-reaching. Behind the warlike words, their fury and violence, loomed the great thought, truly holy, that lay behind the Revolution, a thought that decades later Beethoven would realize musically in the Ninth Symphony: the liberation of humanity. Drawing upon the words of both Schiller and Rouget de Lisle in that work, he would compose a new "Marseillaise" to advocate a future world on the march.[35]

঺

Departure

On November 2, 1792, a month short of his twenty-second birthday, Beethoven left Bonn for Vienna. Ironically, Beethoven's coach encountered Hessian troops intent on recapturing Mainz from the French. The passengers experienced a few tense moments as the coach approached Hessian lines. They gladly paid the coachman extra to get through them. The coach then went eastwards toward the Hapsburg capital. Coaches accomplished the 550-mile journey in about a week, following the route Beethoven had taken five years before. The passengers may even have heard the "Marseillaise" along the way. In Vienna the song would not have been unknown, just too dangerous for people to sing in public.

None of Beethoven's Bonn friends expected his absence from his native city to be permanent. Neither did he. As late as 1794 he expressed his intention to return to Bonn. But the invasion and conquest of the Rhineland by French revolutionary troops in 1792, and for a second and final time in 1794, had resulted in the forced departure from Bonn of the Elector Max Franz. It also made a return by Beethoven to his beloved fatherland and its familiar landscapes inadvisable.

5

Brutus and the Egyptian Mysteries

Tyrants conduct monologues above a million solitudes.

ALBERT CAMUS, *THE REBEL*

From the mid-1790s on, Beethoven gradually became aware that his hearing was slowly fading. For a composer and performer of music good hearing is of primary importance. This gradual loss must have been much on his mind during these years. *"Plutarch has shown me the path of resignation."* So Beethoven wrote his old Bonn friend Franz Wegeler in 1801. Plutarch, the second-century C.E. chronicler of leading Greeks and Romans, taught Beethoven much about lives well lived, but he could not teach him happiness. "Resignation," the composer continues, "what a wretched resource! Yet it is all that is left to me—."[1] Characteristically, Beethoven, in his moments of greatest suffering, turned to the literature of ancient Greece and Rome to renew his spirit's strength. In the Heiligenstadt Testament set down the next year he observed, "It is virtue that upheld me in misery."[2] Encroaching deafness had by then become a terrifying reality for him, and it was Plutarch's larger fortitude that gave him strength to continue. His *Parallel Lives* fed a curiosity about the ancient world, instigated by recent archaeological discoveries in Greece and especially in southern Italy. In the theater Voltaire's *Brutus* (1730) helped promote a republican sensibility. The French historian Charles Rollin drew heavily on Plutarch in his long-standard texts *Ancient History* (1731–38) and *Roman History* (1738–48) .

Plutarch points out that "virtue" in Latin (*virtus*) means "manly valor." He espoused *virtus* as the basis for a person's life. *Virtus* encompasses not only moral rectitude but overall strength of being. Beethoven set about achieving *virtus* as his life-goal. For him, Plutarchian resignation and virtue became key elements in his being. To explore Beethoven as a revolutionary requires that we take up his fascination with Plutarch.

From the Renaissance onward the Greek author enjoyed vast popularity across Europe. Along with the Bible, his *Parallel Lives* and *Moralia* rank among the formative books of European civilization. Anyone who read at all in Beethoven's lifetime would have known his writings inside out, whether in the original Greek or, more likely, in translations. Even that most autocratic ruler, Louis XIV, the Sun King, an individual who read few books in an age in which Plutarch was widely known, had delved into his work. In France the heroes of the Roman Republic portrayed by Plutarch and Livy had by the early 1790s become exemplary models for a free political society. The composer's first major biographer, Anton Schindler, recalled that Plutarch "accompanied Beethoven through his whole life."[3] Preeminent in Plutarch among the revolutionaries of the past was Lucius Junius Brutus, who outwitted the Tarquin dynasty, established the Roman Republic, and served as its first consul.

In Europe as in far-off America, the eighteenth century became a veritable age of Plutarch. Rousseau counted himself among Plutarch's greatest admirers, as did Benjamin Franklin.[4] With the outbreak of the French Revolution in 1789, Latin authors—and the Roman ethos they embodied and wrote about—came dramatically to the fore in both Europe and America. Well into the nineteenth century, a Roman sensibility dominated not only the rhetoric of public life but also French, English, German, and American art, architecture, and sculpture. In creating his painting *The Lictors Bringing to Brutus the Bodies of His Sons* (Louvre), Jacques Louis David consecrates Brutus's uncompromising

belief in the ideals of the newly founded republic. Another hero he celebrates was Socrates, whose death, after that of Jesus, was for Beethoven
the most memorable in all history. David's *Death of Socrates* (also in the
Louvre) commemorates the greatness of an individual who wished to
purge the world of injustice. Unafraid, he sought even in death new
worlds to explore.

Late in life Beethoven would claim, "*Socrates* and *Jesus* are my models."[5] A contemporary averred in 1823 that Beethoven preferred Plutarch
to "all the rest."[6] He had read Schiller's play *The Robbers* in 1785 at age
fourteen. The first words uttered by Karl Moor, its tortured protagonist,
suggest why: "When I read about great men in my Plutarch, / Then this
ink-smudging age nauseates me."[7] The words resonate throughout the
play. Moor's anguished utterance encapsulates the thinking of the rising generation influenced by Enlightenment thought. Plutarch not only
shaped Schiller's, and through him Karl Moor's, conception of virtue
and greatness but, most likely, shaped that of young Beethoven as well.

Plutarch's writings never ceased to delight, guide, and make bear-
able to Beethoven the difficulties of existence. From him the composer
learned of the history, political institutions, and great men of Greece
and Rome. One reason for this admiration is that Beethoven thought of
himself among the Plutarchian great. "His judgment even concerning
classic authors," recalled his pupil Carl Czerny, "was severe, as a rule,
and uttered as if he felt his equality."[8] Although Plutarch provided inspiration and stimulus, Beethoven did not think his own life inferior to or
less important than those recounted by the Greek author.

Madame Roland, a French revolutionary guillotined in 1794,
had proudly proclaimed, "Plutarch had disposed me to become a
Republican"—this at age eight or nine.[9] She treasured Plutarch chiefly
"because he was Virtue, teaching by example."[10] Even the Creature in
Mary Shelley's *Frankenstein* had read Plutarch. George Bernard Shaw,
the Irish playwright, considered Plutarch's *Lives* a revolutionist's hand-
book.[11] Not all readers of Plutarch became revolutionaries. Every line in
Gilbert Stuart's portraits of George Washington, no revolutionary but

a reader of Plutarch, reveals Plutarchian rectitude. Along with Benjamin Franklin, the artist John Trumbull and later Ralph Waldo Emerson became notable Plutarchians but not revolutionaries.[12] No less did Plutarch seize the imagination of an unusual young man educating himself in the intellectually lively Rhineland town of Bonn.

ও

Brutus and Beethoven

Beethoven was an avid collector. Because he changed residences constantly, most of what he collected disappeared over the years or after his death. Some of the survivors—a candleholder, bronze paperweights, a clock, a small bell—we might consider among the normal accouterments for daily living. But there is one survivor of a more philosophical nature: a statue of Brutus on Beethoven's work desk.[13] This statue, now in the Beethoven House in Bonn and only six and a half inches tall, deserves close attention. First of all, it is not of the well-known Brutus who killed Julius Caesar. Today he is the better-known Brutus, the Brutus whom most Beethoven scholars, if they mention the statue at all, and most do not, assume it represents.[14] Beethoven knew about Marcus Junius Brutus, but he is not the Brutus who captured his imagination. His statue is of Lucius Junius Brutus, who came to Beethoven's attention through his reading of Plutarch. Some five hundred years before Caesar's Brutus, this Brutus led a successful overthrow of the Tarquin dynasty of Rome. A composite picture of his deeds and being emerges chiefly from Livy and Plutarch. Beethoven, a student of history no less than of humanity, would likely have read both—as well as hearing much about him—during the early years of the French Revolution. He was then far and away the better-known Brutus, his name on every revolutionary's lips.

The story of Lucius Junius Brutus had riveted artists and writers since the Renaissance. Brutus's uncle, the tyrannical king of Rome, Tarquinius Superbus (the Proud), had murdered the previous king (his new wife's father), a number of senators, and most of Brutus's family, including his father and brother. Realizing that Lucius Junius Brutus might well be seeking revenge, Tarquinius had him watched closely. According to Livy, Brutus was well aware of the danger he was in and deliberately assumed a mask to hide his true character. He survived in the royal household, Livy tells us, by pretending to be inept and stupid, and even submitted to being known publicly as the "Dullard" (the meaning of "Brutus" in English), so that under cover of that opprobrious title the great spirit that gave Rome her freedom might be able to bide its time.[15] Brutus, however, was anything but stupid. Traveling in Greece with Tarquinius's two brothers, he along with them consulted the oracle at Delphi. It prophesied that the man who first kissed his mother would become the next king of Rome. While the brothers pondered the oracle's meaning, Brutus pretended to trip, fell on his face, and kissed "the Earth—the mother of all living things."[16] He had understood the oracle. The brothers had not.

Subsequently, Sextus, one of Tarquinius's sons, raped the virtuous Lucretia, wife of the prefect of Rome, who, to expiate the stain on her honor, stabbed herself.[17] Lucius Junius Brutus swore on her dying body to rid Rome of the Tarquins. Realizing that only a change in the form of Rome's government could save the city, he gave a speech before the assembled populace in which he convinced them to expel the Tarquins and establish a republic. Livy writes that his unexpected eloquence amazed those present. "All looked at him in astonishment," he observes: "a miracle had happened—he was a changed man."[18] It is thus Lucius Junius Brutus who in 508 B.C.E. essentially founded the long-lived Roman Republic, served as one of its first two consuls, and remains its finest hero. Later, Brutus led armies against the Tarquins in defense of the republic. Livy tells us that in rashly engaging Tarquinius in single combat he along with his opponent was killed. Thus he made the ultimate sacrifice for his beliefs. Soon afterwards the Tarquins underwent a final defeat.

European and American statesmen traced the principle that laws are made for everyone to Brutus's introduction into Roman society of elected law-abiding magistrates. The young Beethoven would have read about such concepts of civic rectitude in Cicero, unrivaled as an authority on republican politics; in Livy, who has left us the fullest account of the career of Lucius Junius Brutus; and, most of all, in Plutarch, eloquent on republican forms of government. Plutarch's composite portrait of Lucius Junius Brutus is more psychologically complex than Livy's. He points out that great personal tragedy had scarred Brutus's political achievement. His two sons had joined the exiled Tarquins in their plot to overthrow the newly established Republic. During the campaign that followed, Brutus's sons were captured. As consul, Lucius Junius Brutus had to condemn them to death and watch them die. This act puzzled Plutarch. It led him to probe deeply into the mixed nature of Brutus's being: he found the Roman "of a severe and inflexible nature, like steel of too hard a temper, and having never had his character softened by study and thought, he let himself be so far transported with his rage and hatred against tyrants that, for conspiring with them, he proceeded to the execution even of his own sons."[19] Trying to comprehend the paradoxes of his nature, Plutarch spoke of Brutus's deed as "an action truly open to the highest commendation and the strongest censure; for either the greatness of his virtue raised him above the impressions of sorrow, or the extravagance of his misery took away all sense of it; but neither seemed common, or the result of humanity, but either divine or brutish."[20] Though admired for his single-minded devotion to his country and his republican ideals, Brutus's pronouncing the death sentence upon his rebellious sons cast, for Plutarch and for others, a troubling shadow over his heroic achievements.

Plutarch's depiction of Brutus suggests personality traits characteristic of Beethoven: direct, uncompromising, determined, of inflexible will and capable of immense emotional control, traits much admired in him later by the young Viennese dramatist Franz Grillparzer. Yet Beethoven was prone to sudden outbursts of anger, capriciousness, and he could be erratic in judgment. Like Brutus amid the corrupt Tarquins, this transplanted Rhinelander felt himself temperamentally unlike the frivolous Viennese. Beethoven, in short, may well have fancied himself in Vienna as a modern Brutus. The Roman's devotion to republican values corresponded to the composer's equally passionate devotion to expressing republican ideals in his music. Like Coriolanus, another noble Roman who came to fascinate Beethoven, Brutus was immensely able if personally problematic. Both Coriolanus and Beethoven possessed greatness of being; both were tragic figures. However, like Brutus, but unlike Coriolanus, Beethoven did not bend or break.

ॐ

Brutus in Revolutionary France

By the early 1790s Lucius Junius Brutus had emerged as a figure of tremendous interest to Beethoven's European contemporaries. Individuals in France who valued republican ideals saw themselves as inheritors of a cultural tradition stretching back more than two thousand years. Neoclassical artists presented Brutus both as a paradigm of heroic virtue and as one caught in a shocking conflict of duty. Foremost among those who idolized him was Jacques Louis David. His magnificent painting *The Lictors Bringing to Brutus the Bodies of His Sons* (1788–89), depicts Brutus, his visage deep in shadow, clearly distraught. The artist intended his work as a powerful witness to legal necessity, even if at devastating emotional cost, to sacrifice family members in support of a free republic.

When displayed at the Salon in September 1789, three months after the Revolution had begun, the painting caused a sensation. Its message was clear: anyone could stand before David's *Brutus* in the Salon and, with the Revolution just outside the walls, feel its significance. An *exemplum virtutis* (example of virtue) for the French people, the painting was designed to burn an indelible lesson into the viewer. Visiting France in 1790, the German traveler Gerhard Anton von Halem commented, "It was at the exhibition of *Brutus* that I saw the strongest manifestations of that spirit of liberty that reigns today."[21]

Brutus appeared in drama as well as in art. On November 17, 1790, the National Theater revived Voltaire's early play *Brutus*, itself an inspiration for David's painting. During the French Republic's early years, what those who enthused ardently over the Brutuses of Voltaire and David wanted most were notions of "regeneration," of a better world coming into being, at once physical, political, moral, and social. The idea of a "new man," this time in Brutus's image, was itself hardly new. Images of a second birth for mankind were at the heart of the eighteenth century's dreams. Joseph Fouché, later to become Napoleon's formidable minister of police, inaugurated a civic religion, its focus a "Feast of Brutus" celebrated on September 22, 1793. Towns and streets were renamed after Brutus. Many French patriots changed their names to Brutus, and in the Paris region alone parents registered some three hundred newborn children with the first name Brutus. Other depictions of Brutus, including busts modeled upon those of antiquity, were installed in public buildings, most notably before the bar of the orators in the assembly room prepared for the Convention in 1793. Smaller versions, presumably similar to that acquired by Beethoven, also appeared.

In June 1791 Louis XVI, attempting to flee France, was captured just short of the frontier. On his person was found a proclamation in which he renounced his previous adherence to the new republic. Patriotic citizens compared the heroic behavior of Brutus to the repugnant behavior of their weak king, who lacked the "virtue" to stand up for the new French Republic. Termed a "Tarquin," Louis was executed in January 1792. Virtuous French Republicans now felt themselves worthy of being deemed "Romans." During the Terror of 1793–94 Brutus, who had had his own rebellious sons executed, stood as the emblematic figure of republican duty.

Voltaire's *Brutus* marked the emergence of the young actor François-Joseph Talma in the role of Titus, one of Lucius Junius Brutus's errant sons. Talma's friend David designed his costume consisting of a simple cloth mantle and robe. It led to a complete revolution in people's fashion. No more plumed hats and silken doublets! Greek and Roman heroes now strode the boards in tunics and helmets designed by David. For his role Talma had his hair cut short. On stage amid bewigged actors, his closely cropped hair style caused a sensation. His abbreviated locks associated him not just with classical antiquity, but also with the virtues of simplicity, frugality, and naturalness. The new hair style soon became known as *à la Tite* or *à la Titus*. Among those who adopted it were the young Napoleone Buonaparte (as he then spelled his name) and the even younger Beethoven.

Whereas in conservative Vienna the older generation of Haydn and Salieri dressed carefully in buckled shoes, silk hose, and old-fashioned powdered wigs, Beethoven wore informal Rhenish attire based on the new French style, that is, worn by those who favored the Revolution. Aware of Napoleon's new look (and of its origin in Talma's portrayal of Brutus's son), Beethoven also had his hair cut in the new French style. It did not please everyone. In the 1790s hair style often pointed toward a person's beliefs, or politics. Beethoven, by his hair and attire, intended to make a statement. Though hardly a sansculotte, that is, a radical revolutionary, his appearance indicated support of the Revolution. About 1801 Beethoven's young student Carl Czerny observed that his shock of "jet-black hair, cut *à la Titus*, made him look shaggy."[22]

Napoleone Buonaparte was well aware of the heroic fortitude of Brutus in sacrificing his sons who had betrayed the new republic. Having ordered the execution of the French turncoats responsible for the British occupation of Toulon, General Buonaparte signed his report to the commissioners of the Convention, "BRUTUS BUONAPARTE, citoyen sans-culotte."[23] Upon his return to Paris he sat for David, who painted his portrait. He conquered the artist. David thought Napoleon was Brutus reincarnate, the potential father of a new republic. He was, for David, "a man to whom in Antiquity people would have raised altars."[24]

In the German states Brutus was hardly less valued than in France. Initially, for fear of repression, German enthusiasm for Brutus remained subterranean. The situation soon changed. Christian Gottlob Heyne, the German dramatist, asserted in his autobiography that "his hero was Brutus, the prototype of those who fight against the oppressors of the poor."[25] Schiller regarded Brutus as a social and revolutionary moral force and posited him as a model for William the Silent in his *History of the Revolt of the Netherlands* (1788).[26] Similarly, Goethe valued Brutus as a political and moral ideal, a republican, a murderer of tyrants, and inserted him in his play *Egmont*, first sketched in the early 1770s.[27]

Brutus even managed to make his way to absolutist Vienna. When the Saxon traveler Johann Gottfried Seume passed through the capital on his way south in 1800–1801 he visited the leading Viennese artist Heinrich Friedrich Füger, then hard at work on a painting of Brutus. Seume later thought it bore a remarkable similarity to David's.[28] Beethoven, who knew Füger and had visited his studio, might well have seen there his painting of Brutus. He had likely read about Füger's painting in his copy of Seume's book, to which we shall return shortly.

Although in Hapsburg Vienna the authorities ruthlessly suppressed revolutionary impulses, Beethoven did not despair. A revolutionary in a revolutionary era, he knew he could re-create in musical, if not in political, terms the renewed world that the Revolution had heralded. Few thoughtful contemporaries who listened carefully to his music could have doubted that he approved of the ideals of France's First Republic. But even while Beethoven admired those fighting for the Revolution, Lucius Junius Brutus's strength of character held huge significance for him. He stood foremost in Beethoven's pantheon of greatness.

The Joseph cantata provides initial musical evidence of Beethoven's fascination with a leader who tried to change the world. The *Eroica* Symphony of 1803–04, inspired in part by Napoleon and his deeds, would mark a second climax of his revolutionary idealism. Many then alive considered Napoleon a hero out of Plutarch. Beethoven, while he worked on this symphony, had similar thoughts. He compared Napoleon to "the greatest Roman consuls"—and who stood greater among the consuls than Lucius Junius Brutus?[29]

ঽ

Johann Gottfried Seume Ponders Brutus the Elder

Another who pondered the meaning of Brutus in this era of revolution was Johann Gottfried Seume in his travel narrative *A Walk to Syracuse* (1803), a book whose marked influence on Beethoven I take up in a later chapter. On his way south Seume, in early 1801, passed through Vienna. He arrived with his close associate in his native Saxony, the painter Veit Hanns Friedrich Schnorr von Carolsfeld, director of the Leipzig Art Academy.

The two travelers enjoyed a memorable visit to the studio of Füger, director of the Vienna Art Academy, which under his teaching and leadership had attracted students from all over Europe who sought to specialize in then-popular majestic historical paintings depicting scenes in the lives of classical heroes and heroines. The artist had completed, or nearly so, a painting depicting Brutus the Elder, which Seume describes in *A Walk to Syracuse*. As had many contemporaries, including Beethoven, he had learned about the elder Brutus through his readings of Plutarch and Livy. Now, thanks to Füger's painting, Seume gained a vivid visual awareness of the courageous yet traumatized Roman consul, an *exemplum virtutis*, a man of integrity, who felt he had to condemn his two sons to death for treason. Seume's detailed description of Füger's *Brutus the Elder* indicates that he responded to art depicting the great heroes of classical antiquity.[30] Füger, he realized, had seen engravings of David's initially notorious painting *The Lictors Bringing the Bodies of His Sons to Brutus*. Even for so well regarded an artist as Füger, painting Brutus the Elder in Vienna entailed significant risk. Art no less than literature had to pass the censor. In 1809, after Prince Klemens von Metternich, now Franz I's chief minister, decreed that works of art not embody criticism of Austrian society, censorship tightened even further.

❧

The Egyptian Mysteries

In his compositions, words, ideas, mental playfulness, and range of interests, Beethoven rarely fails to surprise us. His infrequent comments about the meaning of his compositions are often cryptic, occasionally humorous, sometimes deliberately misleading. Early on, he realized that many contemporaries found his music unfathomable, but this awareness apparently gave him little concern. The thought that people had to struggle to wrest his often-concealed meanings often delighted him. Understanding his compositions might well be a slow process, but Beethoven did not doubt that eventually those who cared about them would appreciate, perhaps even grasp, his intent, or some aspect of it. Several later compositions—the *Grand Fugue* (*Grosse Fuge*), op. 133, for instance—remain to this day as challenging and mysterious in meaning as when first composed. In them Beethoven wrote less, it seems, for his patrons or for his contemporaries than for an ideal future audience.

Such a hypothesis gains substance when we consider three gnomic sayings deriving from ancient Egyptian sources that Beethoven came upon in Schiller's essay *The Mission of Moses*. Beethoven valued them so much that he had them framed and placed them on his work desk near his cherished statue of Brutus.

> I am that which is.
> I am everything that is, was, and will be—no mortal man has
>   lifted my veil.
> He is of himself alone, and it is to this aloneness that all things
>   owe their being.[31]

Schiller seems to have come upon the Egyptian sayings in an essay by Voltaire, *On the Egyptian Rites*.[32] Like the Brutus statue, the sayings help us understand key aspects of Beethoven's sense of himself and of his mission as a creator. If we consider the sayings within the context of Schiller's essay, itself an interpretation of the career of Moses, they shed light upon the mask that hid the mystery that lies at the core of Beethoven's being. Unusual as it may appear, they tell us how through his music he came to conceive of himself and of his role as an interpreter of the future of society.

When Pharaoh ordered the slaughter of all male Hebrew infants in Egypt, Miriam, Moses's sister, hid him in the bulrushes along the Nile. Discovered by Pharoah's daughter and adopted by her, Moses was raised by Egyptians, received an Egyptian education, and learned of the Egyptian mysteries. The seat of the select society of Egyptian priests who tightly controlled the mysteries was the temple of Isis and Serapis. Between the mysteries and Moses's later deeds and legislation Schiller posits "a remarkable similarity." In the mysteries, he surmises, "the idea of the unity of the Supreme Being was first thought in a human mind." Given that the Egyptian state religion was polytheistic, secrecy regarding a belief in monotheism was essential.

Moses early manifested a heroism inspired by the highest ideals and pursued with steadfast courage. "Nothing is more unbearable to his great soul than to tolerate injustice," Schiller insists. Moses had no illusions about the task before him. After three centuries of servitude in Egypt, the Hebrews were "the coarsest, the most malicious, the most despised people of the Earth." Professing monotheism to his people, Moses "made Him the only God . . . and cast all other gods around back into their nothingness." God is supposedly the speaker of the sayings. Moses realized all too well his chief challenge: that "from this people itself he can expect nothing, and yet without these people he can accomplish nothing." Still, confident in his own relationship to God, Moses wanted "to found his work for eternity."

Words by Schiller had for Beethoven especial resonance, and in Bonn he had read Schiller's early poetry and plays, and probably saw several of the latter performed. Beethoven came to own several editions of Schiller. It is not known when he first read *The Mission of Moses*. He could have read the essay as early as 1790, when it first appeared, though that seems unlikely. Thoughts stimulated by Schiller often underwent a long maturation in his mind, as in the case of the poem that decades later he reworked into the "Ode to Joy" for his Ninth Symphony. Even if he read Schiller's essay later, he had been thinking along the lines it develops for a good while.

Emperor Franz I feared secret societies and in 1792, at the beginning of his reign, banned all Masonic activity.[33] Mozart had earlier joined a lodge, participated in its rituals, and valued its ideals. Even if Beethoven had had similar inclinations, which is likely, it would have been madness for him and for his career as a musician in Vienna to avow them. While Beethoven biographer Maynard Solomon investigates with exemplary thoroughness Masonic activities in Vienna as well as Beethoven's own Masonic leanings and their possible reflection in various compositions, in explaining what the Egyptian mysteries may have meant for Beethoven he misses, I think, the forest for the trees. Even if we grant that the sayings cited by Schiller correspond to Masonic beliefs and that Beethoven may have been aware of the connection, they would not, in my view, have been the main reason why he treasured them.

So, what drew Beethoven so powerfully to these sayings? Art can imply meaning indirectly. Moses had to hide from the Egyptians his plans for the Hebrews. Only when the right time had come did he reveal his mission to free them. In his need for concealment Moses was a model with whom the reticent and sometimes enigmatically reserved Beethoven could identify. Beethoven saw himself as a Moses figure. God's words resonated for Beethoven. They became for him the ultimate mantra. They indicate him to be a fiercely independent spirit, one almost terrifyingly secure in his awareness of his own high genius, a spirit unafraid of being misunderstood, strong in its knowledge that the future would validate his mastery of his art.

The "veil" in the second of these sayings is usually interpreted as the "veil of truth" or, more specifically, the veil of the goddess Sais, or Isis. In a letter of 1815 to his student Countess Erdödy, Beethoven describes the Temple of Isis as a place of purification and rebirth.[34] Only there, he tells her, can the mystery be unlocked, the veil lifted. The mystery that lies at Beethoven's core, the sense of an unusual power, a divinity even, that he felt within himself, particularly in later years, seems manifest in these words. The three sayings that Beethoven understood as guides to life consoled him for the lack of understanding with which most of the Viennese public regarded his music. Whether, if ever, the veil would be lifted and the moment of understanding or revelation be at hand, depended upon the individual listener. Most likely, only a select few would grasp Beethoven's message.

Schiller in his essay had described the oppressed Hebrews in Egypt as uneducated and barbarous; for Beethoven, they may well have borne an all too close resemblance to the Viennese among whom he lived and worked—and by extension—to much of the rest of uncomprehending mankind. Yet it was through Moses that the Hebrews became aware of the glorious possibilities that awaited them in the Promised Land. Beethoven, then, in this reading, saw himself as the Moses of music. His compositions embodied the messianic impetus of the French Revolution. They would lead those who grasped their import to an understanding of the possibility of a world in which liberty and equality, truth and justice, existed.

As with Brutus, Moses for Beethoven represented political rectitude. Schiller's words—"nothing is more unbearable to his great soul than to tolerate injustice"—would have resonated deeply for Beethoven. He hoped his music would support the growth and spread of political justice. No less than Schiller's Moses, the composer wanted "to found his work for eternity." In short, the cryptic yet hugely significant sayings on his desk—no less than the equally important figurine of Brutus— reminded Beethoven daily of his purpose on earth. Both Brutus and

Moses had recourse to concealment, both maintained the faith, and neither ever compromised his vision of the ideal.[35]

Although Brutus died in defending the republic he had brought into being, and God denied Moses entry into the Promised Land, both figures served as models for Beethoven to emulate. Like Brutus at Delphi and Moses on Mount Sinai, Beethoven understood the divine command. God had spoken to him as He had spoken to them, and he was as certain of his mission as they were of theirs. No less would Beethoven employ music to enlighten mankind. His instrumental music, he realized, was difficult to fathom, but clues exist. Recall, in regard to the explosive Finale of the Fifth Symphony, Exodus 13:21, in which the Lord led the Israelites to the Promised Land by night: "The pillar of fire lighting up the path before us."[36] No more veils, but the free spirit of enlightened man proclaimed and on the march! "Politically," it has been observed, "romanticism was the continuation of the French Revolution 'by other means.'"[37] For Beethoven, the "other means" was his music. The Egyptian sayings, along with the Brutus statuette, tell us why.

6

Hapsburg Vienna

Vienna makes everyone crazy.

LEOPOLD MOZART[1]

In spite of everything I still greatly loved the prison
from which I have been released.

SIGMUND FREUD[2]

Vienna in the 1790s

During the turmoil of the Revolution and the Napoleonic years, Vienna supplanted Paris as the unofficial capital of Europe, at least among absolutist regimes. An international metropolis, hub of the vast Austrian empire, a city whose diverse peoples spoke many different languages, it also served as a cosmopolitan rendezvous, at least for the wealthy and noble-born. In Austria as in many areas of Germany, the fresh winds from France did not often make themselves felt. Instead, class consciousness continued, along with the state's strict control over society. But beneath the glittering surface all was not well. Vienna's social life had its dark sides. After Hungary (then part of the Austrian empire), Austria itself had the highest suicide rate in Europe. Moral laxity was pervasive. The city's numerous streetwalkers, Casanova pointed out, all carried rosaries so that they could tell the police they were on their way to church. The heavy hand of censorship upon Viennese life led the populace to concern itself chiefly with amusements and food.

Public perception of the Austria of Joseph II, at least by those outside of Hapsburg-controlled lands, might well have deemed it among

Europe's most enlightened nations. Few who lived within Austria's
borders held this opinion. In Bonn, at the time of his Joseph cantata,
Beethoven regarded the vast Hapsburg realm positively. Once settled in
Vienna his views altered. He no longer spoke of Joseph II. The city he
had moved to expressed outright hostility to Joseph's proposed reforms
and to the new ideas from France. Governmental unease had led in 1794
to the rapid and drastic suppression of a Jacobin uprising in the capital. Most of the public displayed little interest in revolutionary ideas. In
Beethoven's view, a reordering of society required belief in new ideas
and the courage to accept them. For that to happen the Viennese lacked
both the imagination and the will.

At the city's heart rose the dominating tower of St. Stephen's Cathedral. Massive city walls, with wings of stone projecting outwards, provided a defensive ring around the old city, and seen from above they
made the city look like a giant starfish. Within the walls lived about a
fifth of the population, some fifty thousand, in a closely woven pattern
of streets. Everyone in Vienna dreamed of living in the inner city, with
its palaces and fine abodes, in short, a place of privilege. The open area
beyond the walls, called the Glacis, extended as far as nineteen hundred
feet across, beyond, it was hoped, the range of eighteenth-century cannon. Then came suburbs, afterwards open fields. Whereas the infra-
structure of the old city was barely adequate, roads into the suburbs
were unpaved. A day of rain turned them into a mud bath.

A building spree during the early eighteenth century had shaped
the Vienna of Beethoven's day. Even today a large number of these residences front the city's streets. A century before, the city's most gifted
architect, Johann Fischer von Erlach, had designed the palaces of the
aristocracy. Today most serve as civic or office buildings. Thus much of
old Vienna, at least in its street plan, narrow lanes, and often its buildings, is close to Beethoven's Vienna. Pretty villages, many visible from
the tower of St. Stephen's, lay amid the fields or hugged the nearby foot-
hills. The more outlying villages—Heiligenstadt, Grinzing—reach well
into those hills. On clear days we glimpse from St. Stephen's tower high

mountains to the south, the Austrian Alps. They reminded a Romantic generation of solitude and grandeur, though perhaps not Beethoven, who never mentions them.

During the more than three decades Beethoven lived in Vienna, natives and visitors alike considered Austria an old-fashioned country, a stagnant society, a country without ambition, one which sought to preserve itself in the evolving European domain by opposing all radical developments. Changes in social mores were hardly discernible. "Everything in our almost thousand-year-old Austrian monarchy seemed based on permanency," observed Stefan Zweig, whose classic study *The World of Yesterday* (1942) vividly evokes pre–World War I Vienna, "and the State itself was the chief guarantor of this stability."[3] Even then, the city looked back to the imagined harmonies and balances of an earlier time.

Vienna has long prided itself as being the most theatrical of cities. Many Viennese perceived life as a drama or a Baroque opera. As its older architecture testifies, the Baroque appealed to the aristocracy's sensuous love for beauty and gracefulness, as well as complemented its perennial fascination with drama and music. The theater and opera both enjoyed huge popularity, but throughout the eighteenth century opera reigned supreme. In plays and operas the populace followed the fortunes of its leading performers with greater interest than they did the careers of their creators. Wherever one went in Beethoven's Vienna, people were ready to discuss the plays or operas offered at the old Burgtheater, attached to the Hofburg, or the Kärntnertortheater, near the city gate from which ran the road to its southernmost province, Carinthia.

Economic progress came slowly to the Hapsburg capital. Vienna in its business activities lacked boldness. During the eighteenth century the city suffered from a shortage of capital. Austria's longstanding virtuosity in dramatizing its own myth bolstered the city's conservatism. By the time of the French Revolution, no industrial or financial bourgeoisie of substance or cohesion had emerged. "It was as if in Vienna any attempt at modernity was doomed," comments Frederic Morton, by birth Viennese and a frequent writer on the city.[4] Styles in fashion in the capital also evolved slowly. Throughout Europe the powdered wig gradually disappeared, and the heavy, ornate brocades of the early eighteenth century quietly gave way to simpler, untrimmed, lighter fabrics.[5] Morton speaks of "the Viennese brand of courtliness—that is, the art of maintaining an entirely pleasant mask over a psyche of usually mixed emotions."[6] Later, Freud thought the city combined the frivolous with the narrow-minded. A few things—tastes in fashion and music among them—gradually changed. But change was glacial, and invariably resisted. The Viennese disdain for complexity continued well after Beethoven's time. Still, whatever the city's imperfections, for many of its inhabitants—at least those of the aristocracy and the sufficiently well-off middle class—Vienna offered a seemingly irresistible charm.

Under Hapsburg rule Austria retained its ancient traditions. In the eighteenth century the Hapsburgs revived the strict court ritual derived from Spain. Spanish melancholy, not the long overdue rationalism that had spread across the rest of Europe, became preponderant. The rigidity of the court etiquette was such that it became a noxious, time-consuming affair. Most foreign travelers agreed that the Viennese notion of ceremonial presence was the most obsessive they had ever encountered. The gulf between rich and poor in the mid-eighteenth century shocked the British philosopher David Hume. In Mozart's Vienna of the 1780s aristocratic control of society reached its apogee. The poor were subject to the whims of the powerful, and taxed to support the luxurious life of their betters.

᛬

City of the Phaecians

When Beethoven's younger contemporary, the Austrian dramatist Franz Grillparzer, called the city "a Capua of the mind," he wished to remind people that "Capua," or Capri, was in Roman times the favorite haunt of decadent emperors and their acolytes. Schiller in a 1797 epigram in

his *Xenie* did the same: "Round me abide with lustrous eyes the Phae-
cian people. / Every day is Sunday, the spit turns without cease on the
hearth."[7] He recalled the notoriously gluttonous, sensual, yet extremely
pleasant people whom Homer in his *Odyssey* depicted on the island of
Scheria.[8] A mysterious society in which stress was unknown, it became
Odysseus's last stop before reaching his home island of Ithaca. Disgusted by this degenerate life, Beethoven condemned Vienna as "this all
powerful *land of the Phaecians*."[9] To live amid such people often appalled
the serious-minded young musician. Already Tannhäuser in the Middle
Ages, to characterize Vienna's sybaritic ways, had spoken of "Phaecian-
ism" in which "underground dwellings," that is, taverns, seemed more
numerous than dwellings above ground.[10] Images of decadence continued to haunt Vienna throughout the nineteenth century and into the
early twentieth.

Hypocrisy pervaded Viennese life, nowhere more so than in its sexual mores. Vienna, if religiously conservative and politically repressed,
was sexually open. "No city perhaps can present such scenes of affected
sanctity and real licentiousness," remarked Henry Reeve, a Scottish
traveler who surveyed the city in 1805 and whom we shall encounter
again.[11] Beethoven was no prude, but he often prided himself on having
high moral standards. The abundant licentious behavior around him
would have confirmed his notions of Viennese decadence.

Karoline Pichler, a contemporary of Beethoven and a chronicler
of Viennese life, termed her decades in the city as the *Backhendlzeit*,
that is, the time when the populace became obsessed with consum-
ing roast chicken.[12] Beethoven agreed. He found the Viennese *leicht-
sinnig* (light-headed). His contempt for their frivolous ways waxed and
waned over the years but never disappeared. The populace's passivity,
its overall indifference to social and political issues, its focus on eating,
amazed—and disgusted—the newly arrived Rhinelander. The Viennese, he found, delighted in their "brown ale and little sausages."[13] A
familiar combination in Germanic lands then as now, they were con-
sumed morning, noon, and night. That is not to say that Beethoven

did not relish them himself or, even more, a fine meal accompanied by a good wine. But to him it seemed that the Viennese concerned themselves with little else than food and gossip, maybe with some light music thrown in. Neither the political nor the martial capabilities of his new compatriots impressed him. He criticized Viennese indifference to ideas, to politics, to thoughts of improving their lot in life, even the capacity of the military to defend the country. More important matters occupied Ludwig van Beethoven. Paramount among them was the creation of the music that he felt lay in the depths of his soul.

Despite the many musical luminaries and masterpieces associated with Vienna, few have regarded the city, at least in Beethoven's epoch, as a haven for artistic creativity. For those who could afford it life went along in such an environment so pleasantly that intellectual effort became almost impossible. Noted authors hardly vary in their critiques of the city, from Lady Wortley Montagu in the early eighteenth century to Madame de Staël in the early nineteenth, from Stefan Zweig a century later to Nicholas T. Parsons today. Yet Beethoven, though appalled by lax Viennese ways, initially felt a kind of liberation upon his immersion in a metropolis teeming with varieties of bustling life.

Austrians of German descent lived as a tiny minority in a vast country surrounded by more than a dozen major and many minor nationalities, each with its own customs and speaking its own language. In the face of societal ills that they felt could not be cured, or even comprehended, they experienced a pervasive failure to face reality. The Austrian empire, believes the acute American historian of the country, William M. Johnson, "conducted its affairs in a semi-permanent state of self-deception."[14] The city exhibited a "preference for self-glorification over self-analysis." In all the assessments of Vienna by Viennese "there is something inflated or askew."[15] Thinking individuals in other European capitals were generally more self-aware. "The Austrian has a hidden soul," observes Friedrich Heer, himself Austrian; "he does not reveal himself or say what he 'really' thinks, or believes, or feels deep inside, over the things that touch him most deeply—religion and the state."[16]

The refusal by Austrians to understand their own society reached a turning point in the decade of the 1790s, when Beethoven first moved to the city.

~

Pezzl's Vienna

The most acute local commentator on late eighteenth-century Vienna is Johann Pezzl. His *Sketches of Vienna* (1786–90) offers a detailed, comprehensive, and immensely intriguing account of Josephinist Vienna, the decade from 1780 to 1790. Like Joseph II and Mozart, Pezzl believed in Enlightenment ideas. Hence he strongly supported Joseph's reforms. In many, but not all, ways Pezzl's "sketches" "hymn the same humanitarian principles that inform Mozart's *Le nozze di Figaro* and *Die Zauberflöte*."[17] Covering a wide range of subjects, Pezzl casts a shrewd yet critical eye upon life in Vienna in the decade before the Revolution exploded in France.

The dust enveloping the city appalled Pezzl. "If you leave your house at eight o'clock on a Sunday evening after a lovely warm day," he observes, "it is like entering a fog; one can only make out the lanterns flickering through the dust; and if one leaves by one of the city gates, a dense dust-cloud covers the whole Esplanade."[18] By esplanade Pezzl means the Glacis mentioned earlier, the large open area beyond the city walls. We need read no further in Pezzl to discover why Beethoven, as soon as he could afford to, spent summers in villages well beyond this dustbowl. If Vienna's water supply now ranks among Europe's finest, in Beethoven's time it was truly dreadful. "The water drunk by the Viennese is not the best," Pezzl cheerfully informs us; "it acts like a purgative and any foreigner who has been here for a few weeks usually suffers from diarrhea for a month."[19] Not only short-term visitors suffered. During most of his more than three decades in Vienna, Beethoven, a foreigner, suffered from intermittent and sometimes severe intestinal troubles.

The notoriously built-up and overcrowded inner city contributed to the water pollution. Pezzl speaks of the difficulty of walking its streets. Beethoven, having grown up in compact Bonn, may well have relished such density, for a number of the lodgings he occupied over the years lay within the city walls. The population constituted a microcosm of the vast multinational Hapsburg empire. Its bouillabaisse of peoples—among them, Germans, Hungarians, Czechs, Poles, Armenians, Turks, Slavs, Greeks, Wallachians and Moldavians, Serbians, Gypsies, Muslims, Croats, Polish Jews, Bohemian peasants, Transylvanian waggoners—congregated in their own districts. "A pleasant feast for the eyes here," observes Pezzl, who admired the variety of national costumes of different countries. Walking the streets, the inhabitants presented a colorful scene.[20] In 1794, two years after Beethoven arrived in the city, the Prince de Ligne deemed "Vienna a perfect Babel of tongues." The linguistic mayhem distinguished the city from other European capitals. Here one met "with many men and women who can speak five or six languages, and almost all at least three—French, German and Italian."[21] The empire's German inhabitants still identified themselves as Saxons, Swabians, Frisians, Bavarians, and Rhinelanders. In Vienna people considered Beethoven a Rhinelander. He never became an Austrian, never wished to.

The reticence of the Viennese to express their innermost thoughts, their avoidance of critical discussion, Pezzl found disillusioning. "On formal social occasions one never speaks openly, and never about matters of importance."[22] In contrasting old with new Vienna, he favored the former. "It is true," admits Pezzl, "that the soft character of the Viennese is not calculated to produce heroic virtues."[23] Beethoven would have agreed. The Viennese, he found, lacked not only revolutionary fervor but even basic political curiosity. In a 1794 letter Beethoven dismissed the typical Viennese burgher as a simple hedonist, uninterested in politics, and content as long as he ate well.

Discussions of politics had to be avoided at all costs. Even among friends political conversations could become tense. A swarm of paid informers and spies infested society. The situation gradually worsened during the decades the composer resided in the city. Pezzl viewed Vienna as an entity in decline. Where before the authorities had permitted casual talk about affairs of state, now "a ridiculous secrecy" surrounded "the most unimportant matters." Although Pezzl claimed for pre-1789 Vienna "an unconstrained freedom of speech," the first edition of his book appeared before Joseph tightened censorship, and well before the severe repression that occurred under Franz I.

꒒

Music

Music was the great exception to the city's cultural torpor. Though the tastes of the populace remained resolutely conservative, Vienna retained the strongest musical traditions of any German-speaking city. Encouraged by the example of a highly musical court, every member of which had received training in music and had learned to sing or to play an instrument with proficiency, music prospered. Whatever disadvantages Vienna posed to a young pianist-composer, the city in 1792 was still the place to go—for musicians, especially—to have a chance at success and a better life. All the same, Beethoven's decision to move to Vienna not only took the physical courage required to cross battle lines but also the even greater courage needed to leave home, friends, and supporters.

Vienna's musical traditions had long had a cosmopolitan flavor. During Beethoven's time there Italian music, particularly Italian opera, dominated the musical scene. Music in Vienna entered upon a golden age of melodic clarity and accessibility, both Enlightenment characteristics. If its rulers during this period totally lacked the political savvy and imagination of Pericles or the Borgias or Queen Elizabeth, in music over nearly five decades it housed within its walls four geniuses— Mozart, Haydn, Beethoven, and Schubert.

ꕔ

An Intellectual Backwater

If cultured Europeans regarded Vienna as musically rich but intellectually stagnant, it was not entirely the fault of the citizens. The censorship
permitted few serious books to enter Austrian domains. Such volumes
might disturb people's minds. From a populace forbidden the classics of
Enlightenment thought as well as the plays and narratives of the German
Sturm und Drang, of Lessing and Herder, of most of Schiller and early
Goethe, what could one expect? The radical writings that poured forth in
these decades had given many late eighteenth-century Europeans a galva-
nizing political shock regarding the nature of society and its possibilities
for improvement. But Austrians had little or no access to these writings.

"Everything," noted Henry Reeve in 1805, "is regulated more by force
and formality than by freedom and good will."[24] Cultural life—the life
of the mind—stood at a standstill. "With regard to literature, arts, and
sciences," Reeve believed, "Vienna is far behind other towns even in
Germany." He thought that "reading is in a manner forbidden by the
Government not allowing the free circulation even of classical books."
The lack of places or opportunities for political discourse appalled him.
"Politics are seldom talked of; the people are indifferent upon every topic
but mere idle objects of amusement."[25] The Viennese adored festivals,
as Madame de Staël observed a few years later. Hapsburg authorities
liked them too, for festivals distracted the citizenry and allowed them to
forget they were living in a police state. For those unhappy under such
a regime, the only possible way to achieve a fuller life involved a kind of
internal emigration. One of those who decided to emigrate internally,
though the decision took him years to make, was Beethoven.

ꕔ

The Weight of Censorship

"To love liberty above all else," Schiller had written in *Don Carlos,* a play Beethoven knew well. He quoted the line in 1793 in the autograph book of a Viennese friend. In the liberal atmosphere of Bonn and its progressive university, radical ideas had flowed freely and Beethoven could have exposed himself to them to whatever degree he wished. Vienna reversed the situation. Official censorship was omnipresent, thorough, and strict. Though more liberal under Joseph II than under Maria Theresa, the censorship was still formidable. It included material likely to undermine the enlightened notions that the monarch himself proclaimed. Joseph II had had little use for higher education, except in specialist fields like medicine, and insofar as it served to form efficient state officials, who, viewing "the universities [as] the breeding ground for all sorts of outrage," purged their faculties thoroughly during Joseph's reign.[26] The circulation of books was affected. Although Joseph reduced the list of forbidden titles from 4,500 to 900, many classics, among them works by Lessing, Schiller, and Goethe, remained officially banned in Hapsburg lands. In the 1790s, after Joseph's death, censorship in Austria under Leopold increasingly reverted to a prior pervasiveness. His successor, Franz, even more uneasy about upsets to the state than his uncle and father, feared those with active intelligences and kept his distance from them.

Banning books then was not as unusual a practice as it may seem now. The Austrian and German states developed their own traditions of coping with what the authorities considered seditious writings. The growing severity of censorship forced newspaper editors to exercise caution in informing their readers about politics or about radical ideas. Censorship also paralyzed the literary scene. The situation was not totally the government's fault. Pezzl faults the Viennese for a lack of intensity in what little reading they did. They showed a reluctance to deal with the new ideas pervading Europe, a point Madame de Staël reiterated in her *Of Germany* twenty years later. For the Viennese dandy, she observed, "the deadly sins are a sensible discussion—A useful book—Hard work—and a bad meal."[27]

Despite Pezzl's dislike of secrecy and the negative aspects of Viennese culture, he was no revolutionary. Vienna banned what he called "the masterpieces of monstrosity by Klinger, Lenz, Schiller." Like many proper Austrians, he found recent literary developments abhorrent. Early Goethe of the *Sturm und Drang* decade of the 1770s fared particularly badly. In direct contrast to Pezzl, the indifferent Viennese response to new ideas and new writings did not please Beethoven at all. In liberal Bonn he had read widely in *Sturm und Drang* literature, including Goethe's *Werther* and his somewhat scabrous play *Götz von Berlichingen*. Schiller's dramas, banned in Austria, he had read or seen in Bonn.

The modest *Wiener Zeitung*, the city's principal newspaper in Beethoven's day, appeared every Wednesday and Saturday. It consisted of four pages. Officials of Joseph II's court exercised only light censorship over its contents. After his death, during the brief reign of Leopold II, censorship moderated still further. The police reported directly to Leopold, who was no friend of secret police methods. Although he did organize his own service, it was a small one, and he used it chiefly for purposes of information. But with the accession of Franz I in 1792, emperor at age twenty-four, censorship returned with greater vigor than ever. Franz felt unsure of his abilities. Even before he succeeded to the throne he had taken an interest in police restrictions.[28] They soon became a notorious feature of his reign. The initial duty of informers was to watch closely civil servants and officers; later foreigners and other suspicious elements came under similar supervision. In 1805, the year of *Leonore*, the first version of Beethoven's *Fidelio*, the censorship bureau became an official government organ. A cumbersome, often ineffective, but nevertheless pervasive system of strict censorship of newspapers and journals as well as of books persisted for decades to come.

Franz recalled to duty Count Pergen, in charge of censorship under Joseph but dismissed by Leopold. Under his rule restrictions were once again tightened. Franz asked Pergen to turn his attention to the many

Freemasons residing in Vienna. Pergen made censorship of their activities more stringent still. He forbade all works that criticized and blamed the government. He also forbade the reproduction of foreign writings, or parts of them. Their spreading of dangerous doctrines, he believed, would disturb public tranquility. Furthermore, Franz entrusted Pergen with the task of suppressing all manifestations of either sympathy or support for the French revolutionaries. Vice Chancellor Cobenzl opined that people who gave speeches approving of their activities belonged in a dungeon. Hapsburg censorship also persecuted dissenters. Consequently, what Viennese radicals there were learned to cultivate discretion and even outward conformity. Franz, to maintain his standing and unwilling that the general public should lose faith in its emperor, from whom it expected fatherly concern for the rights of all, even at one point made a show of imposing a few restrictions on his own virtually arbitrary power. Because Pergen ordered the police to keep all foreigners under the strictest observation, one wonders if Beethoven, that young stranger from the far-off French-influenced (and after 1794 French-controlled) Rhineland, was among the observed.

In spite of the censorship, the Viennese press kept an eye on day-to-day happenings elsewhere. The Austrian court viewed the revolt in the American colonies as the first in a chain of related conspiracies. From the outset Austria responded to the challenge of the French Revolution by repression and aggression abroad rather than by preventive reform at home.[29] Contemporary travelers found the police presence in Vienna more evident than anywhere else in Europe. "Not only was the purchase of books from elsewhere limited but also no circulating libraries were permitted," noted Reeve in 1805, after the censorship had further tightened. Books and libraries, he continued,

> are suppressed by order of government. No reading-rooms or
> clubs are permitted; and every book and every newspaper passes
> through a censor's hands (probably not through his head), before

it is permitted to be given to the purchaser or proprietor. The English newspapers are stopped many days at the post-office to pass through this formality. The consequence of this arbitrary prohibition is, that the public mind is dull and torpid, or rather no public mind exists. *Bread* and *shows* are procured for the people in politic profusion; amusement is the only object of their lives.[30]

Given so repressive a society, politics, observed Reeve, "very seldom are made the subject of conversation." In the best company "they are never mentioned." He found "no public voice" in the city, "no means of expressing public opinion."[31] So completely did the state control the lives of its citizens that most Viennese, especially the poor, could not even marry without the permission of the authorities. Thus did the bureaucracy regulate life from birth to death. Resignation became the general response. People accepted rather than combated restrictions.

Although in letters Beethoven rarely wrote openly of Viennese intellectual lassitude, he indicated on one of his sets of variations that he wished it to be played *alla Austriaca*, that is, in a relaxed Austrian manner. The bluntness of Beethoven's ways in Vienna astounded Austrian-born and -bred Haydn. Early letters Beethoven wrote from Vienna show a man who did not hesitate to express contempt for those among whom he lived. In Vienna most people remained attached to the monarch, and their basically easygoing character kept them from becoming a revolutionary people. Of the various mental burdens Beethoven faced in Vienna, the increasing state suppression of basic freedoms must have been the most galling. He felt he differed greatly from those among whom he had chosen to live. Sensing and perhaps already believing himself the heir of Haydn and Mozart, Beethoven claimed genius for himself.

Well before the outbreak of war between Austria and France in 1792, the authorities had put in place tighter regulations. Fearing the spread of the French revolutionary poison to Austria, Franz exerted pressure on officials to turn the Hapsburg domains into a full-fledged police state. Austria soon became, claims Ernst Wangermann, one of its most distinguished historians, Spain transported to the fortress of Kufstein, where in the 1790s Austria put most of its political prisoners, without benefit of trial or hearing. The societal unease previously felt under Joseph II increased greatly. The secret police readily equated Freemasons and Illuminati with Jacobinism. Besides them, they also feared Theosophists, Eclectics, Rosenkreuzer (Rosicrucians), and Americans. After all, had not the last-named managed a successful rebellion?

ᡃᢄ

French Ideas and Language

In the middle decades of the eighteenth century a sea change in European thought and taste had taken place. Many educated people at this time regarded France as the greatest nation in the world, the center of fashion, the arbiter of taste, the source of new ideas. Across Europe and deep into Russia, French ideas and the French language had become the currency of the educated and the aristocratic. French became the court language of innumerable German states. Well before the Revolution, the German nobility had wholeheartedly adopted French manners. Despising his native German, Frederick the Great wrote and spoke only in French. He once quipped that he spoke German only to his servants and to his horses. Even native speakers of German had trouble using their language. Gluck's written German was awkward. Metternich's remained uncertain all his life. Their French was much better. Italian was also much in evidence in Vienna, particularly in the court, and among the musically inclined aristocracy. Beethoven learned Italian reasonably well. To sum up, the French language, lively Italian music, rigid Spanish court ceremony, and a reluctance to speak German were the inheritance of well-born Austrians. To add to the mix, Latin remained the official language of adjacent Hungary well into the nineteenth century.

At dinner parties in Vienna during 1805, Reeve expressed surprise to discover that "the language employed was French; the German

language is seldom or never spoken in the best company of Vienna."
Despite Austria being often at war with France, the French language
remained a preserve of the aristocracy and the educated. German, Reeve
quickly learned, was for dealing with servants.[32] In Vienna, the capital
of Europe's largest German-speaking political entity, Beethoven felt he
lived in a foreign country even when speaking German. The spoken
German of the educated classes differed measurably from that in Bonn,
and the shopkeepers and servants spoke a quite different dialect. Any
Viennese would have recognized from the moment Beethoven opened
his mouth that he was not a native. He never became one.

sq

Freemasonry and the Revolution

Without ever himself becoming a Mason, Beethoven had acquired in
Bonn a favorable opinion of Masonic ideals. In Vienna many of his
new friends were or had been Masons, including Gottfried van Swieten and Baron Nikolaus Zmeskall von Domanovecz, as well as his first
patrons in the city, the Lichnowsky family. Haydn and Mozart were
both Masons. Indeed, most of Vienna's cultural elite had some kind of
Masonic connection. But in 1792 Franz—fearful of religious toleration,
political compromise, loyalty to local instead of royal authority, and rel-
ishing the power of secrecy—banned Freemasonry altogether. Despite
protests, he did not rescind his ban.

For Beethoven the Revolution remained a vision of what might have
been, a vision, as has been suggested, of "a lost paradise."[33] In the
imperfect society of Hapsburg Vienna the revolutionary impulse flick-
ered and died or went underground. But the ideal world that the Revolution heralded continued to excite Beethoven's imagination. He knew
that he could re-create that world in musical, if not in political, terms.
A century later, Ferruccio Busoni looked back upon Beethoven as "the
product of 1793," that is, "a revolutionary before the excesses of the Terror that year and the next, left many disillusioned." He was, for Busoni,

"the first great democrat in music."[34] Language may fail us when we try to render Beethoven's thoughts into words, but his music speaks its own language. On the basis of what we hear, few can doubt his vibrant approval of the ideals of the First French Republic.

During the first twenty-two years of Beethoven's life in Vienna, that is, until 1814, French Enlightenment ideas and influence posed the greatest threat to Austria's absolutist emperor and Austrian aristocrats. During this time few in Austria dared to express a relish for French political influence. For a while, in part because of the revulsion Vienna's aristocrats felt for the French Revolution, German again became in many palaces the first language, as it had been before Maria Theresa acceded to the throne in 1740. Within a few years, however, the French language reasserted its preeminence. Conversation in Vienna again became French. The nobility, which remained apart from the city's diverse population, wrote its diaries in French. In short, it was more open to Italian influences in music and to French influences in everyday conversation than to German. Despite Austria's several wars with republican and later with Napoleonic France, educated and aristocratic Viennese retained discourse in the French language as a cherished preserve.

Though patronized soon after his arrival in Vienna by the aristocracy, Beethoven did not quite rank as an aristocrat (the controversy over the "van" in his name lay far in the future), yet his patrons certainly regarded him as more than a mere plebeian. Dubious about aristocrats of birth, Beethoven valued aristocrats of talent and character. They were, for him, the only undeniable nobility.

ঽ

Beethoven's Languages

While Beethoven responded to French Enlightenment and revolutionary ideals, he disliked the affected use of Francophile language in German-speaking Austria. In his native Rhineland, where France had long maintained a cultural presence, use of French was widespread, and in Bonn he had attained some fluency in the language. Even his awkward, imperfect French proved useful in Vienna. All the same, using French made him uncomfortable. Richard Wagner, as late as his 1870 study of the composer, expressed resentment "that the French are the ruling people of the civilization of our day."[35] He claimed that Beethoven had fought against this domination. Only after World War I did French cultural and linguistic hegemony in European upper-class life decline.

Beethoven took his Rhineland dialect with him to Vienna, and he kept his local accent all his life. Despite living in the city for over thirty-five years, he never gained acceptance as Austrian or, despite claims by some Austrian musicologists to the contrary, as an Austrian patriot. Nor, we should remember, did that appear to be his wish. As the Austrian historian Friedrich Heer succinctly put it: "Goethe remained a Frankfurter all his life, Schiller was a Swabian in exile, and Beethoven's 'fatherland' was Bonn."[36]

Proud of being a Rhinelander and unwilling or unable to learn the local Viennese dialect, Beethoven stood out in the cosmopolitan city. Not only did people think of him as an outsider but he felt himself one. He had distinguished literary precedents in that belief. In effect, once he had moved to Vienna, he felt himself as much an outsider as did Saint-Preux in Rousseau's novel *Julie, or the New Héloïse*. In Vienna he would have encountered Enlightenment thinking far less frequently than in Bonn, certainly not in bookstores (where books promoting new ways of thinking were unavailable or, if available, heavily censored) and probably not in the mansions of his aristocratic patrons. Just possibly Beethoven might have encountered such thinking among his friends in Vienna, such as Baron Zmeskall and, later, Karl Amenda, both outsiders.

❧

Franz I

Leopold II died in March 1792, his reign having lasted barely two years. Four months later, on July 14, 1792, his son received the crown in Frankfurt as the new Holy Roman Emperor of the Hapsburg lands, Franz I. Joseph II, who had studied his nephew shrewdly, had been unimpressed. Franz, he thought, had "a good memory but a barren one"; also "a sensitive fear of the truth"; he showed "irresolution, nonchalance in thought and action"; most damning of all, he had an "incapacity for great affairs."[37] An older contemporary, the Prince de Ligne, later described Franz as a "swimmer": "after each defeat he changed his ministers and re-entered Vienna to the cheers of his loyal subjects."[38] A modern German historian sums him up thus: "Franz was young and mistrustful, lantern jawed, with cold, languid, ungracious eyes, and a stony expression."[39] It was this individual, born in 1768, who became emperor of the vast Austrian empire soon after Beethoven arrived. Franz labored to stop time. His constituents with active minds made him nervous. He kept his distance from them.

Few contemporaries praised Franz either for his character or for his achievements. His long and increasingly repressive reign lasted until 1835, nearly a decade after Beethoven's death. Conservative, indeed reactionary in his social views, Franz as he aged became ever more fearful of new ideas, of change of any kind. A passable violinist, he did show early on some slight interest in the city's musical life, the last Hapsburg ruler to do so. But he did not respond to Beethoven's music. During their joint time together in the city, he and Beethoven, two years apart in age, apparently never met nor connected in any way.

Beethoven's failure to establish any kind of relationship with Franz had unfortunate consequences. The emperor's indifference, indeed active dislike of him and his music, deprived the composer of official or governmental patronage. Beethoven, who welcomed support wherever he could find it, is not known to have criticized Franz publicly. Privately, it was no doubt another matter. If Franz had cared to interest himself in the man whom contemporaries soon acknowledged as the city's, and then Europe's, greatest living composer, a worthy successor to Haydn and Mozart, he might have garnered praise from music lovers and posterity. But the individual who could have become Beethoven's most important patron made a point of never attending a concert of his music, or according him even minimal attention.

Other members of the royal family came to regard Beethoven more favorably. Franz's second wife, Maria Theresa, empress from 1792 until her death in 1807, was passionate about music. An admired singer, she often took an active role in Vienna's musical life. Although Beethoven never entered her innermost music circle, she recognized his merit and his frequent criticisms of the Vienna musical scene never extended to her. To Maria Theresa he dedicated his Septet, Op. 20, a major triumph and long a favorite work among Viennese audiences. Only her active intervention, as we shall see, made it possible for Beethoven's opera *Leonore* to get past the censor. With Franz's third wife, Maria Ludovica, Beethoven also came to establish a rapport of sorts. A general atrophy in musical matters seemed to have overtaken Hapsburg monarchs. The first Empress Maria Theresa (reigned 1740–80) had had Gluck instruct her daughters. Joseph II ably discussed with Mozart his operas, and Leopold II composed music.[40] Franz, perhaps afraid of music's power to move people, kept his distance from such a dangerous mode of expression.

Mozart's Vienna years, from 1781 to 1791, offer a pointed contrast to Beethoven's first decade in the city. Profoundly immersed in Enlightenment concepts, Mozart was an idealist. Though not a political radical, he was, as *The Abduction from the Seraglio*, *The Marriage of Figaro*, and *Don Giovanni* all reveal, an astute social critic. Mozart's *Figaro*, drawing on Beaumarchais' play, had so little sting left in its libretto that it passed the suspicious court censorship. Vienna's gradual disenchantment with Mozart's music came about not because of any advanced political views he had but because operagoers thought him a kind of unbridled emotionalist. The position of the musician, in Vienna, as Mozart's career illustrates, remained uncertain, at times lowly. His art transcended limits set by court and Church. He was never able to achieve personal independence or financial security. He died, as Beethoven no doubt well knew, in considerable debt. The precise location of his burial place is not known.

When Mozart decided in 1786 to set to music Beaumarchais' play, he clearly approved of its social message. Figaro, though a servant, feels himself the equal, perhaps more than the equal, of the Count, his master. Mozart no doubt thought himself as good as any count. Necessarily, for opera performances in Vienna the composer had to tone down Beaumarchais' egalitarian sentiments. Notably he had to leave out Figaro's long monologue in Act 5, scene 3, in which the clever servant muses upon the injustices of society. A few years before, in the Finale to Act 1 of *Don Giovanni* (1787), Mozart has the Don utter, *"Viva la libertà!"* Liberty in the German-speaking world always meant political more than personal freedom. The words could be sung during the reign of Joseph II, but no one dared utter them in the Vienna of Franz.

Even Haydn did not at first conquer the Viennese: there are six "Paris" Symphonies and twelve "London" Symphonies, but no "Vienna" Symphonies. What struck contemporary observers most strongly about Haydn's music was its unorthodoxies, its wit, surprise, and what these days we call irony. Typical is Haydn's Symphony No. 88, which plumbs neither the heroic nor the tragic level of experience. Only with *The Creation* and *The Seasons*, on either side of 1800, did the Viennese take Haydn fully to heart.

ℒ

The ideals of the revolution in France had affected Beethoven's Bonn and altered life in the Rhineland. As they moved across Germany, they had sometimes led to violent repercussions. Yet they hardly disturbed Austria. The reasons are simple: Austria was distant, and there was no pretext there, nor support available, on which dissidents could base a successful revolutionary movement. Besides, the Terror that convulsed Paris and other French cities during 1793–94 led to a gradual diminution of fervor across Europe in support of the Revolution. More and more Germans distanced themselves from revolutionary ideas. In time, distance would yield to hostility. In most of the German states Jacobinism had never really caught on. Except for Spain, Portugal, and Austria,

revolutionary activity could least be found in many of the German entities. Besides, how long would the Revolution last, wondered officials? As
the years went by, its success fueled a rise in counterrevolutionary reac-
tions. All the same, given the varied nature of the vast Hapsburg lands,
the dynasty had cause for worry. In the wake of perceived threats to its
sovereignty, Franz sought to strengthen counterrevolutionary forces.
The Vienna in which Beethoven lived thus became the heart of resistance to French republican ideas.

Yet, though hundreds of miles further east of Paris than Bonn, the
city paradoxically did not altogether escape the Terror. By the summer
of 1794 a small group of individuals sympathetic to the Revolution had
formed in Vienna. On one occasion it even raised a Tree of Liberty,
a symbol of protest first seen in the revolution in America, then vigorously adopted by the French revolutionaries, subsequently by their
followers across Europe. But in Vienna the government had quickly
suppressed the movement and it soon collapsed. Its arrested members
received death penalties, long prison terms, or were exiled. The Jacobin trials in Vienna, however, subverted already strict laws. The inevitable guilty verdicts and the harsh sentences handed out undercut the
unwritten understanding that the will of the sovereign was circum-
scribed by law. Even after the Viennese authorities had dissolved the
local "Jacobins," a good deal of discontent remained in the city.

The chief reason why Beethoven never returned to his homeland
was that he could not. By late 1794 the French had occupied the Rhine's
Left Bank. The Elector Max Franz, his supporter and protector in
Bonn, had dissolved the court and its orchestra before himself taking refuge in Vienna. The stipend as a court musician he had regularly sent Beethoven ceased in March 1794. Whatever status Beethoven
had acquired in Bonn no longer existed. He may also have felt he had
outgrown the city, which would be under direct French rule for the
next twenty years. Echoes of the French Revolution had engendered in
Beethoven revolutionary and liberal aspirations. "He was a passionate
democrat, a convinced republican, even in his youth," comments Hugo

Leichtentritt, who regards him as "in fact, the first German musician to have strong political interests, ideals, and ambitions."[41] Not wishing to live under French rule, he had no desire to return. Vienna was now, for better or worse, his home. The opportunities offered him in the Austrian capital soon confirmed him in his decision to stay.

7

Beethoven's Vienna

Never *outwardly* show people the contempt they deserve,
because one cannot know when one may need them.

BEETHOVEN[1]

O f the three main musical forms that flourished in the Vienna of
Beethoven's day—opera, dance music, orchestral and chamber
music—opera, a field long dominated by Italians, was far and away the
most popular. Often written by Italian-born but Paris-based composers, French rescue operas, in which a main character is rescued from
danger and a happy resolution occurs, began in the 1790s to enjoy a
considerable vogue. Beethoven expressed great interest in opera, but
German-language operas were far fewer. He lacked a native tradition on
which to build. He considered librettos and possible subjects over the
course of his life, but in the end wrote but one, *Fidelio*, originally titled
Leonore. First performed in 1805, this version was revised in 1806, and
again, extensively, in 1814 under the title of *Fidelio*. Only the last version
achieved a full measure of success.

The second of Vienna's musical universes was dance music. During Beethoven's time in Vienna he witnessed the rise and amazing
success of the waltz, which gradually replaced the more stately minuet
long favored by the aristocracy. Though he wrote much dance music,
including waltzes, during his life, Beethoven mostly devoted his genius

to more complex music. With his orchestral and chamber music—symphonies, concertos, sonatas, string quartets, as well as songs, two masses, and several cantatas—he soon achieved a significant if always controversial presence within Vienna's music scene.

The city's music lovers valued outstanding, brilliant individuals and performers. Well-connected patrons soon became aware of the talents of the young Rhinelander in their midst. He seemed to have had patrons virtually from the day he arrived. Several of them recognized immediately the force that lay within him. He accepted their support but did not consider himself beholden to them. We may search in vain for consistency in his personal behavior, but in the extraordinary music he created during his first years in the Hapsburg capital we find it without fail. Thanks to Haydn and the interest he mustered for Beethoven among the aristocracy, the young composer soon gained renown as a virtuoso pianist, among the city's finest and most gifted. As an improviser on the piano he left listeners spellbound, but as a composer success came more gradually. Beethoven apparently passed at this time among the Viennese as being of noble birth. They equated the Flemish "van" in his name with the German "von." "Von" usually came with a patent of nobility, "van" did not, but that lack did not become a problem for Beethoven for some time to come. Such an individual as he, blunt and direct in speech and a stranger from French-influenced Bonn, we might expect to have had difficulties in making his way among the cultivated Viennese aristocracy. But Beethoven judged his powers as a musician early and rightly. He had published compositions in Bonn during the 1780s and early 1790s. After he moved to Vienna he decided to hold off further publications until he had fully readied his new and often startling works written in a variety of genres and styles. No less did he intend to make the greatest possible impact as a virtuoso pianist.

♪

Haydn

To become a successful composer Beethoven felt he needed to deepen his musical knowledge. Upon his arrival in Vienna he determined to work with the best available teachers. Hard as it may be to think of Beethoven as a student, he not only continued during these first Vienna years to deepen his study of the basics but also learned to respond more thoroughly to the subtleties and varieties of past achievement in each genre of music. Aware that his musical skills went well beyond the ordinary, he honed them by discipline, by studying with teachers he respected, and by listening carefully to what he heard, perhaps even more by watching musicians as they played, and by conferring particularly with those more advanced than he was. He was always listening, always learning. No music schools existed then in Vienna or anywhere else. The increasing sophistication of Beethoven's compositions testifies to a lifelong willingness to explore new modes within music's vast realm. Only by constant effort, he knew, could he fulfill his musical promise. Haydn had already given him encouragement in Bonn and invited him to study with him in Vienna. The praise of the most famous composer in the world meant much to young Beethoven. Haydn was a master of counterpoint, as Bach had been, and from him Beethoven hoped to learn much.

The letters Haydn and Beethoven wrote indicate their respective characters. Haydn's letters to his noble employer, Prince Nikolaus Esterházy, use the deferential language of formal titles expected between plebian servant and aristocratic master. Beethoven, however, though well aware of the lowly status of musicians, uses the stilted court language sparingly. A decade earlier, Mozart had attempted to make his way in Vienna on his own. He had impressive successes but also failures and humiliations. Embarrassingly, when in 1781 he announced his departure from the Archbishop of Salzburg's entourage and his decision to stay in Vienna, a flunkey of his early patron kicked him out of the room.

A decade later Mozart died impoverished. No doubt aware of Haydn's modest status under his longstanding patron, Prince Esterházy, and of Mozart's trials and humiliations, Beethoven determined to forge for himself as independent a career in music as he could.

When Haydn was released from service after Prince Esterházy died in 1790, he moved to Vienna, where he lived off his generous pension. Under his tutelage Beethoven studied counterpoint, which signaled a development between the canon and fugue of the Baroque in Bach and Handel and the mature Classical style of Haydn and Mozart. Young Beethoven's genius impressed but did not awe Haydn, as Mozart's had. Beethoven highly valued Haydn's conscientious correction of his exercises.[2] Relations between student and teacher remained cordial, and in 1793 Haydn took his student to Eisenstadt, the Esterházy seat southeast of Vienna, now in Hungary, where he introduced the young composer to members of the family. What they thought of him at the time we do not know. But years later, the son of Haydn's former patron, also named Nikolaus, would commission Beethoven to compose a mass in honor of his father.

Haydn had grown up dirt poor and under difficult family circumstances. He sympathized with Beethoven, who in his traumatic early years had suffered comparable hardships. During his youth Haydn had revealed a genius for misbehaving. All his life he nourished a taste for jokes, musical as well as verbal. Beethoven, too, had a sense of humor, sometimes witty, sometimes coarse, sometimes ironic, always unpredictable. Although Haydn may have wondered about the oddities in Beethoven's music, its sudden stopping and starting, for example, he proved a true friend to the young composer. In November 1793 he wrote to Max Franz, elector of Cologne, praising Beethoven's compositions and asking him to increase Beethoven's allowance. Alas, Haydn did not know that the works he cited as evidence of his student's progress Beethoven had written the first version of while in Bonn. But the musically literate elector, who had known of them, saw through the deception and informed Haydn of it. His response mortified Haydn, as well it might. What Beethoven's response was we do not know.

Teacher and student made good progress together. Beethoven's studies underwent a lengthy interruption when Haydn left for a second stay in London. His works met with great success there, as did Haydn himself, so he extended his visit. Haydn had more impact upon Beethoven than the young composer liked to acknowledge. In light of Haydn's suggestions Beethoven revised and made tighter his C-Minor Piano Trio. Given the popularity of folksongs at this time throughout Europe, Haydn had derived significant income from British publishers by setting Scottish and English songs to music. Beethoven would later do the same and for the same reason. Even as a pianist he owed a debt to Haydn. After Haydn returned from his second trip to London, the two sometimes gave concerts together, with Beethoven at the piano and Haydn conducting his new "London" Symphonies.

On occasion, as a result of what he perceived as Beethoven's lofty ways, Haydn would refer privately to his sometimes imperious charge as "the Grand Mogul." Haydn may have been drawing upon Samuel Johnson's nickname as the Great Cham of literature. (The epithet refers to a Tartar monarch of the day.) The English critic was called this in later years because of his authoritative mode of expression. Like most despots, Johnson and Beethoven did not tolerate dissent easily. However, cordiality between teacher and student usually prevailed. Well before May 1809, when he last saw Haydn a few weeks before his death, Beethoven had only kind words for his mentor. The kind words continued long after Haydn's death.

Early in January 1794 Beethoven began instruction in counterpoint from Johann Georg Albrechtsberger, a respected teacher and scholar, probably the most famous music pedagogue of the day and an expert in counterpoint, a musical skill Beethoven wished to master fully. Though several of Beethoven's string trios reflect formulas based on Haydn (and Mozart), they also show that he had learned from Albrechtsberger. Despite differences in temperament, Beethoven expressed himself well pleased with his new teacher. He also studied with Johann Baptist Schenk, with whom he became friends. Like all musicians of the time, Beethoven was familiar with J. J. Fux's long-standard text on counterpoint, the *Gradus ad Parnassum*, literally, the "path to Parnassus." Beethoven would also have read works by another early eighteenth-century theorist, Johann Joseph Sulzer. Later, between 1799 and 1801, he studied how to set texts for opera with Antonio Salieri, the court opera director, already controversial in the posthumous history of Mozart biography. Beethoven also learned informally from the composer Luigi Cherubini, the gifted violinist and conductor Franz Clement, and Carl Friedrich Zelter, Goethe's friend and devoted correspondent, whom he probably first came to know during his stay in Berlin in 1796.

ৎ

Patrons

Thanks to support from patrons, mainly aristocrats like the Lichnowskys and other prosperous noble families, Beethoven paid his teachers' fees as well as covered his living expenses. Vienna's musical cognoscenti soon recognized the young virtuoso as the city's most gifted and dynamic young pianist. For over a decade, they gave him extraordinary, often unstinting moral, musical, and, in several instances, financial support. They also competed for the privilege of having him perform in their palaces. Several of his patrons were devoted to him personally. Although differences in social rank kept them from becoming close friends, they stood by him despite his occasionally obstreperous nature, which he made little effort to hide. Their names would change as the years went by. Several would undergo major financial crises. One died early, a few departed the city, while others took their places. At least until 1814, when the Congress of Vienna began, such support as Beethoven needed he had. His patrons came to value him (in the words of Martin Geck, a leading German Beethoven scholar) "as their very own 'Bonaparte.'"[3]

In linking the young Beethoven to "Bonaparte," Geck may have intended only a passing aside, yet he anticipates a development that would soon hold true. In view of Beethoven's (and Napoleon's) subsequent careers, it is an enlightening juxtaposition. The young general had shown enormous promise in recapturing Toulon from the British in 1792, in putting down a royalist revolt in Paris in 1795, and in triumphing on the battlefields of Italy in 1796–97. Like him ambitious, Beethoven forged a torrid path through the city's intensely competitive musical scene. As the French regarded the young Napoleon as an outsider, proud and frequently touchy but immensely competent, the Viennese gradually recognized the force that dwelled in Beethoven. Self-aware as well as self-confident, he was early an independent soul— and remained one. In the career that he relentlessly willed into being, he became the first European musician to live life on his own terms.[4]

Beethoven had come to the Hapsburg capital with a reputation as a pianist, his instrument of choice, and as a pianist he made his name. Of his abundant musical skills, perhaps the greatest was his pianistic virtuosity. Many regarded improvisation, for which Beethoven possessed a remarkable gift, as the severest test of a musician's genius. Only gradually did he become known as a composer of new and startling compositions. The thirty-five piano sonatas he wrote over his lifetime and the numerous cycles of variations, nearly seventy by one count, are essentially improvisations set down on paper and shaped by compositional logic. Though he could play the viola, clavichord, and harpsichord (he wrote his earliest keyboard works for these instruments), Beethoven soon favored the increasingly more powerful and resonant piano. All his life he would seek either larger or more advanced new pianos, instruments that rendered more fully the subtlety and range of tones he heard in his head.

The new turn in his life brought him fame, but also unease. Accompanying the growth of his personal freedom was the loss of much of the support that had nourished him in Bonn. He did not establish in Vienna as close a circle of friends as he had had in his native city. Nor did his talent lead him to receive a court appointment of any kind. The security of such a position would have reined in his ever-present financial anxieties. Throughout his life he never quite abandoned hopes of obtaining such an appointment. Even in his last years he still yearned for one.

While the Hapsburgs would pay little attention to Beethoven, shortly after he arrived in Vienna in November 1792 Prince Karl von Lichnowsky gave him lodging in his palace at Alsergrund 45 (now Alsergasse), on the recommendation either of Haydn or of a well-connected Bonn friend like Count Waldstein, who had returned to Vienna about the same time as Beethoven. Prince Karl was an enlightened aristocrat with a Masonic background who had studied music with Mozart. For several years, Beethoven became, in effect, almost a family member.

Vienna at this time had no specifically designed concert halls, just theaters used for concerts. Fortunately, a number of the city's music-loving aristocratic or wealthy families owned palaces that often had specifically designated music rooms. "Chamber music" was intended for such rooms, not for concert halls. If family members could play an instrument, and many could, they would perform chamber pieces in their homes for their own pleasure. If the family were less skilled, they might invite three or four more advanced musicians to play for them.

Every Friday morning Prince Lichnowsky sponsored performances of the highest quality. In his employ were three outstanding young musicians: Ignaz Schuppanzigh, first violinist; Nikolaus Kraft, cellist; Louis Sina, second violinist. With this trio of teenagers Beethoven would begin a lifelong professional relationship. Another new friend, Nikolaus Zmeskall, a competent amateur cellist, frequently joined the group. From them all Beethoven benefited, but it was Zmeskall who became his lifetime admirer and most loyal supporter.

During his first Vienna years the Lichnowsky family meant much to Beethoven. Besides Prince Karl, they included Princess Lichnowsky and the prince's younger brother, Count Moritz. Prince Karl, himself an accomplished amateur musician, sometimes participated as a performer in the Friday morning concerts in which Beethoven often played a leading role. In 1795 he subsidized the publication of Beethoven's first major work, the beautifully engraved score of Three Piano Trios, Op. 1. As Beethoven's Maecenas during his early years in Vienna, he gave the composer many personal gifts, including a valuable set of stringed instruments, and from 1800 to 1806 provided him with an annuity of six hundred florins.

In 1795 Beethoven, wishing to live more independently, left Lichnowsky's premises. Subsequently, he resided in a variety of domiciles, many but not all within the walls of Vienna's central district. Tenants in the city signed leases twice yearly, in the spring and fall, so frequent changes of residence were not unusual. Beethoven, but also Mozart, later Brahms, and to a lesser extent even Bruckner, went from apartment to apartment, from the city to the suburbs and country, and often back to the city. And not just musicians. Others as well appeared to be constantly in transit. There was then a restless quality to life in Vienna.

Old Viennese families like the Lichnowskys had often served as patrons to promising musicians. Earlier, the Lobkowitzes and the Kinskys had supported Gluck. Both these families eventually gave their support to Beethoven. He must have come to know the seventh Prince Lobkowitz (or Lobkowicz, to give the name its Czech spelling), another of his important patrons, fairly early during his first decade in the city. Lobkowitz sponsored, among other works, Beethoven's Third, Fifth, and Sixth Symphonies. In 1809 he would formalize his admiration for Beethoven's genius by becoming one of the three benefactors who agreed to support him financially. Prince Kinsky would become another, along with the young Archduke Rudolph. All three agreed to pay Beethoven a pension for life. Yet despite the attention they lavished upon him, Beethoven always kept a certain reserve, a psychological distance, from his patrons. He often dealt with them imperiously, as though they were beneath him, instead of vice versa. Another generous friend to the young Beethoven at this time was Joseph von Sonnenfels, who in 1793–94 had been the force behind and protector of the Vienna Jacobins.[5]

Gossip about Beethoven's huge gift, his exceptional virtuosity, his "genius," circulated within the capital's aristocratic circles. Talk about his brusque ways, his odd behavior, his indifference to social conventions, enhanced the aura he conveyed through his skill. They were signs of the genius he appeared to manifest so effortlessly. His improvisations, which displayed the full range of his emotional moods, moved audience members powerfully, at times even to tears. He seemed to take pleasure in mocking their responses. Carl Czerny cites one of Beethoven's outbursts: "You are fools. Who can live among such spoiled children!" Beethoven's unpredictable moods and behavior may have reminded civilized Vienna of that archetypal character in the eighteenth-century novel, the noble savage. Although he professed to hold in contempt lachrymose exhibitions of emotion, they reflect the visceral effect his playing had upon auditors. He sat down before the piano and played, often for hours, the music he heard in his head. It stayed in his head too, for he claimed that he never forgot anything he had "composed" mentally. His playing and his seemingly natural creativity totally dazzled audiences. The bigger types of classical music—symphonies, concertos, opera—he had begun to think about by the mid-1790s and even to sketch movements, but he delayed completing them or having them performed *until* he had mastered the interactive instrumentation of chamber music. He soon achieved an outstanding reputation as a composer of piano trios, piano sonatas, and string quartets. Vienna's musical connoisseurs clamored for his chamber works. One reason for their popularity is that they needed only one, two, three, or four talented people to play them.

Inevitably, Beethoven's talent for improvising led to contests of skill with rival pianists. Aristocratic supporters of his talent, meeting in small groups at private domiciles, often asked two pianists to compete against each other. Beethoven did not initiate such contests and professed to dislike them, but by engaging with other musicians in piano "duels" he strengthened his reputation in Vienna. Sometimes his "opponents" were locals like the Abbé Gelinek; others, visitors like Daniel Steibelt. He bested both, as he bested all other aspiring competitors.

Beethoven learned early to accept the limitations of Viennese life. Occasionally he rebelled; more usually, commonsense prevailed. His priorities remained constant: to further his career as a practicing musician and as a composer. He also had what was left of his family to consider, in his case the two younger brothers who had soon afterwards followed him to the Austrian capital. For better or for worse, he remained devoted to them far more than their personal worth merited.

ᘐ

Friends

Beethoven lived in an era that fostered marriages arranged for social or financial purposes. Separations or divorces were uncommon. This social pattern may have contributed to the contemporary German cult of friendship, especially male friendship. Particularly in the late eighteenth century and the early decades of the nineteenth, friendship was viewed as an art. Individuals spent much effort and attention in cultivating their friendships. Think of Goethe and Schiller, Wilhelm von Humboldt and Friedrich Gentz, Wordsworth and Coleridge, Chateaubriand and Fontanes. Beethoven, despite a strong, sometimes irritable, nature, showed himself capable of deep, lasting, indeed lifelong friendships, with both men and women. I shall mention a few.

In Vienna Beethoven's closest ties were, as was then usual, with people on social levels near his own. Of the friends he made, Beethoven valued greatly Karl Amenda. Though temperamentally dissimilar, Beethoven seems to have gotten along particularly well with a man whose musical skills and character deeply impressed him. But after a year's residence in the city (1798–99) Amenda returned to Courland, in his native Latvia. Although Beethoven would never see him again, the few surviving letters between them indicate a deep-seated rapport. When Beethoven finally brought himself to admit to others his growing deafness, he confided in none of his friends in Vienna but wrote to Lorenz Wegeler in Bonn and Amenda in Courland. Their relationship illustrates beautifully the age's ideal of male friendship. Beethoven rarely dropped someone whom he considered a good friend. Amenda was a good friend and, though far away, remained one.

Of those friends who lived in Vienna, Nikolaus Zmeskall ranked high. Hungarian, noble-born, a diplomat long attached to his country's embassy in Vienna, Zmeskall was also an accomplished cellist. He quickly became utterly devoted to Beethoven, and remained his staunchest supporter in the capital. Beethoven used and misused him at will, often making him the butt of jokes and puns, and well aware that he did. Zmeskall happily served Beethoven's genius in any way he could. The composer addressed a number of his wittiest letters to him. The friendship, more engaged on Zmeskall's part than on Beethoven's, may have lacked depth but the two men remained close, perhaps because Zmeskall was always reliable, always there whenever Beethoven needed him.

Another friend was Ignaz Schuppanzigh, the first violinist of Prince Lichnowsky's private quartet. Before he reached the age of twenty he had achieved a high rank among Vienna's gifted violinists. He premiered a number of Beethoven's string compositions; later he and his quartet regularly performed them. Schuppanzigh left Vienna in 1815 and toured in the German states, a fragmented Poland, and Russia. When he returned to Vienna in 1823 he and Beethoven resumed their friendship. Schuppanzigh, along with his musical associates, all virtuosos, premiered several of the composer's immensely difficult last quartets. Always plump, he became over the years enormously heavy. Beethoven teased him mercilessly about his Falstaffian girth.

Among Beethoven's oldest friends was Johann Andreas Streicher, who had been a student with Schiller at the military academy in Stuttgart. In 1782, fearing possible persecution by the Duke of Württemberg, Schiller and Streicher fled from Stuttgart across the border to Mannheim in neighboring Baden. Much later Streicher would write the first biography of the poet-dramatist, in which he movingly depicted Schiller's youthful sufferings and his own.[6] In 1792 Beethoven, on his way to Vienna, had stopped in Augsburg at the home of Johann Andreas Stein, a well-known piano maker whom Mozart had visited. The next year Streicher married Stein's daughter Nannette. In 1794, husband and wife moved to Vienna, where they established a piano factory. In Vienna, the good friend of Schiller now became, along with his new wife, the loyal and devoted friend of Beethoven. They welcomed him into their home, lent him pianos, supplied him with creature comforts. Given Beethoven's enthusiastic response to Schiller's poems and plays, conversations with Streicher must often have turned to the poet and dramatist whom both revered. Nannette proved herself helpful to Beethoven as well. At different times, particularly in 1817–18, she took on domestic chores the composer had difficulty dealing with. For a while she also served as general watcher-over and caretaker of Beethoven's chaotic household and his often troubled domestic dealings with servants. She purchased clothes for him, had them washed, threw out the old and torn, and supervised the servants' preparation of meals.

Another friend and supporter of Beethoven during his first decade in Vienna was Baron Gottfried van Swieten. A man of wide-ranging abilities and interests, he kept a sense of balance amid the swirl of omnipresent governmental change and repression. His father, Gerhard, originally from Holland, had served as Maria Theresa's personal physician and had not feared to antagonize her beloved Jesuits. Over the decades Gerhard had worked as a diplomat and civil servant and had held important government posts in Vienna. Maria Theresa even allowed him to introduce Enlightenment ideals into Austria. His son, Gottfried, became a bastion of Enlightenment influence. During the reign of Joseph II, Gottfried had his hand in almost all of the emperor's attempts at reform. After 1782 he served as director of the imperial and royal library. A patron of both music and musicians, he sponsored concerts of rarely heard choral music. He befriended both Haydn and Mozart. "No one has satisfactorily explained," write the authors of a recent Haydn biography, "why in 1789 Mozart's subscription invitation for concerts in the next season should have come back with but a single name."[7] That name was van Swieten's. He furthered the reputation of Handel in German lands and wrote the libretti for Haydn's *Creation* and *Seasons*. His own magnificent library contained impressive collections of the works of both Handel and Bach. He allowed both Haydn and Mozart to study the scores and manuscripts of earlier but still under-appreciated masters. Now, near his life's end, he became a patron of Beethoven, that proud, touchy young genius who wished to establish himself as their successor. With Beethoven he shared his collection of Handel scores. To van Swieten Beethoven dedicated his First Symphony.

Baron Pasqualati also befriended the composer. In his building on the Mölkerbastei, rising above a still-standing section of Vienna's city walls, he allowed Beethoven to live in an apartment rent-free on and off until 1816. When Beethoven chose not to occupy the apartment, Pasqualati kept it empty for him to use should he wish to return, which on occasion he did. A man who could elicit such regard from others need fear little.

ᘐ

The meager state of journalism in Vienna makes it difficult to measure the critical reception of Beethoven's music during his first decade and even afterwards. Few journalistic outlets for music criticism existed in the city. Young artists had no concert series that they could tap into. As we have seen, Vienna also had no concert halls per se, only theaters or buildings meant primarily for other purposes, chiefly plays or operas. Concerts also took place in churches or in the homes of the aristocracy. The general public was not invited to attend. Those who did go to concerts in public venues often found Beethoven's music too loud, too unusual, too complex to grasp.

Given Vienna's history of oppression, Beethoven had to limit his responses to contemporary events. Yet, from the Joseph and Leopold cantatas of 1790 to the Ninth Symphony more than three decades later, his compositions entwine themselves around the political ideas of the age. They also reflect a basic consistency of outlook. The Joseph cantata lamented the death of the most enlightened emperor Beethoven would ever live under; the cantata for Leopold expressed hope that the new emperor would continue Joseph's progressive policies. The hope for enlightened rule embedded in these early cantatas anticipates his belief that wise civic leadership can heal the ills inherent in human behavior. His final symphony urges mankind to come together in brotherhood and joy. In between we have the *Eroica*, his opera *Leonore/Fidelio*, and his music to accompany Goethe's *Egmont*. These works hymn liberty and advocate freedom from oppression. Although Beethoven did not write the texts he set to music, the words corresponded with his values. He did not hesitate, if it suited his purposes, to add, change, abridge, or otherwise rearrange what he took from others. *Leonore/Fidelio*, the one opera libretto he deemed worthy of a sustained effort, reflected views held strongly. Once he had composed its music, he vigorously resisted attempts by friends and well-wishers who wanted to alter it.

ॐ

Beethoven as a Political Being

Beethoven considered himself a man of the new age, a maker of music certainly, but also an intellectual, a thinker. Even in Bonn, poor and with little formal education, early the main support of a dysfunctional family, he claimed he fully intended to take part in the era's cultural discourse. He considered it his duty to engage with the exciting present—in works of history, literature, philosophy—as well as with important writings from earlier epochs. "I have striven to understand," he wrote in 1809, *"what the better and wiser people* of every age were driving at in their works."[8] "Scarcely any other composer drew on the intellectual springs of his time," claims the German musicologist Martin Geck, "from youth onwards, with such eagerness and determination."[9]

Throughout the 1790s Beethoven monitored events abroad as best he could. That he maintained his republican beliefs is beyond question. When the Bonn publisher Nikolaus Simrock referred to a proposal Beethoven had made in a letter as "*Cavalier* Sprache" (courtier speech), the young composer replied testily in a letter of August 1794. "Fie," he chides Simrock, "who in these democratic times of ours would indulge in that kind of talk?"[10] He alludes here to the persecution of the Vienna Jacobins, which was taking place as he wrote. He wanted his old friend to realize that a new era had arrived, and he had no qualms about enlightening him. Ideally, Beethoven preferred a republic, but failing that, he could accept a monarchy with a liberal and constitutional base. His views, from a modernist perspective, were distinctly liberal, not radical. But the Hapsburg authorities would unquestionably have stamped them—and him—as radical.

With few exceptions, Beethoven spent almost all his adult life within Austrian domains. Often outraged by Vienna's political stagnation and repression, he remained an outsider. Life in the capital he regarded as a kind of exile. Yet exile can have positive benefits. Exile can broaden horizons, limit parochialism, further skepticism and impartiality. But if exile can stimulate, it can also harden. For Beethoven it did both. Though he never warmed to the Austrian state or to most of its inhabitants, living in an attractive city populated by many different peoples gave him ample opportunity to exercise his phenomenal talent. For its full development he knew that he alone bore responsibility.

It was unusual at this time for musicians to express political opinions. Not until Prussia's twin defeats by Napoleon's armies at Jena and Auerstädt in October 1806 did an active political awareness begin to develop in German-speaking lands. But even before France took over the Rhineland Beethoven's political awareness had already been active. He was not indifferent. Though few surviving letters take up politics, silence does not indicate lack of interest. With the censor active and omnipotent in Hapsburg Vienna, with government spies everywhere, with Europe roiling with intrigue and uncertainty, and with war between Austria and France either lurking or in process, it seemed safer not to express views about potentially subversive subjects.

Censorship was a tricky business not only for the censored but also for those who censored. Uncertainty was common for both. The censor's office almost certainly opened letters to destinations outside the Austrian empire. If it found comments critical of Hapsburg rule or ways, retribution could be swift and sure. Many initial supporters of the French Revolution, disappointed in their hopes, eventually became disillusioned. But not, I think, Beethoven. For him the Revolution continued to offer a vision of what might have been, even of what might still be. Lack of progress did not prevent Beethoven from imagining a better world. Such thoughts excited his imagination. Whatever the degree to which Beethoven breathed the ideals of the Revolution, he knew that in Vienna he could not openly talk or write about them. Words criticizing Hapsburg rule, whether written or spoken, would—if the authorities learned of them—have ended his career in Vienna.

Over the decades Beethoven became more and more disillusioned with Viennese life and Austrian rule. Although he never returned to the Rhineland, he retained a lifelong attachment to his native soil. In 1801 he distinguished between a Rhineland friend and a "Viennese friend."[11] He had no doubt who was the more true. Though he had friends in Vienna, he remained wary of Austrian ways.[12] "Cursed, damned, execrable, abominable rabble of Vienna!" Beethoven cried out in frustration in 1819 over a schoolmaster's incompetence in dealing with his nephew Karl.[13] Yet despite such frustrations, he remained put.

ᔥ

The Development of Beethoven

Biographers have roughly divided Beethoven's creative life into three periods. Until about 1802, when he turned thirty-two, Beethoven often experimented in different musical genres, seeing what he could or couldn't do. Wishing to revitalize music in German lands, he produced during his first Vienna decade (1792–1802) trios, quartets, and sonatas, as well as three piano concertos, a ballet score, and two symphonies. For Beethoven the years between the publication of his Opus 1 Trios in 1795 and the first sketches of the *Eroica* in 1802 mark a time of transition, immensely fruitful but often difficult to grasp. He tested his strength in various genres and did not find it wanting. Though not yet fully what we mean by the mature "Beethoven," these compositions reveal impressive stirrings in that direction.

In the middle, or "heroic," period, from about 1802 to 1814, we see Beethoven developing a profoundly original style of his own. This body of work achieves a climax in the mighty *Eroica* and in an opera, *Leonore*. The Fifth and Sixth Symphonies follow, along with several overtures of great power, including the *Coriolan*, a Violin Concerto, and the Fourth and Fifth Piano Concertos. Then come *Egmont*, the Seventh and Eighth Symphonies, and the revised *Leonore* as *Fidelio*. Though many still found his music disturbing, an increasing number of the city's more discerning music lovers, along with admirers elsewhere, had come to appreciate it.

During the nineteenth century and well into the twentieth, audiences responded most to Beethoven's heroic-period works, especially the symphonies and concertos. Even if we think of Beethoven mostly as a composer of large-scale compositions, all his life he wrote chamber music that both exhilarated and puzzled contemporaries. These compositions have gained increasing favor. Perhaps in the twenty-first century the works composed *before* the advent of the heroic period will also gain the appreciation they have long deserved.

8

Beethoven as Traveler and Composer

My art is winning me friends and renown, and what
more do I want? At this time I shall make a good deal
of money. I shall remain here a few weeks longer and
then travel to *Dresden, Leipzig and Berlin.*

BEETHOVEN, FEBRUARY 1796[1]

Traveler

Compared to Mozart, Gluck, Handel, or Haydn, Beethoven saw little
of the world elsewhere. Travel at this time was arduous and slow.
The roads were bad, the inns uncertain. Berlin was as far from Vienna as
the mature man ever went. In addition, encroaching deafness that began
about 1796, as well as the uncertain state of his finances, made extended
or complex trips problematic. Upon his return from Berlin, Beethoven
occasionally took shorter excursions, to Pressburg (now Bratislava), and
to Buda and Pest (not officially one city until well after Beethoven's
death). He also visited the country estate of the Brunswick family at
Martonvásár, west of Pest. He returned to Prague on several occasions,
and in 1806 he spent time at Prince Lichnowsky's country estate near
Troppau in Silesia (in present-day Poland). In the summers of 1811 and
1812 he went via Prague to take the healing waters in Teplitz (now Tec-
sin) and Karlsbad in Bohemia, both today within the Czech Republic.
But 1796 was the last time he left Hapsburg-controlled territory.

His 1796 trip was in length and consequences the most important. It proved to be an eye-opening and beneficial experience since the cities he visited, Prague somewhat excepted, lay in German-speaking lands not under Hapsburg control. In later years, ever fascinated by the human and cultural diversity of Europe, Beethoven sought to bring up his young nephew as a world-citizen, a *Weltbürger.*

Beethoven early developed a perspective on life and society as large as the music he composed. Along with traveling, he explored the interior world of the imagination. Whatever the origins of his compositions, they bespeak an awareness, even a vision, of humanity that transcended national and linguistic borders. Beethoven perforce became a mental traveler. Like Thoreau, he traveled widely elsewhere. Except for his restorative summer sojourns after 1802 in villages neighboring or near Vienna, Beethoven lived much of his life within the boundaries of what is now called the capital's Central District or in its near suburbs. In Beethoven's day defensive military walls (now defined by the horseshoe-shaped Ringstrasse) enclosed the city. Much of the area beyond the walls was then attractive open space. Parts of it remain open today. Once Beethoven had established himself in Vienna, he would leave the city in late spring and return when the leaves began to fall. Most summers he passed in one or more of the outlying villages, from Heiligenstadt (then separated from Vienna by fields) to Baden, some sixteen miles to the south. Walking in the meadows and the valleys, exploring the forested terrain, rocks, and streams, looking up at the cliffs and hills—several crowned with ruined castles—following paths that led through fields and along streams, he unwound and rejoiced in the bounty of rural life and nature. While composing in these environs he celebrated the beauty of what he felt was God's creation.

ی

North to Berlin

Beethoven's early experiences in Vienna held the promise of a wider acquaintance with Europe. "My world is the universe," he exclaimed in

1795. The brave new world heralded by the French Revolution augured infinite possibilities. Beethoven had always yearned to travel, to explore new cities, to see new faces, to hear new ideas. He wished to visit the music-loving cities of fabled Italy that had long produced many of Europe's leading composers and musicians. With his mother he had visited Rotterdam and The Hague in 1783. In 1790 he spent part of the summer in Mergentheim, as one of the elector's musicians, where his playing drew much praise. Perhaps most of all he hoped to spend time in the great capitals of music, Paris and London. Both, however, were far away, and though he could manage some French, he had no English.

Now in 1796, thanks to Prince Lichnowsky, a major trip became possible. The prospect of his first extended venture elsewhere since arriving in Vienna must have been exhilarating. He would test the waters at several German cities—Prague with its significant German-speaking population, then Dresden and Leipzig in Saxony, finally Berlin in Prussia—all four famous as venues for music.

Lichnowsky's chief residence and property lay in Prague and its environs, within the vast Hapsburg-controlled realm of Moravia. Beethoven's route followed that of an illustrious model, for Mozart, also in the company of Lichnowsky, once Mozart's student, had made a similar voyage to the same four cities from April to June in 1789. In Prague Beethoven stayed at an inn not far from the Charles Bridge, the still-standing "Goldene Eichhorn." Thanks to Lichnowsky's connections and patronage, the elite of Prague's musical society, particularly Count Christian Philip von Clam, received Beethoven warmly.

In Prague Beethoven found time to compose. Drawing upon a text attributed to the Italian poet and dramatist Metastasio, he wrote a concert aria for soprano, *Ah, perfido!* for Countess Josephine Clary, who presumably sang it for him during his visit. While working on it, Beethoven recalled Mozart's magnificent arias for soprano, violin, and orchestra, particularly his "Bella mia fiamma" in *Don Giovanni*. Haydn also had a hand in Beethoven's *Ah, perfido!* His *Scena di Berenice*, one of the great cantatas of the age, served as a model for Beethoven's own *scena*. The well-known concert singer Josepha Duschek would sing it in Leipzig with great success, and again in Vienna in 1798.

In Prague Beethoven composed another splendid concert aria, his setting of Friedrich Matthison's "Adelaide," an unusual, still controversial poem of a lover haunted by recollections of his beloved who appears to him everywhere in nature. Praised by Johann Friedrich Reichardt, dismissed by Vincent d'Indy, but admired by Beethoven, it has its own particular beauty.[2] For such an endeavor Haydn and Mozart again stood as models. Though Matthison complained that the theatrical outbursts in Beethoven's musical setting of the poem showed little sensitivity to his words, most subsequent hearers find the aria an impressive achievement. Subsequently he would write music for a number of lieder and also for songs in half a dozen European languages.

Beethoven, now on his own, continued north to Dresden and Leipzig, the two chief cities of Saxony, then an independent grand duchy that included the western part of Poland. Citizens in both cities lived under conditions less restrictive than those that chafed Vienna's population. Dresden, well situated on the Elbe, was the capital of the court. Paintings by Bernardo Bellotto—the nephew of Canaletto, the famed artist of urban scenes—had earlier celebrated its natural and architectural beauty. Beethoven stayed there thirteen days; in Leipzig, the next stop, his stay was shorter. Both had vibrant musical traditions. He would have experienced in them what he may not yet have known existed outside of Bonn: a freer urban life.

Unfortunately, we know almost nothing regarding Beethoven's musical activities in either city. Leipzig, whose fairs—cultural, literary, and commercial—had earned it wide renown, radiated prosperity. After Vienna, it was the second city in the German-speaking lands for music. Its resident orchestra, the Gewandhaus, founded in 1743, was and is Europe's oldest. During Beethoven's lifetime, however, civic orchestras such as the Gewandhaus remained the exception, not the rule. Leipzig had also become the center of the German book trade, the base of many publishers, several of whom would issue Beethoven's scores. Here in 1798 would be launched the *Allgemeine musikalische Zeitung* (*General Musical Journal*), which rapidly became the leading music periodical of the day. Although Beethoven never returned to Dresden or Leipzig, he must have sensed that both cities offered urban and musical possibilities other than those in Vienna. Fond of mocking the Viennese for their pliant nature, coupled with their love of food and drink and lighthearted entertainment, he must have relished German cities in which repression was less in evidence and serious music more in favor. The north German states were reading nations; the Austrian empire was not.

ৎ

Berlin

Beethoven's final stop was Berlin, the rapidly growing capital of Prussia, where he stayed longest. Frederick the Great had consistently worked during his long rule (1740–86) to elevate his country's power and status. After his death, the capital continued to prosper. Beethoven no doubt contrasted new Berlin with old Vienna. At the end of the eighteenth century Berlin's rapidly growing population of 150,000 still stood well below Vienna's 231,000. Vienna's great building era had occurred a century before. Though Berlin lacked Vienna's long historical past, several esteemed architects—Karl Friedrich Schinkel is today the best known—lived in the city and endowed it with their genius. Already, it had begun to grow much more quickly than its southern rival. Frederick had died childless, but long after his death his achievements radiated a glow over his dominions. His unimpressive successor, his nephew Frederick William II, held reactionary views in politics and religion. To his credit, however, he allowed many freedoms not found elsewhere. In 1795 Prussia had negotiated a ten-year truce with republican France. It seemed to promise for the country an era of peace and continued growth.

Berlin exuded a liberal cultural atmosphere. The hugely popular playwright August von Kotzebue, a frequent visitor to the city and a pungent observer of European urban life, contrasted Berlin's remarkable freedom of expression with Vienna's repression. Returning from a trip to Italy, he found there an equality to which Beethoven would have responded. Frederick William's enthusiasm for music had led Haydn in 1786 to write for the newly crowned king his Opus 50, consisting of six quartets, works that became known as the "Prussian" Quartets. Frederick William subsequently summoned Mozart to Berlin. Unable to come, Mozart dedicated to him his last three quartets.

During Beethoven's months in Berlin the city's musical elite had ample opportunities to admire his gifts as a pianist, composer, and improviser. His was an expedition of conquest, and it succeeded brilliantly. He was repeatedly asked to play before Frederick William, a passionate devotee of the cello as well as an accomplished cellist himself. Beethoven wrote, most likely for Jean-Louis Duport, the famous court cellist, his Sonatas in F Major and G Minor for Piano and Cello, Op. 5, nos. 1 and 2. Beethoven also played the piano in their initial performance at court. As a reward the king sent him a magnificent snuffbox. It was "full of louis d'or," crowed Beethoven, in effect a gift "like those given to ambassadors." He long kept fond memories of Prussia's capital and its welcoming musicians. His positive reception in Berlin may even have led to an invitation to join the Prussian court, but this cannot be confirmed. In November 1797 Frederick William II died and his son, Frederick William III, born the same year as Beethoven, succeeded him. His long reign lasted until 1840.

While in Berlin Beethoven also composed, presumably inspired by Duport, his lively F-Major Variations on Mozart's "Ein Mädchen oder ein Weibchen" for cello and piano. Not least was the first of several versions of Beethoven's *Opferlied* (*Song of Sacrifice*). He must have held the subject of sacrifice close to his heart, for often he returned to it. In short, his months away from Vienna further matured the young musician.

§

Louis Ferdinand

Among Beethoven's friends we may also count Louis Ferdinand, nephew of Frederick William II. In Berlin Beethoven became acquainted with this morally flawed young prince. Born in 1772, thus two years younger than the composer, Louis Ferdinand was a charismatic being. Brilliant but eccentric, he exerted a charm upon the leading poets, philosophers, thinkers, and musicians of the time, among them Goethe, Freiligrath, Fouqué, Clausewitz—and, not least, Beethoven. A frequent attendee at the salons of Berlin's leading hostesses, Rahel Levin and Dorothea Schlegel, Louis Ferdinand dazzled the city's elite. Beethoven responded positively both to the man and to his virtuosity on the piano. His pianistic abilities the composer rated more highly than those of the court Kapellmeister, Heinrich Himmel, who, he maintained, "had a fair amount of talent but no more." The prince, for his part, quickly became an admirer of Beethoven's genius, and a friend.

Beethoven and Louis Ferdinand apparently kept up ties. When in 1805 the prince visited Vienna, he and Beethoven again met and made music together. At a formal dinner Beethoven attended, the hostess put those without titles of nobility, Beethoven among them, at a lower table. The composer vented to his royal friend his ire at the snub. A few days later when the prince arranged a dinner of his own, he made Beethoven the guest of honor, placing him at his right hand. Such a courtesy would have pleased the composer immensely. But Louis Ferdinand's life was soon cut short. He immediately rejoined his regiment when Napoleon invaded Prussia early in October 1806. A few days later, on October 10, he died on the battlefield of Saalfeld.

౨

Composer

As the eighteenth century yielded to the nineteenth, many thoughtful individuals came to regard music as the greatest of the arts, a perspective that arose out of philosophical and literary works by, among others, Kant, Schiller, and Goethe. Through their writings people became increasingly aware that listening to music required more than a passive awareness of pleasant sounds. An eighteenth-century concert of music by Haydn or Mozart could be a relaxing listening experience, an enjoyable entertainment. A nineteenth-century concert of music by Beethoven (and the Romantic composers who followed him) was meant to be a participatory experience. Audiences were expected to pay close attention to the music being performed, to engage with it, to exert their mental and imaginative faculties upon it, and, if at all possible, to let the music become part of their inner beings.

Beethoven sought this new appreciation for his music. Early on he thought of himself not simply as a composer but more as a *Tondichter*, a poet of tones, a poet who had something important to express. One way in which Beethoven inaugurated a new era in the history of music was that he forced listeners to pay attention to music in new ways, to respond to its drama, its unexpected juxtapositions of instruments, the intensity of its sounds—and not just in his music but in the music of his time. Those in attendance had to stretch their imaginations, to extend the range of their capacity to hear that music, to feel it. Listening to music, if not exactly a religious occasion, was not mere entertainment. It was a serious experience.

ა

Three Piano Trios

The year before he left on his travels, 1795, had marked a turning point in Beethoven's life. On March 29, lovers of music assembled on a Friday morning in the palace of Prince Karl von Lichnowsky to hear a largely unknown young composer perform three trios of his own composition, along with his Piano Concerto in B-flat Major. Beethoven rightly dedicated his trios to Lichnowsky, for since his arrival from Bonn his patron had given him considerable support. In this successful and well-attended concert the young composer formally launched his career as a musical presence before the aristocratic world of Vienna.

Beethoven had worked hard on his trios during 1793 and 1794. Composers often create within each other's shadows, and although the first trio of Opus 1 clearly reflects the influence of Mozart and Haydn, it compares impressively to similar compositions by either figure. In the third of the trios, in the key of C minor, Beethoven stretched the parameters of the genre, and in so doing entered a different realm. He need not have worried. These trios for piano, violin, and cello, written with Beethoven's characteristic assurance, did bring out his talents. Whatever new developments were to come—and there would be many—Beethoven had arrived. Contemporaries recognized the trios as a significant achievement, and subsequent Viennese audiences received them enthusiastically. He even endowed his trios with an opus number, the first of his creations to receive one.

All three trios reflect Mozart and Haydn, yet all three also oppose both composers. Opposition linked with novelty would become Beethoven's signature tactic over the next half-dozen years. The first of the trios, unusual in that it has four movements (most trios before this time had but three), hints at Beethoven's originality. The second trio is crowned by its slow movement, Largo con espressione, one of Beethoven's first truly subjective utterances. Beethoven's idea for his first two trios was to write scherzi instead of minuets. The minuet was fading as a dance, and after the Revolution it seemed on its way to mummification. The third trio in C minor, what would become a favorite key of Beethoven's, the public greeted with particular approval. Its innovative qualities have gained it recognition as the finest of the three. Clearly this piece has more than a purely musical purpose. Beethoven intended its unexpected vigor to jolt listeners. Some responded positively, others did not. Beethoven would continue to write piano trios, among them such masterpieces as the "Archduke," Op. 97, and the *Kakadu* Variations, Op. 121b. The three trios of Opus 1 made for a superb beginning on this path.

Beethoven had intended his trios to be played by amateur musicians. The violin and cello parts are of limited difficulty. Yet the trios are already overpowering, symphonic in scale and sonority. They even feature "Mannheim rockets," that is, sudden explosions of sound, popularized a half-century earlier in concerts in the Rhine city of Mannheim. Though more traditionally minded listeners found the newness of the trios perplexing, others, amazed at what they heard, felt that greatness for the young composer loomed on the horizon.

As he would in Berlin, Beethoven had triumphed before a most sophisticated audience, here elite aristocratic Viennese music patrons. The concert at Prince Lichnowsky's signified in effect that he had arrived. His dazzling performance on the piano convinced those in attendance that, with the deaths of Gluck and Mozart in recent memory, and the frequent absence of Haydn in London, a new star was in the ascendant over Vienna. Though in England at this time, Haydn had heard the trios the previous year. All three had impressed him, but, discomfited by the third trio's boldness, he had urged Beethoven not to publish it until he had smoothed out a few difficult passages. Beethoven, perhaps thinking Haydn envious, took mild offense. Already and always his own man, he did publish the trio as it was, though after Haydn's death he revised it. Haydn in later years expressed regret over the misunderstanding. Artaria, a leading Viennese music firm, sent forth the trios in an elaborate production. The Lichnowsky family worked hard and well to persuade their aristocratic acquaintances to acquire copies. As a result, the long subscription list for the trios contained an extraordinary number of the city's wealthy musical patrons, a veritable Who's Who of the Viennese music aristocracy.

৵

String Trios

Wishing to inspire and revitalize music in the German lands, Beethoven during this first decade in Vienna began or produced a bevy of major

works. This body of music culminates with sketches for the commence-
ment of the mighty *Eroica* and for the opera *Leonore*. Most of these
compositions embody in one way or another Beethoven's revolutionary
enthusiasm. During the 1790s he would often combine several related
works under one opus number. In the future he usually gave each individual work its own opus number.

The three equally remarkable trios that he wrote for violin, viola,
and cello in 1797–98 he designated as Op. 9, nos. 1, 2, and 3. They are
Beethoven's first important works for stringed instruments. If less well
known than the earlier piano trios, they offer listeners a greater palette
of tones to savor. The stringed instruments interrelate well with each
other. The result was that these trios are among the most dazzling—if
least played—of his early works. Many find them equal in verve and
brilliance to the piano trios. Mozart, who died the year before Beethoven
had arrived in Vienna to stay, would long exert a powerful influence on
him. Several of the string trios reflect formulas inherited not only from
that supremely gifted genius but also reveal that Beethoven had benefited from Albrechtsberger's teaching. We can trace a certain progress
in Beethoven's music in these years: from piano trios, to string trios,
eventually to string quartets.

Beethoven dedicated his three string trios to Count Johann Georg
von Browne-Camus, whose father came from Ireland. He had served
in the Russian army and thought of himself as Russian. He had retired
to Vienna, in which lived a colony of titled Russians, the best known of
whom, and not only among Beethoven admirers, was Count Andreas
Razumovsky. Judging from the number of works—seven in all—he
dedicated to Count Browne-Camus or to his wife, the count quickly
became one of Beethoven's most fervent admirers and patrons. He
hailed him as "the first benefactor of his Muse." Beethoven told the
count that he thought his string trios the "best of my works." In fact,
several of the movements in them can stand comparison with the best
of those in the six Opus 18 Quartets set down a couple of years later. In
the quartets the second violin allows a level of contrast unavailable in

the string trios. Presumably Beethoven recognized that it is often the second violin that makes a quartet come together. The quartets, though better known, need not overshadow the trios.

ᔐ

Piano Concertos

In 1784, when not yet fourteen, Beethoven had sketched an early piano concerto, WoO 4. The piano part, which has survived, has great energy. But he put it aside. As a young piano virtuoso and composer, Beethoven knew that in Vienna's competitive music world he needed concertos to make his mark. Displaying his mastery of that instrument was surely the best means to achieve success. During his early years in Vienna he composed his first two piano concertos. Although listed as his second piano concerto, the composition of Opus 19 preceded the first. Opus 19, in B-flat major, lacks the intensity, the controlled energy, that would mark its successor, Opus 15 in C major, in 1798. In that year, well after he had supposedly completed it, Beethoven worked on and revised Opus 15. A few years later, he completed the second of his first two string quartets, Opus 18, before the first. To anticipate: this reverse duality holds true for the Fourth and Fifth Symphonies, with the Fifth completed before the Fourth.

Back to Opus 19. Even though Mozart's later piano concertos, particularly those in C minor (for example, No. 24, K. 491), may have somewhat intimidated Beethoven, they seem to have influenced his Opus 19. Beethoven had played a primitive version of it at his Vienna debut on March 29, 1795. Fast-paced and charming, Opus 19 comes close to lifting Mozart's opening theme for his own. It is the force that infuses his themes, Beethoven's already remarkable power of momentum, that brings them to life. One hears the Revolution in the distance. The first movement, a revolutionary quick-march, the music critic Alfred Einstein has wittily observed, "should have earned Beethoven, like Schiller, an honorary citizenship in the French Republic."[3]

❧

Sonatas

Sonatas during these years also occupied his thoughts. Beginning in the late 1790s, Beethoven wrote a number for violin with piano accompaniment. Of the second, the Sonata in A Major, Op. 12, no. 2, we might say, "Beethoven is about Haydn, while not being about Haydn at all." Admittedly, Haydn is the dedicatee, the music speaks his language, and there is also the older man's fearless eccentricity. But wholly original are the strange detached-note accompaniments of the slow movement. Obsessive in a way that Haydn's sonatas never were, Beethoven fixes on the idea of quick rising scales and won't let it go. Fierce in the first movement, the scales become graceful flurries in the finale. In one of the two named violin sonatas, "Spring," Op. 24, the light–dark contrast reflects the popular Enlightenment belief that from darkness emerges light. This Beethoven had already done in his Joseph cantata.

A key work of these years is the Piano Sonata Op. 13 (1797–98).[4] Serious music for serious times, this sonata, known as the "Pathétique," emerged out of Germany's *Sturm und Drang* movement of the 1770s and early '80s. The *Sturm und Drang*, at its most vigorous during Beethoven's youth, retained a presence in German literature and music well into the 1790s. Unlike many of the names attached by publishers or later admirers of Beethoven to his compositions, Beethoven named this sonata himself. *Pathetisch*, or "pathetic," derives from Greek *pathos*, an intense emotional feeling that verges on the tragic. Beethoven introduces his "Pathétique" Sonata with heavy Haydnesque chords, which are then repeated; soon "Mozartian" lightness arrives. The piano takes off. Powerful chords are again heard, then quiet melodic music that at first hearing seems unexpected. At this point in his development he seems to be internalizing Mozart's piano sonatas, copying and imitating the music, but also making it his own. His themes have a distinct sound. Mozartian lyricism does not die in Beethoven's hands. Rather, it gains new life. Its second movement is titled "Funeral March on the Death of a Hero" (*Marcia funebre sulla morte d'un eroe*). A French funeral march celebrates human greatness, a greatness that often encompasses the sacrifice of death for the greater good. The march's stoic strength appears in other works, including the *Contradances*, WoO 14 (1795–1801). Did Beethoven already have it in mind for the *Eroica*'s slow movement? Had he even begun thinking about a new symphony? In this sonata as in the symphony's *Marcia funebre*, Beethoven implies both the tragedy and the human greatness that "pathos" embodies.

Another piano sonata of this time, Opus 27, no. 2, marked "quasi una fantasia" (fantasylike), has become popularly known as the "Moonlight" Sonata. Ludwig Rellstab gave it its name in 1832 because it evoked for him a moonlit boat ride on the Lake of the Four Cantons (Lake Lucerne) in central Switzerland.[5] Beethoven composed it in 1801. Its unusual but soon famous opening movement, somber and meditative, is as revolutionary as anything he ever wrote.

9

The Rise of Napoleon

I should like such matters to be differently
ordered in this world.

BEETHOVEN[1]

The Revolution in France and Its Aftermath

Without the Revolution, followed a few years later by the astonishing rise of Napoleon Bonaparte, we cannot truly begin to
understand Beethoven. Echoes of the Revolution engendered in him
aspirations to change the nature of society. The Revolution had fatally
eroded the foundations on which rested the ancien régime. The internal
tumult, the departure of many royalists into exile, the need to replace
military officers who had resigned or left the country—these factors
opened possibilities for those Frenchmen who remained. New concepts
about the nature of society, highly upsetting to many, found expression
in philosophy, art, architecture, literature, and music. They percolated
within France, spread across Europe, and exerted their sway overseas.
Even when those in power managed to channel or deflect revolutionary
energies, they feared that the principles of 1789 might triumph, if not
in their lifetimes, then eventually. But Humpty Dumpty had fallen: no
one could put the ancien régime back together, at least not fully, without
the cracks being glaringly visible.

Three years after angry dissidents had stormed the Bastille on July 14,
1789, the surprising French victory over Austrian and Prussian troops

at Valmy led, as we've seen, to the birth of the First French Republic. Shortly afterwards the Revolution underwent a new and ominous
phase: the Terror of 1793–94, when many of the original Jacobins like
Marat and Robespierre met the guillotine. In the blood of its citizens
the Revolution had in just a few years gone through what in the Roman
republic, its ostensible model, had taken centuries. Understandably, the
populace, after the chaos and instability of these years, looked forward
to quieter times.

In April 1795 France's newly formed Directory, composed of five civil-
ians, signed the Treaty of Basel with Prussia. In it, Prussia, having lost
at Valmy in 1792, acknowledged the legitimacy of the revolutionary government and accepted France's subsequent occupation of the west bank
of the Rhine. Not only did the treaty neutralize Prussia for ten years
but it essentially removed the danger that the Revolution might spread
into German-speaking lands across the Rhine, in effect deferring the
ultimate fate of these territories until later.

The chaotic situation in France made possible the meteoric career
of Napoleon Bonaparte. During the early 1790s he demonstrated his
mettle in areas far from Paris. The British had occupied Toulon, a key
port city, one of France's main gateways to the Mediterranean. In 1792
Napoleon directed the cannon fire that proved crucial in ejecting the
invaders. Under the Directory, he came into greater prominence. In
early October 1795 rumors abounded that royalist-backed dissidents
intended to topple the Directory from power. To quell the anticipated
revolt, the Directory turned to the promising young general. On October 13, after intense fighting before Saint-Roch Church on Paris's Right
Bank, Napoleon, in a brilliantly executed plan, scattered the insurgents.
Early the next year the Directory appointed Napoleon, only twenty-six
years old and now *général de division*, to lead the Army of Italy based in
the south of France for a planned invasion of Austrian-held Italy. Leaving behind his new bride, the former Josephine Duharnais in Paris, he
set off to assume his command.

૭

Napoleon in Italy

While Beethoven went north from Vienna in 1796 to Prague and eventually to Berlin, Napoleon led an army from southern France into
Austrian-controlled northern Italy. After defeating Piedmontese troops
in several battles, he found himself before Lodi, a small city south of
Milan, then capital of the Hapsburg-controlled kingdom of Lombardy.
The Adda River flows before Lodi. A long wooden bridge spanned the
river, with Austrian-led troops and cannon stationed at its far end. To
take the city Napoleon would have to storm the bridge under heavy fire;
his generals said it was madness. Napoleon sent cavalry upstream to
ford the Adda and to attack from the side at an agreed-upon time. After
the French artillery silenced the Austrian cannon across the river, Napoleon, mounted on a white horse, exhorted his troops to advance over the
bridge. To the drums and fifes of popular revolutionary songs, "Heroes
Dying for Liberty" and the "Marseillaise," the main force hurled itself
at the enemy. The cavalry, though delayed in finding a ford, had managed to come down upon the Austrian flank at the crucial moment. The
charge succeeded—barely. The Austrian troops, mostly Croatian auxil-
iaries, broke and ran. The battle was soon over. Lodi, mused Napoleon
later, "made me conceive the ambition of doing great things."[2]

After Lodi, Napoleon's foot soldiers, appreciating his courage, fondly
nicknamed their young general *"le Petit Caporal"* (the Little Corpo-
ral). The name stuck. But they worried when he threw himself in the
immediate chaos of battle and urged him to stay in the rear. In later
engagements, Napoleon might remain toward the rear, but each night
he bivouacked amid his troops. He spent time with them, got to know
some of them, and did not hesitate to reward those who showed exceptional bravery. He made them feel that they were in the capable hands of
a courageous man, and that if they persevered, victory would be theirs.

Napoleon's strategic brilliance and personal bravery at Lodi became the stuff of legend. His dazzling exploits there awoke the imagination of Europe. Before 1796 only a few attentive observers had heard of the man with the unusual name. After Lodi it was on everyone's lips. In England Lodi enchanted a schoolboy named George Gordon Byron. Throughout life he venerated it as a touchstone, indeed *the* touchstone, of heroic greatness. Even Walter Scott, in most ways hostile to Napoleon, felt obliged in his 1815 poem "The Field of Waterloo" to commemorate "He of Lodi's bridge."

Five days after Lodi, General Bonaparte entered Milan, the queen city of Lombardy, in triumph. "A whole nation became aware," wrote the French novelist Stendhal in *The Charterhouse of Parma*, "that everything it had respected up till then was supremely ridiculous. . . . The departure of the last Austrian regiment marked the collapse of the old ideas; to risk one's life became the fashion. People saw that . . . they must love their country with genuine affection and seek to perform heroic actions."[3] After Napoleon had driven the Austrians out of Milan, the Hapsburg foreign minister, Johann von Thugut, remarked that he was "more afraid of anti-war feeling in Vienna than of the French army."[4]

Napoleon's heroics at Arcole (November 15–17, 1796) became almost as well known as those at Lodi. When the general leading the attack was wounded, Napoleon took command of his division, picked up the revolutionary tricolor flag that a dying soldier had dropped, and led the troops back into the thick of the fighting. Attempting to cross a bridge already filled with troops, Napoleon fell into a water-filled ditch, from which an aide-de-camp rescued him. Victory took three hard days of desperate, often hand-to-hand fighting, but victory did come. Antoine Gros would celebrate Napoleon's heroics in a famous painting. Subsequently, Rivoli (January 14, 1797), equally hard-fought, provided another major triumph. After it, both sides knew that the tide had turned.

In relief of forces repeatedly defeated in the field, the Austrian high command had sent out to Italy four successive armies. After a sequence of epic encounters with Napoleon's citizen soldiers and his dazzling strategy, all four went down to defeat. Victory followed victory for the young general. However closely contested the battles, however difficult the physical circumstances of combat or precarious the odds against victory, General Bonaparte somehow managed to emerge triumphant. He suffered no defeats. Finally, the successful capture of the fortress of Mantua (February 2, 1797), the last major Austrian stronghold, clinched French hegemony in northern Italy. After he had cleared Lombardy, only the neutral territory of Venice lay between him and the loosely guarded imperial frontier.

General Bonaparte and his troops had achieved a series of brilliant victories against the numerically superior veterans of the multinational Hapsburg army. He and his troops became demigods overnight. No less a personage than the British consul in Bologna reported how impossible it was to convey an adequate idea of the terror and astonishment that accompanied the Republic's armies in their conquest of Italy, where they were venerated as a superior order of beings to whom nothing was impossible.

With Austria's troops routed in northern Italy, Napoleon now led his army across the Alps toward Vienna. The Viennese talked of nothing else but him and his approaching forces. From his base camp at Leoben in Styria, about seventy miles southwest of Vienna, Napoleon, at the head of seasoned and undefeated troops, stood poised to assault the capital—less than three days' march away. With a military leader of surpassing skill and determination at their doorstep, the Hapsburgs rightly regarded Napoleon as a major threat. No foreign potentate in his right mind would wish to trifle with such a man.

Discontented Viennese might see Napoleon as a redeemer, one who would rescue them from repressive Hapsburg rule. Given the lack of success of his armies in the field, Emperor Franz wisely made no attempt to confront Napoleon, who offered terms for a truce. On April 18, 1797, his minister Thugut signed, as a stopgap, the Preliminary Peace of Leoben. Further negotiations now took place. Austrian delegates claimed they could not sign a treaty since Austria had not recognized the new French Republic. Napoleon had an irrefutable answer for them: "The French Republic is like the rising sun; it doesn't need your approval."[5] After further negotiations, Franz, on October 17–18, agreed to the Treaty of Campo-Formio, a treaty favorable to French interests. It was the first and least humiliating of the four subsequent treaties Austria would sign with the French Republic. Though less favorable to Austria than the Preliminary Peace, it succeeded in its chief purpose: it kept Napoleon from advancing upon Vienna.

Austria also agreed to recognize the new republic across the Rhine and deeded to France the Austrian Netherlands and its territories on the river's left bank. In return, Austria received, along with a portion of its former holdings in northern Italy, the once-free city of Venice, an act that scandalized liberals across Europe, especially those in Britain. The treaty also provided for an exchange of ambassadors. Two years before, Prussia had signed a treaty of peace in Basel with the French Republic. That may have made it a little easier for the Austrian delegation to come to an agreement with an individual whom opponents had already begun to vilify as "the Corsican Ogre."

Having succeeded beyond his wildest dreams, General Bonaparte returned in triumph to Paris on December 10, 1797. The Directory that ruled France gratefully accorded the young general—Napoleon was but twenty-eight—a hero's reception. Two hundred musicians performed Méhul's *Song of the Return* in his honor.

The Italian plains served as the cradle in which the Napoleonic legend came into being. No general of ancient or modern times had won so many major battles so quickly, with such limited resources and against such strong enemies. Thus observed an admiring Stendhal, not inaccurately, in his *Life of Napoleon* (1818). Even Napoleon's adversaries hailed the dazzling Italian campaign as the most brilliant in Europe since antiquity. Besides boosting French morale and restoring international respect to his country, Napoleon's success inspired peoples elsewhere to believe they could realize in their own countries the ideals of the French Revolution. Napoleon continued (and continues) to awe later generations, by his achievements certainly, but even more by the aura of his being. Napoleon's troops, most of his officers, Napoleon himself, had the energies of youth with which to tackle new and apparently insuperable situations.

ৎ

Beethoven Responds to Napoleon

Beethoven never met Napoleon. Yet Napoleon's career mesmerized the young composer, who followed it as best he could in distant Vienna. He began to see himself in the world of music as the equivalent of Napoleon in the world of arms. It does not appear that Napoleon ever attended a concert, either in Paris or elsewhere, in which he might have heard a work by Beethoven. He left behind no known comment regarding the composer. That Beethoven would write works inspired, at least in part, by him seems never to have entered his musical awareness. Drawn to harmonious, uplifting music such as Paisiello's, Napoleon, like many other contemporaries, might well have found Beethoven's tumultuous scores disturbing. Oddly, he liked quiet music. For his part Beethoven, well aware of the lively contemporary Paris music scene, no doubt wondered about what Napoleon's musical tastes might be. Even though his works achieved a certain repute in Paris during his lifetime, only after his death did they explode in popularity there.

The Revolution of 1789 had marked a major turning point in Beethoven's life no less than it did in Napoleon's.[6] Joseph II's death in 1790 had cut short administrative and social progress in Austria, but Napoleon's successes revived hopes elsewhere for change: in the early 1800s France appeared to have embarked upon a path similar to Joseph's. Not only did legends circulate about Napoleon, but from the start there also existed a Napoleonic myth that assimilated Napoleon with the Messiah. Indeed, myth early enveloped the hero who had brought order into the chaos of the revolutionary decade.

ঞ

Beethoven's Songs for the Austrian War Effort

In the heady weeks and months after the Bastille's destruction on July 14, 1789, song had captured the essence, the excitement, even the energy of the unfolding Revolution, not only in France but in nearby German-speaking lands. Revolutionary propaganda deemed essential the composition and dissemination of songs, often of a military cast. Statesmen on both sides of the conflict dividing Europe, those in absolutist Austria no less than those in republican France, took note of the potent effect songs had upon the people. Many, if not most, at this time could not read, but they could sing. Thus, to counter French revolutionary songs the Hapsburgs commissioned music and songs of their own.

Haydn had earlier placed himself in the forefront of this musical propaganda. His Symphony No. 100, the "Military" (1793–94), composed after a French citizen army had defeated Austrian and Prussian regulars at Valmy on September 21, 1792, was, claim his biographers, "one of the earliest, and certainly one of the most distinguished, in a long series of works generated by the revolutionary and Napoleonic wars."[7] In 1796, as General Bonaparte inflicted defeat after defeat upon the armies of Austrian-controlled northern Italy, the Hapsburgs organized several volunteer corps to send in aid of their battered regulars. To encourage civic ardor they asked local composers to write appropriate martial music. Haydn's *Missa in tempore belli* (*Mass in Time of War*) of 1796 was his most sustained effort in the combat against revolutionary France. Of lasting effect was a slighter piece, Haydn's variously titled folk song, "God Preserve Emperor Franz," which served as an Austrian rejoinder to the "Marseillaise." Clearly inspired by Britain's "God Save the King" as well as the "Marseillaise," it became the second movement of Haydn's "Kaiser" String Quartet, and, with adjustments since to the title and words, the Austrian, and still later, the German national anthem.

Defeats of Austrian armies in 1796–97 appeared to justify Beethoven's low opinion of their military endurance. Called upon by the authorities to express his civic ardor by writing patriotic songs in support of Austrian troops, he approached the task with little enthusiasm. Around November 15, 1796, the day of Napoleon's victory at Arcole, he composed music for a "Farewell Song to the Citizens of Vienna." Written to words by Joseph Friedelberg, it was intended to cheer volunteers departing for the front. The song, however, did not stop General Bonaparte from continuing his series of triumphs in Italy. On April 14 Friedelberg wrote a second poem and Beethoven again set it to music. "War Song of the Austrians" begins, "We are a great German people."

Friedelberg's texts for his songs are trite, even clumsy. Beethoven thought his music for the songs ephemeral work. Although he no doubt lamented the sacrifice of young lives in war, I find no evidence that he responded strongly to the Hapsburg cause. Compared to Haydn's arias in his contemporaneous *Mass in Time of War*, Beethoven's efforts hardly rise above the commonplace. In short, his musical contributions to the Austrian war effort lack inspiration, passion, depth, even credibility. As usual when Beethoven fulfilled requests or accepted commissions, he did not assign opus numbers to these works. Generally speaking, the composer regarded them as insignificant. Unrevealing of his deeper feelings, they come across as puny efforts, little more than the required "patriotic" exercises.

ঙ

Twelve Variations on "See, the conqu'ring hero comes"

During his Berlin sojourn in 1796 Beethoven had begun to set down his Twelve Variations on "See, the conqu'ring hero comes," WoO 45, for cello and piano on Handel's theme in his oratorio *Judas Maccabaeus* (1746). He published the Variations in 1797, just in time, it seems, for Napoleon's return to Paris late that year. What, we might wonder, did Beethoven have in mind by writing and publishing a work with this title at a time of Austrian humiliation? He had witnessed performances of Handel's oratorio in Vienna in 1794 and in Berlin two years later. He based his Variations on the triumphal air near its close. During the 1795–96 winter the Berlin Singakademie had extensively rehearsed *Judas Maccabaeus*.[8] Next to *Messiah* (1741), it had become the most popular of Handel's oratorios. The air's huge success when premiered in *Judas Maccabaeus* induced Handel to include it subsequently as well in *Messiah*.

Over the past fifty years Judas Maccabaeus, the hero of Handel's oratorio, had morphed in German-speaking lands into Jesus Christ. Even the rigorous Viennese censorship would have had difficulty faulting the publication of Beethoven's Variations. Nevertheless, the censor might have wondered what exactly Beethoven intended. Either the composer was being tactless, indeed foolish—possibly he had himself in mind as a "conqu'ring hero," one who would "take" Vienna (not an impossible supposition, for Beethoven had an unusual sense of humor)—or, equally likely, a particular "conqu'ring hero" had impressed him greatly. In 1797 there was no Austrian candidate for a "conqu'ring hero." In Austria and all over Europe the being and exploits of one individual were on everyone's lips, an individual with whom Beethoven had begun to grapple, mentally and psychologically. And that was Napoleon.

Handel had written *Judas Maccabaeus* for a different hero. Having moved to England in 1710, he soon revealed himself increasingly aware of English history and sensitive to contemporary events in his new homeland. He responded there to the progressive ideas and philosophical concepts of the Enlightenment. In 1745 English forces under the Duke of Cumberland successfully repelled an invasion of England led by Bonnie Prince Charlie, the Stuart pretender to the throne. The duke's victory over the Jacobite Scots at Culloden (1746) ended hostilities. When writing *Judas Maccabaeus* shortly afterwards, Handel implied a parallel between the duke and the biblical hero of his title.

Judas Maccabaeus draws on the story of how the Seleucid monarch, Antiochus IV, based in present-day Syria, had in 164 B.C.E. desecrated the Temple in Jerusalem, persecuted the Jews, and tried to destroy their identity. Among those who resisted was Judas Maccabaeus. An able military leader, he led a revolt the next year, in which he defeated an expedition sent to suppress the Israelite uprising. Upon reoccupying Jerusalem, Maccabaeus destroyed the pagan gods and restored and rededicated the Temple that Antiochus had defiled. By defeating the Syrians, Maccabaeus saved the Jewish state. To this day the feast of Hanukkah celebrates his achievement.

Similarly, the Duke of Cumberland's victory over the Scots kept Britain free and the Church of England Protestant. Few at the time failed to recognize that in depicting an ancient hero Handel also celebrated a modern one. The words soon developed wider associations. One well-known nineteenth-century rendering begins, "Thine is the glory, risen, conqu'ring Son / Endless is the vict'ry thou o'er death hast won." In subsequent times when Lutherans (and Christians generally) heard these words, they would have brought to mind Jesus. A contemporary painting by the French artist Pierre Subleyras, *Judas Maccabaeus Destroys the Altar and the Statue of Jupiter*, draws a parallel, one often made since, between Judas Maccabaeus's scourging of the Temple of pagan relics and Jesus's later purification of that same Temple.

The choruses of *Judas Maccabaeus* have a rugged elemental beauty. Thanks to the patronage of the Jews of London who came to celebrate their national hero, the oratorio became an instant hit. In the fifty years that followed the first performance of *Judas Maccabaeus*, the work remained extremely popular not only in England but elsewhere as well. "See, the conqu'ring hero comes" inspired numerous hymns as well as other arrangements. By the century's end Handel's music stood high in esteem among Germans favoring the French Revolution.

Upon this triumphal air Beethoven built his Twelve Variations. He dedicated it to Princess Maria Christiane von Lichnowsky, wife of his patron, Prince Karl. The Twelve Variations, one of nearly seventy sets of variations he composed over his lifetime, are among the few examples available of the then unusual combination of cello and piano. Though Handel's oratorios had few performances in Vienna at this time, the suggestion to use the theme from *Judas Maccabaeus* may have come from Baron Gottfried van Swieten, Beethoven's early patron and admirer, who had long championed Handel's works. The presence in Berlin of the famed cellist Jean-Louis Duport to accompany Beethoven on the piano may also have been decisive. Composed in the decorative, high Classical style, Beethoven's Twelve Variations maintain the harmonic movement of the theme with a virtuosity and control unparalleled in his other early works.

Viennese audiences had probably not heard of the Duke of Cumberland; they might well have wondered who Judas Maccabaeus was. More likely, they may have assumed that in this energetic and tuneful work Beethoven had Jesus in mind. Although audiences probably would not have known who had inspired its composition, they may have noted its marked contrast to Beethoven's two lukewarm songs of 1796 and 1797 in support of Austrian forces. In writing his Variations Beethoven was perhaps being cunning, seeing what he, living in an absolutist state, could get away with without incurring the censor's wrath. His decision hardly seems accidental. It appears to gauge more truly his intentions. Besides, he apparently published his Variations on "See the conqu'ring hero comes" just before Napoleon's triumphal return to Paris in December 1797. The young general had indeed come home in glory. It seems quite likely that Beethoven's Variations commemorate less the achievement of Judas Maccabaeus than that of Napoleon Bonaparte, whose meteoric career had already begun to inspire the composer. Thomas Carlyle grudgingly conceded that Napoleon "had words in him that are like Austerlitz battles."[9] Such language—decisive, overwhelming, triumphant—Beethoven wished to achieve in his music.

ℒ

First Consul

Beginning in 1795, France's ruling Directory maintained an uneasy civic existence. No one loved the Directory. During its years in power

Paris roiled with political tension. Several of its five members gained notoriety for their blatant corruption. The city's *jeunesse dorée* (golden youth) publicly scoffed at this unpopular government. By September 1799 the Directory had reached a crisis point. It faced dissolution. But after a decade of instability it had found a solution. It decided to set up a new government modeled on the Roman Republic. A month of intense negotiations followed. Executive power, it was decided, would devolve upon three consuls. Less than two months after Napoleon returned to France from Egypt in November 1799, an expedition of mixed success but with far-reaching results, he capped a stunning rise to power by being chosen First Consul. Two other consuls were also chosen, but only he had real power. In effect he was ruler of France at age thirty. His becoming First Consul marked a decisive turn in French political life. Napoleon promoted enlightened policies for France. He replaced the chaos and corruption he had inherited with a stable and efficient regime. During his five years as First Consul (1799–1804) he reorganized the government, modernized its older institutions, and created many new ones. Awareness of his progressive rule spread across the Continent. His larger vision, as yet unstated, was to bring Europe gradually under French hegemony.

The Revolution's vibrant and enduring ideals had inspired many. As First Consul, Napoleon presented himself as the man who would preserve these ideals. Among them were equality before the law, fairness in taxes, suppression of feudal rights, and protection of the rights of property. By ending societal disorder, Napoleon sought to bring the Revolution to a close, which he did, although gradually. Not even Napoleon could control all the diverse currents that the Revolution had set in motion.

While Napoleon effected groundbreaking changes in the political sphere, Beethoven set out upon what was in effect a new path in music. To Beethoven the French leader appeared to be the greatest of contemporaries. The reforms he instituted in French society had elicited hopes in many, Beethoven not least, that they might lead to change elsewhere. Like other liberal-minded Europeans, Beethoven admired what Napoleon had accomplished and expressed that admiration in his music. He even gave serious thought to moving to Paris.

"That which seduces in Napoleon" for Jean Tulard, interpreting him via Balzac, "is the will, that 'iron will,' with which [Balzac] endows Louis Lambert, the will that stands behind all forms of power."[10] Napoleon indeed possessed a powerful will. With such innate gifts of leadership, how could he fail? Perhaps Elie Faure best summed up Napoleon's equivocal character: "But why . . . were there so few among those who saw him either a god or a devil, to realize that the Devil is but another face of God?"[11] No less did Beethoven possess a steel-like will. He had a vision of what he wanted to do, and the resolve to follow through with it. On lesser matters he could compromise and adapt. In business dealings, he revealed himself a skillful negotiator; in life, he often appeared a poor money manager. But in writing music he trusted himself.

❧

Why Europe Feared France

Napoleon's nearness terrified some Viennese; many appeared indifferent; still others rejoiced. The Hapsburgs elicited little loyalty. Even more than Napoleon's victories, France's republican government threatened the foundations of long-established Hapsburg rule. The young Hapsburg emperor, Franz I, recognizing the seriousness of the situation, had already taken extreme measures to repress disloyalty. In 1794 Austrian authorities had severely punished those who favored France's revolution. They now prodded, with but modest success, the placid Viennese to express patriotic furor *against* the new French Republic.

Besides boosting French morale and restoring international respect to his beleaguered country, Napoleon's Italian campaign had inspired other peoples to believe that they could realize the ideals of the French Revolution in their own lands. Many in Europe regarded the advancing French armies as furthering prospects for national liberty. With the advent of Napoleon, the old regimes began to lose their hold upon the minds and hearts of the populace. When even well-trained Hapsburg regulars retreated before the onslaught of revolutionary forces, people knew that more than a new age had dawned. Even though the Hapsburgs managed to postpone the physical disintegration of their empire for more than a century, many observers already regarded its eventual collapse as inevitable. In addition, Enlightenment thinking had weakened Christianity across Europe. New faiths and ideologies strove to fill spiritual voids. Even in Catholic Vienna skepticism gained a foothold. Over the next two decades the young general would inherit a goodly share of the era's energy.

10

Parallel Lives, Beethoven and Napoleon

Conqueror and captive of the earth art thou!
She trembles at thee still, and thy wild name
Was ne'er more bruited in men's minds than now.

BYRON ON NAPOLEON[1]

Alexis de Tocqueville, coolly analytical and not even slightly a Napoleonist, had only one reservation about the First Consul, large though it was: Napoleon, for him, "was as great as a man can be without morality." Young Beethoven may have sensed this. One way the composer differed from the French leader—there are others—is that he was both a genius *and* a moral man. Long before he became fascinated with Napoleon, Beethoven had espoused revolutionary ideals. After Napoleon's Italian campaign had gained him renown, all Europe watched his career carefully. Beethoven, sure of his own genius, early regarded Napoleon not in reverent adulation, but level-eyed, as an equal. Napoleon knew he had the wherewithal to attain his goals; Beethoven knew he had the capacity to conquer the world through music. Both Napoleon and Beethoven viewed themselves as outsiders. The Rhinelander Beethoven stood apart in Vienna nearly as much as the Corsican Napoleon did in Paris. Neither felt wholly at home or at one with the people or the country where he would spend his maturity. Each looked upon the society in which he lived from without as much as from within.

No less than young General Bonaparte did Beethoven desire to learn about the world. He wished to change the Europe into which he had been born, in both its core beliefs and its structure. Like Napoleon, Beethoven had a transcendent vision of life's possibilities. He also had an acute sense of the rough practicalities involved in any difficult undertaking. Though he wished to realize his imaginative longings for a world elsewhere—to explore Italy, go to Paris, take London by storm like Haydn—daily realities forced him to rein in such thoughts. Of necessity more a mental than a physical traveler, Beethoven journeyed to the clichéd East by listening to unusual and exotic Turkish or Turkish-influenced music, a favorite of Viennese street musicians and popular with the public.

After his stunning victory at Lodi in 1796, Napoleon savored a moment when he realized that all was possible for him, that the future lay before him, there to make of it what he wished and could. About this time Beethoven may well have undergone a similar experience. Already Vienna's star piano virtuoso, he was yet determined to become more a creator than a performer of music. Though still learning his craft, he had by the mid to late 1790s begun to shake off his teachers and by composing dramatic, powerful, even unnerving music become the "Beethoven" we know today.

If not close to Beethoven as a physical presence, Napoleon yet loomed large before him as a man of almost mythic achievement. By the autumn of 1803, perhaps before, Beethoven had decided to dedicate the *Eroica* Symphony to him. That proved impossible, but in years to come he kept alive the thought of associating Napoleon with a major work, notably in 1810 his Mass in C. The dominant figure in Europe, soon to become its virtual master, Napoleon was the one man whose career Beethoven thought worthy of emulation. Even in a sphere as different from war as music, he felt that he could equal Napoleon's achievements and, just possibly, surpass them.

To Beethoven, Napoleon as First Consul may have seemed the heir to Joseph II, in fact, a more successful Joseph II, for Napoleon had conquered and Joseph had not. Whereas Joseph had largely failed in his domestic reforms, Napoleon appeared to have succeeded brilliantly. Once in power after 1799, he gradually reorganized the economic, religious, and educational institutions of the French state. His achievements reinforced Beethoven's deep and passionate commitment to the destruction of feudalism and the establishment of equitable laws for the populace. Beethoven intended to reinvigorate the world of music, to do what Ezra Pound a century and more later claimed necessary for literature: "Make it new." He played the piano with tremendous élan, his stubby fingers racing up and down the keyboard. Surviving metronome markings indicate he wished his works performed at extraordinarily fast tempi, a rapidity that later generations rarely dare attempt. If (as Egon Friedell has observed) "Napoleon conquered space with time,"[2] Beethoven sought to conquer sound with time.

૭

The Revolution Invades Vienna

The Peace of Leoben, signed on October 15, 1797, provided for an exchange of ambassadors between France and Austria. To represent revolutionary France, the most liberally inclined state in Europe, the decision to place General Jean-Baptiste Bernadotte in the capital of the archconservative Austrian monarchy might appear unwise. In 1796 Bernadotte had fought along the Rhine. The next year he helped General Bonaparte conclude his Italian campaign. To the most aristocratic, antirepublican court in Europe, the French Republic now appointed a general of plebeian background, a republican who had served under Napoleon, and who had commanded troops that had recently camped in Austrian territory. While acknowledging Bonaparte's brilliance in the field, Bernadotte had reservations about the man. He apparently disliked what he perceived as his "domineering ways and dictatorial aims."[3] He was certainly jealous of Napoleon's virtually instant fame. Though Bernadotte may not have gone out of his way to speak favorably in Vienna of Napoleon's achievements, among his diplomatic entourage revolutionary ideas and enthusiasm percolated. How the appointment had come his way remains uncertain. Possibly Napoleon, sensing in him a potential rival, persuaded Prince Talleyrand and the ruling Directory to shunt Bernadotte off to distant Vienna. But then again, possibly the Directory may have felt he would represent revolutionary ideals abroad positively.

General Bernadotte arrived in Vienna on February 8, 1798. With his appearance the French Revolution itself entered Vienna. He set up quarters in the heart of the city, the still-standing Lichtenstein Palace on Wallnerstrasse, then owned by the banker Johann Geymüller. To make sure no one misunderstood him or his beliefs, Bernadotte appeared in Vienna dressed in his military uniform. A tricolor plume adorned his hat. His superiors in Paris had requested that he and his staff display republican emblems in the embassy and wear the republican colors wherever they went. And wear them they did. Many Viennese of conservative persuasion took offense. It was not an auspicious beginning.

Vienna, like other European cities outside of France, teemed with royalist emigrés self-exiled from France and bitterly hostile to the revolutionary government of the country that had guillotined the aunt of the current Austrian emperor along with the French king. Many Viennese felt the same. They along with the discontented French refugees avoided all contact with the embassy republicans, who found themselves socially isolated.

Little is known about Bernadotte's sojourn in Vienna, even less about the impact it may have had on Beethoven. But some interaction between Beethoven and the general's staff, and possibly with Bernadotte himself, seems likely. Despite a meager education, the general was thought to favor the arts and music. According to one reliable source, the embassy soon became a rendezvous of artists and musicians. Bernadotte during his stay allegedly spoke with animation about music in a meeting with the current Austrian empress Maria Theresa, the second wife of Franz

I. And music, as we shall discover in taking up Beethoven's Akademie of 1800, was Maria Theresa's great passion.

According to Anton Schindler, Beethoven's late-in-life secretary and future biographer, Beethoven frequented the French Embassy at this time and apparently came to know members of the ambassador's entourage, particularly the talented violinist and composer Rodolphe Kreutzer. He may even have come to know Bernadotte himself, for one evening, it appears, Bernadotte had Kreutzer and Beethoven as dinner guests.[4] Kreutzer, French but of German background, was at this time a radical in politics. His career had flourished along with the Revolution. In 1796, after Napoleon invaded Italy, Kreutzer joined the general and his army in Milan. Given his experiences, he could have told Beethoven much about the young hero's adventures in Italy. In frequenting Bernadotte's circle Beethoven could also have become acquainted with the French musical scene, particularly the martial French revolutionary music now frequently heard in Paris.

How much Bernadotte and others at the French Embassy influenced Beethoven is impossible to determine. At the least, their company and conversation would have deepened his awareness of a more liberated world elsewhere. Even the mere presence in Vienna of Bernadotte himself, an avowed republican, could not but have strengthened Beethoven's own leanings toward a representative form of government.

Older accounts of Beethoven's life, following Schindler, sometimes claim that Bernadotte not only shaped the composer's response to Napoleon but suggested, indirectly, that he write a symphony commemorating Napoleon's life and achievement, that is, the work we know as the *Eroica*. Even though leading Beethoven scholars accept this scenario as likely, it must remain conjectural. Yet Beethoven would have heard discussed specific revolutionary compositions with their increased use of percussion and wind instruments. Whatever the level or intensity of his relationship to Bernadotte, Beethoven responded positively to Kreutzer's company and to that of the liberal-minded embassy staff.

The Austrian government was not impressed. Not until nearly two months after his arrival, on April 8, 1798, did Bernadotte present his credentials to Emperor Franz. The meeting of the fiery Gascon with the fearful young monarch did not go well. Six days later, on April 14, Bernadotte decided to hoist the tricolor from the embassy balcony. Embassies in Vienna did not fly national flags, and the Viennese construed his doing so as an act of defiance. It set off riots, and a crowd gathered calling for its removal. Stones crashed through embassy windows. The flag was soon torn down and burned. Outraged at the desecration, Bernadotte requested, and received from the Viennese authorities, passports allowing him and his staff to leave Austria. It was suggested that they slip away during the night. Instead, courageous and defiant to the end, Bernadotte and his staff proudly left at noon on April 15. Despite the assembled crowds, they entered their carriages displaying their tricolor plumes and cockades. Bernadotte's brief stint as French ambassador to the Austrian empire had been unsuccessful. The Viennese fiasco, a nine days' wonder all over Europe, was not quickly forgotten. And not forgotten, apparently, by Beethoven. One significant result of Bernadotte's brief stay in Vienna remains to be considered.

᠍

A Revolutionary Sonata?

Even if he had wanted to write one, Beethoven, living in archconservative Vienna, realized that the time for writing a revolutionary sonata had long passed. Austria had already lost two wars to France, one to a French revolutionary army at Valmy in 1792, another to Napoleon in Italy during 1796–97. Writing a revolutionary sonata in Vienna would have caused trouble for him at any time, but in 1802, four years after Bernadotte's departure and a year after Napoleon had humiliated an Austrian army at Marengo, it would have been madness. If he wished to prosper in the imperial capital, Beethoven had to accord the regime at least surface allegiance. The grim alternative was retribution, most likely severe, or exile. Besides, even in Paris, after 1799 when Napoleon became First Consul, revolutionary euphoria had waned, at least publicly. No longer did the people openly celebrate the Revolution's achievements; no longer did composers write overtly revolutionary music.

In a letter to the Leipzig publisher Franz Hoffmeister Beethoven, speaking frankly, explained, "There are rascals in the Imperial City as there are at the Imperial Court." Though Beethoven dismissed the idea of composing "a revolutionary sonata," he may not have dismissed it from his thoughts. This brings us to the "Kreutzer" Sonata. Beethoven had originally intended to dedicate it to George Bridgetower, a biracial English violinist who visited Vienna in 1803 and whose virtuoso playing he had admired. Even though Beethoven had, as so often, barely finished the score in time, Bridgetower performed it on May 24 of that year—and, by all accounts, performed it well. But Beethoven subsequently became disillusioned with Bridgetower, rumor having it that a young woman was involved. Pondering a new dedicatee, he remembered Kreutzer, his acquaintance of five years before. "This *Kreutzer* is a dear kind fellow," he recalled, "who during his stay in Vienna gave me a great deal of pleasure."[5] In recollection of that friendship, he now dedicated to him his most challenging, passionate, and daringly complex violin sonata.

Kreutzer, unfortunately, did not reciprocate Beethoven's admiration of his talent. Like many contemporaries, he expressed strong reservations about the composer's dynamic new music. He also showed no interest in playing the sonata named after him. That even a trained musician, a composer of impressive talent, could not respond to the revolutionary genius behind Beethoven's turbulent music helps us understand why the far more cautious Viennese audiences found it perplexing, if not off-putting.

Anyone who doubts the powerful and even contradictory emotional responses that the *Kreutzer* Sonata arouses in those who hear it would do well to listen to it as attentively as did Leo Tolstoy. Tolstoy's son recorded that music would sometimes affect his father against his will and even torment him. He would ask, paraphrasing the writer Bernard de Fontenelle, "Que me veut cette musique?" (What does this music do to me?).

An accomplished pianist, Tolstoy knew the "Kreutzer" Sonata well. It disturbed him profoundly. In the spring of 1888 he had it performed in his Moscow residence. The performance left an especially strong impression upon him and inspired him to write his riveting tale, *The Kreutzer Sonata*.

Pozdnyshev, the narrator, claims not to understand music's power over people. While affirming music as "the most noble of arts," he yet finds that it "generally is a fearful thing." "Music," he thinks, immediately "transports me directly into the inner state of the one who wrote the music." Hearing Beethoven's "Kreutzer" Sonata affects him profoundly; his own inner being, he imagines, resembles Beethoven's, whose music "had a terrible effect" on him. It unhinged Pozdnyshev's balance. It revealed to him "pernicious new feelings, new possibilities, which I hadn't known until then." Tolstoy's grim tale illustrates the power of that music, whose emotional depths can lead to good or evil.

❧

On July 15, 1801, First Consul Bonaparte, signed with Pope Pius VII a Concordat that reestablished the Catholic Church in France. Napoleon's signing stirred in Beethoven long-held anticlerical sentiments. His distress over the Concordat elicited, in an 1802 letter to Hoffmeister, one of his few recorded comments on Napoleon's legislative achievements. Given his justified reservations about taking up political or religious issues in letters for fear of Austrian censorship or imprisonment, the words in which Beethoven expressed his scorn of Napoleon's Concordat are unusually frank. "Everything is trying to slip back into the old rut," he lamented, "now that Buonaparte has concluded his Concordat with the Pope."[6] In this same letter Beethoven scornfully refused to write a sonata addressing the French Revolution, a request made to Hoffmeister by a woman he knew. Beethoven, omitting a salutation, responded brusquely: "Has the devil got hold of you all, gentlemen?— that you suggest *I should compose such a sonata*—Well, perhaps at the time of the revolutionary fever—such a thing might have been possible. . . . But, good Heavens, such a sonata—in these newly develop-

ing Christian times—Ho ho—there you must leave me out." Although
aspects of the Concordat of 1801 seemed a step in the right direction,
Napoleon's apparently full restoration of the Church galled Beethoven.
The composer objected to the Concordat on political as well as on religious grounds. Concerned about the loss of freedom for religions other
than Catholicism, or for those practicing no religion, he feared that
by privileging Catholicism the Concordat would have adverse political
ramifications. With it in place, France might well regress to the bad old
ways of the ancien régime.

Beethoven's dismay is understandable. The Revolution had seemed
to herald a more secular society. A staunch anticlerical throughout his
life, he held established religion in contempt. In his response in 1802
he once again demonstrates his apartness from the Viennese, many of
whom remained attached to their clerics, their devotions, and Roman
Catholic traditions. As an admirer of republics and Joseph II, Beethoven
would have recalled that by disbanding monastic orders and granting
Protestants and Jews near equality before the law, Joseph had promoted
religious toleration. Beethoven believed the Concordat threatened progress already achieved. Religious freedom, one of the Revolution's major
achievements, would now vanish.

In his *Cantata on the Death of Joseph II*, written more than a decade
before, Beethoven had bitterly attacked the Church for its fanaticism
and bigotry. Although raised loosely as a Catholic, he seems later to
have had little regard for the religion he inherited. He is not known to
have attended church services as an adult. The two masses he wrote are
so irregular that no church would wish or be allowed to perform them.
Beethoven remained, however, a deeply spiritual being, a believer in
God and in ethical behavior. Though after Joseph's death his successors had repealed many of his reforms, Josephinism—which included
a belief that a part of progress was in establishing a secular state—
maintained for decades to come an underground presence in Vienna
and throughout Austria. Although Hapsburg monarchs had suppressed

the liberal-leaning Masonic lodges in the early 1790s, Masonic ideas continued to influence progressive-minded thinkers during Beethoven's lifetime and well beyond. Even if the state considered such ideas subversive, Beethoven did not. In all likelihood he remained all his life, along with several other close friends in Vienna, more or less a Josephinist.

Actually, the Concordat did not fully restore the Church's position in France. As events were to play out, it became clear that Napoleon and Pope Pius VII did not share the same vision. Whereas Pius thought that the Concordat presaged the return of Catholicism to its predominant position, Napoleon had in mind a French state in which the Church would return but would have no special status. By putting it under state control, Napoleon effectively made the Church subservient to his administration.

Though Beethoven's comments indicate displeasure with the Concordat, it seems unlikely he held any lasting resentment against Napoleon for his actions. If he had understood how limited the provisions of the Concordat were, how much the state retained the upper hand, he might have responded to the new arrangement more positively. Sudden outbursts in letters or in person against someone or something were not unusual for him. After eruptions, apologies, sometimes early the next day, almost invariably followed. Beethoven had too much mental energy invested in Napoleon's being and career to abandon the hopes he had placed in him. To reject Napoleon would be, in effect, tantamount to rejecting a vital part of himself. And that he would not do.

უ

Even after rejecting the idea of composing an overtly revolutionary sonata, music, not politics, came first for Beethoven, at least whenever his realistic self took control. To prosper in his adopted city required suppressing impulses that might well harm his image as the rising man in music. He had already aroused the suspicions of the Viennese authorities. In his political awareness Beethoven pursued practical ends. If he intended to celebrate in music the Revolution—or its latter-day champion, Napoleon—he would have to disguise his intent, to proceed cautiously.

In the 1840s Alexander Herzen—social reformer, idealist Russian emigré, and exiled wanderer around midcentury Europe—looked back upon the world before he had been born.

> At the end of the eighteenth century men for the first time—not in books but in actual fact—began to free themselves from the fatal, mysteriously oppressive world of theological tradition, and were trying to base on conscious understanding the whole political system which had grown up apart from will and consciousness. In the attempt at a rational state, as in the attempt to found a religion of reason, there was in 1793 a mighty, titanic poetry, which bore its fruits.[7]

That new world was Beethoven's world. Of its "titanic poetry" Beethoven was the herald in music. Yet when Herzen set down his *Memoirs*, that poetry had "weakened and withered." Though Beethoven's early music had gained admirers in France, Austria, Germany, and Russia, absolutism continued triumphant.

ช

Power

"*Power* is the moral principle of those who excel others." So Beethoven had asserted in a letter of 1798 to Zmeskall, concluding, "and it is also mine."[8] Such a candid admission may give us a momentary jolt. It may even bring to mind Nietzsche's scorn for the feeble and ignorant. All the same, can we imagine Beethoven making a more Napoleonic statement? "My mistress is power," the composer claimed, "but it is as an artist that I love power—as a musician loves his violin." Beethoven may even have regarded Napoleon as a "fellow-artist," observes W. J. Turner, one of the composer's biographers, "a creator in another sphere of action, the creator of a good world."[9]

Napoleon's fascination with power subsequently became part of his legend. Even in countries he didn't conquer, power and Napoleon went hand in hand. But what of the situation of powerless people in the absolutist states that made up most of Europe, particularly Russia? Pushkin commented cynically but realistically, "We all aim at being Napoleon." Tolstoy in *War and Peace* wrote brilliantly of Napoleon's mastery at Austerlitz. In Dostoevsky's *Crime and Punishment* Raskolnikov pathetically craves power. And not only in Russia. Did not Freud, when he later claimed, "I am by temperament nothing but a conquistador," echo Napoleon as well as generations of earlier power-hungry male leaders? Freud judged truly: he *was* a conquistador in his new field of psychoanalysis; and if we keep in mind all the disciples jettisoned along the way, a conquistador who took few prisoners.

Beethoven kept before him the astonishing career of Napoleon, the daring young general of Italy, the conqueror of Egypt. Only after Napoleon had become First Consul did Beethoven claim "power" as the proper morality for exceptional beings like himself. He viewed his music as the display of his power and an ultimate force for the good. By it he asserted his independence, his apartness from others, his domination in his art. After 1799 he based his admiration for Napoleon on the evidence that, within a few years, he had brought order to a state deeply shaken by revolution. Yet from that revolution Beethoven had learned much. Just as he struggled to express the music in him, so Napoleon had struggled to bring order out of chaos. Now the leader of Europe's most populous and powerful state, he bestrode the world like a colossus, or so it seemed to contemporaries. "All *Talent* has a propensity to attack the *Strong*," claimed Byron, translating from Madame de Staël.[10] No less than did Byron, Beethoven numbered himself among the *Strong*.

❦

Napoleon Dominates Europe

During his years in power Napoleon was a force for change. He transformed the lives of the inhabitants of continental Europe. He dissolved the old monarchies, reconstituted European society, sought greater individual freedom. He introduced into European life "a completely new factor, an unheard-of *tempo*."[11] "Activité, activité. Vitesse!" (Activity, activity. Speed!) became his watchwords. No less were they Beethoven's. The composer identified himself with ceaseless *activité*, his music hurtling along at a *vitesse* hitherto unimagined. The years preceding the *Eroica* witnessed a period of phenomenal creativity. As Napoleon had shaken the royalty of the ancien régime of France (and older ways of thinking everywhere else), Beethoven began to shake the "Classical" era in music.

Despite its absolutist monarchy, prerevolutionary France personified for Beethoven the Enlightenment. It had produced Voltaire and Rousseau, two in a galaxy of geniuses. After 1789 it projected progressive ideas as well as revolutionary ideals. A decade later, under the direction of a brilliant young general, now First Consul, it sought to emulate the governmental forms of the Roman Republic. By 1800 the time seemed right for a *pax napoleonica*. Beethoven was a man of hope. Not until Napoleon's final defeat at Waterloo in 1815 did he fully despair that political change might yet sweep across Europe. Even then he continued to believe that his music might give strength to, perhaps even renew, an imperfect world, if not immediately, then in time.

After all, of those then alive in Europe, who besides the young Napoleon could Beethoven measure himself against? He knew his hero possessed flaws of character no less than of deed, but he also knew that Napoleon towered above other European leaders. "If Bonaparte was a conqueror," wrote William Hazlitt in his 1830 biography of Napoleon, "he conquered the grand conspiracy of Kings against the right of the human race to be free . . . if he was arbitrary and a tyrant, France . . .

was in a state of military blockade . . . and not to be defended by mere paper bullets of the brain." With a man who symbolized for him, as he did for Hazlitt, "the right of the human race to be free," Beethoven felt affinities. Napoleon might make mistakes, indeed had made mistakes, but who else in Europe could rival him in determination and deed?

In these years Napoleon became very much Beethoven's idol. His successes left the composer determined to create music worthy of a new age. Whereas the First Consul reorganized the institutions of the French state, creating new ones when necessary, Beethoven, largely working within inherited forms but transforming them utterly, composed music of pioneering, often revolutionary significance. Passionate each in his own way to create order, they toiled virtually without rest, one through legislative reform that transformed France, the other through creating compositions that relentlessly pursued (so Beethoven claimed) a "new path." The century that began in 1800 appeared to bode well for both. Within a few years each had succeeded magnificently. Whereas Napoleon stretched Europe's conception of the possibilities of its political life, Beethoven intended to stretch notions of the possibilities of music.

11

The Rise of Beethoven

There is much to be done on earth, do it soon!

BEETHOVEN[1]

Beethoven in the New Century

Compositions on either side of 1800 give evidence of Beethoven's sense of confidence, even of power. From sonatas, trios, string quartets, and other forms of chamber music he now ventured into realms hitherto unknown, realms in which Wordsworth, in a late addition to his epic poem *The Prelude*, termed "strange seas of Thought, alone."[2] On such seas the poet had envisioned Newton embarking. The seas on which Beethoven ventured to sail also churned. At times they nearly capsized his vessel. But he sailed on, composing works within his epic vision, even if not always knowing where he was going, or when he would come upon the desired harbor, or even knowing if it existed. Inspiration came unaided to his creative imagination. "Tell her 'that I still have now and then a raptus,'" he informed Franz Wegeler in 1801.[3] "Her" is Wegeler's wife, the former Eleanor von Breuning, whom a younger Beethoven had once also admired. "Raptus" encapsulates a sudden moment of heightened inspiration, a Wordsworthian spot of time, a Joycean epiphany, a satori, a moment when darkness yields to light, that is, to enlightenment. Such revelations now announced themselves to Beethoven with increasing frequency.

The year 1800 marked a high point in Beethoven's first period in Vienna. With the Classical models of Haydn and Mozart behind him, he had sought to develop his own distinctive voice, yet for his first Akademie, or concert performance, that spring he wisely chose to include compositions by both composers. Clearly he wished to position himself as the successor to Mozart, dead nearly ten years, and Haydn, back in Vienna from London and now writing another mass for Prince Esterházy.[4] The Viennese public was ready to hear music by the man who viewed himself as heir to both these giants. Thus Beethoven carefully thought out what compositions he would include. Believing that his creative gift rivaled, perhaps even surpassed, those of Mozart and Haydn, he stood poised to act upon this awareness, to express through his music the power he felt within himself.

Even though the Viennese took their time in acknowledging Beethoven's gift, the progressive-minded sensed that they had among them an unusual genius. At this moment, writes Martin Geck, "Beethoven—like Napoleon—took the initiative and crowned himself."[5] Geck's point is valid: already by 1800 Beethoven viewed himself as the new emperor of music, one capable of compositions of dimensions never before imagined. During the summer and fall of 1800, Beethoven in a creative surge completed the six quartets that constitute Opus 18, works he had begun in 1798. String quartets, invented and developed by Haydn, rethought and reworked by Mozart, had become increasingly popular in Vienna. Up to a point Beethoven followed the practice of his mentors. He began each with the traditional sonata-allegro movement, followed by an andante. Use of a scherzo, an Italian word that can mean "joke," allowed Beethoven to indulge in humor, even tricks. Usually the fourth and final movement is a rondo.

Before Beethoven, string quartets usually gave precedence to the first violin. The other players—second violin, viola, and cello—had supporting roles. As had Haydn and Mozart, Beethoven gave active roles to all four instruments. With his love of deep bass sounds, the cello in his quartets received lots of play. Players had to readjust. The resultant Opus 18 Quartets are very dramatic, full of fire and brimstone. They stop and start, mix and match, and in the process display an energy the genre had rarely manifested before.

◡

The Akademie of April 2, 1800

A month before Napoleon crossed the Alps to reconquer northern Italy, Beethoven held his first Akademie. In the musical parlance of the day, an Akademie meant a kind of benefit or subscription concert, one organized by a composer or performer in order to display his talents. He put on a concert at his own risk and for his own benefit. Almost all of Beethoven's previous appearances in Vienna, many playing his own works, had taken place in the palaces of the aristocracy. He didn't attempt an Akademie until the city's musical elite had confirmed him both as Vienna's leading pianist and as a leading composer of chamber music: that is, piano and string trios, sonatas, and string quartets. Beethoven's decision to have an Akademie reflected an increasing confidence in his own music. The Akademie of 1800 marked the first time he appeared before the general public. By it he intended to draw attention to himself as a composer as well as a performer.

Akademies help us understand both Beethoven and the music he created. Not only did they allow him to present recent works before a musically sophisticated public, but their inclusion in such a concert also indicates that he thought them important, or at least characteristic of his genius. So he rented the Hoftheater, the court theater, and made the other arrangements, including selling tickets himself. First up was a "grand symphony" by Mozart (we don't know which one), then an aria and a duet from Haydn's recent oratorio *The Creation*. Beethoven followed this with his own Septet, Op. 20, dedicated to the Austrian empress, the music-loving Maria Theresa. A savvy move. Almost immediately, greatly to Beethoven's benefit though somewhat to his annoyance later, the Septet became one of his most popular pieces.

After the intermission the audience heard Beethoven play his First Piano Concerto, Op. 15, actually the second written. The concerto and the Septet are often performed today. Then he improvised for a while on the piano. This is where he truly dazzled. The concert concluded with his First Symphony. If you're counting, that's two pieces by Haydn and three by Mozart, but only two by Beethoven. Draw your own conclusions. One might be that a new man had appeared on the musical scene, one respectful of his distinguished predecessors, but one who intended to command the future. Beethoven wished to leave no doubt who it was.

During Beethoven's lifetime the symphony gradually became the most elevated type of instrumental music. It owed its preeminence to Haydn and Mozart. As a prospective composer of symphonies, Beethoven knew that in the achievement of his famous predecessors he faced formidable competition. The memory of Mozart, an early and internationally acclaimed prodigy, still gleamed fresh among Vienna's music-going public. At his death in 1791, he had left behind forty-one symphonies, of which the last three, perhaps the most impressive of them all, held special meaning for Beethoven. Haydn, too, remained a potent challenge. Beethoven had learned much from him in the early 1790s. Later in the decade Haydn had twice taken London by storm, and his last twelve symphonies, known as the "London" Symphonies, rank among his best. In 1800, Haydn, who had recently composed his *Creation*, stood at the peak of his fame. Together with Mozart, he had opened up a European concert world in which language posed no barrier.

"Romanticism" as a word and as a movement varied from country to country. At this time it applied more to Germany and Italy than to Britain or France. Political and social Romanticism defended individual rights and eliminated the bonds of servitude; it championed personal religious values over ecclesiastical authority. Many listeners today respond to Beethoven, along with Haydn and Mozart, within the context of Classicism in music. I believe Beethoven more a Romantic, and in many ways, possibly most, a revolutionary. Though Beethoven worked within the accepted styles of the 1790s, he always seems to be making changes to them, changes that no one had thought to do before. He was not only an innovator, but a radical innovator. The revolutionary age in which he lived called for larger-scaled works. He rose to the challenge. In its daring, its originality, its vigor, the First Symphony formally announces a new voice, the voice of the Beethoven to come.

He closed his 1800 Akademie with that symphony. He had made lengthy preparations for writing it. During the previous decade he had composed ten piano sonatas, among them the "Pathétique." While writing his first six string quartets and his first eight trios, he was determined not to attempt a symphony until he had mastered different kinds of chamber music, which domain included most modes of composition at this time, opera and choral music excepted. Several of Beethoven's early compositions exhibit distinctly symphonic elements. Over the previous fifteen years he had in fact begun several symphonies, including one in C major and another in C minor, before completing what became his First Symphony, it too in C major. He took his time because he knew it had to be good. Mozart had used the key of C major for his "Linz" (No. 36) and "Jupiter" (No. 41) Symphonies, and throughout his own symphony Beethoven shows himself aware of Mozart's (and Haydn's) achievements. Trying to rival these titans as a composer of symphonies proved to be among the toughest hurdles in his rising career. He was nearly thirty when he completed his First Symphony. Though it has much of the character of one by Mozart or Haydn and ranks with the best of theirs, it sounds distinctively different. It has a ruggedness, a certain vigorous humor and originality in form, in detail, and in imagination. Clearly, upstart Beethoven wanted to issue a challenge. He intended to dedicate it to his former employer, Maximilian Franz, the elector of Cologne who had so generously supported his musical devel-

opment in Bonn. But when Max Franz died suddenly, Beethoven dedicated it to that most cultured individual, Baron Gottfried van Swieten.

The First Symphony foreshadows later Beethoven. His purpose in
writing music was not to soothe people's nerves or just to give pleasure, but to surprise their ears, to give their beings a good shaking,
at times (it may seem) even to frighten them. Though the work had
a raft of precursors, going as far back as Beethoven's compositions in
Bonn during the 1780s, it formally introduced to the Viennese public
the new worlds of music he wished to conquer. With his stocky figure,
indifference to proper attire, lack of wig, and hair in the new French
revolutionary *à la Titus* style, he seemed a man who by his presence and
music was unafraid to affront his alleged superiors. Beethoven never
feared being different. As a human being he is full of contradictions, of
surprises. They never stop. His compositions overflow with the unexpected. Themes disappear and reappear as occasions arise. If audiences
found his music not to their tastes, he expected them to adjust and learn
from it. Their tastes could change, his vision would not.

The First Symphony received a mixed reception. Most audience
members responded favorably; others felt baffled. Then as now, musical
tastes in Vienna were conservative. Musically inclined citizens brought
up on Haydn and Mozart felt that a new symphony should sound somewhat like those they had heard before. Five years later, the first public
performances of the *Eroica* would upset many of the city's music lovers. The First Symphony, by then, upset no one, at least on the surface.
For that reason conservative Viennese audiences long made it the most
popular of Beethoven's symphonies.

Several decades afterwards, when Hector Berlioz, an early French
admirer of Beethoven, heard the First Symphony, it impressed him by
"its form, its melodic style, and its sobriety of harmony and instrumentation." Yet he found the symphony "not Beethoven"; or at least not yet,
or not quite, "Beethoven." It struck him as altogether distinct from his
later compositions. For Berlioz, as for Beethoven's Viennese contem-

poraries and subsequent hearers, it was more aligned with the masterpieces of Mozart and Haydn than with Beethoven's next symphony.

Beethoven's 1800 Akademie received its only review from the *Allgemeine musikalische Zeitung*. Recently established in Leipzig, it was the first German journal specifically devoted to music. Its Vienna-based critic described Beethoven's program thus: "Truly the most interesting concert we have heard in a long time. It finished with a symphony of his own composition, which contained much art, many 'new things' and a 'wealth of ideas.' "[6] What were these "new things," what were the "wealth of ideas"? The reviewer does not say. Perhaps the vocabulary to describe them did not yet exist.

᠊ᢒ

The Prometheus Myth

Beethoven himself said on several occasions that his works had meaning. We should believe him. He loaded his compositions with ideas, but what they are has long puzzled admirers. Though we may never fully divine what he had in mind, clearly the European cultural explosion that followed the French Revolution influenced both his thought and his works. One theme integral to Beethoven's music is encapsulated in the Prometheus myth. He infused his First Symphony with Promethean dynamism and drive. Soon afterwards he composed music for his ballet *The Creatures of Prometheus*. Behind this work, and climaxing in the *Eroica*, lies the myth of Prometheus, the benevolent Titan forbidden by the gods of Olympus to create human beings. He disobeyed the gods by empowering his creations by giving them the gift of fire. An icon of Enlightenment idealism, Prometheus brought light and benefited humanity. For this deed Zeus had Prometheus chained to a peak in the Caucasus. Each day an eagle devoured his liver, each night it grew back.

Literary treatments of Prometheus have a long history, from Aeschylus to the present. By the late eighteenth century the myth had become extremely topical. The young Goethe in his poem "Prometheus" (1774) commemorated the Greek Titan for his "crime" in creating humanity. No less did the Prometheus myth, with its emphasis on constant striving, affect the way Goethe chose to live his life.

Goethe was not the only creator to fall under Prometheus's spell. Even before General Bonaparte became First Consul, contemporaries associated him with the story of mankind's redeemer. During the Italian campaign of 1796–97 Italian Jacobins saluted him as the new Prometheus. They interpreted his career as a literal and startling instance of Promethean daring and hubris. The young Vincenzo Monti in his *Il prometeo* (1797), intoxicated by his youthful reading of Aeschylus's *Prometheus Bound*, drew upon the legend for his Prometheus creating, or reviving, a humanity new, enlightened, joyous, and free. Monti viewed Napoleon as a modern incarnation of Prometheus. Though he later adjusted his thinking to whatever political winds wafted through Italy at the time, his early enthusiasm for the young Napoleon was genuine. Another Italian, Salvatore Viganò, responded to Prometheus in the ballet that Beethoven set to music.[7]

Prometheus also loomed large within Byron's creativity. In "Prometheus," one of his finest poems, written during the summer of 1816 in self-imposed exile in Switzerland, he drew upon the suffering Titan as an emblem of endurance. As the narrator plumbs the depths of his personal despair, he learns to accept his fate. In his determined resignation, Prometheus served Byron as a model to emulate. Writing "Prometheus" stimulated the poet to a torrent of creativity. The eponymous hero of his dramatic poem *Manfred* fights a valiant but losing battle against fate within a universe he deems hostile. High in the Alps, Manfred contemplates suicide, only to be prevented by a chamois hunter.

◆

The Creatures of Prometheus

Late in 1799, about the time Napoleon became First Consul, Beethoven began to rethink the Prometheus myth. Both as creator and as suffering savior, Prometheus captured his imagination. The Titan prompted him to create several of his greatest compositions. Embodying most aspects of the myth—rebellion, creation, punishment, redemption—they lead, above all, to freedom. Belief in freedom, for himself and for others, observed Schindler, courses like a leitmotif through Beethoven's life. The composer even came to envision *himself* as a modern Prometheus. Through his creation he would bring light not only to the realm of music but also to the intellectual life of his and future ages. Prometheus was a model for the composer to live by. "You are dealing with a true artist," he told the Scottish publisher George Thomson a decade later, "who is never content with himself and tries always to go further and make yet greater progress in his art."[8]

In turn-of-the-century Vienna, ballet as a serious musical form ran a close second to opera. Instrumental music limped along, a distant third. Understandably, when a commission to compose a ballet score based on the Prometheus myth came along in that year of wonders, 1800, Beethoven quickly accepted it. He had long wished to write for the stage. Viganò, a distinguished ballet-master, would create the choreography. Given dynamic life by Beethoven's music, Viganò's *Creatures of Prometheus* enjoyed considerable popular success in Vienna. Publicly performed twelve times in 1801, the work was repeated fourteen times in 1802 and thirteen times in the next year. It boosted Beethoven's fame substantially. Performances subsequently took place across Europe.

Lasting more than an hour, the eighteen sections of *The Creatures of Prometheus* make it one of Beethoven's longest works. The music travels through a variety of moods, from comic to playful, tragic to heroic. The final movement includes a gently swinging little tune that Beethoven associated with thoughts of the Titan. We hear what we now call the Prometheus theme adumbrated in the Scherzo of the Piano Sonata No.

12 in A-flat Major, Op. 26, written in 1802, and in several other works, including the seventh of his Twelve Contradances, WoO 14, in the key of E-flat major, from the 1790s. The theme, vastly more powerful and resonant, will resound in the Finale of the *Eroica*.

Given our awareness of Beethoven's subsequent use of this theme, for him to base a ballet on it may seem puzzling at first. But the message is clear: whatever Prometheus's misfortunes—Zeus's threats against humans, his own sufferings—the Titan's benevolence and good deeds will inspire humankind to resist tyranny, to continue to better itself. Despite his hellish torture, Prometheus will have triumphed. The vibrant, lively, dynamic music of this work signals a departure for Beethoven: a step forward that would lead to the majestic harmonies of the years ahead.

❧

Beethoven's "New Path"

A revolutionary impetus had stirred Beethoven around 1802. He wrote of developing a style "completely new for me," one that treated music in "a wholly different manner." Who can gainsay him? Even if we limit ourselves to piano works—the three sonatas that comprise Opus 31; the Bagatelles, Op. 33; and the Variations, Opp. 34 and 35—all bear the marks of outstanding originality. By speaking of his desire to follow a "new way" or "new paths," Beethoven, claimed Carl Czerny, "intended to deepen his music, to venture in new directions."[9] Once launched on that path, he sought structures to encompass the roiling tide of music he felt within him. During the next few years he completed work after work of increasing vigor and significance.

In the years between his claim in 1798 that "*power*" in music was the proper morality and completing the *Eroica* in 1804, he faced one challenge after another. Hapsburg power he believed immoral, whereas power in music should work for the common good. Pondering and working concurrently on the *Eroica* and *Leonore/Fidelio*, he kept at the same time other compositions in his head and on his desk. Ideas for still others lay deep in his imagination. In Vienna during winters, and in summers, at least after 1802, more peacefully in a nearby village, he composed feverishly. Unusual as were Beethoven's ideas about creativity, they were not radical. Composing music meant for him going on a "journey," destination unknown. "My voyage is in the skies," he once claimed. Though coddled by some of Vienna's aristocrats, he never forgot his painfully difficult childhood, the borderline existence his fragmented family had eked out in Bonn. Even in the relative security of his early Vienna years he evaluated his circumstances from the perspective of someone brought up poor.

A strong surge of creativity marks the years preceding the *Eroica*. "Why, at the moment I feel equal to anything," Beethoven told a correspondent in 1801.[10] That same year he wrote Wegeler, "I will seize Fate by the throat."[11] And so he did, and did not relax his grip. Many of his works we can consider as "manifestos" demanding the recognition of "a new mode of creation."[12] He sensed he was becoming a great composer but wished to become one still greater. He would allow nothing to prevent him from attaining the goals he had set for himself.

ૐ

"Gracchus" Babeuf

Babeuf is a name that appears rarely in books on Beethoven.[13] But it should. Among the more unusual ideas about the present and future state of humanity circulating in turn-of-the-century Europe were the egalitarian notions expressed by the French revolutionary and social theorist François Noel Babeuf (1760–1797). His father had nicknamed him "Gracchus" after Caius Gracchus, the heroic Roman. On his deathbed he bequeathed to his son his personal copy of Plutarch. Stimulated by his paternal example and by the heroic lives he read about in Plutarch, young Babeuf created with others a "Society of the Equals." Its

Manifesto of the Equals describes what was in effect a socialistic society, in which its members were interdependent and property was common to all. "The French Revolution," Babeuf claimed, "is but the forerunner of another revolution far more grand, far more solemn, which will be the last." Society in this idealized world would support those who worked to remove barriers inhibiting creativity. It would pay those who wished to make art for their creations.[14] Babeuf's ideas exerted considerable appeal—mostly underground—to European radicals and intellectuals in the later 1790s and well into the nineteenth century.

In a letter to Franz Hoffmeister of January 1, 1801, Beethoven echoed Babeuf's ideas. "There ought to be in the world *a market for* art," he wondered, "where the artist would only have to bring his works and take as much money as he needed."[15] At this time and under the present system, Beethoven realized, creative figures had to be not only devoted to their art but men of business as well. Selling "art" involved commercial haggling, a practice the composer could do quite well and generally with success, but which he claimed to dislike thoroughly. Despite or perhaps even because of its presumed impracticability, the concept of a reformed society that supported its creative artists—with workers in the arts being compensated fairly for their work—appealed to Beethoven. Besides, he noted on several occasions that he "wished to practice his art solely for the benefit of the poor," believing it would give them hope and comfort. His vision of expressing in music an ideal world in many ways parallels the utopian thinking of his high-born aristocratic contemporaries, Claude Henri de Saint-Simon (1760–1828) and Charles Fournier (1772–1857). They along with Babeuf are among the starry-eyed idealists to whom few listened at the time but whose ideas have had a long afterlife. Through his music Beethoven saw himself continuing their work.

Babeuf in wishing to remake society on a fairer and more just basis served as an ideological soulmate to the composer. Not that Babeuf himself was terribly hopeful that the Directory ruling France in the later 1790s would take his ideas seriously. "We have but to reflect for a moment," he wrote, "on the multitude of passions in the ascendancy in this period of corruption we have come to, to convince ourselves that the chances against the possibility of realizing such a project are in the proportion of more than a hundred to one."[16] Babeuf and his collaborators wished to replace the bourgeois republican government of the Directory with a dictatorship of Jacobin inspiration, which would involve a second revolution and a new and more equitable division of property, perhaps even its abolishment altogether. His thought (known as "babouviste") found adherents then, and subsequently among others, including Richard Wagner.

Alas, in March 1796 France's ruling Directory—with its hands already full dealing with poverty, corruption, and internal chaos—deemed Babeuf's ideas far too radical. Along with his followers in the Society of the Equals, he fell a victim to the guillotine. At his trial Babeuf, an extremely intelligent man, defended his principles with eloquence and conviction. His defense, in the opinion of the literary critic Edmund Wilson, possesses "moments of grandeur which it is not absurd to compare to Socrates' *Apology*."[17]

❧

The Heiligenstadt Testament (1802)

Heiligenstadt in Beethoven's day was a well-situated village clinging to the Vienna hills a few miles northwest of the capital. A lively brook descends through the village. Above looms the Kahlenberg, thick with vineyards, fields of grain, and pasture. Though now part of greater Vienna, the village retains a rustic charm. With its old stone houses, its *Heuriger*—taverns where every autumn Viennese and others gather to enjoy the harvest's new wine—its fields and its forests, its unhurried pace, it proved attractive to Beethoven. In 1802 he decided to pass the summer there.

Beethoven possessed a strong, exuberant disposition, neither melancholic nor pessimistic, though capable of both moods. A child of the

Enlightenment and its values, he was yet even in so idyllic a landscape as Heiligenstadt subject to bouts of depression. He had good cause to worry. For several years already his hearing had shown signs of decline. As autumn approached his unease grew. On October 6 he began an anguished epistle to his brothers Karl and Johann. The letter, known to posterity as the Heiligenstadt Testament, is a cri de coeur in which Beethoven bewails his growing deafness, first sensed years before, but now getting worse.

Beethoven seems to have first experienced hearing difficulties around 1796. For a few years he tried to hide its gradual progress in public, first by listening closely, then by pretending to hear, finally, by 1800, if not before, by gradually withdrawing from society. But he sensed that others had noticed his failing hearing and wondered about it—and about him. He tried to imagine a pianist unable to hear the notes he played, a conductor unable to hear the instruments of the orchestra. Whether as a soloist, or playing with or conducting others, a musician needs to hear well. What kind of future did a deaf pianist, a deaf composer face? Both for the development of his art and, more practically, for his future financial well-being, Beethoven had reason to despair. His virtuosity on the piano and as a teacher of piano had earned him a major part of his livelihood. His triumphs as a performer might soon be of the past.

The Heiligenstadt Testament, the most powerful and moving prose statement Beethoven ever set down, describes his unhappy state of mind. Such an expression of despair was unusual at this time. Beethoven had obtained considerable success as a musician, but he could no longer hide from himself, nor, he feared, from others, this new reality. "For six years," he tells his brothers,

> I have been suffering an incurable affliction. . . . Year after year deceived by the hope of an improvement, finally forced to contemplate the prospect of a lasting illness, whose cure may take years or may even be impossible. . . . I was yet compelled early in my life to isolate myself, to spend my life in solitude . . . and yet I could

not prevail upon myself to say to men: speak louder, shout, for I am deaf. . . . My affliction is all the more painful to me because it leads to such misinterpretations of my conduct. Recreation in human society, refined conversation, mutual effusions of thought are denied to me. . . . But what a humiliation when someone standing next to me heard a flute in the distance and I heard nothing, or when someone heard the shepherd sing and, again, I heard nothing. Such occurrences brought me to the verge of despair. I might easily have put an end to my life. Only one thing, Art, held me back. . . . Now it is done. It is with joy that I hasten to meet my death.[18]

For a career as a musician once so promising, what would deafness mean if he could no longer hear the sounds of nature around him during his walks, nor the voices of actors on stage, nor people speaking to him? How could a deaf man continue to create music—music gradually recognized by an increasing number of listeners as brilliant, even earthshaking? Still more tragically, how could he bring about the even greater works of the future that he envisioned? Anyone who reads this letter cannot but be overwhelmed by the anguish it expresses.

Yet the language is ambiguous. Some interpret the letter as an expression of suicide, but that was not the path Beethoven chose. The eminent scholar Walter Riezler hears in it instead "the despairing cry of a man who sees no future but a life of isolation, who fears he may not have the strength to bear such a fate; the cry of a heart, overflowing with love for mankind and a longing for fellowship, but tormented by the fear of being misunderstood."[19] "This famous document," observes the musicologist Joseph Kerman, "reads less as a letter or a will than as a great unburdening cry of grief at his deafness and solitude—mingled with apology, self-justification, self-pity, pathos, pride, hints of suicide, and presentiments of death."[20] The Viennese writer Hans Gal places the letter within the context of Beethoven's beloved classics. "It is as in ancient tragedy," he comments, "when the hero in his moment of triumph is suddenly smashed by the hand of an outraged god, punished for his *hubris*."[21]

Since this letter was found in his desk after his death, presumably Beethoven never sent it to its intended recipients. Even *before* he wrote the Testament, the climax of the crisis may have passed, or he may have set down his anguish so that he could look at it more dispassionately. Beethoven had now begun his Second Symphony, one of his sunniest works. In any case, soon after October 1802, a marked change in his creativity occurred. While expressing his emotional despair in the Heiligenstadt Testament, he was working steadily on this warm and buoyant work that radiates cheer. Of it he wrote, "Artists are fiery by nature and do not weep." The symphony does not weep. If the artist who composed it did weep, we do not know of it. Published in 1804 after still more revisions, the symphony precedes the *Eroica*, on which he had already made good progress—and whose creation may offer to the despair expressed in the Heiligenstadt Testament the best possible answer.

When Beethoven turned again to piano sonatas, they too underwent a sea change. Genius we expect from him, at any stage in his life, but the endless yet riveting repetitions in the first movement of the "Waldstein" Sonata, Op. 53, take even seasoned listeners aback. Yet, once heard, the movement is never forgotten. The "Appassionata" Sonata, Op. 57, with its meditative, haunting Andante, is an even more complex wonder. Both sonatas in their dynamism and the range of emotion have more in common in mood and energy with the *Eroica* and *Leonore* than with the sonatas that preceded them.

Though staggering to contemplate, Beethoven's personal anguish and his efforts to cope with his deafness may well have allowed him to reach a further level in the realm of music. We shall never know for sure. All the same, the emotional price seems almost unbearably high. An individual growing deaf tends to spend ever more time in the silent world of his thoughts. Beethoven did that, but he did much else too.

The composer had an impassioned nature. To those who knew him well, his buoyancy of being might not always have seemed such.

But he loved life, and creating music was his most cherished activity. As he wrote in the Testament, a person growing deaf over a span of years soon realizes his hearing will probably not get better. More likely it will get worse. In Beethoven's case, over a future abundant with promise loomed a dark cloud already ominous. Part of coping with an increasingly noiseless world was that, without someone to help him manage, travel would become more difficult. Imagine the challenges a nearly deaf person in Beethoven's day faced on the road. If the coachman called out a change of coach or the destination, and the traveler could not hear or distinguish between "Koblenz" and "Königsberg," an unpleasant surprise awaited him or her. "Learn through suffering," Aeschylus could have told Beethoven, and he would have understood.

Violinist Yehudi Menuhin, discussing Beethoven's torment at the loss of his hearing, once asked how he could face "so fateful and shattering a curse." It led Menuhin to draw an analogy between Beethoven and Prometheus: "Prometheus stole fire from the gods and gave it to man; the gods punished him by chaining him to a rock. For Beethoven, overflowing with genius and desirous of sharing it with humanity, the rock was his deafness."[22] He endured "a mental agony all the fiercer," the Beethoven biographer Marion Scott pointed out, "in that for the most part he suffered in silence as proud as that of Prometheus towards his captors."[23] The outpouring of grief in the Heiligenstadt Testament, although putatively addressed to his brothers, seems intended as much for the world at large. Beethoven was Promethean in grandeur, Promethean in his suffering, and never less than Promethean in his determination to continue creating music.

ᔥ

The Akademie of April 5, 1803

We know less about Beethoven's second Akademie than about the first. Unfortunately, no copy of the program has survived. We do know that, again, Beethoven conducted. In addition to the adventurous Second Symphony, Beethoven also included the more traditional First, which many in the audience preferred. *The Magazine of the Elegant World* deemed the First "better . . . because it is developed with a lightness and is less forced, while in the second the striving for the new and surprising is already more apparent."[24] Once again, we find Beethoven marching a few steps ahead of his listeners. This dilemma lasted all his life. The program, again somewhat overlong, also included the splendid Third Piano Concerto, Op. 37, and the oratorio *Christ on the Mount of Olives*. Beethoven presumably interspersed the above works with a few shorter, lighter compositions, but we do not know which ones. More likely due to his loss of hearing, he did not perform extempore as he had in his first Akademie.

In his Akademies, Beethoven would premiere his first four concertos with himself as soloist. Only the fifth and last, the so-called "Emperor" Concerto, dating from 1809, did he not play in public. By then his fading hearing did not permit a nuanced performance. Once Beethoven realized fully that his time as a piano virtuoso was over, he wrote no further piano concertos.

Although scholars usually date the Third Piano Concerto to 1800, Beethoven had likely worked on it already for several years. He employed his favored key of C minor. As was his wont, he continued to revise it right up to the hour of its first performance. Even then he still had not finished it. For the piano part he had only his erratically pencil-scrawled manuscript. Ignaz von Seyfried, who turned pages for him, recalled how the first performance went:

> I saw almost nothing but empty leaves; at the most, on one page or the other a few Egyptian hieroglyphics wholly unintelligible to me scribbled down to serve as clues for him, for he played nearly all of the solo part from memory, since, as so often the case, he had not had time to put it all down on paper. He gave me a secret glance whenever he was at the end of one of the invisible passages, and

my scarcely concealable anxiety not to miss the decisive moment amused him greatly.[25]

Not finishing a work on time was not unusual for Beethoven. Nor did it overly bother him. He had lodged the concerto's piano part deep in memory. He wasted nothing. Soloists then, unlike most today, did not play from memory. Audiences would have regarded doing so as too eccentric. Only decades later did Franz Liszt begin the practice of playing from memory.

Also included in Beethoven's Akademie was his first major work on a religious theme, *Christ on the Mount of Olives*. In this work Beethoven measured himself against Handel as well as Haydn. But the oratorio's mood differs from works by either composer. It tells of Christ's agony as he is called upon to make the ultimate sacrifice. His responses indicate a measure of resentment. Jesus addresses his divine Father: "Your power makes all possible. / Take the goblet of suffering from me!" Feeling completely abandoned by his Father, Christ suffers unbearable torture. He despairs and welcomes Death, "from which I on the cross / die bleeding for the salvation of mankind." Especially moving is Christ's final recitative: "My torment is soon gone, / the work of salvation completed." At the close, a chorus of angels sings a rousing climax, one of Beethoven's most powerful. Given the composer's indifference toward formal worship, the meaning of the work within the context of Beethoven's life must remain highly speculative. He had, however, often pondered the reality of death. He may even at times have welcomed the thought of dying, but, the Heiligenstadt Testament informs us, he had resolved to live and to continue to create. Christ hoped his sacrifice would result in mankind's salvation. By creating music worthy of heroic suffering, his own and humanity's, Beethoven held similar hopes. Many in the audience received *Christ on the Mount of Olives* with extraordinary approval. But not everyone, Beethoven perhaps among them. Continuing to rethink and rewrite the work, he waited until 1811 to have it published. Though the oratorio receives few modern performances, it has slowly gained recognition as a major work in the Beethoven canon.

The Akademie started at six in the evening, but lasted so long that a few pieces were not performed. Alas, we do not know which they were. All the same, despite its extraordinary length, the Akademie proved a success financially as well as musically. Beethoven had priced tickets far higher for this Akademie than for that preceding. He did well by it, emerging eighteen hundred florins richer. With the Second Symphony, the score for *The Creatures of Prometheus*, and the Third Piano Concerto in C Minor, all full of strident militarism, Beethoven indicated he had begun in earnest his conquest of the musical world. With these works he announced himself as a new, perhaps now the dominant, voice in European music. He wanted to have an impact upon the musical world as powerful as Napoleon's had had upon the European continent. Napoleonic determination and energy, the sheer brilliance of his achievement, helped give Beethoven the courage to continue.

12

The *Eroica*

MEANING AND DEDICATION

The *Eroica* is the noblest piece of absolute music ever
written in sonata form, and it is the noblest piece of
programme music. In Beethoven, indeed, the distinction
between the two became purely imaginary.

H. L. MENCKEN[1]

The characteristic of the great compositions of
Beethoven is that they are veritable poems, in which
it is sought to bring a real subject to representation.
The obstacle to their comprehension lies in the difficulty
in finding the subject that is represented.

RICHARD WAGNER[2]

The most staggering novelty in the history of music.

HANS GAL[3]

Even if Beethoven dismissed the idea of "a revolutionary sonata" in
1803, he may not have dismissed a revolutionary work. Might he
not write a revolutionary symphony? Whatever the circumstances, after
completing the "Kreutzer" Sonata in 1803, Beethoven turned to the *Eroica*. Work on it occupied him for at least six months, followed by months
of revisions. Although the "Kreutzer" Sonata does not engage the symphony's heroic first movement, the two works share a common origin,
for the sonata possesses the *Eroica*'s dynamism, its breadth of vision. In
both works, Beethoven intended to disturb, even upset, listeners.

The earliest surviving sketches of the *Eroica* date from early in 1802, the year of the Heiligenstadt Testament. Able to articulate in the Testament his fears concerning his increasing deafness, cognizant that it might worsen, even last his lifetime, Beethoven struggled against what seemed to him to be an unkind destiny. He had contemplated, but stoically rejected, suicide. Plutarch, particularly his admonition to accept "resignation," came to his rescue. No doubt Beethoven did despair, but he was a fighter, and fight he would. Fate would not conquer *him*. The *Eroica* may strike those aware of Beethoven's subsequent career as his most difficult, most challenging work. Twice as long as a typical symphony by Mozart or Haydn, it runs to what contemporaries regarded as an inordinate length, in modern recordings from forty-five to fifty-five minutes. It is also the first of his named symphonies.

During the spring of 1803 he began what was perhaps *the* crucial work of his career. He rented a cottage for the summer in Oberdöbling, a village closer to Vienna than Heiligenstadt but still well outside the then city limits.[4] His sketches make clear that ideas for the symphony matured slowly. There in the rural peace he loved, Beethoven worked on his new symphony during the autumn and, once back in the capital, throughout the winter of 1803–04.

Perhaps Beethoven's increasing deafness even escalated the extraordinarily creative years that followed. Besides the *Eroica*, he conceived, or began, or continued work on the "Appassionata" and "Waldstein" Piano Sonatas, the Triple Concerto, and *Leonore*. He did preliminary work on the Fourth and Fifth Symphonies. Having over the past decade absorbed revolutionary and Napoleonic energy, he now re-created it in music. All the above works embody a heightened dynamism. The "new path" Beethoven had announced in 1801 or 1802 became a credo, a challenge, for the man who now took giant strides on it. In the *Eroica* Beethoven conceived the possibilities of life in a Europe renewed by Napoleon. "He saw in his idol," writes Anton Schindler, "the promise of a new age, the embodied spirit of a world reborn." Such thoughts sum up, in a nutshell, Beethoven's purpose and achievement in his symphony.

The *Eroica* marks an epoch in the history of music. No one before had essayed a symphonic work of such complex design, intricate structure, and great length. The symphony rushes along at a ferocious velocity, a veritable torrent of sound at white-hot intensity. With the *Eroica*, Beethoven's music began to evolve faster than many contemporaries could comprehend. Most of them, however, considered the *Eroica* a musical aberration. Listeners since have found it an astonishing work, a source of frustration to some, a masterpiece for others. From the first, it had its passionate devotees.

Edmund Burke's almost instantly famous *Philosophical Inquiry into the Sublime and the Beautiful* (1756) had put the idea of the sublime in the air. The emotional and aesthetic pleasure of sublime works derived from the sense of terror, of fear, that they conveyed, combined with a transcendent awareness of beauty. "The feeling for sublimity is the direction of my soul," Herder wrote three years after Burke; "the sublime determines my love, my hatred, my admiration, my dreams of happiness and unhappiness, my purpose to live in the world."[5]

Many early hearers of the *Eroica* did not rise to the occasion. But a few did. Upon first hearing the symphony in Paris, Berlioz felt *foudroyé*, that is, thunderstruck. For him, "it was Beethoven, and only Beethoven, who had ushered in a new age of limitless possibility."[6] Berlioz never referred to Beethoven as a musician. Doing so, he felt, would have belittled him and misled others. Indeed, "he always called him poet, or poet-musician, or giant of music or poetry."[7] The word "poet" Berlioz reserved exclusively for creators of "the lasting works and revelations of musical art." Romantic creators, Leo Schrade, the French expatriate who taught at Yale, tells us, "from now on, and not only in France, were to speak in these terms; and it is to poetry that they ascribed all the breadth and depth of musical form."[8] Yet Beethoven thought the poet's realm more restricted than the musician's. Comparing music with poetry, he believed music opened access to a higher realm. "It allowed him," he wrote, "to consider himself to be more favoured than any Muse: our sphere extended further into other regions and our empire cannot be so easily reached."[9]

To triumph Beethoven needed, he once said, to "seize Fate by the throat."[10] In years to come he would do just that. Fate became his greatest adversary. But the combat had rewards. As Thomas Mann once put it, "The breath of the rolling sea of epic would not so expand our lungs with living air if it did not bring with it the astringent quickening spice of the spiritual and the divine."[11] For Beethoven, the music of transcendent greatness, which he knew lay within him, constituted the "spice of the spiritual and the divine." In his oratorio *Christ on the Mount of Olives* death comes as a release; in *Leonore* (which became *Fidelio*) a woman's love rescues her imprisoned husband. The *Eroica*, preceding these two works, implies an immersion by Beethoven in his art so total that we cannot easily summarize, much less comprehend, its scope. It is the signature work of Beethoven's so-called "heroic," or middle, period of composition.

With the *Eroica* we enter an expanding universe, one seemingly without bounds, one that vigorously extols freedom's possibilities. Erich Leinsdorf, the twentieth-century American conductor, compared the *Eroica*'s stunning newness, with pardonable exaggeration, to "man's first orbital flight in a spacecraft after many years of being confined within the earth's atmosphere."[12] Bruno Walter, interpreting Mahler, speaks of works of genius having "that element of ultimate immeasurability which is the hallmark of greatness."[13] In other words, there exist creations—whether in art, music, or literature—that we cannot fully measure, cannot fully understand, creations comparable to the *Eroica* in their depth and insight into humanity. We read *Hamlet, Lear, The Divine Comedy*; we look up at the Sistine ceiling or at the Parthenon frieze; we listen to a symphony by Beethoven or Bruckner or Mahler. We grasp something of what we read, or see, or hear of these creations, but we may not understand more than a fraction of their meaning. They remain for us, to use a German word, *unheimlich*. Its usual translation is "uncanny," that is, it refers to something essentially beyond our normal ken, outside our usual sphere of reference. In 1838 the music publisher Léon Escudier presciently observed, "the *Eroica* Symphony is not yet understood; but it will be."[14] Nearly two centuries have passed since then. Have we come closer to understanding the *Eroica*?

❧

Meaning

Neither Bach nor Beethoven, observes Wilfrid Mellers, "doubted that their music had 'meanings' discussible in terms simultaneously musical, theological and philosophical."[15] Unlike Stravinsky, who insisted that his music meant "nothing by itself," Beethoven intended his music to mean something beyond the sounds heard. Occasionally the composer dropped hints to friends regarding what had inspired him. But he rarely commented at length on his works, and when he did his remarks are often more cryptic than enlightening. Only slightly less tantalizing are Beethoven's terse recommendations to those wishing to understand his compositions. For Piano Sonata, No. 17, Op. 31, no. 2 (known as the "Tempest") he refers to Shakespeare's play of that name. For Opus 18, no. 1, he simply states, "Read *Romeo and Juliet*." He does not mean that he based these works upon these plays, only that by reading them we might understand better what he had done. By comparing his creations to Shakespeare's he implies that they possess something of the poet's complexity and depth. Beethoven professed to want the music-loving public to know what he had in mind. "For approximately ten years," Schindler tells us, he "considered preparing an edition of his works in which he would have described the extramusical ideas or the psychological state that had led in each case to the composing of the work."[16] Once aware of his intent, the public would presumably understand, or appreciate better—so Beethoven believed—what he had done. Unfortunately he never set down his thoughts. Beethoven's contemporaries sensed that he often rooted his compositions deeply in the events, imaginatively reconceived, of his own life. But not always. His devoted student and lifelong friend Carl Czerny posited that

Beethoven was excited to work on many of his most beautiful compositions through similar *visions* and images created from readings or from his own active fantasy, and that we would find the true key to his compositions and their performance only through an accurate knowledge of their circumstances.[17]

The challenge for us is to penetrate that fantasy. Within the *Eroica* Beethoven intertwines at least three levels of meaning—the mythic, the personal, and the historical. This study will focus on the historical, on how it relates to the French Revolution and Napoleon.

More attention has been given to the classical influences on the *Eroica* than to the political ones, chiefly the Revolution and the First Consul. Yet the symphony clearly reflects the ideas and tragedies of the upheavals occasioned by the recent events in France. "French music inspired by the Revolution celebrated liberty, camaraderie, love of country, and victory over tyranny," writes Elisabeth Brisson in her well-named study *The Consecration of the Musician*: "Beethoven adapts this music, gives it a heroic accent, a warlike élan, until it becomes his own mode of expression. The category '*Eroica*,' or Heroic, was destined to maintain the fundamental values of a free and happy humanity marching toward its *épanouissement*" (apotheosis).[18]

❧

Heroism

Notions of heroism pervaded the nineteenth century. "I want a hero." So Byron begins his comic epic poem *Don Juan*. "Want" implies "lack," or possibly, "need." Byron most likely meant both. Understood as "need," "want" implies that Byron thinks heroes desirable, even necessary. But in one way or another all the candidates he takes up, Napoleon among them, fail him. Who, in his view, might qualify? For the present, only a sixteen-year-old boy, his titular hero. Byron may be echoing Voltaire. "I hate heroes," said the *philosophe;* "they are so noisy."[19] No doubt Voltaire recalled the *miles gloriosus* (braggart hero) of Roman comedy as well as the pompous court buffoons of his own day. What he would have liked to admire he was forced to mock. Byron probably felt the same unease regarding heroes. Yet during his life Napoleon remained a hero for him. Heroism does not exist in a vacuum. It needs an antagonist. Inevitably the question arises, does the work have a hero—and if it has one, who might it be? The object and even the nature of Beethoven's conception of heroism remain debated subjects. Even if we accept the symphony's heroic nature, what kind of heroism does it hymn? True heroism is less about battles and campaigns and more about courage, integrity, determination, a striving for greatness, even the heroic spirit of mankind. The antagonist can be another person or a cause, even oneself, for, in reality, the toughest conflicts often involve the self. This was certainly true for Beethoven.

Plutarch in his *Lives* praised the conduct under duress of Greek and Roman heroes. Such individuals, to whom the ancient Greeks devoted a cult, were by their lives *and* deaths considered as intermediaries between the gods and mankind. According to the Greek author, heroism lay in imitating the courage of these past heroes. As we have seen, Beethoven had developed an abiding fascination with the Prometheus myth. In the Enlightenment the Titan personified the liberation and aspirations of humanity. In Shelley's *Prometheus Unbound* (1819) Prometheus symbolized man's best and most creative qualities. In his Preface Shelley calls Prometheus "the type of the highest perfection of moral and intellectual nature, impelled by the purest and the truest motives to the best and noblest ends." After Zeus had mistreated humans, Prometheus championed their cause. His defiant facing of adversity and his overcoming it testify to his immensely resilient nature. This behavior helps us interpret the symphony. It reflects Beethoven's near-obsession with the Titan. The Prometheus theme enters dramatically in the Scherzo. It will dominate the exultant Finale, whose dynamic music well renders the energy of its creator's mighty being.

The *Eroica* also looks back to *The Creatures of Prometheus*. By re-creating the Prometheus myth in music, Beethoven could express his thoughts about Hapsburg hegemony in ways he could not in words. He did not relish oppressors, whether in the mythic shapes of the ancient Greek gods or in a living Hapsburg emperor. Beethoven depicted liberators positively: best (as we shall discover) were those like Leonore who succeeded, but even a failed liberator like Egmont, or a would-be liberator like Coriolanus, held appeal for him.

If we superimpose the mythic upon the personal, the fire-stealing and god-defying Titan served Beethoven as an ideal of heroism. Promethean fire enabled women and men to raise themselves above other creatures. It also gave them the possibility of creating what became civilization. Promethean fire enabled men and women to raise themselves above other creatures. It also gave them the possibility of creating what became civilization. As discussed earlier, by giving fire to humankind Prometheus had disobeyed Zeus, who had him chained to a rock where he seemed destined to undergo an eternity of suffering. Only the thought that one day he would triumph over the gods enabled him to endure. Heinrich Eduard Jacob, the biographer of Mendelssohn, once drew a parallel between the Greek Titan and Beethoven. The composer "was a man of immeasurable greatness; like Prometheus, who had brought the gift of fire to mankind, Beethoven had given his age a new music. And like Prometheus, so cruelly punished for his temerity, Beethoven suffered punishment by the loss of his hearing."[20] The composer's despair over this loss strengthened his character and gave him the courage to survive and continue to compose.

The *Eroica* revolves as much around Beethoven's own life as a creative work can. The dissonances he experienced within himself—the result of a titanic struggle within and without—terrified even Wagner. If you want to become an epic hero, and Beethoven seems to have envisioned himself as such, you need to confront an opponent or antagonist, or fight for a cause, or remedy a situation. Achilles had Hector; Prometheus, Zeus; Aeneas, Turnus; Roland, the Moslem forces at Roncesvalles. Epics often revolve around or end with a catastrophe: the death of Hector in *The Iliad*, of Roland and of Charlemagne's rear guard in *The Song of Roland*, of the German knights in *The Nibelungenlied*. Or the adversary may be, as it was for Beethoven, a personal dilemma to face, his loss of hearing. In short, to be heroic you need to strive against a force equal to or greater than yourself. Beethoven's worsening deafness proved a worthy antagonist. By threatening to derail his public career, it imperiled his livelihood as a pianist. It made living a normal life (he believed) virtually impossible. Worst of all, it questioned his capacity to create. Against this opponent he engaged in a long and desperate combat. The odds were on the side of deafness, but instead of succumbing to despair Beethoven went on to achieve new heights of creativity. His physical ear had failed him, but his mental ear refused to acquiesce.

The *Eroica* incarnates Beethoven's life in music as he had thus far lived it. The Heiligenstadt Testament of October 1802 had affirmed his will to continue. "It seemed impossible to bid farewell to the world," he tells us in it, "before having given all that for which I felt myself gifted."[21] The first movement of the *Eroica* affirms his heroic being, his determination to proceed; the second embodies his despair over his encroaching deafness; the third reveals his determination to overcome this grave handicap, even if he could not cure it, by affirming his joyous love of life; the fourth celebrates his triumph of the will and emblazons his continued creativity. Another way to describe or interpret the movement-by-movement scheme is through a biographical context: I. Beethoven's triumphs during the first Vienna decade; II. his awareness of the loss of his hearing; III. the renewal of his confidence; IV. his optimism as he joyously contemplates his hopes for future creativity. Like Napoleon, Beethoven incarnated in the symphony not just the end of the ancien régime but the possibilities of change, of human progress. His music would undermine absolutism, promote liberty, and encourage fraternity.

᠄

Listening to the *Eroica*

Introductory Chords

Two E-flat chords, whiplashes of sound, hit us like cannon shots, or cosmic blasts. Why commence a symphony so dramatically? Doing so astounded, indeed shocked, early audiences. It can shock listeners today. What, in beginning thus, did Beethoven intend? What prompted these chords? They pay homage to the cannon fired by the *Eroica*'s original dedicatee, young General Bonaparte, now First Consul. Directing cannon fire was his specialty, as the British forces holding Toulon discovered to their cost in 1792. The chords recall the world of the Revolution: exuberant, over-the-top, colossal. They are wake-up calls to jolt somnolent audiences, in Vienna certainly, but elsewhere as well. They unite two of the greatest figures of the era. Warriors both, one wished to conquer by arms, the other by music. Things hitherto unimaginable, the chords tell us, are on our doorstep. Who can predict what will happen next?

�℘

Allegro con brio

The revolution that began in France has changed things everywhere else as well, Vienna included. A new era is about to dawn, in fact has arrived—and those listening to the *Eroica* are, like it or not, participating in it. In the rapidity of the movement that follows, the symphony appears to sweep away symmetry and balance. The music assails our ears. It offers us a heightened awareness of ourselves and of our own time. No less does it announce the advent of a terrifyingly new world.

The revolution Beethoven heralds in the *Eroica* is one of wide, potentially universal, import, one still ongoing. Napoleon in 1803–04 is its herald. A magnetic being, he strides across the landscape of Europe.

Armies molded by him march at his pace; its commanders think quickly, urge an advance rather than a retreat, hold terrain only as long as needed to attack. The rapidity with which Napoleon moved his troops during his Italian campaign of 1796–97 left European military leaders gasping. The *Eroica*'s first movement mimics that pace—and incarnates the myth of Napoleon as it has developed, by leaps and bounds, since that time. Its 691 measures constitute a single directed span; or, to recall Goethe's language in regard to nature, "a single organic growth." This movement demands from the listener a degree of mental and emotional engagement that little previous music had.

ھ

Marcia funebre

Is not the Marcia funebre (Funeral March) "to be ranked," asks an American music critic of an earlier era, Lawrence Gilman, "together with the Crucifixus from Bach's B-Minor Mass and Wagner's *Funeral Hymn* for Siegfried among the unapproachable trio of music's supreme laments?"[22] For Romain Rolland, the Marcia funebre is "the modern poem that comes nearest to the elegiac choruses of Greek Tragedy."[23] John Updike believed that in the Marcia funebre Beethoven "projected a personality Napoleonic in its insatiability and capacity for heroic defeat."[24]

With its "great phrases, long passages, and wide deviations," the Funeral March expressed for Schopenhauer "a great and noble effort towards a distant goal, and its final attainment."[25] Opinion divides, however, on what reaching the "distant goal," that is, death, might achieve. Whose funeral does the Marcia funebre commemorate? For Schopenhauer it speaks "to the man who gives himself up entirely to the impression of the symphony, it is as if he saw all the possible events of life and of the world passing by within himself."[26] He regards the movement as "the memory of an ideal, a reminder of our mortality, of our shared humanity, of the divinity that resides in all of us." Though we lament the death of individuals, the greatness in our lives—and the greatness in what we create—lives on. Individuals depart, but their accomplishments can leave the world in a better state than before. We experience as well the world on a metaphysical level: as a journey through the valley of death into a new realm where earthly cares no longer predominate. Even emperors are mortal. Eventually they must die as we must die.

Commemorating the departed through music, visual art, and words has a long history. Beethoven was well aware of the vogue for solemn funeral music. Neefe, his teacher in Bonn, had written a Funeral Cantata in honor of Lessing. Beethoven's own Joseph cantata is in this tradition. Funeral music, or *Trauermusik*, by medieval and Renaissance masters includes works by Josquin Després, Alexander Agricola, and Conrad Paumann. Paintings by Raphael, Bellini, and Poussin, among earlier artists, depict the death of heroes of classical antiquity and of Christian saints. Purcell in the seventeenth century wrote a *Funeral March for Queen Mary*. Bossuet in his *Funeral Orations* celebrated in unsurpassed rhetorical splendor the virtues and greatness of the illustrious dead. Handel created a "Dead March" in his *Saul* (1739); before that, his *Israel in Egypt* (1736) had pondered a "Funeral Anthem for Queen Caroline." Behind Beethoven's Marcia funebre also lurks the solemn military music spawned by the French Revolution. Countless songs, chief among them the instantly popular "Marseillaise" and "La Carmagnole," raced across Europe. All the same, the Marcia funebre has puzzled hearers since at least 1838, the year Franz Wegeler and Stephan von Breuning published their memorial tome on Beethoven in which they linked the *Eroica* to Napoleon. Well before Bonaparte's death in 1821, even before his coronation in 1804, several of Beethoven's intimates knew how greatly he had admired him. Only a few, however, were aware he had originally named *Bonaparte* the symphony they knew as the *Eroica*, and that he had initially intended to dedicate it to the French leader.

Beethoven viewed French revolutionary composers as harbingers of a desired future. Drawing inspiration from Gossec's *Marche lugubre*

(Funeral March), Beethoven's Marcia funebre, at once *lugubre* and *héroïque*, owes much to the feats of the revolutionary armies and the music they inspired. However we interpret it, the Marcia funebre is the symphony's core. No funeral march since has equaled it. But why put a *marcia funebre* in a symphony—particularly a symphony that celebrates heroism and the heroic? Does Beethoven anticipate Napoleon's funeral? Or, if not Napoleon's, someone else's? Does the Marcia funebre even commemorate a particular person? Is it not, implied a contemporary reviewer, "too big to lead to the tomb of a single man"?[27] Is the Marcia funebre, to the extent that it concerns the young Bonaparte, more about his greatness as a human being than about his death? These questions remain open.

Behind this titanic movement, indeed the whole symphony, looms the French Revolution, its music and its deeds, its ideals and its tragedies. Honoring a hero with a funeral march provided a means for citizens to participate in a revolution that many believed would lead to a new age for mankind. French composers of funeral marches in the Revolution's "National Guard" style wrote them in a tempo that people could walk or march to. So did Beethoven. He grasped the democratic aspect of French revolutionary music. The musicians of the National Guard would have recognized in him their prophet. Thanks to funeral marches, people viewed death with greater intensity, and perhaps with greater understanding, than before. Celebrating the Republic's triumphs and the progressive spirit of the age, such music signaled that in the ultimate sacrifice lay hopes for a better future for mankind everywhere. The music written for these *fêtes* also helped shape the *Eroica*. Soon afterwards, the symphony, roughly contemporary with the *Chant national*, began to emerge from the recesses of Beethoven's creative imagination.

Between the music's contemporary roots in the *Chant national* and other such works and its epic transfiguration in the Marcia funebre we sense a communion. This revolutionary music with its warlike élan, somber dignity, and heroic vitality Beethoven adapts until it becomes a mode of expression uniquely his own. By implication, the Marcia funebre celebrates no less the ongoing revolution in men's minds that the Revolution in France had ignited and furthered. His Marcia funebre is thus an epic transfiguration of a long tradition inspired by heroic greatness.

Beethoven's Marcia funebre limns the intensity of death. No wistful sweetness softens it, nor is Beethoven's music, as Keats once put it, "half in love with easeful death." Like the French *marche funèbre* tradition, including the "Marseillaise" upon which it draws, Beethoven confronts death squarely. His Marcia funebre represents the deepest sense of tragedy. Heroes must be willing to die for their ideals. Without this commitment, without sacrifice, there can be no heroism and no glory. The Marcia funebre, with its deliberate pace and somber tone, validates the heroic striving heard in the other movements. These movements affirm that those who died in the cause for freedom, as well as those who died in fighting tyranny, will participate in the glory of a new life.

ৎ

Scherzo

The brief Scherzo that follows, exhilarating and life-affirming, stretches the span of emotion further than before. From deepest tragedy in the Marcia funebre we move to ecstatic joy. The movement's basic structure introduces a theme, then stops it, then repeats it, several times. The variations suggest the extraordinary variety of human life. The Prometheus theme now enters after the fifth or sixth variation, where it is played by the woodwinds accompanied by the strings. The French horns when they enter are not military or strident, but joyful, as if on a hunt. Like the Marcia funebre, the Scherzo commemorates less a particular hero than it does all heroes who have fallen for their respective fatherlands. For his Scherzo Beethoven added a third French horn, one more than in any of his previous works. Their sonority offers relief and hope.

In the "Knocking at the Gate" scene in *Macbeth* a drunken porter staggers onstage after Macbeth has murdered Duncan, the sanctified king of Scotland. The porter's crude behavior and crass language initially shock us. Did Shakespeare miscalculate by such a juxtaposition? Not likely, for Shakespeare knew what he was about. As Thomas De Quincey pointed out two centuries ago, the introduction of low comedy heightens the tragic effect. Contrasting the comic with the tragic puts into truer perspective Shakespeare's encompassing vision of life. Likewise, Beethoven's joyous Scherzo offers relief from the tragic Marcia funebre.

ℒ

Prometheus

The *Eroica*'s last movement, composed first, served Beethoven as a basic springboard with which to prepare the first three. Not only did he destine the Prometheus theme from the outset to be the work's Finale, but he also composed the other three movements with it in mind. Introducing the Prometheus theme in the Scherzo gives the symphony an unprecedented unity. Upon hearing the *Eroica*'s Finale, a Viennese audience, conservative in taste but long of memory, may well have recalled the simple English dance with which Beethoven, a few years earlier, had closed the music for his ballet *The Creatures of Prometheus*.

ℒ

Reception

According to a review of the public premiere of the symphony at the Theater an der Wien on April 7, 1805, audience reaction was divided into three distinct groups:

> One group, Beethoven's very special friends, maintains that precisely this symphony is a masterpiece, . . . that if it does not please at present, it is because the public is not sufficiently educated in art to be able to grasp all of these elevated beauties. After a thou-

sand years, however, they will not fail to have their effect. [An]other group utterly denies this work any artistic value and feels that it manifests a completely unbounded striving for distinction and oddity, which, however, has produced neither beauty nor true sublimity and power. Through strange modulations and violent transitions, by placing together the most heterogeneous things, as when, for example, a pastorale is played through in the grandest style, with abundant scratchings in the bass, with three horns and so forth, a true if not desirable originality can indeed be gained without much effort. However, genius does not proclaim itself by simply bringing forth the unusual and the fantastic, but rather by creating the beautiful and the sublime. The third, very small group stands in the middle; they admit that the symphony contains many beautiful qualities, but admit that the context often seems completely disjointed, and that the endless duration of this longest and perhaps also most difficult of all symphonies exhausts even connoisseurs, becoming unbearable to the mere amateur.[28]

Only Beethoven's "very special friends" were able to grasp fully the revolutionary nature of the *Eroica*, to believe in the "masterpiece" they had experienced, and to proclaim that, given Viennese torpor toward newness, it might need a thousand years to have its intended effect.

～

Dedication

From Haydn and Mozart Beethoven had inherited a Classical vocabulary. In the *Eroica* he radically enlarged and extended, but did not shatter, this earlier vocabulary. Too shrewd and savvy to be a utopian, Beethoven had yet mulled over ideas propounded by "Gracchus" Babeuf, particularly Babeuf's notion that society should support artists by allowing them to draw upon a common fund. The *Eroica* envisages a future in which society would repress humans less and allow creation more.

Thus the symphony's originality and power. A decade and more earlier, his *Cantata on the Death of Joseph II* had indicated Beethoven's reverence before human greatness.

Until May 1804 Beethoven had intended to dedicate his new symphony, the greatest work he had written to date, to the modern Prometheus, Napoleon Bonaparte. Who, after all, among contemporaries better embodied the heroic spirit? Napoleon "was a monarch," claimed the Comte de Ségur, "but he was the monarch of the Revolution."[29] However, upon hearing of his imminent coronation as emperor Beethoven uttered angry words and withdrew the dedication. Yet only three months later he claimed to a publisher that the symphony "was really named Bonaparte."

The story of the *Eroica*'s dedication to "Bonaparte"—and its abrupt termination—has become the best-known anecdote in music history. While the original manuscript of the *Eroica* does not survive, the conducting copy of the score does. At the top of the first page Beethoven wrote *"Sinfonia grande"* in large letters in ink, and underneath it *"intitolata Bonaparte"* (named Bonaparte). Then follows the date *"[1]804 im August," "Del Sigr.,"* and beneath both, *"Luigi van Beethoven."*

To render in music Napoleon's forceful persona required new means. The French scholar and statesman Édouard Herriot posits "an ideal Bonaparte" dominating the symphony.[30] It evokes, he observes, "those feelings that Napoleon's career inspired in the beholder, here Beethoven."[31] Does not the dramatic music that Beethoven gives us tell us that the French leader has changed the world and, not least, the way people think of the world? But not everyone has seen it that way.

Among those who wished to distance the symphony from the First Consul, Wagner ranks foremost. The *Eroica* fascinated him. Following Schindler, he believed that Napoleon's intention to become emperor shattered Beethoven's admiration of the French Titan. Heaven forfend!—nowhere in the *Eroica*, cried Wagner, can Napoleon be found. Gradually the work's meaning, though not his understanding of Napoleon's impact upon it, widened for Wagner. "The real hero of the *Eroica*," he claimed in 1851, "is humanity itself."[32] But in arguing for the *Eroica*'s appeal to a broader humanity, Wagner evades Beethoven's political philosophy and historical context. The designation "heroic" in no wise relates merely to a military hero but implies rather a fully rounded human being. Though Wagner can no longer accept Napoleon as the symphony's hero, in comparing Beethoven with Napoleon he did make a valid point: both figures, he thought, had territory to conquer. Wagner also claimed the symphony portrayed Beethoven's career musically. "He, too," he writes, "must have felt *his* powers aroused to an extraordinary pitch, his valiant courage spurred on to a grand and unheard of deed! He was no general—he was a musician; and thus in *his* realm he saw before him the territory within which he could accomplish the same thing that Bonaparte had achieved in the fields of Italy."[33] But Wagner's remains a minority view.

Complementary to the amazing career of the young Napoleon are Beethoven's own travails. Placing Beethoven in Napoleon's company, comments Elisabeth Brisson, implies that the composer deserves a consecration, a *sacre*, of his own. Beethoven thought himself more than life-sized. His controlling, even demanding, temperament bore remarkable similarities to Napoleon's. He believed in power, bowed to no man, impressed many as arrogant, and thought himself a heroic conqueror. Not only did Beethoven draw upon Napoleon in the *Eroica*, he inserted his thoughts about the Revolution—and himself—into the symphony. "Make it new," urged Ezra Pound. More than a century before Pound, Beethoven did. His band of rabid admirers, few at the time, valued the music's newness. Even though his patron Prince Lobkowitz did not respond positively to the *Eroica*, he recognized its genius and gave the work and Beethoven himself his full support.

Beethoven's creative life had moved in rough counterpoint to the stages of the Revolution and Napoleon's career. Much of his music, at least in these years, reflects his responses to the ebb and flow of the Revolution, subsequently to Napoleon's role in it. When Beethoven began work on the *Eroica*, Napoleon had become, in ways still imperfectly understood, a huge, even dominant presence in his imagination. Behind Napoleon loomed the specter of the Revolution and the promise of a new and enlightened society. The propulsive movement, inherent in the *Eroica*, mirrors Beethoven's—and the First Consul's—ceaseless energy.

Names, as so often, come loaded with significance. Napoleon, about the time he began his Italian campaign in 1796, had altered the spelling of "Buonaparte," his name in its Italian or Corsican form, to the somewhat more French-sounding "Bonaparte." English Tories, refusing to acknowledge the change, continued to refer to him as "Buonaparte." Doing so implied that Napoleon was not really French. They recognized the Bourbons (in exile in England) as France's legitimate rulers. Beethoven usually speaks of "Bonaparte," not "Napoleon," because for him, as for Byron and liberals elsewhere, the difference had significance. Byron, by using "Buonaparte" in his "Ode to Napoleon Buonaparte" (1814), wished to remind people of the greatness the young general had achieved in Italy. "Napoleon" for Byron smacked of the imperial purple. For Beethoven too, "Bonaparte" meant, not the emperor, but the leader of the first French Republic.

Napoleon's awareness of Beethoven is difficult to ascertain. While he occasionally attended musical events in Paris, few featured Beethoven's music, not yet often performed. All the same, Beethoven's gradually became a talked-about name in Paris during Napoleon's reign, and the First Consul probably had some awareness of who he was. Of Beethoven's major compositions, the *Eroica* is the work most closely associated with Napoleon. The association did not come about suddenly. In fact, the decision to dedicate the *Eroica* to "Bonaparte" must have arisen early, perhaps near the symphony's conception. Most probably, Beethoven had long nurtured the regard he expressed for Napoleon in 1803–04. An admiration of such intensity does not, after all, emerge in a moment.

Beethoven had written the first sketches for his Third Symphony in late 1802. A year later, in the autumn of 1803, he began serious work on it. By then, he was planning on honoring Napoleon. A letter of October 22 of that year from Ferdinand Ries to the publisher Simrock, written on Beethoven's behalf, states that the composer "is very much inclined to dedicate it [the symphony] to Bonaparte." However "because [Prince Joseph von] Lobkowitz wants to have it for half a year and will give 400 [ducats], [only] then will he entitle it Bonaparte."[34] The practice of such a "rental" was fairly common at the time. After the initial period expired, Beethoven could reap whatever other subsequent reward he could glean from the symphony, even if he wished to dedicate it to "Bonaparte." By the spring of 1804 he had completed it. He had already chosen who would perform it. Apart from the Esterházy Kapelle, of the local private orchestras Lobkowitz's was probably the best and best known. Haydn, as well as Beethoven, appeared regularly at its concerts. Given that Vienna at this time lacked public orchestras, or even suitable spaces for public performances, Beethoven had chosen a fitting environment for the first private hearing of his new symphony.

ふ

Emperor of the French

But then, on May 18, 1804, the French Council of State decreed Napoleon Bonaparte emperor of the French, to be crowned six months later. In that year and for several years afterwards France still regarded itself as a republic. But it was a republic born of revolution. In crowning Bonaparte emperor, the Senate in effect crowned the Revolution and its principles. By reaffirming them, it hoped the new emperor would do the same. Reference to the French Republic was maintained in official acts and on coins until 1807. Besides, Napoleon at his coronation was crowned "emperor of the French," not "emperor of France." That is, he was emperor of a people, not of a state, the implication being that he represented the people. All regulations and laws regarding the Roman state long ago had come freighted with these words: *"Senatus populusque romanus"* (the Senate and populace of Rome). The French Senate followed the model of Rome. But "emperor," particularly "emperor of the French," awakened national aspirations for glory going back to Charlemagne. Napoleon, needless to say, understood these subtleties very well.

Ferdinand Ries, encountering Beethoven, told him of the Senate's decree. Upon hearing the news, Beethoven expressed outrage. It shattered his idealized image of the French leader. "So he too is nothing more than an ordinary man," he exclaimed angrily. "Now he also will trample all human rights underfoot, and only pander to his own ambition; he will place himself above everyone else and become a tyrant!" Beethoven, according to Ries, "ripped" off the title page of his newly completed symphony and "flung it on the floor." He now rejected the man he had previously revered. On the surviving conducting copy Beethoven scratched out part of the dedication so violently that he left two holes in the title page.

A believer in republics, Beethoven felt that Napoleon, by having himself declared emperor, had betrayed him on both a personal and a political level. No longer was Bonaparte the head of a republic, no longer Europe's true leader, no longer the man Beethoven had greatly esteemed, no longer the man European liberals had believed would bring about a new order. How could this individual upon whom he had placed such hopes shatter the dreams of so many?

Anton Schindler, who in 1840 wrote the first full biography of the composer, claims that Beethoven's rejection of Napoleon lasted his lifetime. Leading twentieth-century Beethoven scholars, including Leo Schrade and Maynard Solomon, agree. But the facts argue the contrary. In a letter of August 26, 1804, Beethoven offered, along with other works, the completed *Eroica* to the Leipzig publisher Breitkopf & Härtel. He termed it "a *new grand symphony*." He then asserted, "Die Simphonie ist eigentlich betitelt Ponaparte." (The *P* was presumably a slip of the pen.) Do the words mean "the symphony is *originally* entitled Bonaparte"—or "the symphony is *really* entitled Bonaparte"?[35] The language, as Konrad Küster has pointed out, is ambiguous.[36] The weight of evidence tips toward the latter translation. As the erased words in Italian on the title page of the conducting copy indicate, the symphony was truly *"intitolata [B]onaparte."*

Beethoven stated both when he began intensive work on the symphony and some months after he had completed it that he had done what he had never done before: dedicate to and *name* a major work after an individual. As the erased words in Italian on the title page of the conducting copy indicate, the symphony was *"intitolata [B]onaparte."* Presumably his anger with Napoleon, so vividly described by Ries, had quickly dissipated. Whatever specific program we may wish to read into the *Eroica*, Beethoven makes clear that he wrote it with Napoleon in mind and that he dedicated it to him because he admired him. Those who deny that Napoleon influenced the symphony, or had little or no relationship to it, have to slip past Beethoven's repeated affirmations that it does.

"The inner, ideal association of the work is with Napoleon."[37] So concludes Carl Dahlhaus, a leading German music scholar of the later twentieth century. In sharp contrast to the halfhearted supposedly patriotic songs of 1796, the *Eroica* radiates energy, energy that stems from Beethoven's youthful republicanism, his belief that Napoleon inherited the goals of the Revolution. The dedication may appear idealistic and even utopian. It certainly entailed huge risks, both for Beethoven's career in Vienna and for his personal well-being.

Napoleon remained a hero for Beethoven, perhaps *the* essential figure in his creative imagination. In years to come he often resented Napoleon, at times set himself in opposition to him. But the initial enthusiasm survived. He was the individual against whom Beethoven chose to measure himself. In his own realm of music he felt himself Napoleon's equal, an emperor unto himself, whose achievements in music rivaled, and might well outlast, Napoleon's on the battlefield and as a statesman.

᪥

"Intitolata Bonaparte"

On the title page of the conducting copy of the *Eroica* Beethoven wrote his name and scribbled in pencil under it, presumably later (and now barely legible in reproductions), the words "*intitolata [B]onaparte.*" Although Beethoven attempted to scratch out the words, no one has doubted that they are in Beethoven's hand. The erasure may indicate uncertainty, perhaps even unease, on his part. But the words remained.

It may at first seem puzzling that Beethoven signs his name "Luigi van Beethoven," but Italian was then (and largely remains) the language of classical music. Whereas Napoleon had made his name less Italian-sounding ("Napoleone" to "Napoleon," "Buonaparte" to "Bonaparte"), Beethoven, we have seen, often made his more international ("Ludwig" became "Luigi" or French "Louis"). At a time when Napoleon avoided Italian forms, Beethoven adopted one. What do we make of this? A fit of pique by the mercurial composer? Possibly. By 1804 most of his dedications had gone to titled aristocrats, and he would continue this practice. Possibly Beethoven inscribed his name in Italian so that he might show rapport with the symphony's Italian-speaking dedicatee.

Liberally inclined Europeans no doubt found Beethoven's violent reaction to Napoleon's decision to proclaim himself emperor surprising. Actually, given the intensity of the tie he felt with Napoleon, Beethoven had good reason to respond positively toward him. In March 1804 Napoleon introduced into France the Civil Code, subsequently known as the Napoleonic Code. It determined the equality of man before the law, abolished the privileges of the landed gentry, and recognized the freedom of the individual and of property, as well as the separation of church and state. The entire work breathed the spirit of the Revolution. In the course of Napoleon's campaigns the Civil Code, introduced in altered form, took effect in the territories on the left bank of the Rhine annexed by France in 1794. The code's fame spread across Germany. This body of law also established the civic order in several German states. However positively Beethoven's beloved Rhineland welcomed the

Statuette of Lucius Junius Brutus. The founder of the Roman republic, Lucius Junius Brutus, was Beethoven's lifelong hero. This statuette never left his work desk.

Beethoven-Haus Bonn

Jakob Alt, *View of Vienna from the Spinner on the Cross*, 1817. The Vienna of Beethoven's day was encompassed by rural areas where he loved to walk. In the center of the far distance is St. Stephen's Cathedral.

English School, *Storming the Bastille.* Women played a significant role in the French Revolution. The woman featured here is dressed in French Revolutionary attire with sword in hand, urging the burning of the Bastille. The French Revolution stands behind Leonore's heroic courage in Beethoven's *Fidelio.* *Private collection; © Look and Learn / Bridgeman Images*

Leonore points her pistol at the villain, Don Pizarro. Wilhelmine Schröder-Devrient made her debut in *Fidelio* as Leonore in 1822. Her interpretation of this role made her famous all over Europe. *De Agostini Picture Library / Bridgeman Images*

Joseph Willibrord Mähler, Beethoven, 1804–05. This portrait reveals Beethoven's revolutionary thinking at the time.

Johann Heinrich Wilhelm Tischbein, *Goethe in the Roman Campagna*, 1787. I compare this portrait of Goethe to Mähler's of Beethoven. Beethoven and Goethe were the great cultural figures of the age.

Thomas Sully, *Byron*, 1827. Byron's response to the French Revolution and to Napoleon parallels Beethoven's. *Private collection; photo by James Hart*

Antoine Gros, *Napoleon at the Bridge of Arcole*, 1796. The battle of Arcole was the young General Napoleon's most brilliant victory in his dazzling Italian campaign of 1796–97 against Austria. The focus on his tricolor sash celebrates his support of French Revolutionary ideals.

Jean Auguste Dominique Ingres, *Napoleon I on His Imperial Throne*, 1806. In his rose-hued imperial robes Napoleon appears as an enhanced Louis XIV, the "Sun King." Beethoven reviled this concept of Napoleon. In pique he crossed out his dedication to him of the *Eroica* Symphony. © *Musée de l'Armée / Dist. RMN–Grand Palais / Art Resource, New York*

Jacques-Louis David, *Napoleon in His Study at the Tuileries*, 1812. David portrays Napoleon working through the night to benefit his country. His tailored red-white-and-blue attire tells us that he at this point wanted to emphasize his role as the inheritor of the ideals of the French Revolution, a view he promoted in writings toward the end of his life. Beethoven in later years realized that whatever flaws Napoleon had, he still towered over the reactionary monarchs of Austria and its allies.

National Gallery of Art, Washington, D.C.

Giovanni Battista Piranesi, *The Drawbridge, plate VII from the series Carceri d'Invenzione*, 1745. Typical of the age, Piranesi was obsessed with the horrors of prison life. No less obsessed was Beethoven in his opera *Fidelio*.

Eugène Delacroix, *The Prisoner of Chillon*, 1834. Delacroix was inspired by Byron's famous poem of this name, which takes place entirely in a dungeon.
RMN-Grand Palais / Art Resource, NY

Joseph Karl Stieler, *Beethoven*, 1819–20. The strong revolutionary colors in this portrait tell us that even in late maturity Beethoven remained a revolutionary.

Ferdinand Waldmüller, *Beethoven*, 1824. Beethoven fell out with Ferdinand Georg Waldmüller during his first and only sitting for the artist. Waldmüller depicts the composer in an intensely realistic foul mood, but also as a man determined, resolute, unwilling to yield.

Bettmann / Getty Images

Johann Nepomuk Höchle, *Beethoven's Room*, 1827. By depicting the empty chair before the piano in Beethoven's last residence, the Schwarzspanier Haus, this image, drawn three days before Beethoven's death in 1827, mourns his absence.

Karl Sterrer, poster for the 1920 Secession exhibition in Vienna focused on Beethoven. Sterrer superimposed on the Höchle image a huge half-length portrait of Beethoven. Its full-blooded dynamism powerfully depicts the composing Beethoven as intensely present, not absent as in the Höchle. The Hapsburg empire had collapsed the year before, but Beethoven "lives on." *Private collection; photo by James Hart*

news of the Civil Code, none of its provisions had a prayer of becoming law in Hapsburg Austria.

Although Beethoven canceled the initial dedication, his doing so does not deny his faith in Napoleon's strategy. "Geschrieben auf Bonaparte" (written for Bonaparte) can still be deciphered on the title page. Beethoven does not alter the music. He thought Napoleon shared the values of freedom and justice in which he believed. These values his symphony expresses. He wrote it for the one man in Europe who could realize them.

Finally, how trustworthy is Ferdinand Ries's account of the dedication and its retraction? Scholars have questioned details of his "biographical notices" since their first appearance in 1838. The skeptical Dahlhaus, who studied the evidence carefully, regrets that Ries's account has become "a permanent fixture in the Beethoven myth."[38] He has grounds for his unease. Ries did not publish his memoir of Beethoven until thirty-four years after the incident of the torn dedication. He apparently did not set it down during Beethoven's lifetime. The son of Franz Ries, a close family friend of Beethoven in Bonn, Ferdinand studied in Vienna for several years after 1803. He was an honest man, clearly fond of and devoted to Beethoven. But when he wrote the memoir, presumably in the 1830s, his health was declining, and his memory of Beethoven's words in 1804 may have blurred. He would die before the book's publication. Even under the best of circumstances he may have distorted the recollection of an incident so distant in time. Also, Ries's memoir misdates his own arrival in Vienna by three years, putting it in 1800 instead of 1803. If Ries errs on this matter, he could easily have misremembered details of the composer's response to the news of Napoleon's impending coronation. Still, even if Beethoven's fury did not occur exactly as Ries remembered it, we should not dismiss his account outright. His anger bears the stamp of reality.

The story of the destroyed dedication also rests on the often dubious and much criticized recollections of Anton Schindler. In the first German edition of his Beethoven biography (1840) he mentions the incident. He claims that Beethoven's friend and admirer Count Moritz

Lichnowsky accompanied Ries that day. But if Lichnowsky was there (Ries does not say so), he made no mention of the incident himself. In short, the authors of both accounts, however well intentioned, may have misremembered or embellished what happened.

Ries's narrative, however trustworthy in essence, is questionable on other grounds. Did a transitory fit of pique against Napoleon on Beethoven's part metamorphose into a towering rage and lasting resentment? By August 26, barely three months after Ries's encounter with Beethoven, Napoleon had returned to the composer's good graces. Lasting anger on his part seems unlikely. Beethoven had a mercurial temperament. Full of passion and energy, moody, somewhat unstable, easily piqued at real or imaginary slights, he was quick to anger. He could argue furiously with a friend one day; on the next, the tempest having passed, he would apologize profusely by letter or in person. As Ries tells us, he may have torn off the dedication to Napoleon on the *Eroica*'s original manuscript. We shall never know for sure. Then Beethoven, or perhaps someone else, scratched out Napoleon's name on the conducting copy. But the composer's extremely positive response to Napoleon rests on his letters of October 22, 1803, and August 26, 1804. The latter epistle, written three months after hearing the news of Napoleon's intended coronation, indicates that he did not take lasting offense. Beethoven's rage, as so often, proved temporary.

In dedicating a symphony to Bonaparte, Beethoven faced a larger issue. For a citizen of the Austrian empire to name and dedicate a major work to the French emperor involved a huge risk, if not outright foolhardiness. Dedicating a work to the king of Prussia or the emperor of Russia (Beethoven had done both) had little political significance—as long as these countries remained neutral or allied to Austria. But dedicating a work to the archenemy, a man anathema to the Hapsburgs, who saw him as the embodiment of the dreaded Revolution—that would have been regarded as tantamount to a declaration of principles—which meant, within the Hapsburg context, republican principles. Hapsburg authorities actively persecuted individuals who expressed ideas hostile to the state. Such individuals faced imprisonment, even death. Appealing as Beethoven found the idea of a dedication to "Bonaparte," he knew that if he wished to pursue his career in music in Vienna such a dedication had to go. Sometime after August 26, 1804, with another war with France looming on the horizon, he wisely jettisoned "Bonaparte" as the *Eroica*'s dedicatee. When finally published in October 1806, the *Eroica* bore a quite different dedication.

Again, Byron serves as a useful parallel figure to Beethoven. Ten years after Beethoven erased his dedication of the *Eroica* to Napoleon, Byron underwent a stunning, if similar, disillusionment with the French emperor, whose fortunes waned after his failed Russian campaign of 1812. After the allies finaly defeated Napoleon and captured Paris on the last day of March 1814, Napoleon did not commit suicide, as Byron thought he should have, but abdicated. Upon hearing the news in London, the poet, on April 6, 1814, wrote his "Ode to Napoleon Buonaparte." In it he berated the fallen emperor for his unwillingness to continue the fight or die trying. Byron, like Beethoven, believed in republics and, like Beethoven, saw in Napoleon the only realistic hope for a reformed Europe. Thus his rejection of Napoleon hardly lasted longer than Beethoven's. Within a year he would compose the most pro-Napoleon poems of his career. Years later, in *The Age of Bronze* (1823), a survey of the European scene, Byron looked back upon Napoleon's crowning himself emperor and termed it his "single step into the wrong."[39] His other steps, presumably, were right, or at least could be justified.

In short, it took staggering courage on Beethoven's part even to think of dedicating a symphony to—and naming it—"Bonaparte." Nothing he had ever done, or would in future do, quite compares with this bold act. In sheer audacity it astounds to this day. If Beethoven had held to his original intention to dedicate the *Eroica* to Napoleon, he would have had to move to Paris or another pro-Bonapartist city. Two Napoleonic invasions of Austria would have to pass before Beethoven gained a fuller awareness of the hard realities of Napoleonic rule.

13

The *Eroica* in Its Literary and Artistic Contexts

SEUME'S *WALK TO SYRACUSE* AND MÄHLER'S PORTRAIT OF BEETHOVEN

There reigns such a reverent silence in the coffeehouses.

JOHANN GOTTFRIED SEUME[1]

I find that there are never too many points of view from which to take in a work of art, and Beethoven's works present aspects numerous enough and varied enough to call for examination from all sides.

ROMAIN ROLLAND[2]

Rolland's wise words help bring into perspective a book that Beethoven read and admired. In 1803, while he pondered the *Eroica*, Johann Gottfried Seume published a travel tale, *A Walk to Syracuse in the Year 1802*. Soon popular, it is actually more than a travel tale, for it offers acute observations on the contemporary political scene in Austria, Italy, and France. After Beethoven's death a marked-up copy of this volume was found among his effects. What may seem like a digression is not, for the views Seume expresses significantly help us assess the composer's intent in the *Eroica*. By documenting the harsh conditions under which Beethoven lived and composed in Hapsburg Vienna, *A Walk to Syracuse* offers further evidence of Beethoven as a highly political being.

֍

Johann Gottfried Seume

Surviving letters by Beethoven do not mention Seume, but one that has apparently not survived did. "You wrote me," Georg Christoph Grosheim informed the composer on November 10, 1819, "that you had placed yourself among the admirers at Seume's grave. He deserves your esteem." Seume had died on June 13, 1810, at the age of forty-seven, in the spa town of Teplitz and had been buried there. "He was a great man," continues Grosheim in the same letter, "a fortunate man," who "was permitted to express aloud his *vitam imponere vero* [willingness to stake one's life on the truth]—and was loved; Rousseau, for his motto—was stoned."[3] Rousseau was pilloried, metaphorically at least, by many, including several Enlightenment figures. Seume, like Rousseau, suffered much from the injustices done to him. But he also possessed courage comparable to Rousseau's, and, as had Rousseau, he found devoted readers who admired him for his integrity and unflinching sense of expressing what he believed was right. One of the readers who admired his work was Beethoven. Seume did indeed merit the esteem in which the composer held him.

While on vacation in Teplitz in 1811 or 1812 Beethoven visited Seume's grave. It is the only instance I am aware of in which he visited anyone's grave. Surely this mark of respect suggests that Beethoven held Seume in high regard. In 1828, the year after the composer's death, Grosheim published a note in the music periodical *Cäcilia* that underscores the importance of the composer's lost letter of 1819: "Beethoven's thoughts at Seume's grave, which I still protect like a noble jewel, give an exact report of his magnanimous outlook on the world's misfortune."[4] Of Beethoven's modern biographers, only Piero Buscaroli has dealt seriously with the significance in Beethoven's life of this interesting but still little-known individual. Buscaroli argues that Seume was "the most convincing example of a brother in spirit and opinion that Beethoven could find in the Germany of his day."[5] Seume's ironic, progressive outlook on life and society accorded well with Beethoven's. The *Walk to Syracuse,* published while Beethoven was composing the *Eroica,* offers clues to understanding the composer as he struggled to create that great work.[6]

Among Beethoven's contemporaries it is Seume whose forthright, iconoclastic opinions best help us come to grips with the composer's political thinking during these years. They rival the impact upon him of Eulogius Schneider, the radical revolutionary whose lectures Beethoven attended in Bonn in 1789 and whose volume of poetry, published early in 1790, he subscribed to. Seume's strongly expressed societal and political views, if less openly radical than Schneider's, would have resonated equally in Beethoven's mind.

Seume and Beethoven were both rebels. In an era when clothing denoted personality, position in society, and even political orientation, Seume, like Beethoven, dressed casually. He sported a head of short curly hair, a *Tituskopf,* or *à la Titus,* a coiffure that had emerged in the early years of the Revolution and which Beethoven had also adopted. Replacing the wigs and formal attire characteristic of male dress in the ancien régime, such an appearance indicated an individual who supported liberal, even revolutionary, causes. Seume's democratic vistas, his droll humor, his contempt for absolutist monarchs, his love of Plutarch and Schiller, and his uncomplaining determination in facing the injustices and challenges of life would have touched chords deep in Beethoven's nature. His life and his book, in short, have much to tell us about the composer.

Seven years older than Beethoven, Seume was born in Poserna, near Leipzig, in 1763. The son of poor farmers, he was destined to lead an existence both adventuresome and hard. He began theological studies in Leipzig, but under the influence of Enlightenment thinkers he abandoned theology and instead turned to law, philosophy, philology, and history. On his way to further study in Paris in 1781, the eighteen-year-old student was seized in Hessian territory and conscripted into the army of the Landgraf of Hessen-Kassel, who sold him, along with nine thousand other impressed soldiers, to Britain.[7] In 1782 he was shipped to Canada to join the fight against the forces in the American states that had rebelled against British rule. He arrived too late, however, to see combat. On his return to Germany in 1783, he was transferred from Hessian to Prussian control, escaped twice and was recaptured each time, then condemned to death as a deserter. Finally in 1787, thanks to a benefactor, he was freed from his bondage of six years.[8] The experience of being held against his will in military servitude left Seume with a detestation of absolutism.

Upon gaining his freedom, Seume again pursued the education that his impressments had so forcibly interrupted. By studying history, he hoped to discover a societal development toward reason and freedom, but he did not find it. Subsequently, from 1793 to 1795 he served in the Russian army as secretary and adjutant to the Russian general of Swedish descent Josef Andreyevich Igelström, who quelled the Warsaw uprising of 1795, in which Seume just missed getting killed. Returning to his native Saxony, he became first a private tutor in Leipzig and then a proofreader in the well-known publishing house of Goschen in nearby Grimma.

Long a lover of classical Greek literature, Seume determined around 1800 to ground and deepen his knowledge of ancient Greek poetry by visiting the land where it had been written. With mainland Greece still part of the Ottoman empire and difficult to enter, Seume decided to explore Sicily, long an outlying area of *magna Graecia,* a land of Greek temples and pastoral landscapes. Syracuse, in its heyday a major rival to Athens, lies at the southeastern tip of Sicily. Seume's route, which followed generations of German travelers who went on the Grand Tour in the eighteenth century, took him through Dresden, Prague, Vienna, Trieste, Venice, Rome, and Naples. Like many other travelers, he continued his journey by sea to the Italian boot and then walked across Sicily. His return via Paris and Frankfurt covered, again on foot, several thousand more miles. In his knapsack Seume carried treasured copies of Homer, Theocritus, and Virgil. What was truly unusual about his journey was not so much its length and difficulty but the fact that he was among the few travelers who accomplished almost all of it in an unusual way: by walking.

ଽ

A Walk to Syracuse

The narrative of his adventures, *A Walk to Syracuse*, came out in the spring of 1803, eight months after Seume arrived back in his native Saxony. In 1805 a revised edition appeared. The work proved popular, in part because it recounts in vivid prose a difficult but event-filled journey. Goethe had written *Wilhelm Meister's Apprenticeship* in 1795–96, after his own trip to Italy. Italy changed both him and Seume. Whereas Goethe experienced a "new birth" and became aware of himself less as an artist and administrator and more as a poet and sage, Seume instead realized that the political injustices he had experienced in German lands also occurred in Italy and France—in short, that absolutism poisoned the lives of the populace everywhere it existed.[9]

Though Seume's *Walk* was immediately banned in Hapsburg domains, it enjoyed wide distribution and immense popularity in most of Germany, especially among liberals. In 1827 seventeen-year-old Robert Schumann hung an engraved portrait of Seume on the wall of his parents' home in Leipzig; once Schumann began his studies at the university there, the portrait went with him.[10] The *Walk* remained in print in Germany for decades to come. New editions continue to appear to this day.

Given Hapsburg censorship, Beethoven must have acquired his copy surreptitiously. We do not know precisely when he read it, but read it he did, most likely during the time of the *Eroica*'s composition.[11] The book's narrative vigor, political insights, sensitivity to people, places, and customs, its stylistic verve and broad humor—irreverent, fresh, perky but, in Hapsburg eyes, clearly subversive—would doubtless have appealed to the composer. Seume's use of irony, expressed in a laconic, informal tone, evidences the liveliness of his mind. His sense of intimacy—he addresses his reader informally as "you, dear reader"—no doubt further contributed to the book's wide appeal.[12]

One of the few German-language biographers of Beethoven to give Seume some attention is the German scholar W. A. Thomas-San Galli, who a century ago found a "strong similarity of character" between Seume and Beethoven.[13] Seume protested that he was not a revolutionary, but like Beethoven's former professor in Bonn, Eulogius Schneider, he was deeply critical of the European status quo. But whereas Schneider became overtly bold in speech and deed, Seume analyzed the contemporary political scene in prose of acuteness and subtlety.

The *Walk* may well have influenced Beethoven's understanding of the contemporary scene, for Seume's liberal political views are close to what we know of Beethoven's own. As we'll see below, Seume's narrative also gives us clues as to why Beethoven introduced the *Eroica* with those two monumental chords. In fact, Seume's pages on Vienna and the Viennese have special resonance for our understanding of the contemporaneous symphony. What Seume achieved through force of language, Beethoven rendered through force of music. Observing at first hand the harsh realities of European society, Seume found the city musically sophisticated but culturally backward—and politically oppressed. It was an environment where he felt he had to watch his every move and word. Beethoven too chafed against its restrictions and rules. His unease could appear paranoid, for he believed, as he often claimed, that "nobody in Vienna has more private enemies than I have."[14]

Seume was a man of wide experience, a democrat, whose adventuresome personality had in the past caused him difficulties. Though claiming early on he was "not at all a revolutionary," he conceded he tended to speak on controversial subjects more forcefully than discreetly.[15] In Vienna he encountered a cowed, frightened populace courteous but wary of outsiders, timid, afraid to speak out in public, fearful of even overhearing murmurs of revolutionary ideas, in short, the inhabitants of a virtual police state. If officials were polite, the reticent Viennese, he soon discovered, lacked imagination and courage. The prevailing atmosphere of fear dampened the spirits of many. Beethoven, we remember, had felt much the same. "You dare not raise your voice here or the police will take you into custody," the composer wrote in 1794, after nearly two years in the Austrian capital.

Seume found disconcerting the "reverent" silence he encountered in Vienna's coffee houses:

> Public affairs are almost never commented on in Vienna, and you can go to the public houses for perhaps months at a time before you will hear a single word that refers to politics; one finds that orthodoxy regarding the state as well as the church is strictly enforced. There is a reverent silence everywhere in the cafes, as though High Mass were being celebrated, so that everyone hardly dares to breathe. Although I am accustomed to speak out not too loudly, I do, however, speak my mind freely and uninhibitedly, and for this reason one time I received friendly instruction from my acquaintances, who warned me about the invisible ones [police spies]. I do not know if they were right; however, I have very often observed that people have suffered from injustice caused by the invisible ones.[16]

One day Seume began to hum the "Marseillaise" in a public place.[17] The song had long since swept across Europe, even penetrating Hapsburg lands. His humming "affected those present like a damper." Merely being in the presence of anyone who hummed this mantra of revolution incurred risks.

Seume tells us of a "not very political" veteran lieutenant colonel in the Austrian army who found himself in a coffeehouse near the Hofburg, the Hapsburg royal palace. Like Seume, he experienced the "quiet of a cloister." Irritated by the eerie silence, he decided to speak out:

"What the Devil, what sort of damned pious ways do you have here in Vienna? Can't one speak here? Or is the whole capital a huge Carthusian monastery? Here you are in danger of forgetting how to talk. Or is one not allowed to talk here? I have heard something about this, that one must always be on the watch here: is that true? Damn this mumbling! I cannot stand it, and I am going to speak loudly and be happy." You should have seen the people's faces at this overture! Some were serious, others shocked; others smiled, others nodded obligingly and significantly at the joke: however, no one joined the old soldier. "I will," he said, "return to the army; the ways of the dead do not please me."[18]

The silence Seume experienced in 1801 was not new. Beethoven, who frequently took his meals at a nearby coffeehouse or tavern, had experienced it from the time of his arrival in 1792.[19]

The composer experienced daily what Seume endured briefly. Over Beethoven's lifetime fear and repression in Vienna gradually intensified. The coffeehouses became ever more silent. With government spies everywhere, where could one go to communicate with friends? Beethoven would have daily asked the same questions that intrigued Seume. The city's stultifying atmosphere was one reason why the *Eroica*, instead of beginning with the more traditional slow first movement introduction, hits us immediately with two hammer-stroke E-flat major chords. Whereas Seume hummed the "Marseillaise" to arouse silent coffeehouse patrons, Beethoven intended the dramatic chords to startle his audience. Both succeeded.

Seume had as hard a time leaving Vienna as he had entering it. The Viennese official he dealt with proved recalcitrant in allowing him to depart. This individual spoke in the thickest Viennese *Bratwurstdialekt*

(literally, "sausage dialect"), a few nibbles of which Seume wittily reproduces.[20] Only with difficulty did this fearsome individual allow him to
proceed on his way southwards. The irreverent Saxon was happy to leave
Vienna. He never returned.[21]

ॐ

Beethoven and Portraiture

Both Seume's *Walk* and Willibrord Joseph Mähler's portrait of
Beethoven, to which we now turn, sought a new world in which democratic ideals and higher levels of moral and ethical behavior would
prevail. Just as Napoleon had dramatically altered traditional European
politics, so Beethoven intended to alter the course of Western music.
His compositions would effect as extreme a revolution as, he hoped,
would occur among the nations of Europe. From Seume's ironic yet
bitter travelogue we move to a portrait of Beethoven that allows us to
interpret his thoughts as he composed the *Eroica*.

Beethoven liked to look at portraits of other composers. In a journal
entry, likely in 1814–15, he wrote, "Portraits of Handel, Bach, Gluck,
Mozart, Haydn in my room. They can promote my capacity for endurance."[22] When Beethoven felt uncertain about his direction, portraits
of past great composers served as inspiration. He had relatively easy
access to fine art. In 1801 he visited the studio of Vienna's leading artist and director of the city's Art Academy, Heinrich Friedrich Füger, to
secure one of his history paintings for his Bonn friend Franz Wegeler.
There, as well as in the homes of his wealthy patrons, he viewed history
paintings and sketches of ancient Greece and Rome by Füger and others, also busts of classical figures by Füger's close colleague in the Art
Academy, the sculptor Franz Anton Zauner. Füger's and Zauner's work,
combined with his readings in Homer, Plutarch, and Livy, presumably
helped shape Beethoven's conception of antiquity and his republican
political views. His cherished statue of Brutus brought together his love
of art and his political ideals.

In earlier epochs portraits had celebrated military and political leaders as exemplars of valor and endeavor. That tradition continued. Portraits done in the 1790s of leading European figures often seemed to
depict a race of superheroes. Thanks to Enlightenment ideas, artists—
many influenced by Lavater's magisterial four-volume treatise *Essays on
Physiognomy* (1775–78) or redactions of it—now tended to portray with
new insight the physiognomic characteristics of the great and famous
of the day. Thanks to Lavater, portraiture rose in esteem in relation
to history painting. No less than did Lavater, Anton Graff, working in
Dresden in the 1770s, broke with stately representation and narrative
embellishment in seeking to capture the essence of a person's being.
Viewers scanned portraits of contemporaries for revealing character
traits. Artists now presented men in positions of power with even more
elevated features than before; people expected good portraitists to render not only a likeness but to express a point of view. Among well-
known late eighteenth-century paintings and sculptures dedicated to
statesmen, Gilbert Stuart's and Jean Antoine Houdon's lofty renderings
of George Washington emerge from this philosophy.

No less did works of art by Jacques Louis David and Antonio Canova
of Napoleon, among others, play an important role in creating the Napoleonic myth. Their works offer clues as to how the young general conceived his mission. In *Bonaparte at Arcole* (1796) Antoine Gros depicted
a youthful Napoleon leading his troops, sword in one hand, tricolor in
the other. It furthered the emerging Napoleon of legend. A few years
later, David memorialized Napoleon's courage in his *Napoleon Crossing the Alps* (1801), a dazzling image of the young general radiating
confidence upon a rearing stallion. François René de Chateaubriand
comments perceptively how its depiction of the already legendary First
Consul overwhelms by sheer power prosaic renderings of his workaday
self: "This fantastic hero will remain the real person; the other portraits
will disappear."[23] And his claim proved correct. Later, David's *Napoleon
in His Study* (1812) depicted the emperor laboring through the night,
presumably for the benefit of his subjects. By focusing on his mental

discipline, his concentration on work, the long hours he put in to keep France running efficiently, David reveals here a deep regard for Napoleon's gifts as an administrator.

No less valuable to understanding their subject are portraits of Beethoven. Like those of Napoleon (or of another famous contemporary, Byron), they often differ greatly. Artists interpreted their features not only as they appeared to them but also presumably as the subjects wished them to appear. The varying efforts of painters often leave us uncertain how the individual in question actually looked. Yet portraits of Beethoven, examined carefully, do offer clues as to how he wished his music to be understood and interpreted.

Portraits, whatever their merits as likenesses, can also prompt observers to create their own mental portrait of the subject. In 1827, when fourteen-year-old Richard Wagner first heard Beethoven's Seventh Symphony, he characterized its effect upon him as "indescribable." But what excited him as much as or more than the music itself was "the added impact of Beethoven's physiognomy, as shown by lithographs of the time, as well as the knowledge of his deafness and his solitary and withdrawn life. There soon arose in me an image of the highest supernal originality, beyond comparison with anything." Thus even lithographs of a portrait could stun a receptive viewer.[24]

Portraits interested Beethoven intensely. Despite his professed reluctance over a lifetime to have himself painted, the many surviving portraits of him suggest he must have somewhat enjoyed the experience; at least he often liked the result. Just as Seume's *Walk to Syracuse* can tell us much about Beethoven's political thinking, so portraits of the composer can inform us not only about his appearance but about his values and his music. In his first Vienna years casual onlookers might have considered him something of a dandy. While still a musician in the pay of the elector of Cologne, in effect a high-level servant, he dressed accordingly: "green coat, green knee breeches, white silk stockings, three-cornered hat, and sword with silver knot."[25] Once in Vienna, Beethoven took dancing lessons, kept a horse, and spent (we are told) the greater part of his money on clothes.[26] But when released from the elector's service in 1794 as a salaried employee, his appearance changed.

The Revolution divided the generations no less than it divided the eighteenth century from the nineteenth. Just as a sonic divide separates the symphonies of Haydn, Salieri, and Mozart from Beethoven's *Eroica*, so a chasm equally large separates how they presented themselves from how Beethoven did. Unlike them, he was a man of the new order—and he dressed accordingly. Across Europe, as Tim Blanning observes, "music lovers could see that Beethoven's appearance matched his compositions—passionate, indomitable, exciting, untamed, above all *original*."[27]

Unlike Bach and Mozart with few portraits, Beethoven was painted by many artists. His admirers, responsive to the extraordinary dynamism of his music, wanted to know how their hero looked. They examined his behavior, his appearance, his way of life, his clothes. He was the first musician to become a cultural icon in his own lifetime. Thus arose a market for portraits of Beethoven that publishers reproduced endlessly, first as engravings and, later, as the technique evolved in the late 1820s, as lithographs.

Interpreting these portraits poses a continuing challenge. Clearly the composer at most stages in his career cut a striking, even an unusual figure. He lived in the last generation before photography came into more regular use in 1839. We thus depend for evidence of his appearance on oil portraits, pastels, sculptures, miniatures, engravings, even the life mask of 1812. We learn from them that he had piercing eyes and a penetrating gaze. The eyes, small and deeply set under a massive forehead, were most likely brown. His skin was darkish, with some evidence of smallpox (then an almost universal malady) on his cheeks.

Interestingly, Beethoven's portraits sometimes resemble those of Napoleon. Both men were compact, solidly built, with large heads and an intense look. Lean in youth, both became heavier as they aged.[28] Comparing Beethoven's build to Napoleon's, J. A. Stumpff, a harp maker and poet who met Beethoven in Baden in 1824, described him as big-boned, with a short neck and broad shoulders. He and Napoleon, he thought, shared certain similarities of character.[29]

Neat and trim in early maturity, Beethoven grew increasingly indifferent to his appearance as he aged, which accorded with the increasing difficulty of dealing with him as a person. Cherubini, offended by his rough ways, thought Beethoven an "unlicked bear"; Goethe, put off by the composer's brusque candor, spoke of his "totally undisciplined personality."[30] As Beethoven pushed his way through the narrow, often crowded streets of the Austrian capital, he sang and hummed the melodies that overran his brain. Youngsters sometimes heckled this man of unusual attire and odd habits, but overall his presence seems to have left the Viennese bemused.[31]

Mähler's portrait of 1804–05 tells us how Beethoven conceived of himself during the time he composed the *Eroica*. It not only supplies evidence that Beethoven thought of himself as a revolutionary, it supports my argument that the *Eroica* actively advocates revolution. If we knew nothing from other sources about Beethoven's political views during these years, this portrait alone tells us a great deal. But to set its detail in perspective, we turn first to another portrait of the era, the best-known representation of Goethe: that by Johann Heinrich Wilhelm Tischbein.

❧

Tischbein's Goethe

Tischbein, influenced by his friend Lavater, was among the many artists of the time who sought to interpret character through facial features. The Enlightenment cult of genius had increasingly embraced thinkers and artists as worthy of celebration. In the later decades of the eighteenth century Rome exerted an enormous hold upon painters and literary figures. The Eternal City drew visitors less as the center of the Catholic world than as a cradle of classical culture and Renaissance art.

In his 1787 portrait of Goethe, Tischbein depicts the seemingly relaxed author of the travel narrative *Italian Journey* in a Roman setting. He alludes to the breadth of Goethe's interests by presenting him comfortably seated, surveying the antiquities scattered about the Roman countryside. Now in his late thirties, Goethe was well aware that his culturally rich *Wanderjahren*, his years of looking and learning in Italy, would soon end. Tischbein presents him in near half-profile; a wide-brimmed hat serves as a kind of secular nimbus. Goethe had just completed his drama *Iphigenia in Tauris*, influenced by Euripides' treatment of the subject.

Tischbein's life-sized, hero-worshipping likeness presents Goethe as the Prince of Poets. The idea of portraying an individual in a landscape as a subject of sensibility was still new. It derived largely from the writings of Rousseau, particularly the fifth of his *Reveries of a Solitary Wanderer*. Tischbein's recumbent poet evokes antique sculpture. Wrapped in a cream-colored traveling cloak that recalls the togas of antiquity, his bearing at ease yet noble, Goethe gazes pensively upon the desolate yet historically rich scene before him.

A chief source of this love of the ancient was the writings of Johann Joachim Winckelmann, particularly his *Reflections on the Imitation of Greek Art in Painting and Sculpture* (1755) and his *History of Ancient Art* (1764), both of which had enthralled a generation. Winckelmann's concept of "noble simplicity and calm grandeur" greatly influenced Goethe's conception of the ancient world, which in turn influenced Tischbein's portrait. Winckelmann believed in studying ancient models "as a means of penetrating the eternally valid truths which were thought to underlie the superficial diversities of the visible world."[32] The portrait carries this philosophy forward as Goethe seeks to comprehend the ruins before him in their archaeological, artistic, and literary manifestations. He sits on a fallen obelisk with Egyptian hieroglyphics on it. Within his range of vision are ionic capitals, the ruins of a Roman aqueduct, and in the distance the tomb of Cecilia Metella on the Via Appia

Antiqua in Rome. Tischbein even inserts a relief depicting a scene from Goethe's own *Iphigenia in Tauris*, making the connection between the setting and Goethe's literary achievement even clearer.[33]

❧

The Mähler Portrait

Contemplating Mähler's portrait of Beethoven in relation to Tischbein's of Goethe, we discover a new kind of hero portrayed in a new way. Goethe's regard suggests a man in his prime, in full control of his faculties, capable of great action or thought. We might say the same for Mähler's *Beethoven*. Both artists had studied in Dresden with Anton Graff and had sought to capture the essence of the subject before them. But what actions or thoughts preoccupied Beethoven at this time? What story did Mähler wish his portrait to tell? It is the major iconographic representation of the composer at the time of the *Eroica* and *Leonore / Fidelio*. Its significance for Beethoven is comparable to Tischbein's for Goethe nearly twenty years before. As in the earlier collaboration, artist and composer knew each other well. Understanding what they intended to accomplish together should convince us that the composer viewed his new symphony essentially as a hymn to revolution, a revolution in music certainly, but no less a revolution in the nature of society, one that would result in greater freedom for humanity.

Mähler was born in Ehrenbreitstein, a village below the looming rock cliff that lies across the Rhine from Coblenz, upriver from Bonn. Ehrenbreitstein is also, significantly for Beethoven, the birthplace of his cherished mother, Maria Magdalena Keverich. Not long after Mähler arrived in Vienna in the autumn of 1803, Stephan von Breuning, a mutual friend of his and Beethoven, took him out to Baden, a spa town south of Vienna, to visit the composer. After they had conversed a while, Beethoven played the *Eroica*'s first movement on the piano, "then continued, without a pause, a free fantasia for *two hours*."[34] Beethoven did not play for everyone, as members of Vienna's aristocracy had discovered to their regret and annoyance, so we may assume that artist and composer felt comfortable with each other from the start.

For this portrait Mähler clearly drew inspiration from Leopold Radoux's oil portrait of Beethoven's beloved grandfather, circa 1770, which Beethoven had asked Wegeler in Bonn to send to him and which Mähler must have seen in Beethoven's lodgings. The grandfather stares at us, his right hand pointing to a musical manuscript, which has been identified as from Pergolesi's light opera *La serva padrona*.

Like that of Tischbein, Mähler's portrait draws upon history painting as well as current traditions of portraiture. To capture the "Beethoven" the painter had in mind it needed both. Art historians as well as Beethoven scholars have subjected Mähler's *Beethoven* to intense analysis, but major aspects of it remain unexplored. One is its importance as a key to understanding Beethoven's political thinking at this time. As Goethe had experienced a "new birth" in Rome, so Beethoven, a decade after arriving in Vienna, had chosen for his music a "new path." The portrait illumines that path.

If we do not always fathom the meanings in Beethoven's music, we err if we assume they do not exist. That music can be understood in itself or as Beethoven's response to Goethe's insistence in his writings upon *Tätigkeit*, that is, activity.[35] Music was Beethoven's "activity," and he expressed his emotions and thoughts in it far better than in words. So, I shall argue, does the Mähler portrait. By the time the artist painted it the composer had achieved considerable recognition. The portrait reveals Beethoven's mindset as he brought the *Eroica* to completion and worked on *Leonore*.

Mähler painted Beethoven in his mid-thirties, about the same stage in his life's journey as Goethe when Tischbein portrayed him. Tischbein envisaged an iconic portrait, one depicting the poet as well as the artist (Goethe still clung to fading hopes of becoming a painter). By surveying Goethe's interests in the classical world, Tischbein achieved from the outset, as Goethe himself noted, a unity.[36] Mähler also aspired to create an iconic portrait of Beethoven, using pose, expression, gesture, and—not least—the landscape in which he places the composer, to illumine the man, his achievement, his values, even his hopes for the future.

Beethoven suggested or, more likely, insisted upon key details in the portrait. These include the pose in which he is depicted (he appears in motion), his facial expression (utterly serious, but engaging and personable) and, providing crucial clues to the painting's intent, the surrounding landscape. Mähler shows Beethoven, as artists in the eighteenth century often depicted significant individuals, sitting with his weight placed on one leg (usually the right, as in the Beethoven portrait) and with the left used chiefly for balance. Mähler has elongated Beethoven's body and face and made him especially lean and youthful-looking. Like several other artists at this time, among them Christian Hornemann in his 1802 miniature of Beethoven, Mähler portrays the composer with his hair in the short Titus style. This both emphasizes Beethoven's youthful look and conveys his political sympathies. The pose suggests intense energy. Though seated, the composer seems about to spring forth. In his left hand he holds a lyre-guitar, an instrument then popular, and one believed to have been used by Apollo, the ancient Greek divinity chiefly associated with music.[37]

Beethoven was of average height for his day, broad-shouldered, his head massive. Few regarded his appearance as Apollonian. Neither did Mähler in his portrayal. Nor is Beethoven's music usually thought to be Apollonian. Knowledgeable about Greek history and mythology, Beethoven associated himself and his music with the dark, unbridled, passionate side of Greek myth, in short, with Dionysus—or, to call the god by his Roman name, Bacchus. Given the over-the-top exuberance of a number of his compositions, particularly their incandescent finales, Beethoven's pose conveys Bacchic energy rather than Apollonian calm.[38]

Beethoven extends his right arm over what seems to be a pastoral landscape, his palm facing the viewer. His regard serious and confident, the composer invites us to enter the landscape in which he sits. The outstretched hand beckons. The Beethoven scholar Peter Schleuning speaks of it as a gesture of triumph made by the great of antiquity.[39] It reminds another scholar of Beethoven as "a modern Homer."[40] It is no less a welcoming gesture of greeting in portraits, seen, for example, in classic depictions of Washington by Stuart. Mähler stated that "the right [hand] is extended, as if, in a moment of musical enthusiasm, he was beating time."[41] Certainly the gesture implies energy, movement, and purpose; one can interpret the gesture as that of a noble or an emperor. Beethoven thought himself noble by nature and achievement, truly an emperor of music.

᭡

Clues in the Landscape

When first seeing the Mähler portrait we tend to focus primarily on Beethoven's face, less so on the pose, least of all on the landscape. But we need to give this last close attention. The domed circular columned structure (*Rundtempel*) on the extreme left is a Greek *tholos*. Mähler refers to it as a "temple of Apollo," and so we may consider it. Its descendants are the vestal temples in Rome and Tivoli, and, centuries later, such structures as the Temple of Love (1778) on the grounds of Versailles. In the classical era temples might have held within a statue of Apollo or another divinity; in modern times, the statue is often absent. If a statue resides within Mähler's *tholos*, we cannot see it.

But even if the temple is (as the artist claims) dedicated to Apollo, it serves as an "Apollonian reflection" of Beethoven, and even more as a visual symbol of the antiquity that he revered all his life. Apollo symbolizes light, clarity, creativity. His temple stands protective above the landscape—and Beethoven in it—like a guardian angel. From Apollo's being and deeds emerged the republican virtues, subsequently exemplified by the heroic figures of antiquity such as Lucius Junius Brutus.

Temples had as well another dimension for Beethoven. In a letter to Wegeler a few years before, the composer assured his Bonn friend "that the new temple of sacred friendship which you will erect on these qualities will stand firmly and forever, and that no misfortune, no tempest will be able to shake its foundations."[42] In such temples a band of like-minded brothers gather in friendship and in solidarity of belief and purpose. In Schiller's *William Tell*, a drama Beethoven admired (and one exactly contemporaneous with Mähler's portrait), the Swiss rebels unite in a bond of brotherhood dedicated to freedom. Later, in the emotional climax of his Ninth Symphony, Beethoven declares that in times to come all peoples shall be brothers united in a vision of hope. The *tholos*, then, is not limited to Beethoven's Apollonian talent. It is a symbol of people joining together in a common purpose. In turn, we need to place the temple within the context of what is surely the most unusual and revealing (and least discussed) element in the landscape: the two trees standing together in the meadow.

Beethoven's arm extends across both trees. Their vaguely triangular shape indicates they are conifers.[43] Trees and temple, even the lush foreground vegetation, are in balance, and we sense that in some way they complement the upraised arm. The light, coming from the painting's left (as the shadows reveal), falls upon Beethoven's face as well as upon the two trees. His arm and his facial expression—determined, serious, uncompromising—suggest he may be trying to protect the trees.

Landscape design in Beethoven's day had become a much-debated subject. The best-known landscape manuals of the time drew upon newly formed aesthetic concepts of how the natural scene might be shaped and arranged. Even though trees formed an integral part of early nineteenth-century landscape design, no contemporary landscape architect would have planted two conifers in the midst of a flat, otherwise empty meadow. Landscape manuals in Britain and the Continent drew inspiration from "Capability" Brown's work in "improving" country estates. They advocated positioning trees in clumps with undulating greensward in between, as we see in landscapes by John Constable. If a tree was spectacular or in some way unusual, artists might isolate it in the landscape, as Caspar David Friedrich often did. In Beethoven's time a vogue for "English gardens" swept across Europe. With their lush lawns, their "S" curves or "lines of beauty," their meandering streams, their carefully situated bridges, their well-sited classical monuments, such landscapes reflected the aesthetic concepts of the picturesque and the beautiful. Trees, then, were considered as design elements in a carefully planned and idealized garden landscape. Connoisseurs familiar with contemporary landscape esthetics would have considered Mähler's depiction of the isolated trees lacking in good taste. The trees perhaps violate canons of good taste, but they represent another virtue: freedom.

ჟ

Liberty Trees

In the aftermath of the insurrections in France of 1789–90, Gallic townspeople who believed in the ideals of the Revolution planted Trees of Liberty. After electing, usually in May, municipal officials sympathetic to the Revolution, citizens often placed a tree in the town square. The "Trees of May," as they were sometimes called, served at once as symbols of insurrection and of faith in a new future. For example, French revolutionaries, viewing Benjamin Franklin as a hero of their Revolution as well as of the one in America, planted a Tree of Liberty in his honor in the neighborhood in Paris where he had lived.[44] Soon Trees of May became a veritable institution across France. A new symbol had emerged in the public consciousness.

Or rather an old one had gained new life. Many cultures have worshipped trees.[45] Early Christians worshipped beneath elms that became emblems of eternal life. In English folklore, green since the days of Robin Hood has been the color of revolution and freedom. In the years preceding the American Revolution, Liberty Trees played an important role in the American colonies. When Bostonians wished to show their defiance of the Stamp Act imposed by Britain in 1765, they gathered under a large elm. Afterwards they continued to employ it as a meeting place to celebrate their wins or to protest British policies. They called it a Liberty Tree. It became the inspiration for other Liberty Trees. Soon the trees spread throughout New England, then down the coast to South Carolina, even as far as Savannah, Georgia. Given France's active support of the revolutionary cause, the thousands of returning French soldiers who had fought for American freedom likely brought the idea home with them.

As revolutionary ideas took hold, the custom of planting and decorating Trees of Liberty spread beyond France to French-occupied northern Italy, Switzerland, and parts of Germany. Even before the decisive battle of Valmy on September 20, 1792, several Rhineland cities had come under French control. Liberty Trees and the ideals they symbolized gradually sprouted across Beethoven's homeland in at least fifty locales.[46] Soon they sported *cocardes* (military insignia that are often green). In 1794 a Liberty Tree appeared in Bonn's marketplace.[47] Although Beethoven had left his native city nearly two years before, he might have come upon the trees elsewhere or on his journey to Vienna. In hostile Austria, partisans of the Revolution, several of them well-known figures, erected a Tree of Liberty in 1794 in a valley outside Vienna, danced around it, and, inevitably, underwent severe punishment.[48] The trees bade farewell to the Old World. As evergreens, they signaled the birth of a New. Revolutionaries regarded Liberty Trees as symbols of the spirit of freedom and the rights of man. Their presence inspired generations to come.

But the trees in Mähler's portrait—how do we know they are Trees of Liberty? They are not decorated poles, as were many of the original European Trees of Liberty, small and spindly when planted in the early 1790s. Instead, a decade or so later, they are full-grown, healthy conifers. Most conifers grow fast. Even after winter's onset they retain their old needles as well as produce new ones. Austrian authorities no more allowed Trees of Liberty in their domains than did the British in theirs. It would have been foolhardy for Mähler to depict them in art as they appeared in the 1790s—that is, in their decorated, often anorexic form. The large, healthy trees he painted in his Beethoven portrait have survived, and their fulsome appearance bodes well for the future hopes of liberty. In a landscape overlooked by a Greek temple, they symbolize the classically inspired ideals of the Revolution. They also serve as arboreal reminders of Plutarch's self-sacrificing heroes of old, heroes who from their tombs exhorted those then alive to similar sacrifices in resisting tyranny. The trees in Mähler's painting are fulfilling their destiny. They imply that the idea of revolution continues, and that the music of Beethoven proclaims it.

In 1804–05 the *Eroica* and *Leonore* indicate that Beethoven maintained his faith in political liberty. Not everyone possessed similar resolve. After the incredible outburst of revolutionary energy a decade before in Paris and elsewhere, many now felt that Europe had lost its way. The trees in Mähler's portrait tell us, however, that Beethoven believes that liberty still lives and that the Promised Land of freedom lies within reach. "Let me lead you to it," Beethoven's body language seems to say. Whereas he urges viewers to enter this land, his music urges listeners with receptive ears to harken to its revolutionary message. Consider Mähler's portrait, if you will, as a visual complement to the *Eroica* and *Leonore*, even to Seume's *Walk to Syracuse*.

Usually the inhabitants of European towns and villages planted only one Tree of Liberty. In Mähler's portrait, however, we see two. If we look closely, we see that the trees are linked, even interlocked, one slightly in front of the other. What did Beethoven via Mähler intend? Let me present several hypotheses. Might one tree represent Beethoven himself, who in his music celebrates liberty, and the other his new artist friend Mähler? Beethoven generally felt more comfortable with those who shared with him similar political values. It seems likely that Mähler, his fellow Rhinelander and eventual lifelong friend, held similar republican, even revolutionary ideals.

But there may be another, perhaps likelier possibility for the second tree. May it represent the man whom Beethoven had long pondered and whose career he followed closely, namely, Napoleon Bonaparte? He had written the *Eroica* with First Consul Bonaparte in mind, and he had intended to name after as well as dedicate to him his newest and until now greatest work. In 1818, having written eight symphonies in all, he would proclaim the *Eroica* his favorite, and it could have been his favorite earlier. Preceding its composition, Napoleon had achieved a reputation as a brilliant military strategist, one who appeared to champion freedom. He was also recognized by many, at least until 1804, as an enlightened political leader who had restored order and prosperity to his country. Liberals across Europe assessed developments in their own lands by progress in France. To many, the First Consul still seemed the best, indeed virtually the only, hope of effecting lasting change in a Europe ruled by long-powerful dynasties of kings and emperors. By linking the two Trees of Liberty Beethoven via Mähler may have wished to indicate his solidarity with Napoleon. He liked to think that Napoleon shared his belief that in mankind's destiny lay a future era of freedom. Napoleon is omnipresent in the *Eroica* but its true subject, its underlying theme, is revolution. Whereas Beethoven's response to Napoleon fluctuated widely over the years, his faith in the Revolution and its potential for improving the future of mankind remained fairly constant. Napoleon had taken part in a great revolutionary movement, one that had changed the world. In that movement Beethoven viewed himself as a partner. Here he and Napoleon stand together, joint Trees of Liberty, joint beacons of freedom, Beethoven through his music, Napoleon through his statecraft and—so Beethoven must have hoped—as ardent as he in support of liberty.

Still another tree in Mähler's portrait requires our attention. On the right, behind Beethoven's back, looms a large gnarled hardwood, most likely an oak, as its size, branches, and leaves indicate. In art a fallen or devastated tree often stands as a symbol of mortality, our own or that in nature. Such is the "dramatic blasted tree motif" of which Alessandra Comini speaks in this painting.[49] Owen Jander observes that it resembles similar isolated trees seen in sketches and paintings by Friedrich.[50] Such a tree, he points out, was typical of painters trained in Dresden, where Mähler as well as Friedrich studied.[51] But Mähler's oak is clearly dying. Dead or dying trees in earlier European landscape painting symbolize the passing of time, the mortality of generations. It is a frequent motif, for example, in works by the seventeenth-century Dutch artist Jacob van Ruysdael.[52] Mähler's dying oak, then, has a role other than being part of a pastoral landscape. Even though larger than the Trees of Liberty, it represents a past that has no future, at least in a world capable of being enlightened.

Though monarchies still ruled most of Europe in 1804, Beethoven hoped the future lay not with them but with a world the Trees of Liberty anticipated. In contrast to the dying oak, the Trees of Liberty behind Beethoven's arm appear radiantly healthy and green, the color of hope, the color of many revolutionary *cocardes*. Whereas what I shall call the Tree of Absolutism has only limited life remaining, the Trees of Liberty—symbolizing Beethoven's revolutionary fervor—still have ahead of them an impressive longevity.

Beethoven has his back to the Tree of Absolutism. In effect, his pose indicates his disregard for what it represents. As he urges viewers to explore the revolutionary terrain in which thrive the two Trees of Liberty, his dark blue cloak has fallen off his shoulders.[53] A sliver of bright red lining is exposed. The "redlined coat," Comini observes, "twines around his lower torso like a classical garment."[54] So it does. But that red lining—it catches our eye. It serves more than to demarcate the dark cloak from the dark tree. Red was the revolutionaries' color of choice. "The colors of Paris, red and blue," the historian Simon Schama tells us, "became the colors of the uniform of its citizen soldiers." Red represents "the blood to be shed for freedom." It's one of the bands on France's tricolor.

If we accept the complex allegorical reading of Mähler's portrait advocated here, the "red" lining is there to burn down the moribund Tree of Absolutism. The tree will die in time of natural causes, that is certain, but Beethoven wished to hasten its demise by igniting it himself. The red lining adorns the posterior of a man whose correspondence reeks of improprieties and who liked (and did not disdain using) scatological witticisms. We are being offered a visual pun, and a subtly clever one. By having the coat lining so positioned, Beethoven expresses his contempt for what he hoped was dying absolutism. The portrait, in sum, appears to depict a proper bourgeois male in formal attire in a bucolic landscape, but its subtext presents a revolutionary in a landscape saturated with revolutionary symbolism.

Mähler uses his portrait to express in visual terms the message of freedom and liberation conveyed so magnificently in Beethoven's Third Symphony. It beckons us to listen to Beethoven's music carefully. Much of it bears witness to his belief in revolution—one that embraces not only radically changing the nature of society but also raising music to new heights. After all, Prometheus and Napoleon were in themselves revolutionaries, and Beethoven's *Eroica* tells of Promethean and Napoleonic striving. Most of all, both portrait and symphony are Beethoven's embodiments of his utopian hopes. Like his prized statue of Lucius Junius Brutus, the Roman tyrannicide, Beethoven kept the Mähler portrait by him. It did not enter the public domain during his lifetime, nor for some decades after.

14

Toward Beethoven's 1808 Akademie

He mentioned Beethoven.... Then the music started. Mick raised her head and her fist went up to her throat.

She could not listen good enough to hear it all. The music boiled inside her. Which? To hang on to certain wonderful parts and think them over so that later she would not forget—or should she let go and listen to each part that came without thinking or trying to remember. Golly! The whole world was this music and she could not listen hard enough.

CARSON MCCULLERS[1]

Renewed Creativity, 1802–08

The "new path" on which Beethoven set himself in 1802, the year of the Heiligenstadt Testament, inaugurated a major period of creativity, in effect, the advent of a new artistic universe. Joseph Kerman, a leading American musicologist, spoke of it as "somewhat like Keats on first reading Chapman's Homer," that is, a revelation that is transformative. Beethoven's hearing, despite several desperate attempts at cures, showed no signs of improvement, but he often remained, as Ignaz von Seyfried described him, "cheerful, ready for any fun, jovial, sprightly, full of the joy of life, facetious, often satirical."[2]

The despair evoked in the Heiligenstadt Testament had dissolved in creativity. Along with the *Eroica* Symphony and *Leonore*, the works of this time include the piano sonatas "Waldstein" (1803–04) and "Appassionata" (1804–05). Whereas the "Waldstein" Sonata, Op. 53, has both rhythm and melody, with the "Appassionata," Op. 57, we sense the arrival of a new esthetic. Immediately popular, the "Appassionata" in this regard anticipates the Fifth Symphony.

Having begun the *Eroica*, Beethoven turned to the Triple Concerto in late 1803. It too charts new dimensions. The work was first performed privately at Lobkowitz's palace at the same time as the symphony. Whereas the *Eroica* sought the expansion of the symphonic horizon, Beethoven subjected the Triple Concerto to the accommodation of three soloists. In its resolution of this artistic problem, the work is a masterpiece. It may not represent Beethoven at his greatest, but it is still far beyond any but a composer of his caliber. "We must not underestimate the *Triple Concerto*," comments Donald Tovey, a leading Beethoven scholar, "because Beethoven subsequently wrote more wonderful works. This is like ignoring the marvelous *Mass in C major* because the composer overshadowed it later with one of the supreme achievements of the human mind," the Mass in D, the *Missa solemnis*.[3]

After the Triple Concerto, Beethoven again turned to large-scale forms, including the Fourth Symphony and the Fourth Piano Concerto, along with his opera *Fidelio*, originally called *Leonore*. (A later chapter takes up the opera in its final 1814 version.) *Leonore* was first performed in November 20, 1805, one week after the French by a stunning ruse had peacefully entered Vienna. Franz had ordered the Tabor Bridge, across what is now called the Danube Canal, mined. With staggering cool, the French marshals Murat and Lannes sauntered over it on November 8. They engaged the Austrian general, Prince Karl von Auersperg, in conversation. While the marshals talked about a possible armistice, French grenadiers stealthily slipped under the bridge and cut the fuses of the mines. Before the Austrians knew what had happened, the French by this act of daring had taken the bridge—and the initiative. Napoleon had already installed himself at Schonbrünn, the Hapsburg summer palace then well beyond the city limits. Fortunately, the presence of French troops in and around Vienna does not seem to have affected Beethoven's long-term compositional energy.

The incredible period of 1805–06 rivals the creativity of the previous two years. The composer followed these works with the Violin Concerto in D (1806), the overture for Heinrich Joseph von Collin's play *Coriolanus* (1807), the aforementioned Mass in C (1807), the Fifth and Sixth Symphonies (1807–08), and the Choral Fantasy (1808). There was also in the spring of 1806 a revision of *Leonore*, engineered by Stephan von Breuning and accepted, reluctantly, by Beethoven, who tightened the work and produced another overture. After two performances, Beethoven quarreled with the manager of the theater and withdrew his opera.

In May 1806, a month after the last performance of the second version of *Leonore*, Beethoven turned to the composition of three string quartets, commissioned by Prince Andreas Razumovsky, that became Opus 59. Since 1792 this Russian diplomat had served as his country's ambassador to the Austrian empire. The friend and patron of Haydn, Mozart, and now Beethoven, Razumovsky was at the heart of Viennese musical life. Ensconced in his opulent new palace on the Landstrasse, he, like his brother-in-law Prince Lobkowitz, maintained his own private orchestra. He became one of Beethoven's greatest patrons.

The quartets represent the Classical ideal of a conversation among equals. Written about the time as Beethoven's other great revolutionary works, they have in them elements of the *Eroica*, the "Waldstein" and "Appassionata" Sonatas, as well as the earlier "Kreutzer" Sonata and the Triple Concerto. The effect of this trilogy of quartets is virtually "orchestral," closer to the symphony than to their own genre. They have the heft of symphonies. But as with so much of Beethoven's innovative music, when performed at Razumovsky's palace the Viennese who attended received them with indifference.

Beethoven thought of, sketched, rehearsed, or performed all the above works during half a dozen years of feverish creativity. Many, but not all, of them evince militaristic bearing and energy. Clearly in his musical creativity the composer wished to challenge, perhaps even in his works to surpass, the mighty achievements on the battlefield of the man whom he considered his greatest rival, Napoleon.

In October 1806, when Beethoven visited Prince Lichnowsky in his castle at Grätz, near Troppau, the prince had asked him to play for French officers quartered there in preparation for battle with Prussian forces. Beethoven stubbornly and persistently refused. That night he fled the premises on foot, in a heavy rainfall, but not before leaving for his host a note, which in effect stated his credo unequivocally: "Prince, what you are, you are by circumstance and birth, what I am, I am through myself; there are, and always will be, thousands of princes; but there is only one Beethoven."[4]

ᔌ

Violin Concerto

Beethoven had known the violinist Franz Clement since his early teens. He admired his virtuosic skill all his life. A child prodigy, Clement was also a composer. He and Beethoven got along well together. As a result Beethoven agreed to write a violin concerto for Clement's benefit performance on December 23, 1806. Along the way the concerto underwent many revisions. Clement's role in crafting the final version may have been greater than has been supposed. An oft-repeated anecdote has Clement playing the concerto holding the violin upside down. Not so. That occurred in another, lighter piece in the second half of the concert, after he had performed Beethoven's concerto.

The concerto is full of unusual touches. In it Beethoven transformed and spun out the simpler line of the Triple Concerto. What other violin concerto begins with a five-beat timpani solo, one that will reoccur at key moments throughout? The long orchestral introduction that precedes the entry of the violin departed from accepted musical practice. Conservative Viennese taste might also have disliked such an introduction on political grounds. The kettledrums, Elisabeth Brisson suggests, may connote the armies of the French Revolution. Their rhythms, clearly determined, she writes, provide the piece with a sonority. In most performances the first movement alone runs to twenty-five minutes. Unfortunately, a Viennese audience could hardly approve a work of such length and complexity, in effect symphonic in scope. "If we think of Beethoven in his more eruptive and daemonic moods as recognizably Dionysiac, then we can also see that in his music there is a strong counter-balancing pull, an Apollonian sense of order, elevated beauty, and serenity."[5] The concerto combines both moods.

ℒ

Coriolanus *Overture (1807)*

Coriolanus was among Plutarch's model heroes, hugely flawed yet still an *exemplum virtutis*. Beethoven in an extraordinary overture re-created this powerful being, his tragic flaws, his arrogance that led to his downfall, and his death. T. S. Eliot once observed that Shakespeare, another huge admirer of the Greek historian, had "acquired more essential history from Plutarch than most men could from the whole British Museum."[6] To Jacques Louis David, as later to the young Napoleon— and not least to the young Beethoven—Plutarch's heroes and heroines were as familiar as leading contemporaries.

Beethoven wrote the *Coriolanus* Overture to introduce a revival of Collin's play *Coriolanus* (1802). The composer, who knew and liked Collin, had earlier contemplated collaborating with him on a proposed *Macbeth*. Later he considered composing music for an opera based on Collin's *Romulus*. Shakespeare, drawing chiefly upon Plutarch's life of Coriolanus, presents the Roman aristocrat as a tortured being. Though an able general, he expresses scorn for the populace. Exiled from Rome, his native city, Coriolanus joins his chief adversary, the Volscians, raises an army, and besieges the city. We might expect Beethoven, by background and inclination, to have had little sympathy for such an impetuous aristocrat, but Coriolanus was strong-minded, courageous, determined, a genuine though flawed hero. The overture stresses his positive qualities.

Two themes predominate in the overture's first section. One presents the gathering of the army, and, repeated in bits and fragments, suggests the march on Rome. The second theme is a plea to avoid destruction, expressed first by the citizens of Rome, then by Coriolanus's mother, his wife, and two children. Beethoven uses the sonata allegro form—exposition, development, recapitulation—to build tension, a sense of urgency. Torn between losing the trust of his army if he retreats and the love of his family if he sacks his native city, Coriolanus accepts that it must be he who decides his fate. Commentators who speculate that Beethoven felt a spiritual kinship with the intransigence, pride, self-assertion, and self-righteousness of the Roman hero have a point. The internal dissonance in Beethoven's music mirrors that within Coriolanus. He impressively renders in sound the defiant perseverance of his hero, a noble-minded but imperfect man, wronged yet justly repudiated by his people, a man who accepts the death he has brought upon himself.

The overture ends brilliantly. A gradual dispersing and extinguishing of the strong first theme, it is an obvious announcement of the hero's death. Once before, in the Funeral March of his *Eroica* Symphony, Beethoven had commemorated the death of a hero. Here, in the work's four final beats, his heart ceases to function.

E. T. A. Hoffmann believed the *Coriolanus* Overture "too muscle-bound to serve as an introduction to Collin's reflective drama."[7] The famous Allegro, Hoffmann thought, Beethoven conceived in his own characteristic spirit. The overture reminded him of those by Cherubini, which often lurk behind Beethoven's. As Hoffmann listened to *Coriolanus*, he gradually grasped "the psychological relationship of the two masters."[8] Similarly that splendid music interpreter Paul Henry Lang also saw Cherubini as the single greatest influence hovering over the *Coriolanus* and the *Egmont* Overtures, even for that matter over *Leonore*'s. The heroism in the *Coriolanus* and *Egmont* Overtures can be heard in the Third and Fifth Symphonies. Both overtures, each about seven or eight minutes long, exert a greater emotional impact upon listeners than many much longer works.

❧

Heinrich von Kleist

Of all the literary figures in the German states who rose up to fulminate against Napoleon, none was more complex in his emotional responses, more vehement in his protests, more paradoxical in his behavior, than the dramatist, poet, and writer of extraordinary novellas, Heinrich von Kleist. Because he serves as a counterpoint to Beethoven during these years, he receives consideration here. The fascination, the ambivalence—and even, in Kleist's case, the sheer hatred—he felt at different times toward Napoleon allow us to elucidate further Beethoven's responses to the French emperor. Kleist's uncompromising response to Napoleon, in various moods and works, casts light upon Beethoven's own. What Beethoven achieved in symphonies and sonatas, Kleist achieved in plays, poems, and novellas. "In obstinacy, determination, and in genius," his biographer Joachim Maass rightly claims, "Kleist had much in common with Beethoven."[9] To these qualities we may add intransigence, unwillingness to compromise, single-mindedness of purpose. Temperamentally, both had an obsessive personality. Beethoven's own perspective in Hapsburg Austria on Napoleon can appear ominously close to Kleist's in Prussia.

Initially in favor of Napoleon, Kleist around 1803 began to speak of the "damned consul" who was training an army to invade England.[10] Yet, unpredictable as ever, he joined the force that Napoleon was raising. Unlike Beethoven, whose obsession with Napoleon alternated between admiration and anger, Kleist's initial enthusiasm never revived. In maturity, after the battle of Jena in 1806, his hatred of Napoleon and the French went far beyond the requirements of patriotism. "We are," Kleist wrote his like-minded sister shortly after the battle, "the subjugated people of the Romans,"[11] that is, the French. In the catechism Kleist wrote we read: "Who are your enemies, my son?"—"Napoleon and, all the time he is their emperor, the French."[12] When he heard the news of the French capitulation at Bailén in Spain and of Wellington's victory against French forces at Torres Vedras, he rejoiced. French armies were not unbeatable after all.

Several of Kleist's poems, including "The Battle of the Teutoburg Forest," take deliberate aim at Napoleon. His play *Arminius's Battle*, another anti-Napoleonic work, dramatizes the exploits of the ancient Germanic hero Hermann or Arminius, who, centuries before, routed a Roman army under Quintilius Varus. By such works Kleist hoped to encourage his countrymen to fight Napoleon and *his* invading army. He regarded the French emperor as a new Quintilius Varus and gave himself over to a search for a German Arminius who could defeat him.

Kleist's oft-rewritten poem "Germany to Her Children" offers a bitter riposte to the positive message of Schiller's "Ode to Joy." In 1809, inspired by the Austrian campaign against Napoleon, Kleist in his gruesome "German Song of Battle" envisioned an all-out war against the French:

Whiten with these scattered bones
Every hollow, every hill
From what was left by fox and crow
The hungry fish shall eat their fill;
Block the Rhine with their cadavers;
Until, plugged up by so much flesh,
It breaks the banks and surges west
To draw our borderline afresh![13]

If Beethoven is a very unusual composer, no less is Kleist a very unusual writer. Like Beethoven when angered, Kleist's *furor teutonicus* (Teutonic fury) tore into Napoleon. He could be relentless. His long novella *Michael Kohlhaus* depicts a man who tirelessly seeks to right an injustice. Kohlhaus's uncompromising pursuit of justice reveals

Kleist's own obsession to undermine Napoleon. Like Kohlhaus, Kleist determines to follow through, regardless of whatever laws exist, until he achieves the outcome he desires. He never tires in his pursuit, never compromises his principles, never quits or turns aside until he achieves it.

Beethoven, when the mood took him, possessed a determination parallel to that of Kohlhaus—and Kleist. Yet the composer's response to Napoleon differed in degree from Kleist's. Though at times he damned Napoleon, he lived, after all, not in Prussia but in absolutist Hapsburg Vienna. Given the prevailing censorship in Austria, it becomes difficult to gauge his response to nationalistic sentiments elsewhere in German lands. Living within an increasingly harsh and reactionary regime, Beethoven found thinking about Napoleon offered relief, even glimmers of hope, from oppression. But not always. On April 26, 1807, three months after Napoleon had gained a pyrrhic victory over the Russians at Eylau on the Russo-Polish border, Beethoven raged against "the wicked Gauls." He wished he "could drive them away from where they have no right to be."[14]

Kleist lived most of his maturity in Berlin or elsewhere in a Prussia under French rule after 1806. There he experienced an increasingly repressive government. In Berlin he took part in a large resistance movement. German patriots, virtually under the noses of the French occupiers, agitated for and prepared for an eventual uprising. But in 1811, before German resistance to Napoleon had emerged fully, Kleist took his own life, and his inamorata joined him in death.

Kleist was not the only German literary figure who agitated against Napoleon during these years. The title character of Zacharias Werner's play *Attila*, the "scourge of god" (1807), makes so many references to Napoleon that even in fairly liberal French-controlled Berlin the authorities would not allow it to be staged. Napoleon left others puzzled all their lives. Along with Kleist, a host of talented intellectuals—Fichte, Schleiermacher, Arndt, Kotzebue, Jahn, and not least the young Theodor Körner, whom Beethoven knew—began to involve themselves in Germany's future. Many of them, like Kleist, lived in Prussia. Part of the new German self-consciousness, Prussia presented itself as the creator of pro-German feeling. Ominously for Napoleon, in the wake of Prussia's catastrophic defeats in 1806–07, new and more able military leaders came to the fore—chief among them, August von Gneisenau and Gerhard von Scharnhorst.

∿

The Akademie of December 22, 1808

In mid-1808 Beethoven, to resuscitate his uncertain finances, began to plan an Akademie, or benefit concert for himself, to be given that December. This Akademie surely ranks as one of the pivotal moments in his career. What scholars have neglected—in fact barely touched upon—is the role Napoleon played in shaping this concert and the repercussions it had for Beethoven. Most studies investigating Beethoven's response to Napoleon stop with his withdrawal of the dedication to the *Eroica* in 1804 or soon after. Scholars have often probed Beethoven's response to the French leader during the years previous to 1804, but for them Beethoven's emphatic rejection of him in May of that year marks the end of his interest, at least until his death in 1821. But Napoleon's impact on Beethoven does not cease. In fact in 1804 it had hardly begun. Beethoven's deeply felt rivalry with Napoleon was virtually a lifelong experience. The figure of Napoleon goads Beethoven to compose music as great in its very different way as the French emperor's achievements in the military and political realm.

Between October 1806 and October 1810 this rivalry on Beethoven's part may well have been at its most intense. During these years Napoleon was Europe's dominant figure. Those in power elsewhere hated or feared him, but others still viewed him as the main hope for social and political change in a Europe ruled arbitrarily by kings. Whatever opinion people held of him or his accomplishments, friend and foe regarded Napoleon as the most brilliant man of the age. Beethoven believed himself, in the realm of music, to be Napoleon's equal. The Akademie of

December 22, 1808, plays a key role in his ongoing competition with Napoleon. A turning point in his life, the Akademie and its extraordinary if contentious aftermath show Beethoven at his irascible, magnificent best, Napoleon's greatest opponent—and admirer.

In terms of works first performed, this Akademie may be the most significant concert of classical music ever given in Vienna—or for that matter anywhere else. The audience that December day heard seven works, three of which—the Fifth and Sixth Symphonies and the Fourth Piano Concerto—are among Beethoven's acknowledged masterpieces; another, the Choral Fantasy, may well also merit that designation; and a fifth, the Mass in C, long overshadowed by the later Mass in D, is in its own right a splendid achievement. The other two pieces on the program were the concert aria *Ah, perfido!* and what became the Piano Fantasy, Op. 77. Beethoven composed these works in the middle of what many have referred to as the "heroic" period that began in the early 1800s, when the composer said he now intended to embark on a "new path."

The German word *Akademie* means a place of study, or a gathering of scholars, as it does in English, but in German it has, as noted earlier, an older sense as well. An Akademie was a concert sponsored by and paid for by an individual, in this case Beethoven, who secured a location, hired the orchestra members, the singers and soloists, and arranged for the copying of the parts. Since he would conduct himself he did not have to hire a conductor. He would reap the profit or take the loss. Vienna still did not have a regular series of public concerts in the evening at this time. Many concerts then, as noted earlier, were held in the palaces of the aristocracy and were not open to the general public. By contrast, that public probably comprised most of the audience for Beethoven's 1808 Akademie. To hold a concert open to the public, be it noted, also involved a visit to the police to obtain the permit required for any public gathering. Unfortunately, the Tonkünstler Societät also held a concert that evening, and it drew away from Beethoven's Akademie many of the city's professional musicians.

This Akademie took place in Vienna's Theater an der Wien, where the *Eroica* and *Leonore* were first performed publicly. For most people present this mammoth concert seems to have been more an ordeal than a success. It began at 6:30 and ended over four hours later. Concerts in the early nineteenth century were often longer than today, but even so the program's length was exceptional. The concert hall was unheated, and the audience, even those clad in winter coats and furs, got colder and colder, as did the shivering musicians onstage. Not only was the program very long and the audience and performers very cold, the concert included for many too much challenging new music to take in at one time. Works by Beethoven we now regard as classics were then startlingly unfamiliar. Historical imagination is required for us to realize that most of Beethoven's contemporaries found his music, especially when first heard, discordant, bizarre, puzzling, even upsetting.

The Viennese resisted this music, judging it radically different from the music by Haydn and Mozart they had gradually become used to. Even those in the audience favorably disposed to Beethoven's works often did not know how to respond to it. It was easier to dismiss Beethoven as mad and his compositions as chaotic than to listen carefully and with an open mind. Many thus found the concert an almost unbearably hard slog. But for a few it was an unforgettable experience. Those few really loved Beethoven's music and some of them Beethoven himself, several almost from his arrival in Vienna sixteen years before.

Almost everything that can go wrong with a performance did. The audience sensed, quite rightly, that the concert was underprepared. Beethoven had earlier quarreled with the musicians he had hired, to such a degree that he had been banned from rehearsals. As a result there were too few of them, which led to major mishaps in several of the pieces played.

Johann Friedrich Reichardt, a Berlin music critic, editor of an influential music journal, and himself a composer of some stature, was one of the well-known musicians attending the concert. He shared the box of Prince Lobkowitz. Reichardt admired Beethoven as a "prolific genius and untiring worker." He found the music overwhelming, but he also

knew that preparations for the concert had not gone well. He and Lobkowitz shivered "in the bitterest cold, too, from half past six to half past
ten, and experienced the truth that one can easily have too much of
a good thing—and still more of a loud."[15] To contemporaries used to
Classical works by Haydn and Mozart, Beethoven's music was not only
complex to understand but also much too loud. Concerts then took place
in smaller spaces, either private rooms or local halls, which (as Reichardt notes) concentrated the sound, sometimes unpleasantly. To modern
listeners, often conditioned to even louder music using amplification,
with larger orchestras and in larger halls, the sound level of Beethoven's
works may not seem unusual, but to contemporaries it was.

Concerts two hundred years ago, unlike today's semisacral events,
often presented eclectic programs. Audiences at this time listened to
all kinds of music—movements of symphonies and concertos mingled
with solo piano pieces, dances, fashionable concert arias (almost always
Italian) and variations based on them, even popular tunes sung on the
street. Audiences rarely sat still or quieted down. Applause might erupt
after movements or even during them. Artists felt free to embellish
and alter, to add and subtract, and in the solo passages that Beethoven
played, he no doubt did all these things. The unusual selection of works
heard that evening—an all-Beethoven concert in fact—and, from a
modern perspective, the even more unusual order in which they were
played would not have unduly troubled the audience.

Today's standard program (overture, concerto with well-known soloist, symphony after intermission), or variants thereof, is a twentieth-
century formula. Most pieces at concerts today are by composers long
dead. Concerts rarely last more than two hours, often less, followed
by several rounds of polite applause at the close, then a rush for the
exits. Perhaps if contemporary audiences could hear (and survive) a concert as varied and unusual as Beethoven's 1808 Akademie, they would
recapture some of the excitement audiences of yesteryear felt. There are
obvious reasons why Beethoven organized his Akademie. The Viennese
public had not yet heard most of the pieces, and Beethoven understand-

ably wished to introduce them to his friends and admirers. Even more crucial for him, he was broke.

The Akademie began with his Symphony No. 6, the "Pastoral," though still designated in the program Symphony No. 5. Beethoven loved nature, indeed reveled in it, and stayed in villages in the country during the summer, but his new symphony, he insisted, was more the expression of his feelings than a depiction of natural phenomena. His favorite summer residence seems to have been Baden, a small spa town about twenty-six kilometers (sixteen miles) south of Vienna, where he took long walks along the little river Schwechat in the adjoining *Helenental*, literally, "valley of Helen."

"Walking," the American literary pundit Alfred Kazin once wrote, "I always knew how I felt by the music in my head."[16] Likewise Beethoven. Walking in the countryside gave him the emotional stimulus to create, to write down the music in his head. The ongoing forward momentum we hear in many of his works reflects the energy he felt moving his body through space amid nature. As he walked along he composed— humming, singing, talking to himself—then scribbled down notes and ideas for the melodies that overran his brain.

Next on the 1808 program was the concert aria *Ah, perfido!* which translates, awkwardly, into English as "Oh, perfidious one!" Written in Prague in 1796 during the tour that took Beethoven as far north as Berlin, *Ah, perfido!* was first performed in the Czech city by Josepha Duschek. Italian arias, not necessarily part of operas, were a fixture even during instrumental recitals, and the Akademie witnessed the work's Vienna premiere. The words sizzle. The female singer calls her male lover *barbaro traditor,* "barbarous traitor"; *scellerato,* "rascal," but . . . but *voglio morir per lui!,* "I wish to die for him!"

The Gloria, a section of Beethoven's Mass in C, followed. In 1807 Prince Nikolaus Esterházy had persuaded Beethoven to write one for him. It had been performed the year before in the grand ballroom of the Esterházy castle in Eisenstadt. Though he had earlier written

an oratorio, *Christ on the Mount of Olives,* the composer did not usually attempt traditional religious music. The prince, upon hearing the
Mass, was furious. "My dear Beethoven," he asked, "what is this that
you have done again?"[17] The composer, not amused, promptly returned
to Vienna. To his credit, Prince Nikolaus was apparently the only one of
Beethoven's supporters to make a contribution—one hundred gulden—
to the expenses incurred for the Akademie. Obviously Beethoven, as
often happened in his relations with his patrons, had achieved some
kind of reconciliation with the prince. Unfortunately, the Gloria, as well
as the other sections from the Mass performed that evening, also failed
to please the Akademie audience.

The Fourth Piano Concerto closed the first half of the program.
Beethoven placed this now much-admired piece just before the intermission because the audience would thus focus on him, doubly as both
soloist and conductor. Reichardt, who thought the work "of enormous
difficulty," found Beethoven's performance greatly moving. Beethoven
"carried [it] off bravely in the fastest tempos imaginable. . . . The adagio,
a masterful movement of beautiful, deeply felt song, he played truly with
profound, melancholy feeling."[18] The original program of this movement, according to the Beethoven scholar Owen Jander, is based on versions current in Vienna at this time of the Orpheus myth. If we accept
this interpretation, the concert's first half thus closes with Beethoven
presenting himself as the inspired founder of music, Orpheus.

The Fifth Symphony launched the program's second half. Sketches for
the first three movements went back to 1800 and 1801, that earlier flush
period of creativity that had led to the *Eroica* and *Leonore.* Beethoven thus
had much of this symphony in his consciousness while he composed
both these works, and it is conceived in the same revolutionary vein. If
the Sixth Symphony is the expression of humanity in nature, the Fifth
is the expression of humanity face to face with its tragic destiny, the triumph of ultimate victory after fierce resistance, of light and hope over
the dark forces of despair. "A magnificent song of victory," Hector Ber-

lioz said of the Finale, victory achieved after passing through the dark night of the soul.[19] Today the Fifth Symphony, now the most famous of all Beethoven symphonies, along with the Ninth, usually ends a concert. Beethoven may have realized that if he closed a four-hour concert with what he may already have sensed would become his best-known work the audience would have been too tired or too cold to appreciate it.

After another movement from the Mass in C, the Sanctus (Benedictus), the audience would have heard Beethoven play what apparently became the Piano Fantasy, Op. 77. Beethoven dazzled most when improvising, and how closely his performance actually corresponds to the published version is not known. To show the audience how formidable a pianist he still could be despite his growing deafness, he put it in the concert.

The final piece was the Choral Fantasy. Beethoven composed it at the last minute as an appropriate Finale. The work brings together all the various forces—piano, orchestra, solo voice, and choir—he had used earlier in the concert. From piano to full orchestra, chorus and soloists intertwined. Beethoven intended the Choral Fantasy to lift the audience out of its seats. It began with an improvised piano solo eventually written down. Then came an aria based on a poem Beethoven had used earlier, "Gegenliebe," meaning "reciprocal love." It celebrates the liberating "power of music to bring peace and joy." And if the audience understood "Gegenliebe" as Beethoven intended them to, in which words and music solemnly interact to form a magical world of sound, Beethoven also emerges as the work's hero. As so often, he moves from dark to light, from apparent chaos to order. The words imply that music's power lasts longer than that of any secular authority. Years later, when he came to write the Finale of his Ninth Symphony, he found an ideal starting point in the Choral Fantasy.

Unfortunately the Choral Fantasy heard in 1808 was poorly prepared and under-rehearsed. It turned out disastrously. Beethoven had written out the orchestral and choral sections but, as was his wont, improvised the introductory piano part. After he had played with blazing intensity for some minutes, the orchestra failed to enter. Beethoven, conducting from the piano, was much annoyed. He stopped the work and insisted upon beginning again. His friends in the audience winced in embarrassment. Although the Choral Fantasy went well the second time around, Reichardt wished he'd left before having had to witness this mishap.

The story of the extraordinary Akademie of 1808 does not end with the last notes heard on December 22. While preparing for his concert Beethoven had entered into negotiations with Jerome Bonaparte, the emperor's youngest brother, the newly minted king of Westphalia, a subject state in Germany recently decreed into existence by Napoleon. Jerome offered to make Beethoven his Kapellmeister. Disgusted by the cabals and intrigues of Vienna and with his finances at a low ebb, Beethoven pondered the situation for several months. On January 15, 1809—that is, three weeks after the December 1808 Akademie—he formally accepted Jerome's offer. He had, in essence, agreed to join the court of a country created by Napoleon. That Jerome was a Freemason, as was Reichardt, who had just resigned as Kapellmeister there and with whom Beethoven almost certainly conferred about taking the position, may have influenced his decision.

One reason Beethoven made this Akademie of December 22, 1808, so long and full is that it might well have been his last public appearance in Vienna. He gave the concert in part to make the Viennese regret all the more the musical genius they would have lost, humiliatingly, to the youngest brother of the all-conquering Napoleon. Fortunately for Austrian prestige, three of Beethoven's Viennese patrons—Prince Kinsky, Prince Lobkowitz, and Archduke Rudolph—came to the rescue by offering Beethoven an annual stipend that matched Jerome's offer. The contract, which would take effect March 1, 1809, stipulated he remain within Hapsburg territory (which besides Vienna included the major musical cities of Prague and Budapest). Beethoven accepted the terms and remained where he was. But the Viennese had come within a hair of losing their greatest composer.

15

Napoleon in Vienna in 1809; Beethoven Befriends Baron de Trémont

If it were possible to measure such things at all one
might be tempted to claim that the Napoleonic myth
later flourished more strongly in Germany and was
more effective there than in France.

GOLO MANN[1]

War

Eighteen hundred and five had proven to be a dramatic year in
European history. It was the year of Schiller's death, of Nelson's
great sea victory at Trafalgar, off the Spanish coast (October 21); of Napoleon's spectacular triumph at Austerlitz, some eighty miles north of
Vienna (December 2). Countries found themselves either in France's
axis of power or in England's. English naval strength had made even its
allies uneasy. There was a growing sense of moral outrage that any one
nation should gain something like exclusive rights over the high seas.
Likewise, Napoleon's victory at Austerlitz might lead to France exerting
its hegemony over the entire European mainland. Both possibilities
heightened tensions on the Continent.

On April 9, 1809, the Austrian government, propped up by a new coalition, again foolishly declared war against Napoleon's France. With the French emperor now planning a campaign to subdue Spain or to cross the English Channel, Austria had sensed a chance to strike. The government, the army, and the people were all keen to avenge the defeat at Austerlitz four years before. But the decision to go to war proved ill considered. It was indeed a fateful step, one that would cost Austria—and not least Beethoven—dear.

The French army was again soon before Vienna. Napolon ensconced himself once more in Schönbrunn. Emperor Franz and the Viennese aristocracy, along with a number of Beethoven's friends and supporters, again left for Olmütz in Moravia. Unlike the situation in 1805, the civic authorities had received orders to defend Vienna. Napoleon thus ordered its bombardment. It began May 11. Three days later, on May 13, Archduke Michael, left in charge of the defense by his older brother, surrendered, and the first units of the French army entered the undefended city. They encountered only minimal resistance. The main body entered five days afterwards and encountered none. Vienna was theirs. The French emperor—or, as hostile caricaturists liked to call him, the "Corsican Ogre"—was once again in control.

Among those who stayed behind was Beethoven. While French cannon bombarded the city, Beethoven took refuge in the basement of his brother Karl's residence. To protect his ears against the noise of cannonballs crashing into nearby buildings, he covered them with pillows. Whereas in 1805 many Viennese had had pro-French feelings, in 1809 a cooler reception awaited Napoleon and his troops. The French emperor who gave respect to those whom he felt deserved it posted a guard at Haydn's house, where the aged composer was failing. When one of the officers on duty with a fine tenor voice sang the aria "With Majesty and Grandeur" from *The Creation*, Haydn was moved to tears.

❧

Aspern-Essling

Even with Napoleon's main force settled in Vienna, the conflict continued. A body of the French army had set up camp on the Danube's south bank. Hoping to establish a beachhead on the north bank, Napoleon's troops occupied the island of Lobau in the middle of the river. From Lobau they threw pontoon bridges across to the north bank. Napoleon had based about half his troops in Aspern and Essling, two villages across and upstream from Vienna. But he had not taken into account the torrential spring rains that raised the river level hugely. Upstream, Austrian patriots floated tree trunks down the now rapidly flowing stream that damaged or wrecked his bridges. The Danube then overran its banks, cutting communications between the army's two halves.

Sensing a strategic advantage, Austrian forces based on the north bank, led by another of Emperor Franz's brothers, the capable Archduke Karl, attacked the French troops based in Aspern and Essling. A major battle raged furiously on May 21–22. The French suffered heavy losses. Only after Napoleon had reestablished the pontoon bridges could he send reinforcements and supplies and enable survivors to cross back to Lobau and safety.

Even with Napoleon not directly involved, the battle of Aspern-Essling marked Austria's first victory over a Napoleonic army. It was a personal triumph for Archduke Karl, the commander. By his success Karl had aroused the envy of Emperor Franz, his far less able older brother.[2] The news of the French defeat resounded across Europe. Heinrich von Kleist hailed Karl as the conqueror of the unconquerable. In England the twenty-one-year-old Byron, on the verge of setting out to explore the East, expressed his amazement: "The Continent is in a fine state! An insurrection has broken out at Paris, the Austrians are beating Buonaparte, the Tyrolese have risen."[3] Byron had cause to express surprise: his hero had proven himself vulnerable. Two months after Aspern-Essling, a French army suffered another humiliation, surrendering to Spanish forces at Bailén. Though comfortably ensconced in Vienna and not involved in the defeat in Spain, the hero of Beethoven's (and Byron's) imagination was not invincible.

ᔰ

Wagram

While the armies of Austria and France regrouped for the climactic battle both sides knew would come, Napoleon remained at Schön-brunn plotting strategy. In July he defeated the main Austrian army once again, at Wagram, on the Marchfeld across the Danube, within sight of the steeple of St. Stephen's Cathedral. Enclosed by the Danube and the March, its small tributary, it was a plain barely ten miles wide. There three hundred thousand men, more than Vienna's then popula-tion, fought each other in a closely contested struggle that lasted two days, July 5 and 6. Sixty thousand died. Napoleon emerged victorious, yet Wagram proved for him a pyrrhic triumph, for losses on both sides were huge and the gains questionable. What disturbed the French com-manders (and what commentators across Europe observed) was how much closer the Austrians had come to winning than before.

ᔰ

Beethoven in Occupied Vienna

About Vienna's French occupiers Beethoven has little to say. At least initially, he seems not to have found their presence oppressive. All the same, he had to forgo his usual summer departure for the country. Though conceding the "indescribable misery which prevails in Vienna," neither then nor later did he turn against the French. Life in the capi-tal continued much as before. The waltz had emerged, and the modest orchestras of Josef Lanner and the elder Johann Strauss soon popular-ized it further. The Viennese, it has often been said, don't want to be perturbed. They want to be entertained. Joseph Wechsberg, a modern scholar of his native city, has wittily described the situation in Vienna during this summer as "desperate, but not serious."[4] The Viennese returned to their entertainments.

Austrians of Beethoven's day had an obsession with titles. "In Vienna a man with no title has no identity," comments Wechsberg; "Vienna remains a large stage where everybody enjoys himself by playing a part, as in a play." The individual who wrote the play? No one seemed interested in him. "He only wrote the play," I've heard them say. Which leads to the question, what part could a nearly deaf man play? One of Beethoven's lasting regrets was that he never became a musician of the imperial court, the same court he often professed to scorn. A position, with the corresponding title, would have compensated for the social and financial poverty of much of his life in Vienna. But then, Beethoven only wrote the music.

~

Grillparzer and Beethoven

The man who eventually became Austria's most famous dramatist, Franz Grillparzer, knew Beethoven early. Despite divergences in temperament and talent, they became friends. His uncle Joseph Sonnleithner, who ran an art and music bookshop in Vienna, had given young Franz musical instruction. He had also prepared the libretto for the 1805 production of *Leonore*. When Franz first encountered Beethoven in that year, he found him "thin, dark, and even, despite his subsequent habits, elegantly attired." At this time, though rarely afterwards, Beethoven wore glasses. The elegant Beethoven depicted in the Mähler portrait still existed, but in years subsequent the composer had let his appearance slide. During the summer of 1808 Grillparzer and his mother shared with the composer a house in the then-outlying village of Heiligenstadt on Grinzinger Strasse, today number 64. While Beethoven played the piano, Franz's mother used to open the door and surreptitiously listen. One day the composer noticed her, became annoyed, and did not play again.

The next year, 1809, Grillparzer, now a youth of eighteen, participated in the halfhearted defense of the Vienna abandoned by Emperor Franz. The city's rapid surrender on May 13 does not seem to have overly concerned him. But the sight of Napoleon reviewing his troops at Schönbrunn he found unforgettable. It prompted an ambivalent, confused response:

> I myself was no less an enemy of the French than my father, and yet Napoleon fascinated me with a magic power. I had hatred in my heart, I had never been addicted to military displays, and yet I missed not one of his reviews of troops at Schönbrunn and on the parade ground of the so-called Schmelz. I still see him before me . . . standing there cast-iron, hands folded behind his back, to survey his hosts on their march past with the unmoved look of the lord and master. His figure is present to me. . . . He put me under a spell as a snake does a bird.[5]

Grillparzer could not see enough of the man who had cast so potent a spell upon him. Three years before in Jena, Hegel, upon seeing Napoleon riding his horse, felt in effect as if he were watching the "World Spirit," omnipotent and in motion. Like Hegel, Grillparzer felt overwhelmed. On August 15, 1809, a month after Wagram, the Viennese celebrated Napoleon's birthday with great pomp. Civic authorities requested citizens to line the streets for the great march-pass of the troops. Flags flew from houses; church bells rang. Among the Viennese watching, again unable to restrain his curiosity to see the French emperor, was young Grillparzer.

ℒ

Baron de Trémont Visits Beethoven

Another reason Beethoven did not leave for the country in 1809 is that early in the occupation he made the acquaintance of one of the French officers based in Vienna, Louis-Philippe-Joseph Girod de Viennay, later to become Baron de Trémont. With this individual he developed a friendship. Enthralled by music, Trémont read it fluently by the age of five. He could sing and had learned to play various instruments. A cultivated member of Napoleon's staff and an auditor to his Council of State, Trémont had early become an admirer of Beethoven's music. Throughout his life, whenever his duties did not take him away from Paris he held musical reunions in his home. In regard to contemporary composers, his tastes were eclectic. He valued Auber and Cherubini, had reservations about Liszt, disliked Berlioz's music but admired his journalism, and considered Mozart to be a universal musical genius.

Before leaving for Vienna, he had asked Cherubini for a letter of introduction to Beethoven, which Cherubini refused because he thought that Beethoven had too difficult a nature. He did give Trémont a letter for Haydn, who, however, died just before Trémont arrived in Vienna. Anton Reicha, who had known Beethoven well in Bonn days, finally gave Trémont the desired letter of introduction, though Reicha doubted it would be of use. Undaunted by reports of Beethoven's reclusiveness and greatly wishing to meet the man whose compositions he admired, Trémont, with difficulty, at last discovered where Beethoven lived. He knocked three times and was about to go away "when a very ugly and evidently ill-humored man opened the door."[6] The dapper Beethoven of the early portraits had metamorphosed into a stocky, somewhat ill-kempt individual.

Beethoven, who often abruptly turned away uninvited guests, was unexpectedly cordial to Trémont. They began to talk, the composer in bad French, Trémont in even worse German. While each spoke the other's language poorly, they understood it somewhat better. Even with Beethoven's increasing deafness, they managed to communicate.

Despite or perhaps because of such marked differences in temperament they hit it off well.

Trémont's written account of his encounters with Beethoven is one of the more reliable documents of its kind. He left us candid impressions of the man—unkempt appearance, irascibility, surly disposition—as well as of the utter disorder in Beethoven's lodgings. Most physical descriptions of Beethoven's abodes date from later times, but this of 1809 suggests that the composer's scruffy ways had a long history:

> Imagine all that is most filthy and untidy: puddles on the floor, a rather old grand piano covered in dust and laden with piles of music, in manuscript or engraved. Beneath it (I do not exaggerate) an unemptied chamber pot. The little walnut table next to it was evidently accustomed to having the contents of the inkwell spilled over it. A mass of pens encrusted with ink—and more musical scores. The chairs, most of them straw chairs, were covered with plates full of the remains of the previous evening's meal and with clothes, etc.

Granted, Trémont came upon Beethoven unannounced and also at a time when he lacked a servant. Still, he gives us an idea of how the composer lived.

What is also memorable in this account is Beethoven's friendliness, his willingness to talk to and share ideas with an admirer. Beethoven, having taken a fancy to him, Trémont tells us, "gave me many opportunites of meeting him during my stay in Vienna, and for my own benefit he improvised for me no less than one whole hour, no, two whole hours." Sometimes he would break off from playing and talk "about philosophy, religion, politics and especially about Shakespeare, his idol, and always in a language which would have made any listener had there been one burst out laughing." Beethoven, Trémont realized, "was not an *homme d' esprit*, in the sense of making polished and witty remarks. He was too taciturn by nature to permit a conversation with him to be spirited. He uttered his thoughts in jerks, they were exalted and generous, though often erroneous." In this regard Trémont compared him to Rousseau, a byword then for scandalous and erratic behavior. Beethoven was also unpredictable and contrary: "in his splenetic humour he sometimes desired that I should contradict him rather than defer to his own views."

The initial visit lasted three quarters of an hour. Then Trémont took his leave, "feeling prouder than Napoleon when he entered Vienna: I had conquered Beethoven." Parallels between Beethoven and Napoleon were not uncommon at this time, and it was probably easier for people to wangle an introduction to Napoleon than to Beethoven. In their conversations, they discussed the French emperor. When asked "whether he did not feel inclined to get to know France," Beethoven replied that he would have preferred to have done so "before France acquired an Emperor [Napoleon]." In other words, he responded more to the France of the Revolution than to Napoleonic France. Nonetheless, Beethoven said that he would have liked to have listened to Mozart's symphonies in Paris. In response to this Trémont said he "did not mention either his own nor those of Haydn in this connection."

They talked endlessly about the emperor of the French, even about going to Paris together. "The greatness of Napoleon preoccupied him and he often spoke to me about it. . . . He admired Napoleon's ascent from such a low beginning. It suited his democratic ideas." Proudly independent, Beethoven feared that in Napoleon's Paris he might lose the relative freedom he enjoyed in Vienna. He wondered out loud how Napoleon would receive him. He would receive him well, Trémont told him. "One day he remarked, 'If I should go to Paris, should I be obliged to pay a call on your Emperor?' I assured him of the contrary, unless he were expressly invited to do so. 'And do you think he would order me to attend on him?'" To which Trémont replied, "If Napoleon could judge who you are, then he would undoubtedly do so—but you've learned from Cherubini that he knows next to nothing about music."

Trémont explained to him why Napoleon had only a limited interest in music. "Napoleon was no musician—although it is said that he played the viola a little in his youth. His musical memories were bounded by the reign of Paisiello, an Italian composer of melodies and harmonies of a tranquil kind. He considered more clangorous compositions ill-conceived and disorderly; he did not understand them." But, increasingly aware of music's power to move others, Napoleon gradually became more attentive to its possible use as propaganda. "Not until 1806, after he'd heard the music of the Court of Saxony, at Dresden, did the Emperor begin to think that he, too, would like to have a musical establishment of a kind not exclusively religious." And what Napoleon wanted usually happened. "All artists of distinction who arrived in Paris were invited to sing or play at the Emperor's concerts, on the express condition that they would accept, in silver, some honorable recompense, proportionate to their merit." So seemingly generous a patron was unusual at this time.

Little wonder that Beethoven, long hopeful of a court position from the Hapsburgs and no doubt aware by now that he was unlikely to get one, expressed interest in going to Paris and meeting Napoleon. The possibility that Napoleon might have responded to Beethoven's music tantalizes the imagination. Egon Friedell, among the wisest and most sensitive of Vienna's twentieth-century men of letters, believed that if Napoleon had had Beethoven's music ringing in his ears instead of Paisiello's, he might well have transformed not only the history of music but Europe's destiny. On September 8, 1809, the *Eroica* was performed in Vienna. Beethoven must surely have hoped that Napoleon would attend. But at the last moment the emperor was called away.

Trémont offered to take Beethoven back to Paris in his private carriage and lodge him in his apartment, but the composer, who planned many trips but took few, retreated behind excuses. Once he said, "Your Parisians will say that I am a bear." Trémont would have none of it. He adroitly replied, "What does that matter to you?" Extolling the virtues of Parisians' open-mindedness, he tried to convince Beethoven that "distinguished men are accepted there exactly as they please to show themselves, and should one such, especially a stranger, be a trifle eccentric, that contributes to his success." Finally, after more discussion, Beethoven consented to go with him to Paris. As it turned out, Trémont was called away in July for a posting to Moravia and could not fulfill his end of the arrangement. Though he apparently returned to Vienna again for a few weeks in mid-October, whether he renewed his offer to Beethoven is unknown. In any event, the composer stayed put.

Such a relationship as Beethoven's with Trémont during a time of open war between France and Austria may seem an oddity. Trémont had good fortune in gaining access to Beethoven, but Beethoven, too, had good fortune in encountering Trémont. Here was someone on Napoleon's staff, a lover of music as well, who had firsthand knowledge of both the French emperor and Paris's musical scene. No doubt Trémont described and Beethoven visualized an idealized Paris. There was censorship there too, but it was less rigorously applied than in Vienna. Paris also had better doctors, and Beethoven may not yet have quite abandoned hopes of regaining his hearing. So, despite the contract with his patrons, he had been sorely tempted and had indeed agreed to go. A decade later, with the prospect of success and fame in London, he openly expressed the hope of going to the British capital, but again he did not go.

Neither on the surface totally pro or contra Napoleon for any sustained time, Beethoven's idealism would feed his obsession with Europe's dominant figure and most famous man. Although he lived in Vienna and had benefited from the largesse of his Viennese patrons, he had no desire to be considered a dutiful subject of Emperor Franz. Even when angered by Napoleon's actions, Beethoven tended to admire the greatness "in the republican," as Dahlhaus puts it, "and not merely the martial, sense."[7] And how in 1809, with Napoleon actually residing in Vienna, could Beethoven not be interested in him as he dreamed of a more fulfilled life? Napoleon could have become his patron. No man alive in Europe was quite like Napoleon, no man embodied better the possibilities of change. And, in Beethoven's understanding of human genius, no man in Europe was more like Napoleon than himself. Or so he liked to believe. With such thoughts he began a new concerto.

❧

The "Emperor" Concerto

Beethoven had completed his Fifth Piano Concerto, Op. 73, in the autumn of 1809. Though after his Akademie of that year he continued to play occasionally in public and wrote piano pieces until the early 1820s, the Fifth was his last piano concerto. The work bristles with military energy. In the first movement (Allegro) the solo pianist engages in a duel against the full power of the orchestra. In response to the orchestra's majestic opening chords, florid cadenzalike passages roll up and down the keyboard. With these difficult maneuvers, the soloist holds his own, but just. Its vitality established, the orchestra engages in a martial motif. The piano risks being overwhelmed, but rises vigorously to the call. It challenges the orchestra at every moment. It is the orchestra's equal. There is heroism in every note. Seized by a warlike fever, Beethoven—while writing the first movement—annotated the margins of his musical sketches with vibrant commentary: "Song of triumph for combat! Attack! Victory!" The movement proceeds at an unrelenting pace, with never a moment's hesitation. At about twenty minutes it is one of the longest he ever set down. "Certainly when a composer like Beethoven wrote the symphonies and piano concertos that we hear today in the concert hall," the distinguished pianist Emmauel Ax once said, "he expected that if a movement ended in a flourish, such as the first movement of the Fifth Piano Concerto, the audience would leap to its collective feet and let the composer [and pianist] know that they had triumphed." Napoleon had occupied Vienna, but Beethoven reigned as emperor of music. The concerto's second movement (Adagio un poco mosso) opens with a subdued orchestral prelude. The piano then enters quietly. It leads to the final movement (Rondo: Allegro), which begins with another eruption of the piano. Orchestra and piano alternate. The concerto closes with a roaring crescendo by the piano.

The music critic Alfred Einstein termed this E-flat-major Piano Concerto "the apotheosis of the military concept." It was for him "a sister work of the *Eroica*: the heroic element in the guise of the military."[8] France and Austria again confronted each other. In the margin of one of its manuscript pages Beethoven wrote: "Austria should punish Napoleon." Whatever the military realities between France and Austria, his words reveal how extremely polarized thoughts of Napoleon were amid Beethoven's inner tensions. Napoleon had appeared at one time to be a revolutionary, or at least a destroyer of established monarchies, but apparently he no longer was. Perhaps Beethoven during Trémont's visit already envisaged the conflict in this work.

He did not choose to have his new concerto played at this time before the Viennese public. Instead, the work only received its premiere two years later, on November 28, 1811, at Leipzig's Gewandhaus. Beethoven's protégé Carl Czerny was the soloist, and the performance was a triumph. When Czerny introduced it to Vienna in February 1812, it met, unsurprisingly, with failure. This characteristically Beethovenian piece radiates extraordinary energy, but for the Viennese energy in music proved hard to swallow.

Most of his life Beethoven lived within a mile or two of the Hofburg, Emperor Franz's official residence, located in Vienna's heart. The Hapsburgs prided themselves on mixing with all classes of society, and Beethoven on occasion may have seen the emperor in a street or park. But Franz thought his music "revolutionary," and with the probable exception of his youngest brother, Beethoven's pupil Archduke Rudolph, no Hapsburg is known ever to have attended one of his concerts. Furthermore, Franz lacked courage, whereas Beethoven embodied it.

After all, unlike the *Eroica*, Beethoven intended this concerto—his marginal comments leave us in no doubt—as a riposte to Napoleon. Beethoven is here continuing the combat he had launched in October 1806 after the Prussian defeats at Jena and Auerstadt. He had sworn then to contest the ground with Napoleon, and this he had done in his Akademie of December 22, 1808. Now he once again responded with his chosen weapon, the piano. Ultimately the only "emperor" the concerto crowns is Beethoven himself. When he wrote it he regarded himself as a chief opponent of Napoleon, one far more formidable than the Hapsburgs. It seems likely that, in some moods at least, the name his concerto acquired would not have displeased Beethoven. "Österreich lohne Napoleon," he commented on the manuscript, "Austria will make Napoleon pay."[9] The concerto would be a further response, belated but intensely focused, for Jena and Auerstadt and Louis Ferdinand, a battering ram against the emperor of the French, then residing only a few miles away in Schönbrunn.

Pianos at this time, we must remember, were rapidly evolving. In fact, as the eighteenth century yielded to the nineteenth, piano construction underwent a full-scale revolution. The piano was now poised to become one of the great implements of German Romanticism. Companies rivaled each other in the size, structure, and number of octaves of their pianos. The music available for the stronger pianos grew by leaps and bounds. The Fifth Concerto's martial vocabulary made its claim with a vengeance. About the time Napoleon's defeats of Austria's armies in Italy during the 1790s established his heroic credentials, the Romantic piano concerto established the soloist's capacity for pianistic heroism. Only now did a pianist have an instrument with which to play to advantage such a work as the Fifth Concerto.[10] Beethoven had early received a piano from the Streichers, Érard in Paris had sent him one of his, and in 1818 he received a Broadwood. The piano had become Beethoven's battlefield, as later it would become Liszt's. This very grand concerto, written in Beethoven's favorite key of E-flat-major, has the same tonality as the *Eroica* Symphony. Beethoven, at the helm, master of the piano, controls at least the solo part of his Fifth Concerto.

Had he not, this formidable new paladin of the piano, conquered aristocratic Vienna in the 1790s with his piano wizardry? Had he not, in fierce pianistic duels with Daniel Steibelt and others, his fingers fly-

ing across the keyboard, annihilated his opponents in the palaces of
the Viennese nobility? Had he not in his major compositions—the *Eroica*, the "Appassionata" Sonata, the "Razumovsky" Quartets, the Fifth
Symphony—shown himself capable of epic endeavor? The Fifth Concerto ranks among his greatest triumphs in the heroic mode. Beethoven
dedicated his new concerto to a young man he had come to value greatly,
the only Hapsburg for whom he felt affection and to whom he would
dedicate more works than to any other individual: his piano and composition student from 1809, Archduke Rudolph.

The "Emperor" Concerto was not all Beethoven set down during
the summer of 1809. Of his other compositions, a sonata for Archduke
Rudolph is perhaps the best known. Long his student and now his benefactor as well, Rudolph had left the city along with the other Hapsburgs early in May. Starting then, Beethoven wrote his sonata during
the summer of 1809. On the manuscript, at the beginning of the first
movement of "Les adieux," or "Das Lebewohl," Op. 81a, Beethoven has
also put down the date of Rudolph's departure, May 4, 1809. Both its
French and German names come out in English as "The Farewell." In
musical terms Beethoven bids his young friend godspeed on the road
to safety, reflects on his sense of loss, and looks forward to welcoming
him upon his return. His student, companion, and supporter is not
with him to share the discomfort of the French occupation. The pattern
of this sonata is thus one of departure, absence, and return. The first
movement (Adagio—Allegro), meditative and reflective, conveys the
sense of loss. It is followed by a burst of energy, which then leads to a
state of indecision that ends with two strong chords. The second movement (Andante espressivo) begins in an inquisitive mood, the playing
ever more softly, then closing with an explosion of sound. The positive
final movement (Vivacissimamente), looking forward to the return of
Rudolph, closes with a burst of joy. His student had returned. Despite
his relative youth and his status as Beethoven's only student, Rudolph
proved to be a true friend. "The Farewell" is one of only two sonatas to

which Beethoven appended a title. (The other is the "Pathétique.") The result is one of Beethoven's loveliest pieces of music.

Military themes pervade several other Beethoven compositions during the summer of 1809. He poured forth seven marches, band music designed for parades. Presumably they were commissions. Apparently on one occasion an Austrian officer told Beethoven that one of his marches went along too fast for the soldiers to keep up with. The composer replied, wittily if undiplomatically, that it was "for the retreat."

The Austrian army of this era has been characterized as a superb peacetime force with the best military bands in Europe. "The full-scale military parade was the one field on which the Austrian army was unbeatable," claims a leading American historian of Austria.[11] As Stefan Zweig observed a century after Beethoven, Austria was the only Great Power that consistently produced better bandmasters than generals. Austria's soldiers marched in beautiful uniforms. The difference in 1809 between the French forces and the Austrian was not hard to fathom. In the French army the soldiers fought for something and someone they believed in; in the Austrian, conscripts and paid professionals filled the ranks. Beethoven well knew what his military music was worth. "At the present moment," he wrote a friend in the autumn of 1809, "I have to devote far too much time to *potboilers*."[12]

Following the armistice declared at Znaïm in July 1809, the Peace of Vienna (sometimes known as the Treaty of Schönbrunn) was signed on October 14. It formally brought the Franco-Austrian war to a close, and with it ended the Fifth Coalition. Napoleon left Vienna on October 16; Franz slipped back into the city on November 26. The Viennese appeared to be overjoyed. Austria, however, now experienced major economic difficulties. Its coinage declined in value, and its paper notes, which it had produced in great abundance for the war effort, diminished rapidly in value. Napoleon refused to accept them as payment for the large Austrian war indemnity. In years to come the state's economic crisis would grow.

16

Composing *Egmont*

Man is born free, and everywhere he is in chains.

JEAN JACQUES ROUSSEAU

Not long after he composed the Fifth Piano Concerto and his Piano Sonata "Les adieux," Beethoven accepted a commission from the director of the court theater, Joseph Hartt von Luchsenstein, to write an overture and incidental music for Goethe's play *Egmont*. He had been hoping to gain the commission to compose music for a production of Schiller's *William Tell*, but, as Czerny recalled, "a mass of intrigues were hatched—either before the return of Emperor Franz in late November 1809 or shortly afterwards—to see that he got *Egmont*, which (it was hoped) was less suitable for music."[1] The director gave the *Tell* commission to Adalbert Gyrowetz, a Czech who, if forgotten today, had been the court theater's resident composer and conductor since 1804. In government circles Gyrowetz's credentials easily trumped Beethoven's.

Goethe would seem a good match for Beethoven, who deemed him the finest poet of the German-speaking world. Goethe recognized him as one of the few contemporaries equal in genius to himself and longed to meet the man who had achieved so much work that bore the stamp of greatness. *Faust* had seized Beethoven's imagination since its appearance in 1808, and he wished to write music for it, he told the writer Bettina von Arnim, "purely out of love for his poems, which make me feel happy."[2] This hope lasted until his death. He did compose music for several of Goethe's poems, Three Songs by Goethe for singer and piano, Op. 83, and he tackled his epic novel *Wilhelm Meister's Apprenticeship* and recommended it to others.

Goethe had long contemplated writing on the Tell legend. But whereas for Schiller Tell was the stuff of high drama, the trials of Tell were not for Goethe. Once when Beethoven was comparing Schiller with Goethe, he expressed the opinion that "Schiller's poetry is extremely difficult to set [to music]. The composer must be able to rise above the poet. Who can do that with Schiller? There Goethe is much easier!"[3] *Egmont* was the most political of Goethe's plays, yet in writing music for it Beethoven seems to have kept Schiller's *Tell* in mind.

In 1807 Viennese authorities relaxed and allowed several of Schiller's plays, including *Intrigue and Love* and *The Robbers*, to have their first performances in Vienna. During the French occupation in 1809 it became possible to buy complete editions of, among other writers, Schiller and Goethe. That summer we find Beethoven reading not only both authors but also Ossian, the enormously popular mythic bard created by a Scots writer James Macpherson, as well as returning to his longtime favorite, Homer.

Beethoven seems to have read Schiller's *William Tell* soon after its publication in 1804. It achieved a huge success, selling seven thousand copies within three months. When first performed in Weimar on March 17 of that year, it not only put into the shade other accounts of Tell but stamped unforgettably upon future generations the elusive life and spirit of the Swiss hero. Although set in Switzerland, *Tell* with its denunciation of harsh Austrian authority there had little chance of a full Vienna production. Even *Egmont*, which the theater management opted for, held risks, particularly with music by Beethoven, whose *Leonore* had needed the then empress's help to pass censorship and whose music many regarded as revolutionary. Still, even if Beethoven preferred *Tell*, he did splendidly with Goethe's play, providing in the music he wrote for it much of its drama. Yet *Tell*'s influence upon *Egmont*'s composition is significant and deserves recognition.

᷍

Tell vs. *Egmont*

In the Vienna of Franz I Schiller's works led a fitful existence. From 1793 to May 1807 the Austrian government had banned both texts and performances of his plays. Napoleon, upon arriving in the city in May 1809, closed the censorship office. The French occupation opened the city to works foreign, controversial, and containing progressive ideas. Napoleon allowed performances of *William Tell*, but after he left the city in October, Franz's chief minister, Metternich, made sure that performances of *Tell* were rare.

Perhaps in thinking of Schiller's drama as a subject for his music Beethoven recalled his Bonn years, when he had thrilled to performances of *The Robbers* and *Don Carlos*. Although he deemed Goethe the greater writer, he found irresistible the flash and fire in Schiller. He recognized that *Tell* had more of the revolutionary spirit of the *Eroica* and *Leonore* than did Goethe's *Egmont*. Schiller's play had also captured the popular imagination.

Tell's subject matter deals with the early fourteenth-century revolt against Austrian rule in three of the Swiss forest cantons as embodied in the bailiff, Hermann Gessler, the agent of the emperor, unmistakably Austrian. Gessler tyrannizes the local population. His policies include the torture of suspected dissidents. He places a hat upon a pole in the town square of Altdorf, the Austrian base in the canton of Uri, and decrees that since the hat represents Austrian authority, the townspeople must remove their own hats when passing before it. Those who do not face imprisonment or death. Somewhat apart from the main action stands William Tell, a freedom-loving hunter. While direct of speech, he is yet a man of enigmatic silences. Unaware that he is supposed to doff his hat before the pole, he walks by it. Gessler has him arrested and threatens him with death.

After taunting him about his prowess as an archer, Gessler informs Tell that if with his crossbow he can shoot an apple from his (Tell's) young son's head at eighty paces he will not have him executed. Tell undergoes an agonizing mental ordeal, but his aim is true and his son saved. Gessler then asks him why he had set aside a second bolt. Tell replies that if the first had killed his son he would have directed the second at Gessler. Upon hearing this, the bailiff has him placed in chains. They board a boat, a violent storm arises upon the lake, and the experienced Tell is called upon to steer the vessel to safety. His chains are removed and, maneuvering the boat close to shore, he leaps with his crossbow upon a rock.

Having boldly escaped his tormentor, Tell lies in wait for him in a narrow gorge that he knows Gessler's party must pass through. As the bailiff appears, a woman throws herself in front of his horse. She begs for aid in effecting the release of her husband, who languishes in prison. Gessler refuses brusquely, then tramples her under his horse's hooves. Tell, upon hearing him vow to institute harsh new laws to break peasant obstinacy and further reduce Swiss liberties, launches his second bolt— into Gessler's heart. He acts less from a sense of personal vengeance than to prevent the enslavement of his people. There was, after all, no system of justice to which he could appeal. He had to make his own justice and, incapable of untruth, openly admits his deed. The Swiss hero of Schiller's play soon became in German-speaking lands a symbol of the striving of a subject people for freedom and personal dignity.

Instead of the hoped-for deliverance of the Netherlands from Spanish rule adumbrated in *Egmont*, Beethoven preferred to write music depicting Tell's heroic nature. The hunter's belief in personal freedom understandably appealed to him. But recent events had eclipsed Tell's triumph: Napoleon had destroyed the freedom *William Tell* celebrates.

Given what the composer created for Pizarro, the outsized villain of *Leonore* (the opera that would become *Fidelio*), what kind of music would he have written to characterize the wily Gessler of *Tell?* Pizarro's music, harsh and dissonant, would have been appropriate for Gessler. In *Tell* the counterposing forces are the Swiss freedom fighters—and, it turns out, Tell himself. He acts amid other courageous figures young and old: Werner Stauffacher, Walter Fürst, Werner, Freiherr von Attinghausen. His fearless young son holds the promise of a heroism equal to his father's. Like Beethoven in *Leonore*, Schiller in *Tell* leaves no place for an intellectualized, abstract love of all humanity. Only battles fought in the real world would allow a better mankind to emerge.

A key factor in determining Beethoven's preference for Tell is that his being and deeds exemplified for him the bravery characteristic of his favorite hero of antiquity, Lucius Junius Brutus. Whereas Brutus's actions led to the establishment of the Roman Republic, Tell's deeds led to the eventual unification of the Swiss cantons. Brutus had a wife and two sons, as did Tell, yet both come across to posterity as lone individuals, independent, self-willed, perhaps not unlike Beethoven himself. Tell, a man not easily aroused, acts only in the face of injustice. The French revolutionaries had often linked him with Brutus. Like Brutus, Tell is in effect a tyrannicide. That his deed threatened to upset the structure of the society in which he lived did not deter him from acting. Similarly, Beethoven intended his music to serve as a mighty force for change, come what may.

Tell and Brutus often appeared together in France. In 1793 the Jacobin Club organized a festival, to last several days, to honor Tell along with Brutus. On the first day performances of both Voltaire's *Brutus* and A.-M. Lemierre's 1766 play *Tell*, which the Jacobins revised to meet their political needs, took place. Revolutionaries proclaimed that, despite the differing psychological make-up of the Swiss hunter and the Roman consul, a natural kinship existed between Tell and Brutus. Tell was usually, but not always, seen positively. For those unenthusiastic about the Revolution, he was the horrifying messenger of the Terror, a murderer, an accomplice of anarchy.[4] For the Jacobins, however, Tell was the pitiless avenger of an intolerable injustice, the heroic proclaimer of liberty. Tell had acted against Austrian tyranny; so too would Jacobin France. Busts of the two heroes adorned public buildings. For the revolutionaries, Brutus and Tell had both worked in the long struggle for liberty. Along with Brutus and other tyrannicides of the past, Tell served as a saint of the Revolution.

In the *Eroica* and other compositions Beethoven had embedded ideas of revolution. In a Europe ruled by absolutist kings and emperors, he had launched his works like crossbow bolts upon a startled public. And his aim was as true as Tell's. When basic beliefs were at stake, he was, like Tell, not a man to compromise. Freedom remained the fundamental motif of Beethoven's thought and music. If ultimate triumph was not then possible in the Hapsburg world, for the composer the battle was engaged, and he determined to give it his best.

Gyrowetz's production of *William Tell*, no doubt greatly altered and abridged, was performed on June 14, 1810, at the Theater an der Wien. Its fate may be inferred, however, when later that same year Hapsburg censorship again formally banned Schiller's play. Few versions of *Tell* made it past the censor in absolutist Europe. If performed, the official line was to interpret the Swiss hero as being in combat with the tyrant Napoleon, the new Gessler. After Napoleon's downfall in 1815 the Austrian government did allow occasional performances of *Tell* at the Hofburgtheater, the imperial Court Theater. Its popularity was virtually guaranteed to help reduce that playhouse's regular deficit; but with further revolutions in Europe in 1830 *Tell* disappeared from the boards in Vienna for some years.

After Napoleon left Vienna in October 1809, Emperor Franz returned to impose an even more strict censorship. In a Vienna once again under repressive Hapsburg rule, Beethoven's score for Goethe's *Egmont*, though longer and more complex than that for the greatly truncated version that is performed today, would on the surface not have seemed nearly as riot-inducing as music for *Tell* would have been.

ᕽ

Egmont and Goethe

Unlike Schiller, Goethe never gave himself fully to drama. Even in 1806, when Napoleon urged him to write a play on the death of Caesar, Goethe shied away from creating a heroic man of action. Set in Brussels in 1567–68, *Egmont* depicts an early stage of the revolt of the Low Countries against Spanish rule. Goethe had begun his *Egmont* in the early 1770s, when Beethoven was still in swaddling clothes, but only completed it in Rome in 1787. He was not altogether pleased with the result. The young Germans who were his companions in Rome, he commented, "being accustomed to my earlier, vehement, vigorous works, had expected something in the *Berlichingen* style, and could not immediately become reconciled to the calm pace."[5]

Unlike Schiller's Tell, Goethe's Egmont lacks real conflict in his being. Part of the problem lies in the nature of the protagonist himself. We see Egmont largely through the eyes of people who hardly know him and who respond only to his surface being. To them Egmont is a dead shot with the crossbow, ever a victor in battle, carefree, popular, easygoing, generous with money, and in love with a young woman below his station, Klärchen, who adores him. The mother of Egmont's inamorata believes Egmont "amiable and frank and easy," to which her smitten daughter adds courageous and modest. Whereas the citizens of Brussels evince pride in their leader, "his nonchalance and recklessness"— Egmont walks about as if he owned the world—worry and displease the Spanish regent.

The arrival in Brussels of the Duke of Alba precipitates a crisis. Alba would become the general who carried out the Spanish king Philip II's repressive policies in the Netherlands, the man responsible for the massacre of thousands of men, women, and children. He considered it better to lay an entire country waste than to leave it in the hands of Protestant heretics. For contemporaries and for future generations, he came to represent the unacceptable face of Spanish imperialism. Uncompromising, single-minded, determined, ruthless, he is *Egmont*'s Pizarro. He throws Egmont in prison, puts him on trial, and has him condemned to death.

Goethe attempted symbolic rather than literal history. *Egmont* presents dubious historical scenarios. Whereas Beethoven, with a talent for tense situations and strong emotions, expressed politics and passion through music compellingly dramatic, Goethe's dramas do not present a concrete society in time and place in the way that Shakespeare's plays reflect Elizabethan society. Goethe's characters are mythic, and he uses the form of historical drama less to focus on political intrigue than as a medium for advocating a certain idealism.

The opportunity to compose music for *Egmont* revived Beethoven's always latent interest in writing more for the stage and, despite *Leonore*'s problematic reception, more operas. Early in 1807 he had even proposed to the administration of the Theater an der Wien that in return for a fixed stipend he would commit himself to writing one opera a year for them. The directors did not take up his proposal, understandably given Beethoven's known difficulties with *Leonore*. Now, fresh from the Fifth Piano Concerto and a bevy of martial music during the summer of 1809, writing a score for *Egmont*, which became his Opus 84, provided him with a new opportunity. Although Schiller had prepared a three-act version of Goethe's *Egmont* in 1796, Beethoven took on Goethe's original version. During the winter of 1809–10 he worked on the score, which besides the overture comprises four entr'actes, as well as Klärchen's two songs (one a militaristic hymn, the other a larghetto depicting her death), a melodrama, and the concluding miniature, but immensely powerful, *Siegessymphonie*, or "Victory Symphony."

Though *Egmont* lacks the emotional and patriotic fireworks of *Tell*, it appealed to Beethoven, who had first read it with enthusiasm when an adolescent in Bonn. Besides, his beloved grandfather had come from the Low Countries. As his music for *Egmont* indicates, the long and heroic struggle of his ancestors for liberty from Spanish oppression resonated in his imagination. The yearning for liberty that weaves its way through Beethoven's life and music draws strength from his awareness of his Flemish inheritance. Except for a few fleeting periods in their history, Belgians, Flemish as well as Walloon, have rarely enjoyed liberty. Yet the Flemish people had a passionate love of liberty; and not just of liberty, but of independence carried to the farthest limit.

"I wrote it purely out of love for the poet," Beethoven told a correspondent regarding his music for Goethe's *Egmont*.[6] Beethoven's words imply that he set it down in part to keep in the good graces of the man whom he revered. The next year, writing to Goethe himself, he mentioned "my music for Egmont, that glorious Egmont."[7] One reason Beethoven may have found *Egmont* "glorious" was that Goethe set *Egmont* in prose. Thus it retains an affinity to his other early *Sturm und Drang* dramas. In a letter to Therese Malfatti of May 10, 1810, Beethoven cites Egmont's words to Ferdinand, imprisoned and facing death, in Act 5: "People are united not only when they are together; even the distant one, the absent one is present with us."[8] In some ways, Egmont's closest parallel is with the idealistic Marquis of Posa in Schiller's *Don Carlos*. King Philip II punishes his idealism by having both him and Don Carlos killed, just as the Duke of Alba in the play deceives and executes Egmont.

The murder of the historical Egmont galvanized resistance to Spanish rule in the Low Countries. Egmont, though himself a devout Catholic, had urged Philip II of Spain to recognize the yearnings of Protestants for freedom, a position that branded him as a rebel and led to his arrest and punishment. Perhaps in the creation of his *Egmont* Beethoven looked for yearnings for freedom in the Europe of 1809–10. Like *Leonore*, *Egmont* ends with a dramatic hymn to womanly courage and the desire of a people for liberty.

Recalling Schiller's Posa in *Don Carlos* and, even more, the titular hero, Goethe's Egmont is a problematic figure, full of idealism, and even in his naivety displaying impetuosity and courage. Spain kept the Netherlands under tight control. The local situation remained tense. In Goethe's play the Duke of Alba, Spain's harshest commander, is on his way to root out dissent among the disgruntled populace. Egmont is governor of Brussels. Though liked by the people, he has not assessed the dangers of his situation carefully. When we meet him, he has a devil-may-care attitude toward his responsibilities: "It's my good fortune to be cheerful, to take life easy, to travel light and fast, and I will not exchange these for the security of a tomb." He asks, "Should I forbid myself to enjoy the present moment, so as to be certain of the next? And consume the next moment too with cares and apprehensions?"[9] The implied answer, for him at least, would be a resounding no. Yet Egmont is courageous, doesn't fear death, and genuinely loves Klärchen.

Egmont's view of life, romantic, even poetic, is thoroughly impractical. Death, provided it be quick, does not hold terror for him: "If I must fall, let a thunderbolt, a gale, even a false step hurl me down to the depths." When the Prince of Orange recommends caution to him and urges him to leave Brussels, he dismisses his concerns. Egmont lacks "subtlety," says the character Vansen, a man of the people. "He shouldn't be so trusting."[10] But Egmont is trusting, and foolish as well.

Schiller, hugely dissatisfied with Goethe's rendering of character and event, wrote upon the play's publication a sharply critical review entitled "On Goethe—*Egmont*," in which he put his finger squarely on the key issue:

> Is not the intention of the play to present the portrait of a hero? In their fight for freedom the people of the Netherlands have centered their whole love on this Count Egmont; they look to him to liberate them from the Spanish yoke. But in what respect has the amiable Count earned the right to our sympathy? What are his merits? But of these we hear next to nothing; it is only his weaknesses that are paraded for us.[11]

The hero's wavering reflects Goethe's own wavering.

A far more dynamic figure in *Egmont* than the titular hero is his beloved, Klärchen, who wants to wear trousers so that she can follow her lover to war. In her first aria she sings, "To be a man, what happiness without equal!" Mignon in Goethe's *Wilhelm Meister's Apprenticeship* also refuses to dress like a girl, and Leonore dresses like a man to gain employ in the prison that may hold her husband. Klärchen, unlike her fellow citizens whom she harangues, scorns danger. To the citizens of Brussels Klärchen cries out, "I have what all of you lack—courage and contempt for danger!" "My heart beats faster than all your hearts," she tells them. A new Joan of Arc in the offing? An unmarried Leonore? But no, the difficulties are insuperable. After Egmont falls into the trap set for him by the Duke of Alba, she and her ally Brackenberg try, and fail, to organize a popular uprising to save him.

To the sleeping Egmont awaiting execution, Klärchen appears as a vision of "Liberty in heavenly raiment, shining." She embodies the freedom he has lost. "Divine Liberty, borrowing my beloved's features and shape," he cries out. Unlike Florestan and Tell, Egmont dies. Only in Klärchen's radiant words does liberty triumph. When she sees the dead Egmont she utters a cry of horror. Her efforts to save her beloved having failed, she commits suicide by taking poison. Her bold language inevitably recalls the "I have courage and strength" of that other "Angel of Freedom," Leonore.

Though deeply flawed as a leader, Egmont, like Florestan, is a fighter for justice and freedom. Goethe wills that Egmont's life and death inspire future generations to continue the seemingly perpetual combat against invested tyranny. Beethoven's music gives this goal full support. Completing what the initial overture had announced, he climaxes Goethe's play with a brief Finale, a "Victory Symphony" depicting Egmont's death and posthumous triumph. Like the third *Leonore* overture, and even more the second, it encapsulates brilliantly the drama's essence. The "symphony" that closes the work expresses his revolutionary sentiments.

᧞

Egmont Staged

Egmont was initially presented without Beethoven's music on May 24, 1810, at the Hofburgtheater. Not until June 1 did audiences hear it accompanied by his music. Although the composer's vigorous score undergirded the drama onstage, the production does not appear to have been a success. According to contemporary reports, the work was poorly performed and left little impact upon the audience. Amazingly, Austrian authorities did not interfere with the performance, presumably because they had commissioned the work. *Egmont*'s initial audiences, knowing that government spies might be sitting near them, may have responded tepidly to Klärchen's arias and to Beethoven's music. Expressing positive emotion before so dramatically powerful a plea for liberty might have made those attending uneasy. Such enthusiasm could provoke reprisals. The authorities, as they did at *Leonore*'s revival as *Fidelio* four years later, promoted the play as a metaphor of deliverance from Napoleon's yoke. It was not an interpretation intended by Beethoven.

In mid-1810, perhaps because of *Egmont*'s lack of public success, Beethoven had given evidence of depression. A few months before completing the string quartet he called "Serioso" (Serious), Op. 95, he had written to his Bonn friend Franz Wegeler, "If I had not read somewhere that no one should voluntarily quit this life so long as he can still perform a good deed, I would have left this earth long ago—and, what is more, by my own hand."[12] The "Serioso" is the only one of his quartets for which Beethoven himself supplied a name. Creating it slowly relieved his depression.

Egmont's score, published in 1811, reached Goethe in the late spring. Beethoven expressed to him his admiration for *Egmont*, "which I have felt and reproduced in music as intensely as I felt when I read it."[13] Beethoven may have meant that only now had he fully put himself into the lives of its principal characters. He was anxious to know Goethe's response to what he had done and asked him to tell him what he thought, even if he didn't like it. Although generally unresponsive to Beethoven's works, which upset and on occasion even terrified him, Goethe regarded Beethoven's incidental music to his drama favorably, especially the passage during Egmont's sleep: "I expressly gave instruction that his slumbers should be accompanied by music," he commented, "and Beethoven entered into my intentions, admirably demonstrating his genius." Beethoven's score for *Egmont* would be as close as he ever came to an active collaboration with Goethe.

꒦

Meaning in *Egmont*

Beethoven's ideal of heroism in *Egmont* links it to the *Eroica* and the Fifth Symphony. His music conveys Goethe's vision of heroism more effectively than do Goethe's own words. Beethoven was, let us admit, a *Rühestörer*, a "disturber of the peace," a man who wished to remind his fellow citizens that change was possible, if not imminent. So the authorities viewed him, and so he viewed himself. The energy of a revolutionary age pulses through *Egmont*'s score. In this regard Goethe's drama served Beethoven well. Few who heard the *Egmont* Overture would have doubted that it supports public heroism and implies its ultimate triumph. Though Egmont dies, the ideals he represents will prove lasting.

The nineteenth century witnessed the heyday of historical drama. The military theme is everywhere implied in the music for *Egmont*, whose "Victory Symphony" ends with an uplifting glorification of Klärchen's heroism. Beethoven took Goethe's thoughtful play and, to a degree, transformed it into a vibrant Schillerian drama. "But who can escape the onslaughts of tempests raging around him?" the composer asked in a bitter moment (May 2, 1810). Beethoven did not specify which tempests or what caused them, but no doubt Vienna's repressive political situation gnawed at his mental peace. He railed against the authorities. To whatever degree he resented the French occupation of Vienna in

1809, he continued to admire the French emperor. As Trémont's reminiscences (discussed in Chapter 15), indicate, Napoleon's impact upon Beethoven's imagination was as enduring as it was unpredictable.

❧

Napoleon's New Bride

The emperor's victory at Wagram (July 5–6, 1809) had ended the war with Austria. The battle left Vienna full of grieving families; the wounded filled the streets. The Treaty of Vienna signed on October 14, 1809, imposed a huge, ultimately crippling, indemnity upon defeated Austria. As he departed from the Austrian capital, Napoleon ordered sections of the city walls demolished. Furthermore, he now enforced the Continental Blockade more rigorously than before. Designed to prevent trade between Britain and the Continent, it undermined the British economy and further isolated that maritime nation. Its renewed enforcement affected most Europeans adversely.

Austria after Wagram quickly resumed outwardly cordial relations with France. The country's latest military defeat, humiliating in terms of national pride, led to still another treaty with France. In 1809 and for several years afterwards the French emperor, invincible in the field, master of Europe's destiny, appeared at the climax of his career. But he was aware of his empire's fragility. Though Empress Josephine had two children by a previous marriage, she had not provided him with an heir. As a stopgap, he had designated the children of his brother Louis as his heirs, but, still young, would they ensure the survival of his dynasty? Safer would be having an heir of his own. "I want to marry a royal womb," he said, with characteristic bluntness. Reluctantly, for he had loved Josephine, he decided in late 1809 to seek an annulment of their marriage and find another bride. His first choice was a sister of Tsar Alexander, the Grand Duchess Anna, but when she proved recalcitrant (she was but fifteen) and Alexander uninterested, the forty-year-old emperor turned to Europe's most ancient and perennially fruitful dynasty, the Hapsburgs. He courted by proxy the youngest daughter of Emperor Franz, the eighteen-year-old Archduchess Marie Louise.

With an empty treasury, the economy reeling, and Austria hoping to avoid a future war, Franz proved receptive. The Hapsburgs, as one contemporary put it, had no qualms about making an offering to the French Minotaur. As a means to recoup Austria's fortunes, Metternich approved the marriage and set out to displace Russia as France's chief ally. Well aware that the choice of husbands was not hers to make, Marie Louise accepted the inevitable. Napoleon dispatched Marshal Louis-Alexandre Berthier to Vienna to settle the matter. The marriage took place there by proxy on March 11, 1810. Two days later, Marie Louise left for Paris. This union, uniting Europe's two main land powers, was meant to stabilize Europe. Though many in the Austrian empire's vast domains expressed dissatisfaction, the war-weary Viennese rejoiced.

~

A Dedication

Beethoven in 1809 had good reason to complain about his worsening financial condition. Like Woyzeck's anguished cry in Georg Büchner's famous play "I can no longer understand the world," Beethoven no longer understood what was happening. He valued order over disorder. "What do you say to this *dead peace?*" he asked in November after the French had left: "I no longer expect to see any stability in this age."[14] After this second occupation, he became even more disillusioned with the city and its citizenry. But the tone of his letters had been more sharply anti-Viennese than anti-French. Though lamenting his "continually disturbed existence," Beethoven surprisingly does not specifically mention the French occupation. "Curse this war," he says in effect in letters of this time, not "curse the French."[15] At best, Beethoven kept his distance from the Viennese; at worst, he vented his irritation over the discomforts and frustrations of life in his adopted city.

In October 1810, to top off the bizarre concatenation of events during the previous year, Beethoven pondered whether to dedicate his Mass in C, nearly two years after its first performance, to, of all people, Napoleon. Dedicating a mass to the French emperor seemed perfectly logical to Beethoven. The man who had preferred the revolutionary triumphs of *Tell* over the failure in *Egmont* showed in his desired choice of dedicatee for the Mass in C no diminution of his natural feistiness. Given the possibly dire consequences of such an act for him in Vienna, it took courage for Beethoven even to consider a dedication of his Mass to Napoleon.

If by October 1810 the French emperor had returned to Beethoven's favor, it seems unlikely he had ever fallen completely out of it. That in regard to the Mass Napoleon was hardly a believer would have mattered little to Beethoven. Though deeply spiritual, the composer himself was not overtly religious and by no means a devoted son of the Church. Maynard Solomon deems Beethoven's intention to dedicate the Mass in C to the French archdemon Napoleon "extraordinary," which it is, but he misjudges the circumstances. Given the interwoven context of European politics and Beethoven's belief that Napoleon's rule would be better than Franz's, such a dedication made good sense. He saw Napoleon as the only leader who could bring down the monarchies, who could promote change. The greater openness of art and literature during the French occupation of Vienna was preferable to Franz's ever-harsher censorship. Besides, early in 1810 Franz had agreed to allow his youngest daughter to be given in marriage to Napoleon.

Austria's truce with Napoleon's France no doubt made it easier, though still problematic, for Beethoven to wish to dedicate a major work to the former archenemy. It may not have been politic, but it indicates Beethoven's respect for greatness achieved under difficult conditions and maintained under duress. Such greatness had been the achievement of Tell, and such an achievement as Napoleon's Beethoven could and did respect. But even in this year of reconciliation he found such a dedication to the former (and potentially future) archenemy too risky politically, and in default dedicated his Mass to Prince Kinsky, one of his trio of benefactors.

It seems Beethoven could not long remain angry at Napoleon. One reason why he rarely criticized Napoleon during these years—even when he had ample cause—was that in effect he would have been criticizing himself: the heroic figure who both resisted and admired Napoleon, who in his own realm of music sought to reign as triumphant as Napoleon in his. Napoleon was the only man in Europe, Goethe excepted, whom Beethoven deemed worthy of his highest esteem. He and Napoleon may at times have stood on different sides of an ongoing conflict, but in an age before rampant nationalism had overrun Europe, such divergences mattered less than they would a few years later. Not blinded by patriotic sentiment, Beethoven could respond to Napoleon's greatness. So went his attitude toward Napoleon year after year: full of lurking, unpredictable mood swings, back and forth, one day anger, the next adulation: a wildly oscillating reaction, not exactly love, not exactly hate, but reflecting a continuing turbulence of soul. Napoleon, without ever knowing it, held—and kept—Beethoven in thrall.

ꙅ

Finances

Austria had several times devalued its currency to pay the heavy war reparations. The economy tottered. The nation's worsening financial situation began to affect Beethoven's mode of life. Eventually on February 10, 1811, the state decided on a *Finanz-Patent* and three weeks later put it in force. It introduced an emergency paper currency, consisting of redemption bonds for banknotes that reduced the currency to a fifth of its former value. Beethoven's income, stabilized early in 1809 by an agreement with his three patrons, now dropped precipitously in real value. The four thousand gulden guaranteed him monthly in 1809 were by 1811 worth, at best, approximately sixteen hundred. Having a sharp head for business, Beethoven gradually renegotiated his contract.

Even the docile Austrian population, hard put to manage in the difficult times that prevailed, began to show signs of restlessness.

Tensions in Beethoven's Viennese life again came to the fore. Xaver Schnyder von Wartensee, a fellow composer who sought Beethoven's tutelage at this time, recalled that "he rail[ed] against the Viennese and would like to leave [Vienna]. 'From the Emperor down to the last shoe polisher,' he says, 'the Viennese are all a worthless lot.' " Early 1812 seems to have been a particularly onerous time. "Cursed be life here in Austria's barbarous country," wrote Beethoven on February 2.[16] He plotted escape. "If only Heaven will give me patience until I have gone abroad," he lamented.[17] In May he spoke of the city as "the sewer where I am living."[18] In July he sighed, "my life in V[ienna] at present is a miserable life."[19] Even if such statements may occasionally be tongue-in-cheek, they occur so often in Beethoven's letters that they leave us in no doubt that the professions of Austrian patriotism attributed to him by recent Viennese cheerleaders are false. But, though he did not realize it, the situation was already improving dramatically.

17

Bacchus Triumphant

THE SEVENTH SYMPHONY—THE EIGHTH—
WELLINGTON'S VICTORY

The daimonic is the power of nature, poetry,
and music, religion and patriotic enthusiasm of the
wars of liberation. Napoleon and Byron were daimonic.

GOETHE

Thus, usually, when he was ask'd to sing,
He gave the different nations something national;
'Twas all the same to him—"God save the king,"
Or "Ça ira," according to the fashion all.

BYRON[1]

For decades visitors to the Metropolitan Museum of Art in New York, ascending the grand staircase to its upper-floor galleries, could look up and see a huge bust of Beethoven by the French sculptor Émile-Antoine Bourdelle. The composer sits high on his pedestal. He looks down, we look up. Obsessed with Beethoven, Bourdelle created during his lifetime over twenty different interpretations of the composer's countenance. All are dramatic and compelling, but the Metropolitan's bust is among the largest and most powerful. Bourdelle called it *Bacchus*. In so doing he drew upon words written by Bettina Brentano, an acquaintance of both Beethoven and Goethe. In a letter to the poet in 1811, she claimed Beethoven had identified himself to her as Bacchus, a deity the composer venerated. "Music is the wine that stimulates man to new achievements," he had said. Recognizing that music was his special gift, he associated it with the classical divinity. "I am Bacchus, pressing this divine nectar for man in order to make him spiritually drunk."[2] Bourdelle inscribed the words in French at the base of the bust.[3] Of the sculptors who have portrayed Beethoven, Bourdelle captured an essence often overlooked or downplayed by others.

This magnificent yet troubled Beethoven looks down upon us threateningly. Masses of unruly hair hide almost entirely the ears that have failed him.[4] Yet Bourdelle was aware of the composer's ability to enjoy himself. On February 10, 1811, Beethoven tells Bettina Brentano he found himself at a gathering "where I really had to laugh a great deal."[5] For Bourdelle, Beethoven as Bacchus symbolized not only the intoxication of wine but a joyous exuberance, a Schillerian "joy," the joy that Beethoven would later express in the choral movement of his Ninth Symphony as "the Daughter of Elysium."

Beethoven was indeed a devotee of Bacchus. The Roman counterpart of the Greek god Dionysus, he represents both sides of ecstasy, the creative frenzy of the life-affirming side and the destructive frenzy of annihilation that tears things apart. Being a man who enjoyed a night out, Beethoven knew well the outward manifestations of Bacchus's power. Along with wine and laughter, good company formed for him an integral part of any Bacchanalian revelry. Wine could also incite creative fervor. "Music is a higher revelation than all wisdom and philosophy," Beethoven told Bettina. It is "wine which inspires one to new generative processes."[6] Beethoven found this sense of ecstasy in composing music, notably in his Seventh and Eighth Symphonies.

The force behind what Beethoven termed "generative processes" Goethe called "the daimonic," a powerful, often irrational force that drives imaginative beings and can erupt into creativity. The German sage continually pondered the daimonic. Manifest in some humans and in certain cultural practices, it essentially animated natural phenomena. From Goethe's perspective, the daimonic can even underlie a patriotic fervor for revolutionary change, which he found evident in the American Revolution. Among individuals who possessed the daimonic in the highest degree, Goethe included Napoleon, Byron, and Beethoven. His reflections on the daimonic illumine Beethoven's Bacchic dimensions. To understand Beethoven's and Napoleon's lives we need to keep the daimonic in historic context. Its manifestations could be diverse. Whereas in 1812 the daimonic compelled Napoleon to invade Russia, it led Beethoven to create his Seventh and Eighth Symphonies.

⇃

1812

The year 1812 marked another turning point in Beethoven's life. The interwoven strands of turmoil he experienced—emotional, financial, intellectual, and political—taxed his patience and energy. Believing himself unappreciated and at times scorned in Vienna, he felt he lived in a hostile city. In a January 28, 1812, letter to his Leipzig publisher Breitkopf & Härtel he declared himself "a poor Austrian musical drudge."[7] The letter marks one of the very few instances in which the composer spoke of himself as a citizen of his adopted homeland. In letters of this time, as well as others written earlier and later, he railed against Austria and its people, seeing them as a foreign force. Of the dozens of references to both not one can be construed as favorable. Even if his statements are occasionally half-serious, or expressions of frustration, they occur so often that they must have validity. The concatenation of events at home and elsewhere led Beethoven to commence a *Tagebuch*, or journal. Doing so offered him perspective as well as solace. He kept it for six years.

Private orchestras or quartets supported by wealthy aristocrats had nurtured Beethoven's early successes. Now they were failing. His patron Prince Kinsky died in a horseback accident in 1812; his initial patron, Prince Lichnowsky, would die in 1814; Prince Lobkowitz died two years later. On New Year's Eve 1813 Count Razumovsky's huge palace on the Landstrasse, along with his superb art collection, went up in flames.

The crestfallen prince had to dismiss his private orchestra. Few aristo-crats could still support a music group; or if they did, it had to be on a smaller scale than before. Thus Beethoven's income dropped. He sold manuscript scores and earned money from his Akademies, which grad-ually became one of his chief ways to support himself. Even when his compositions proved popular in elite circles, the Hapsburgs remained indifferent, even hostile, to both his music and its creator. Except for Archduke Rudolph, who continued to study piano and composition with him, Beethoven now had no other students.

֍

The Napoleonic Collapse

Napoleon's Russian campaign loomed over the summer of 1812. The French emperor had brought to the Russian border half a million men, the greatest military force ever assembled on European soil. On June 24 Napoleon led it across the river Niemen, thus entering Europe's largest state. The fate of the Continent hung upon the outcome. If Napoleon succeeded in humbling Russia, the balance of power would undergo a further shift in favor of France. If Napoleon should fail, his far-flung empire might collapse. Either outcome would likely affect Beethoven's life and the music he wrote.

That summer vague and often conflicting reports from Russia trick-led back to Western Europe. The Russians refused to negotiate with Napoleon or to engage with his forces. Their troops steadily retreated. Adopting a scorched-earth strategy, they burned their cities behind them. In the autumn Europeans heard reports of the bloody but incon-clusive battle of Borodino (September 7), a hundred miles short of Mos-cow. A week later, French troops entered the undefended city, which the Russians had abandoned and set on fire.

Even now they refused to negotiate. His opponents, Napoleon real-ized belatedly, had outfoxed him. His army, through combat and dis-ease, was down to about one hundred thousand fighting men. On

October 19 it abandoned Moscow and began the slow retreat back to France. Weeks passed as it retraced its path through forests and steppes, fending off Cossack attacks, increasing cold, and snowstorms. The army gradually exhausted itself amid the immensities of an unknown land. Lack of supplies caused thousands to perish. During the crossing of the ice-filled river Beresina (November 25–26) one of the pontoon bridges collapsed, leaving many behind to face the pursuing Cossacks. The survivors plodded on. Increasingly disorganized and now suffering from severe winter conditions, the army gradually disintegrated. When news of an attempted coup d'état in Paris—the conspiracy of General Claude-François de Malet on October 23–26—reached the emperor late in November, he left what remained of his shattered force on December 5 and raced back to his capital. By December 13 a remnant of the once great French army crossed the Niemen. Few of those who had passed the river in June returned alive.

In the autumn and early winter scattered and fragmentary reports of an extraordinary disaster began to filter back to an astonished Europe. That Napoleon's Grande Armée had undergone a catastrophic collapse in Russia seemed almost impossible to credit. With each passing day the reports became more ominous. In effect, they confirmed that Napoleon's army hardly existed anymore. In the face of so unexpected a development, everyone speculated but few dared predict what might happen next. Did the army's ill-fated retreat mark the beginning of the end of Napoleon's vast empire? Would the European powers combine to eject him from Europe? Or would he rally, rise again, and reassert France's hegemony? The debacle in Russia led many to ponder an almost unimaginable state of affairs: for the first time in a decade the possibility of a continent no longer cowering under Napoleon's huge shadow. The emperor had been humbled: a liberating thought for many, but for others dismaying.

♆

The "Immortal Beloved"

While Napoleon struggled in Russia, Beethoven in the summer of 1812 visited the spa town of Teplitz, then in Austria, now in the Czech Republic. There he sought to reconnect with the unknown woman known to posterity as the "Immortal Beloved."

"My angel, my all, my very self." So Beethoven begins his famous letter from Teplitz on July 6 to this lady. In it he passionately expresses his longing for an everlasting union with her. She seems to have been very much in love with him as well. In the course of the letter he repeatedly proclaims his ardent desire for "my only sweetheart, my all." But he also reminds her that such feelings as theirs require perseverance and total commitment. "Can our love endure without sacrifices," he asks, "without our demanding everything from one another?" There is realism here no less than passion. But was this letter, or a version of it, ever sent?

For reasons unknown Beethoven did not succeed in his hopes. The realization that he could not attain the partner of his dreams led to immense anguish. No one to this day has convincingly identified the lady in question, but scholarly speculation continues. Wonderful as it would be to discover the intended recipient of this probably unsent letter, what should interest us even more is what it tells us about Beethoven. For him, this passionate love likely was his greatest and most lasting. Although for complex reasons he never married, the letter presents a man who over the years had thought deeply about what true, enduring love demanded, a man who not only yearned for a committed relationship but who also worked hard to achieve one.

Later that July he met Goethe on several occasions in Teplitz. Perhaps as painful to Beethoven's psyche as the loss of his Immortal Beloved was his failure to achieve a meaningful relationship with the man whose genius and wisdom he then revered above all others. Temperamentally they were far apart, and conversation, given Beethoven's fading hearing, no doubt proved difficult. Goethe found Beethoven's being *ungebändigt*, literally, "untied" or "unpredictable." Beethoven's disillusionment with Goethe in Teplitz, although unstated, must have saddened him immensely. Each a genius, they had a different order of talent and hopes for humanity. The best-known incident of their time together in Teplitz has Beethoven and Goethe walking along an allée as a party of aristocrats, by some accounts members of the Austrian royal family, approached. Goethe stepped deferentially to the side, bowing politely. Beethoven walked right through them, acknowledging no one.

No doubt everyone taking the waters in Teplitz that summer pondered Napoleon's campaign in Russia. Could the French emperor go beyond what he had already accomplished? It seemed unlikely. We might say the same about Beethoven. After the *Eroica, Leonore,* the Fifth and Sixth Symphonies, the Fourth and Fifth Piano Concertos, the Mass in C, and *Egmont,* what peaks remained for him to conquer? In his life he had to deal with financial uncertainty, the stress of living in Vienna, his frustration in not forging a friendship with Goethe, and his failure to achieve union with the Immortal Beloved. But he still had his creative gift.

ৎ

The "Heroic" Period

Beethoven's "heroic" period, roughly the decade from 1802 to 1812 (or, if we include his revised opera, *Fidelio,* to 1814), spans almost exactly the years of Napoleon's empire. During the years in which the emperor controlled most of Europe, when everyone talked about his being and deeds, Beethoven had written music of exceptional energy and power.

The Revolution in France had changed traditional notions of heroism. Napoleon's startling career furthered the belief that, by honing skills and working hard, an able individual, regardless of his social status, could achieve recognition on his own merits. Under the ancien régime, only aristocrats occupied the ranks of officers, which was true across monarchical Europe. By contrast, most of Napoleon's marshals came from the people. Marshal Michel Ney's father worked as a cooper, Joachim Murat's ran a tavern. The sons earned their rank by their bravery and skills. The revolutionary and "Napoleonic" encouragement to live up to one's potential, to realize the new opportunities that life and society offered, inspired a generation. While the decades between the outbreak of the Revolution and Napoleon's fall featured, alongside much idealism, constant wars and ever-evolving political alliances, many liberally inclined Europeans interpreted these seemingly contradictory factors as leading eventually to changes sorely needed in society.

ৎ

Bacchus

Bourdelle, we recall, entitled one of his powerful busts of Beethoven *Bacchus*. Franz Klein's life mask of Beethoven in 1812 also reportedly captures him, presumably at his request, as Bacchus. Beethoven considered himself allied with Bacchus, the Roman god who found ecstasy through drinking wine.

Like Dionysus, the earlier Greek god who emerged from the East and from whom the Roman god derived, Bacchus inhabited a world in which miracles happen. The only god both of whose parents were not divine, he is like no other classical deity. Bacchus spawned bacchantes as his minions, who sang and played music on double-pipe instruments. These mythic followers of Bacchus engaged in revelries, orgiastic rituals, and, frenzied by wine, were filled with a fierce ecstasy. Drink reveals human brutishness in lust and violence, yet it can inspire song. Virgil in his sixth *Georgic* provides an otherworldly perspective: "The music struck the valleys and the valleys tossed it to the stars."[8]

Tolstoy in his *Kreutzer Sonata*, his unsettling tale responding to Beethoven's score of that name, defines music as the "refined lust of the senses."[9] Its power, he believes, is Bacchic. Others agree. For the French writer André Suarès, "the musician is always sublime, always Dionysian."[10] Bacchus, the historian Philip Blom observes, "leads his followers on a frenzied Bacchanalia." He expressed himself chiefly through dance and drama. He had the power, Blom tells us, "to seduce and to intoxicate, a power the god used freely, usually with a fortunate outcome."[11] The influence of Bacchus on music, in short, is thoroughly imaginative, endlessly creative, ceaselessly varied, rampant with ideas. Like a Goethe poem, one word flowing into the next, one line merging with that following, a Beethoven composition overflows with musical ideas. The *Eroica*'s Scherzo and Finale proceed in a state of almost continual ecstasy. The unrelenting Finale of the Fifth Symphony possesses an even more determined frenzy. It lasts a long time, and whenever we expect it to stop, it roars along.

Bacchus is a sufferer, afflicted by his own pain. He dies and rises again. The ethos of Bacchus manifests itself in two ideas: the pursuit of freedom and ecstatic joy on the one hand, the expression of maniacal destruction on the other. And he is long-lived: Bacchus is the only god of Rome who remains a living influence today. Goethe noted that Dionysus, who becomes Bacchus, is the force behind revolution; as a daimonic force, Bacchic urges erupt from primal nature, overwhelming rational social constructs. They lead to vertiginous realms of creation, sensual arousal, the fullest expression of emotions. After the fall of the Bastille and in the initial pre-Terror stages of the French Revolution, many in France and abroad, ecstatic with joy, expressed their exuberance in song.

In *The Birth of Tragedy* Nietzsche developed his influential theory regarding the opposition of the Dionysian and the Apollonian. "Man," thought Nietzsche, "tugs himself in two opposite directions. One is the Greek god of wine, Dionysus, who represents the feeling part of man: vital, creative, inspired but, if carried to excess, deranged and destructive. The other is Apollo, the sun god, who stands for the reasoning part of man, drawn towards order, systems, and justice—with the risk, of course, of deadening over-organization." The question for Nietzsche is, "Can life be passionate, alive, Dionysian, without spinning off into chaos? Can life be orderly, totally reasonable, Apollonian, without becoming as sterile as a dentist's office?" Although Beethoven endeavored to keep emotion under a tight rein, harnessing his creativity required herculean discipline. Music of the ancien régime—of Haydn, Mozart, and their contemporaries—had pleased and soothed Viennese audiences. Not so Beethoven's revolutionary music. It jolted, even terrified them.

Apollo, no less potent in his sphere than Bacchus in his, is the Roman god of light, of reason, of the arts. "Noble simplicity and tranquil grandeur": with these words Johann Joachim Winckelmann, the eighteenth-century German classical scholar, characterized Apollonian genius. Winckelmann, having explored Greek and Roman ruins in southern Italy, enlightened contemporaries about the Apollonian aspects of Greek art. Three centuries before, Michelangelo had sculpted Bacchus in Florence. The Bacchic (or "daimonic," to use Goethe's sometime term) element in Beethoven's music incarnates an essential aspect of his genius. Coleridge in his *Biographia Literaria* insists that poetry needs to embody Apollonian as well as Bacchic elements: "Poetry, even that of the loftiest, and, seemingly, that of the wildest odes, ha[s] a logic of its own, as severe as that of science; and more difficult, because more subtle, more complex, and dependent on more, and more fugitive causes. In the truly great poets . . . there is a reason assignable, not only for every word, but for the position of every word."[12] Similarly does Apollonian discipline loom behind Beethoven's Bacchic exuberance. Even when reveling in Bacchic energy Beethoven never loses control. Bacchic and Apollonian elements vie in his music with each other. The tension created engenders its power.

Eighteenth-century music had often been dance music of one kind or another. Increasingly popular in Beethoven's day was "Turkish" music, Bacchic music, music inspired by the god. For Europeans around 1800 Turkish music often featured fifes, drums, and cymbals. With its liveliness, energy, and strong rhythms, it could also express the comic, as in Mozart's music for Osmin in *The Abduction from the Seraglio,* in which he put Turkish themes into German music.

Bacchic music had long appealed to Beethoven. His ballet *The Crea-*
tures of Prometheus revels in wildness and dissonance. Chthonic forces,
Bacchic in content, lurk beneath the surface of other compositions. In
the Sixth and Seventh Symphonies, Nature—fields and forests, storms
and calm—quietly exults in daimonic energy. Beethoven's music offers
ecstasy to those willing to respond to it. Despite his intellectual side,
he valued the Bacchic, intensely emotional, socially upsetting content
of his music. In regard to his later *Missa solemnis* he wrote, "From the
heart—may it go—into the heart" (Von Herzen—Möge es werden—zu
Herzen gehen).[13] Few interpretations of the resultant music can render fully its emotional impact. Beethoven also valued Bacchic fun. One
of his interpreters writes of the Eighth Symphony, "Such a piece of
music . . . is pure play."[14]

Listening to Bacchic exuberance in Beethoven's music brings to
mind Rabelais's *Gargantua and Pantagruel,* a Bacchic work if ever there
was one, particularly evident in Thomas Urquhart and Pierre Mot-
teux's over-the-top seventeenth-century translation into English. In his
fifth book, Rabelais celebrates the irrational being that is Bacchus. The
sublime humor of Rabelais's boisterous bacchanals at once excites and
upsets us, may at times even overwhelm us. Like Beethoven's music, it
hugely embodies the energy of life. Pantagruel believes wine stimulates
joy and energy. Beyond furthering artistic creation, imbibing wine "is
a symbol of the primal energy in all forms, be it inspiration or action.
It is the blind force in all men that makes them live and act and create despite the counsels of reason."[15] No less did Rabelais revel in "the
tragic suffering, the priapism, the orgiastic festival of the wine god,
everything Nietzsche two centuries later called 'Dionysian.'"[16] Through
Bacchic music Beethoven sought to create new and greater worlds.

Others of Beethoven's generation shared his Rabelaisian propensities.
Hegel in his *Phenomenology of the Spirit* found "truth to be a 'bacchanalian revel,' in other words, an orgy of ideas, a conceptual debauch."[17]
"The chthonic element in Beethoven," Theodor Adorno reminds us,
"cannot be separated from the symphonic. . . . The demonic and the

ideal are thus intertwined."[18] In Beethoven the darkness often lurks just below the surface, then erupts. He was not the first—or last—to experience it. Brahms opined that under different circumstances Beethoven "might have been a master criminal." In *The Colossus,* a painting by Goya, a giant shakes his fist at the heavens while creatures below, animals and people together, flee in terror.[19] Like Balzac's Vautrin, the master criminal par excellence who hovers over *Père Goriot,* the greatness Beethoven embodies is potentially of a menacing kind.

᠌ᢒ

The Seventh Symphony

While Napoleon failed in Russia, the composer used this time of Napoleonic upset and the loss of his great love to rethink his music. Eighteen twelve, with the completion of the Seventh and Eighth Symphonies, became after all a year of major creativity. Though earlier sketches for a Seventh Symphony in A Major existed, Beethoven largely wrote it during the spring and summer. After completing it, he proceeded to the Eighth. In this year Beethoven also made a few sketches for what ultimately became his Ninth Symphony. Not ready to take it further, he did not return to it for almost a decade. But to conceive three such works, as diverse as they are magnificent, and complete two of them constitutes an impressive achievement.

Beethoven's friends organized two Akademies to present his newest works to the public. Lacking any official tie to the court's musical establishment, though friendly with many of the city's musical elite, he—the most famous composer of the day—had to arrange concerts of his music by himself or with the aid of friends. This could be an onerous affair. All public gatherings in Vienna, even small groups, required police authorization. Even established artists had to submit their newest creations to the powers that be in order to have them performed, a procedure that cannot have pleased Beethoven.

The 1813 Akademie took place in the splendid Festival Hall of the old university, where, just a few weeks before his death on May 31, 1809, Haydn had attended a performance of his oratorio *The Creation*. Four years later, Beethoven conducted there his new symphony. The enlarged orchestra taking part in the premiere included Domenico Dragonetti, the most famous double bass player of his day, along with Antonio Salieri and Ludwig Spohr on the violins.

The premiere on December 8 proved, in Spohr's opinion, a "resounding success." A second benefit concert took place on December 12, 1813, a third the following January 2, a fourth on February 27, 1814, and still another on March 16. In all, Beethoven had five benefit concerts filled with his recent music. Subsequent performances, if less successful financially, still drew good crowds. Of the instrumental works Beethoven wrote in the years before, during, and after the Congress of Vienna (1814–15), the Seventh Symphony has become the most lastingly popular.

Beethoven's active involvement in the premiere of the Seventh Symphony raised eyebrows. Spohr, himself a noted composer, left in his journal an account of the event that tells us much about Beethoven's unusual manner of conducting. Watching Beethoven on the podium Spohr found an astonishing experience:

> Although I had heard a good deal about it, the actuality still came as a shock. Beethoven had adopted the habit of communicating his expressive desires to the orchestra by all sorts of odd movements of the body. For a *sforzando* he would throw apart his arms, hitherto held crossed on his heart. For a *piano* he would bend down, the more *piano*, the lower. Then at a *crescendo* he would rise up gradually, and at the onset of the *forte*, literally spring into the air. He often shouted, too, in order to contribute to the *forte*, although probably unconsciously.[20]

Goya's *Colossus* might serve as a visual depiction of the Seventh Symphony. The overwhelming figure of the giant grabs our attention: could it be demonic Beethoven shaking his fist in anger and exultation at the universe, while uncomprehending audience members scurry away in terror? What many regard as liberating could frighten others.

Hearing the first movement of the Seventh, Carl Maria von Weber opined that Beethoven was "ripe for the madhouse." A literary contemporary of Beethoven's, Ludwig Tieck, went so far as to deem the composer's music the product of "a raving lunatic." Tieck was not alone in this opinion. He found the work "a kind of enigma—we had almost said a hoax." Did he intend audiences to regard his new symphony as some kind of titanic joke? So thought the puzzled reviewer for the London *Harmonicon*, more than a dozen years later, in 1826.

What brought about such responses? Admittedly, Beethoven's Seventh hurtles along at an unbelievable, almost unsustainable, pace, particularly in the Finale. We are overwhelmed by sound. Often the instruments—horns, trumpets, kettledrums—play in unusual keys. Given the music's unprecedented rapidity, its explosion of musical energy, it is amazing that anyone in Vienna liked it at all. But many in the initial audience, no doubt amazed by the torrent of sound flowing over them, did like it. Listeners especially admired the second movement, the relatively slow Allegretto. As often happened at the time, the enthusiasm of the audience was such that it asked the orchestra to repeat it. This was done. Its reputation as the work's most popular movement lasted well into the twentieth century. After the Presto, the fast-paced third movement, the last movement projects a realm of pure ecstasy, reckless and headstrong, a Bacchic festival of joy. For Wagner, the frenzied Finale embodied the demonic. The music never lets up. It hurtles forward. Once experienced, it can never be forgotten.

A decade after the premiere, the young Clara Schumann, upon encountering the Seventh, observed that most of the audience thought "the symphony—especially the first and last movements—could have been composed only in an unfortunate drunken condition."[21] Such a response then was not unusual. Madness, as John Dryden observed long ago, "is to genius near allied." The Seventh Symphony, with its popular Allegretto and headlong Finale, truly manifests marked Bacchic elements.

Frida Knight believes the symphony embodies the rise of peoples resisting oppression. Martin Geck traces the work back to Gossec's and Grétry's ecstatic overtures and operas celebrating the French Revolution. "We should not ignore the disciplined and fanfare-like subsidiary theme or the military rigor of the clipped rhythms," Geck reminds us, both of which recall Gossec's revolutionary march in his one-act "lyrique divertissement" *The Triumph of the Republic*, the triumph being that of the French at Valmy in 1792.[22] For the philosopher Ernst Bloch, the Seventh suggests "dancing on the ruins of the Bastille."[23]

Not for the first time in Beethoven's music does the Seventh announce Bacchic energy. That energy lurks almost everywhere in many of his compositions. But the Seventh concentrates it. A decade earlier, the *Eroica*'s final two movements had embodied the frenzy of Bacchic rituals. The Fifth's Finale ends in an orgy of sound. Chords crash down again and again, with hardly a break, and with ever more demonic intensity. A decade after the Seventh, near the end of the *Missa solemnis*, elements of Bacchic energy suddenly, and surprisingly, intrude. For the French scholar Bernard Fournier, Beethoven's music demonstrates, as much in the sonatas and in the quartets as in the larger-scaled works, "a kind of humor, sometimes enlightening, sometimes dark." It appears, he believes, also in the last movement of the Sixth Symphony. Beethoven's Seventh he compares to *Till Eulenspiegel*, whose hero of that name Richard Strauss would make much of. "There is something of this merry prankster in the *farouche* [that is, wild and savage] composer of the quartets; but Eulenspiegel," Fournier reminds us, is "a highly ambiguous figure, in which rascality, sentiment and heroic obstinacy mix."[24] Truly, in Beethoven's great-hearted, almost Rabelaisian perspective on humanity, humor constitutes both in his letters and his music a key element. By contrast, Jean de Solliers finds in this music "Beethoven's ruggedness above all fraternal. A kind of virile tenderness animates him.

He overflows with love for all beings. He is the Bacchus who genuinely distributes."[25]

Beethoven worked on the Seventh Symphony while his brief intimacy with Goethe reached its height. The composer knew Goethe's works well, and the poet may have influenced the composer. Beethoven had recently set to music several of Goethe's songs, including "Do You Know the Land" in *Wilhelm Meister's Apprenticeship*. He allegedly told Bettina Brentano that he wanted Goethe to hear his symphonies.[26] Only Goethe, he felt, could fully understand his music. "Now I have had a raptus," a moment of inspiration, Beethoven sometimes said of the unusual way he composed.[27] Goethe himself, well aware of the power of Bacchus, kept a statue of the divinity in his garden in Weimar, where it remains to this day. But in replying to Brentano's epistolary account of Beethoven's Bacchic nature, Goethe had been courteous, but cool. Unfortunately, he could only respond to the surface of Beethoven's genius in music, and even less to the man himself. Like many whose gift was essentially Apollonian, or imagined that it was, Goethe never fully grasped Beethoven's Bacchic nature or creativity.

Czerny claimed that the Seventh drew inspiration from events of the time. Which events he does not say, but its creation overlapped with the early stages of Napoleon's 1812 Russian campaign. On Russian soil by late June, the emperor appeared to be striding toward yet another conquest. The apparent success of his march to Moscow may have aroused in Beethoven a surge of creative energy. Or completion of this frenzied symphony may reflect his attempt to compensate for the loss of the Immortal Beloved. We may never know for sure who she was, but we do know that for Beethoven she was—and remained—the ideal. Just as he had composed his joyful Second Symphony in the midst of the despair recorded in the Heiligenstadt Testament, he had thrown himself into finishing the Seventh.

When published, Beethoven dedicated the symphony to the Russian tsar, Alexander I, whose armies, along with the vast Russian terrain and the arrival of winter conditions, had defeated Napoleon's forces. Much earlier, Beethoven had dedicated his three Violin Sonatas, Op. 30, of 1801–02 to Alexander. Czerny made a piano redaction of the Seventh Symphony, and Beethoven, hoping for publicity and money, dedicated it two years later to Elizabeth, the tsarina, then present at the Congress of Vienna. In return, Beethoven received from her both a present and a sum of money, testimony both to the regard in which she held Beethoven's music and to its appeal among Russian music lovers.

❧

The Eighth Symphony

The "classical" Eighth Symphony, a sequel of sorts to the exuberant Seventh, came to birth in Beethoven's summer visit to the spas of Bohemia, where he had written his impassioned words to the Immortal Beloved and walked about Teplitz with Goethe. Beethoven finished it in October 1812 at his brother Johann's home in Gneixendorf, outside of Linz, on the Austrian side of the Danube. The Eighth celebrates a triumph over adversity, both personal and, in my view, political.

The first performance of the Eighth Symphony, on February 27, 1814, went nearly as well as that of the Seventh. It recalls both its predecessor's dynamism and the Sixth's generally more relaxed atmosphere and exhibits exuberance comparable to that of the Seventh. While the symphony's structure apparently pays homage to Haydn, Beethoven brilliantly innovates by changing expectations in the thematic discourse. Because it has no true adagio movement, the Eighth gathers force with rapturous intensity. It is also, thought Paul Henry Lang, "an essay on humor in music, a parody on the symphony itself."[28] Humor is especially evident in the second movement, the Allegretto Scherzando, but present to some degree in all of them—humor at least as surprise—even in the third, Tempo di Menuetto. Not everyone at the time perceived or appreciated the symphony's humor. One individual whom it did not penetrate was the reviewer in London's *Harmonicon*, the journal already cited, who in 1827, upon hearing the work, deemed it "eccentric without being amusing, and laborious without effect." The stilted eighteenth-century syntax reveals an old-fashioned perspective and suggests the limitations of a musical taste. Bacchus remained vibrant in Beethoven's imagination. In 1815 his dear friend in faraway Courland in Latvia, Karl Amenda, sent Beethoven *Bacchus*, a lyric drama by one Rudolph vom Berge, to consider for an opera. Though not inspired to create music for it, Beethoven found the subject intriguing, for he made sketches for it. It was "in thinking of a Greek myth—and of a 'feast for Bacchus'" that Beethoven wrote, between 1818 and 1824, the *Missa solemnis* as well as the Ninth Symphony. In 1818 a draft for a possible tenth symphony featured a note: "Im allegro Feier des Bacchus" (in the Allegro a festival of Bacchus). Beethoven's next symphony, the overwhelming Ninth, a decade in the making, tells us that he intended to end as a conqueror. The "Turkish march" lodged in the Ninth's choral Finale constitutes a dramatic Bacchic expression. Last movements in fact seem to inspire Beethoven to call upon the god. In almost all of them, comments Emil Ludwig, with pardonable exaggeration, "the dreamer ends either as conqueror or as Bacchus."[29] As Beethoven's once formidable reputation as a pianist declined, his fame as a composer grew.

ꝸ

Wellington's Victory

Although the audience on December 8, 1813, received the Seventh Symphony enthusiastically, upon hearing *Wellington's Victory* (*Wellingtons Sieg*), the final work on the program, it roared its approval. The proceeds of this concert went to benefit Allied soldiers disabled at the battle of Hanau. Repeated by demand on December 12, *Wellington's Victory* became for many contemporaries Beethoven's best-known work and subsequently the musical top hit of the Congress of Vienna, which opened in September 1814, determined to remake the world left behind by Napoleon. Wellington, as Napoleon's most successful antagonist, was the subject of much praise. As *Wellington's Victory* seems to suggest, Beethoven may have shared to some degree the rejoicing over the defeat of a French force. But that defeat occurred at Vittoria in Spain. Napoleon in Saxony, a thousand miles away, was nowhere near the scene. Musically speaking, *Wellington's Victory*, along with *The Glorious Moment* (*Der glorreiche Augenblick*) of the next year, and a host of even less-known works discussed subsequently, ranks among Beethoven's weakest efforts. Compared to the heroic-period compositions of the past decade, their stridency is blatant, the music less convincing. It's almost as if, while his right hand rested, he wrote new works with his left.

Wellington's Victory emerged from an unusual collaborative effort between Beethoven and Johann Nepomuk Mälzel. Falsely credited as the inventor of the metronome, Mälzel had created an automaton chess player and a mechanical robot in the likeness of a Turk. He hoped to have *Wellington's Victory* played on his latest mechanical creation, the panharmonicon, a complex contraption that combined military band instruments with other devices. When that proved impractical, Beethoven rewrote the piece for orchestral performance. He regarded it as a poet laureate might a poem on a commissioned official theme. Widely acclaimed when first performed and for some time after, it also received plaudits from distinguished musicians.

The well-known performers who had participated in the Seventh Symphony in 1813—among them Domenico Dragonetti, Ludwig Spohr, and Joseph Mayseder, with Johann Nepomuk Hummel and young Giacomo Meyerbeer working the drums—also came through for Beethoven in *Wellington's Victory*. The Viennese public that had earlier found the *Eroica* enormously difficult and challenging now "raved over its antithesis," a work two modern scholars term "a cynical and enormously popular travesty of [Beethoven's] own symphonic ideal."[30] Any one of the several versions of *Wellington's Victory* does not disguise the fact that the work rates among Beethoven's most bathetic compositions.

Overall the nays have dominated. Most admirers of Beethoven's genius have consistently regarded the work negatively. Paul Henry

Lang termed it "a purely exterior *pièce de résistance*, perhaps Beethoven's most insignificant work."[31] Harsher still, J. W. N. Sullivan deemed the piece "the worst that Beethoven ever wrote."[32] Admittedly, *Wellington's Victory* does have a few moments of genuine musical energy, particularly in the first movement's unrelenting forward pace and the Finale's hectic march. But much of it can be considered merely agitated battle music, with perfunctory fanfares, challenges, calls to arms. Given the level of achievement that we expect from the mature Beethoven, it falls far short.

A recent biographer of Beethoven, the Dutch scholar Jan Caeyers, aptly terms the work an "avalanche of noise."[33] One contemporary of Beethoven's who did not like the work, Carl Maria von Weber, ridiculed its orchestral effects. When Beethoven read Weber's review he wrote at the bottom of the page, "Oh you pitiful scoundrel, what I shit is better than anything you have ever thought."[34] Not everyone responded to the piece as negatively as did Weber. The twenty-first-century musicologist Nicholas Mathew deems *Wellington's Victory* "the grandest of all such compositions."[35] One has to wonder what he means by "such compositions." In any case, his claim does not tell us much more than that he likes it. In short, the emperor's actual fall from power in the spring of 1814 affected Beethoven's being at a much deeper level. With it any hopes he had for significant positive change in the European world vanished.

18

Fidelio

The Love of Freedom is a flower of the dungeon.

HEINRICH HEINE

There is a point in Leonore's famous aria when, after the
prayerlike slow section, the French horns come in as if
sounding an invocation. At that moment I wanted to seize
a banner and lead regiments, to break through iron bars,
to liberate prisoners in the name of freedom and the
human spirit. In all the magic of music and stage no
call reverberates with such pure echo.

GALINA VISHNEVSKAYA[1]

Over the years Beethoven would consider and reject dozens of
possible librettos for an opera, but only that of Jean-Nicolas
Bouilly's *Léonore*, adapted into German by Joseph Sonnleithner,
excited him sufficiently to write music for it. Clearly Sonnleithner's
text stirred in him thoughts about marriage, about French revolutionary ideas, and about the political oppression in Vienna of his own day.
In Bouilly's play justice triumphs over despotism, faithful love con-
quers adversity, and courage and individual enterprise carry the day.
A woman's sacrifice, a man's yearning for freedom, the two joined
in a devoted and selfless marriage, the whole action set within the
themes of idealism and liberty: Bouilly's libretto had it all. It matched
Beethoven's own yearnings. Late in life Beethoven told his sometime
factotum Anton Schindler that "of all my children, this is the one . . .
most dear to me." He loved his only opera more than his other works

because, he claimed, he had suffered more in composing it. It was, he told Schindler, "his most beloved child of pain."[2]

The opera Beethoven wanted to be called *Leonore*, but which we know as *Fidelio*, is in genre a rescue opera. Rescue operas spawned by the French Revolution had soon migrated to oppressed Vienna, where their considerable popularity lasted well into the first decade of the new century. Marches and marchlike themes that recall French revolutionary music also found their way into *Leonore*, especially in the exuberant *Leonore* Overtures. As John Eliot Gardner astutely asserts, "With the *Leonore* of 1804–05 Beethoven was struggling to recover the fiery revolutionary fervour and idealism of his Bonn years."[3] The composer also wished his opera to rival the *Eroica* in its revolutionary import. In this "speaking" *Eroica* he intended to present the ideals of the Revolution in human, not abstract, terms. The words of the actors onstage support the music. In *Leonore*, observed Theodor Adorno, "the Revolution is not depicted but re-enacted as in a ritual."[4] It can be interpreted as celebrating the anniversary of the Bastille.

The three-act *Leonore* premiered November 20, 1805, a week after Napoleon's troops entered Vienna. Beethoven shortened and changed the opera for the two-act 1806 production. In 1814 he would revise it again, as *Fidelio*. Interesting as are both *Leonores*, I shall focus here on the *Fidelio* of 1814.

❧

Napoleon Again on the Move

During 1813 the growing tension between France and the Austria of Franz and Metternich, an ally of Napoleon until August of that year, approached a turning point. Whatever the outcome of the conflict, its resolution would surely affect adversely Beethoven's uncertain financial situation. When he lamented that "this disastrous war will hold up the final settlement or render my affairs even worse," he refered to Austria's belatedly joining the coalition against Napoleon and the effect it might have upon his income. Instead of his staying put as he had during the 1809 summer, he determined that "if the surging waves of war roll nearer to Vienna," he would "go to Hungary."[5]

Early in 1813 the French emperor, having put together a new and largely untested army of raw recruits and surviving veterans, sought to hold on to the central European states, several of which were still allied, if precariously, to him. With the exception of Austria, tied by treaty and marriage to Napoleon, Europeans—English, Swedes, Prussians, and Russians—joined together to bring him down. Napoleon, surrounded by hostile forces, found himself at bay in Saxony. Even after the Russian debacle, his opponents so feared his reputation for invincibility that they avoided major engagements in which Napoleon himself was in charge and attacked only those segments of his army not led personally by him. During the spring of 1813 Napoleon achieved initial successes at Lützen (May 2), south of Leipzig, and Bautzen (May 20–21), northeast of Dresden. But having lost many battle-hardened veterans in Russia as well as a vast number of horses, he lacked the capacity to pursue his opponents and thus capitalize on his victories. The sand in his hour-glass inexorably began to run out. Though the summer campaign of 1813 in the German states prolonged the Napoleonic agony, it could not alter an outcome increasingly inevitable. On August 12, Austria, led by Metternich and still allied formally to France, abandoned its alliance and joined the European coalition. Napoleon barely won a major battle at Dresden (August 26–27), but his victory did not daunt the resolution of the Allies to continue the struggle.

Hoping for a determining encounter, the Allied coalition on October 16 engaged Napoleon's armies in and around Leipzig. This so-called Battle of the Nations pitted 300,000 allied troops against 150,000 French. In a hard-fought but decisive victory over Napoleon's forces during four days, the coalition—aided by the defection of several of the emperor's German allies, first the Saxons and then the Bavarians—triumphed. Historians today consider the battle of Leipzig a pivotal moment in modern European history. Beethoven, in his surviving letters of the time, leaves it unmentioned. Nor does he speak of Napoleon, or of Austria joining the coalition, perhaps because he did not want to reveal his lack of enthusiasm for the Allied cause. As Napoleon's control of the European mainland shrank and ultimate defeat loomed, Beethoven seems to have become silent. With the remnant of his army the emperor began a slow retreat back to France. On October 30 at Hanau, east of Frankfurt am Main, the French rear guard turned and defeated its Austrian and Bavarian pursuers. But the retreat continued. By year's end the decades-long European war, though not yet over, seemed close to conclusion. Though Napoleon had failed, he had failed mightily.

᠊ᢞ

The Campaign of France

Early in January, 1814, the Allies, building on the momentum of Leipzig, invaded French territory and continued the campaign. Napoleon, in Paris, put together a new, much smaller, and largely untested army composed mainly of young recruits and surviving veterans. He left the capital on January 25 determined to repel the enemy, now for the first time on French soil. The Campaign of France, as it came to be known, lasted two months, until the end of March. In numbers and equipment the Allies held an overwhelming advantage, but Napoleon was at his best, with his gift for strategy and keen eye for tactical opportunities. He won several battles; in fact, over nine days (February 10–18), he claimed four victories. Defeats predominated, however, and became ever more costly.

In March, hoping to draw the invading armies after him, Napoleon feinted eastwards toward the Rhine. But the Allies, having intercepted a letter by him to his wife, Marie Louise, outlining his strategy, marched westwards and soon reached the outskirts of Paris. Napoleon, realizing he had been outfoxed, reversed himself and returned to set up camp at Fontainebleau, southeast of Paris. Too late! Already several key marshals had surrendered their troops. Paris offered only token resistance, and on March 31 the Allies entered the virtually undefended capital. With only a semblance of an army left, Napoleon faced defeat. The Allies, occupying Paris, controlled the peace negotiations. On April 6, 1814, Napoleon abdicated and accepted exile to Elba, a small island off Italy's Ligurian coast. The most magnetic figure in European history was no longer a factor in the destiny of nations. The ongoing war that had begun in 1792 and which, with only brief intervals of peace, had lasted nearly a quarter of a century was over at last. Or so it seemed. Upon the unenthusiastic French populace, the Allies imposed as king the Bourbon Louis XVIII, younger brother to the guillotined Louis XVI.

Napoleon for nearly two decades had captured Beethoven's imagination. Now he was off the stage, presumably for good. Beethoven's attitude toward Napoleon during the months that followed oscillated between antagonism and ecstasy. For a while he wrote no new compositions of consequence. Though he was not idle, the full flow of creativity hitherto in evidence had become impoverished. Aside from the revised *Fidelio,* patriotic, or rather pseudo-patriotic, works now dominated his output. Beethoven may have pondered what could have been if—a big if—Napoleon had fulfilled his initial promise, and a new Europe had arisen. But his great rival, the one man whose energy and ability he most admired, had been defeated and exiled.

Chateaubriand and Byron

François-René de Chateaubriand in his vast *Memoirs from Beyond the Tomb* recalled the moment when he realized the change from the eighteenth century to the nineteenth, a moment we can also interpret in the light of Beethoven's creativity. For Chateaubriand,

> The artist expresses in his way what he has experienced, the birth of a new order where man masters or senses himself capable of

mastering his full history in giving it a true human aspect, in a
collective conscience until then ignored, and which, at the time
when Beethoven composed his first compositions, the ancient
order momentarily pretends to relegate [them] to the past, as a bad
souvenir.

Born a year after Chateaubriand, Beethoven too had grown up under
the ancien régime. In 1814, after Napoleon's abdication, he watched it
reinstate itself. But the events of 1789 convinced both men that even if
life in the new era appeared tenuous, it had arrived.

No less than Chateaubriand was Byron intensely caught up in
the drama of Napoleon's career. Since his teen years Napoleon had
served him as a precarious idol. Byron's thoughts on Napoleon, like
Beethoven's, both soared and plummeted. The emperor's abdication in
early April 1814 profoundly shocked him. He was shattered even more
by Napoleon's willingness to accept exile. Why, instead of surrendering,
had he not committed suicide? "If thou hadst died as honour dies," he
lamented in his "Ode to Napoleon Buonaparte," set down a few days
after the abdication. But then, perhaps thinking of himself, he continued, "some new Napoleon might arise to shame the world again."[6]

∿

Creating *Fidelio*

The "new Napoleon" turned out to be Beethoven. For ten years he had
lived with the awareness that, in two attempts, he had not brought
Leonore/Fidelio to a fully satisfactory conclusion. Early in 1814 three
opera singers—Ignaz Saal, Johann Michael Vogl, and Karl Friedrich
Joseph Weinmüller—remembered the earlier opera with admiration
sufficient to propose to Beethoven its revival as a benefit performance
for themselves. Given the work's checkered performance history, those
making the request did not lack courage. For the proposed *Fidelio* to
achieve the desired success, the Hofburgtheater management insisted

Beethoven make major changes. Though hesitant to turn once again to a work he had twice regarded as finished, he nonetheless embarked upon a full-scale rethinking of it.

Composing *Leonore* in 1805 and rewriting it in 1806 had challenged Beethoven intensely. Such an effort did not come easily for him. In 1814 he must have wondered whether again undergoing the strain of revising the opera was worth his time if, in the end, the censor rejected it. The censor rarely objected to instrumental music, but an opera? That was another matter. Usually unwilling to return to a composition he believed completed, Beethoven found reworking his troubled stepchild a frustrating, distasteful experience.

Nearly a decade had passed since the first performances of *Leonore* in 1805 and its initial revision in 1806. Although Beethoven had since composed a galaxy of masterpieces, he had not actively worked on his opera. As winter turned to spring, he faced a final struggle with a creation that had already caused him much anguish. How to improve his opera of yesteryear weighed upon his mind. Basically, as he often claimed, he preferred to take up a new work than revise an old one. He had finished the initial version when Napoleon stood at the height of his power and had just occupied Vienna for the first time. In 1814, as he began work on his new revision, Napoleon was fighting several allied armies in the Campaign of France. In all, his opera required two major rewritings and the composition of four different overtures before it would achieve its final form.

Fidelio allowed Beethoven to contemplate once again his idealistic but deeply felt view of married love. His failure to rendezvous with his Immortal Beloved in 1812 likely influenced the revision. In his belief in the saving power of women and in the married state, he also reinforced a message the 1806 version had made more specific. If the woman he idolized could not be his in reality, he would create in music a self-sacrificing Immortal Beloved. In the *Fidelio* of 1814 Leonore displays a full gamut of emotions, from uncertainty and frustration to despair, hope, and triumphant love. Revising the opera while Napoleon fought his Campaign of France, and with the troops of the absolutist monarchs closing in upon him, also gave Beethoven the opportunity to reassert his beliefs in the ideals of the French Revolution. For help in reworking the libretto Beethoven engaged Georg Friedrich Treitschke, an experienced dramaturge and director of the Kärtnertor Theater, located near where the Vienna State Opera is now.

Treitschke proved an excellent choice. Drawing upon the earlier versions, he rethought the entire libretto from top to bottom. While he preserved much of the earlier Sonnleithner and Breuning texts, he also made key changes. He retained most of the 1806 revisions but also returned in places to the longer text of 1805. All the same, whereas the 1805 and 1806 versions are textually linked, the major changes in the 1814 version make it virtually a new work. To most of them Beethoven grudgingly acceded. With Treitschke's encouragement he rewrote the score to accord with them but complained to him about how long it was taking: "In this case the whole of my work is—to a certain extent—scattered in all directions; and I have to think out the entire work again."[7]

The Act 1 introductory *Singspiel* depicts Marzelline, the daughter of the prison jailor Rocco, fending off her importunate suitor Jaquino, his assistant. Marzelline has fallen in love with Fidelio not realizing "he" is Leonore, who has taken on this disguise in order to find her husband, who disappeared two years before. She clings to the hope he may still be alive.

In revolutionary Europe during Beethoven's lifetime a new kind of woman had come to the fore. Leonore emerged out of a tradition of forceful heroines that Schiller had made familiar to the world. Those who argue that we need not take Leonore seriously because she is merely the product of Beethoven's deep fantasies are not only wrong but historically asleep. The achievements of women contemporary with Beethoven—among others, Mary Wollstonecraft, Madame Roland, Madame de Staël, Bettina Brentano, and Annette von Droste-Hülshoff, not to forget Rahel Varnhagen von Ense, née Rahel Levin, the brilliant Jewish salon hostess of Berlin, and her equally capable counterpart in

Vienna, Fanny von Arnstein—set the bar high. Beethoven would have known of them and their accomplishments. His self-directed, heroic Leonore has the same vital spirit.

Hoping she might see her husband among the prisoners, Leonore asks Rocco to allow them out of their cells to enjoy a bit of fresh air. Once in the sunshine, the prisoners mournfully recall their lost freedom. Enter Don Pizarro, the governor of the state prison. Enraged that the prisoners have had this respite, he threatens violent revenge upon them and upon a mysterious unnamed inmate whom we and Leonore suspect may be Florestan. After he departs, Leonore learns that Rocco has been ordered to kill and bury the unnamed prisoner. Though horrified, she insists on helping, hoping that somehow she can still save this person, no matter who he is. One of the more beautiful of all opera choruses is the prisoners' lament upon being told to return to their cells, "Farewell, you poor light of the sun." In 1814 Wilhelmine Schröder-Devrient sang Leonore. The sensational new music Beethoven composed for the conclusion of her aria "Come, Hope" further underscores Leonore's incredible courage.

Beethoven's opera provides the strongest image of a forceful woman in any Romantic art form. In Leonore Beethoven created a woman full of courage, integrity, and determination. Neither the novel nor art itself had yet opened up to women such a field of action, or one with so many revolutionary possibilities. The most powerful female figure in all opera, Leonore is larger than life, a worthy successor to Medea, Antigone, and Electra, yet in a revolutionary age immensely real, the musical equivalent of Marianne in Eugène Delacroix's great canvas *Liberty Leading the People*. That impassioned work of art celebrates *les trois glorieuses* of the 1830 Revolution in France, the "three glorious days" in which Parisians rose up and ejected the last of the Bourbons, Charles X, the successor to Louis XVIII.

❧

Florestan in Chains

After the curtain rises on Act 2 of *Fidelio*, we see (and experience) the misery of prison life. An unidentified figure lies unconscious in his cell. Cold and starving, isolated in the enveloping darkness, the prisoner we assume is Florestan appears near the end of his existence. The discordant music depicting the dungeon is evocative of mental anguish, darkness, and despair. Beethoven rewrote it no fewer than eighteen times. Deliberately unsettling, this music captures the misery and pain of extended solitary confinement. A perceptive comment by the biographer Fritz Zobeley in regard to one of Beethoven's compositions consists of only five words: "It allows one no sleep."[8] Experiencing a Beethoven composition to the full can be potentially shattering. Whether we emerge from it exhilarated, depressed, or, just possibly, enlightened, we may find sleep afterwards difficult or impossible.

Florestan lies in a state prison but, along with other prisoners, he was imprisoned for personal reasons. Legally Florestan isn't a political prisoner, as the more astute in the nineteenth-century audience would have recognized. Though exposing Pizarro's misdeeds has a broad political dimension, Pizarro is primarily settling a private grudge. Florestan's name was never entered in the prison register. In the eyes of the authorities he doesn't exist. His death, as Pizarro well knew, would pass unnoticed. That other prisoners may also have endured incarceration for political reasons few in the audience would have doubted.

The fear of being buried alive permeates the powerful French prison literature of the time. It is also Florestan's fear in *Fidelio*. He had good reason for his fear. Captivity, as the prisoners in Beethoven's opera tell us, was seen as a living death. Prisoners were well aware of their likely obliteration. Imprisonment stripped the prisoners of their identity. The mental ordeal of prison existence often caused more acute suffering than the physical. Many did not survive. Some who did emerged as human wrecks, in no condition to lead normal lives.

A prison in Beethoven's day did not need to be a literal dungeon. It could be an enclosure of the spirit, an entrapment of the soul, the result, in William Blake's memorable phrase, of "mind-forg'd manacles," in short, any oppressive or dangerous enclosed space or situation: a room, a relationship, even a country. It could also be a state of being, deafness, for example, as it was for Beethoven. During the Enlightenment the use of torture had decreased throughout Europe, even in Russia, but it continued all the same. Alexander Herzen, the nineteenth-century Russian intellectual exiled from his native land, described Europe as "one great prison."[9] The words apply no less to conditions in the twentieth-century world, as well as to what we know of the twenty-first.

With the exception of Rossini's *Tancredi* (1813), *Fidelio* is one of the few operas still in the repertory that takes place in a prison. Beethoven's music resonates eerily in our times. The situation it depicts may well have worsened since his day. Hearing and seeing the prisoners in *Fidelio*, we visualize in our imaginations the survivors of a concentration camp being liberated in 1945, or life as endured in the gulags of Russia, or the cell blocks in East Germany after the Wall went up, or the torturing of prisoners in Abu Ghraib, or holding them indefinitely in Guantanamo Bay, or isolating those in federal jails in permanent solitary confinement. Today this last is called "administrative sequestration." (The longer the Latin-based words, it seems, the more they are meant to disguise or conceal the horror of the experience described.) Beethoven, we realize as *Fidelio* unfolds, has been there before us.

৵

Unjust Imprisonment Then and Now

Prisons served as a cradle for the eighteenth- and nineteenth-century imagination. In 1764 the pathbreaking treatise by the Italian prison reformer Cesare Beccaria, *Of Crimes and Punishments*, expressed outrage at the "cold-blooded cruelty" of incarceration. "Prison transforms a human being into an object," Beccaria wrote. The tortures of the mind and spirit, even greater than the physical discomfort, make imprisonment without the possibility of liberation the worldly equivalent of damnation. The few who managed to survive emerged shattered in being. Beccaria's plea against the atrocities permitted in the bastilles of the ancien régime touched the conscience of many.

About the same time Giovanni Piranesi, living in Rome and inspired by the ruins he saw around him, created an extraordinary series of engravings, *Imaginary Prisons* (1745; revised, 1761). Piranesi's sixteen plates become a visual accompaniment to Beccaria's treatise. They depict fantasy dungeons, huge gloomy labyrinths hidden from the sun in which tiny figures trapped in the enveloping gloom wander about aimlessly. Revealing Piranesi's obsessions and hallucinations, the darkness of his visionary mind, the endlessly detailed engravings of *Imaginary Prisons* transformed the substance of Rome into the realm of the irrational. Piranesi's work stirred the burgeoning social imagination and rapidly gained him European renown. Later, Thomas De Quincey, inspired by Samuel Taylor Coleridge's verbal description of Piranesi's engravings, re-created in the visionary prose of "The Pains of Opium" in his *Confessions of an English Opium-Eater* the terror they wreaked within his imagination. Even before Beccaria and Piranesi, William Hogarth had depicted the horrors of prison existence. Almost every novel in eighteenth-century Britain—whether by Defoe, Smollett, Richardson, or Sterne, whether Walpole's *Castle of Otranto* or Beckford's *Vathek*—includes a prison scene. No less does the link between enclosure and inner freedom lie at the heart of the developing Romantic sensibility in Germany.

As a symbol of the injustices of the ancien régime, the prison quickly became the French Revolution's key metaphor. "It was," Simon Schama tells us, "the perfect symbol for the monarchy to be despised as arbitrary, obsessed with secrecy and viewed with capricious powers over the life and death of its citizens."[10] During the 1790s many politically active figures in France landed—often without trial, without cause, sometimes indefinitely—in the prisons of Paris. Madame Roland, Tom

Paine, André Chenier, the Marquis de Sade—all spent time in them. Chenier died in prison. Inspired by the Bastille's fall, an abundant prison literature developed, notably of rescue operas. Every operatic experience of the time, the composer André Grétry wryly remarked, seemed to re-enact the storming of the Bastille.

Prior to 1789 French kings decreed prison sentences through infamous *lettres de cachet* (orders under the king's private seal), which could incarcerate an individual without trial and keep him in prison indefinitely. Although the Hapsburgs did not officially utilize *lettres de cachet*, Austrian reality was no less harsh. Incarceration could occur without cause and with the length of time to be served determined not by judge or jury but by whomever in a position of power had decreed it.

Prisons and imprisonment fill the literature of Beethoven's era. "All the frail creatures cruelly sequestered in the Gothic dungeons and Inquisition cells of the late eighteenth-century novel (*roman noir*) had a definite reality," observes the French historian Jean Staroblinski.[11] Imagination, he claims, "gives us the ability to escape the unhappy reality of our everyday existence." Well, perhaps not everyone's imagination. "If ever I were confined to the Bastille," claimed Rousseau, "then I would draw the picture of beauty."[12] "His image of 'freedom' in prison recurs throughout subsequent French literature—in Stendhal and Hugo, Camus, and Sartre."[13] Idealistic and perhaps occasionally true, it is yet not how Beethoven conceived the realities of prison life.

᭥

Schubart and Schiller

In 1792 Hapsburg authorities seized the Marquis de Lafayette in neutral territory—in fact he was fleeing the radicalized Revolution that had turned against him—and clapped him into successive Austrian prisons, with no apparent hope of release, for five years. Napoleon, in negotiations with Austria at Campo Formio in 1797, insisted he be freed. And he was. Lafayette was but one instance of unjust imprisonment.

Every European then alive knew of others. The ordeal of C. F. D. Schubart of Württemberg was especially notorious and can stand for many. A composer of music, Schubart was consigned in 1777 by Duke Karl Eugen, ruler of the Duchy of Württemberg, to imprisonment in a dark vault at Hohenasperg because of his alleged "criminal outspokenness." There he remained without any means of occupying himself. He never received a sentence, nor did he learn a specific reason for his captivity. Only after ten years of incarceration was he released, a broken man. He died four years later, in 1791.

The injustice done to Schubart profoundly affected the young Friedrich Schiller, also a native of Württemberg. Karl Eugen made his early years a nightmare. His harsh decrees prompted and nourished a spirit of rebellion in Schiller. Virtually everything he wrote became an issue about freedom. Absolute despots in his plays abound, as do strivers after goodness and justice. Among his rebellious, idealistic heroes, many of noble blood, Karl Moor in *The Robbers* is perhaps best known. Behind Florestan in *Fidelio* lie also Ferdinand in Schiller's *Intrigue and Love*, Fiesco in his *Fiesco's Conspiracy in Genoa*, and the Marquis of Posa in his *Don Carlos*. Schiller's unloving, vengeful, immensely complex Emperor Philip in *Don Carlos* led to Beethoven's monomaniacal Don Pizarro. Whereas Philip destroys Don Carlos, his son, as well as his close friend, the idealistic Posa, Leonore succeeds—barely—in foiling Pizarro.

᠕

Back to Florestan

"*Gott!*" (God!) is the first word Florestan utters in Act 2 of *Fidelio*. To it he adds, "welch Dunkel hier!" (what darkness here!). Coming after music exuding pain, the words present the singer with a challenge. Moving forward in the aria, Florestan sings, "In the springtime of life," reaffirming his belief in idealistic values. He ponders his existence and wonders what he has done to deserve so grim a fate. His crime, we learn subsequently, was to have boldly spoken the truth about Pizarro's crimes. "Florestan has done the right thing," he concludes; "my duty I have done." He has exposed the iniquities of Pizarro. That has landed him in prison. In a moment of delirium Florestan imagines Leonore visiting him in the guise of an angel. His vision of her foreshadows the reality to come and gives him a brief respite from his agony. His integrity and belief in the possibility of a just and honest world have kept him alive until now.

One senses a connection between Florestan's aria and Beethoven's Heiligenstadt Testament, in which he had lamented the gradual loss of his hearing and other ills. As Florestan's mind wanders and his body weakens, he hears less, indeed has less to hear, and, like his creator, becomes "deaf." Florestan envisions in his delirium the prison walls opening and an angelic Leonore bathed in rosy light summoning him to the freedom of heaven. At that magical moment, he feels "a soft, gentle breeze," and his wrenching lament changes to lyrical ecstasy. The trembling resembles the "correspondent breeze" between human beings and their environment of which the Romantic poets had spoken.

After Leonore and Rocco enter the scene and dig out the filled-in cistern in which to bury Florestan, Don Pizarro enters raging, intent on murder. Having learned that his superior, the Minister, plans a surprise visit to the prison, he realizes he must dispatch Florestan quickly. He has ordered a trumpeter to sound a warning when he sees the Minister's coach approaching the prison. Pizarro confronts the chained Florestan, tells him who he is, and, gloating in his triumph, pulls out a dagger. When Florestan realizes that it is Pizarro who has had him imprisoned he cries out, "It is his crime, his abuse of power, that I dared uncover." At this moment of crisis Leonore throws herself between Pizarro and her husband. She cries out, "First kill his wife." Amazement reigns: Pizarro, stunned by the unexpected turn of events, is stopped cold; Florestan, thunderstruck, sees before him his prior vision of an angelic Leonore; and Rocco, astonished, realizes his prospective son-in-law is a woman.

In the distance an offstage trumpet is heard faintly. The sound is riveting, indeed electrifying. The moment is hugely melodramatic, yet powerful and among the most genuinely moving in all opera. Everyone stops singing. Upon hearing the trumpet solo, we wonder: can it imply that a rescue of Florestan is at hand? Undeterred, Pizarro again advances to dispatch Florestan, helpless in his chains. Leonore draws forth a concealed pistol. Suddenly a second trumpet solo sounds. It plays the notes of the first, but louder and closer in. Only Pizarro knows that the trumpet solos announce the imminent arrival of the king's minister, Don Fernando. To everyone except Pizarro they bode a rescue, a signal that hope has arrived, the possibility of justice. Intended to warn Pizarro, they in effect prepare for the final apotheosis.

At the close of Part 1 of Goethe's *Faust* Mephistopheles informs the imprisoned Gretchen that, having murdered her infant, she is dammed. But suddenly a "voice from above," cries out, "She is saved." They're the only words the voice utters, and they grant forgiveness. The use of the trumpet in *Fidelio* serves as a voice from above, a voice of hope.

Beethoven did not formally compose a Requiem, observes the philosopher Ernst Bloch, but he "did write one in his *Fidelio*, a completely unequivocal requiem, with *Dies irae* [wrath of God] for Pizarro, and with *Tuba mirum spargens sonum* [the trumpet scattering its amazing sound] for Florestan."[14] The trumpet call for Bloch literally announces not only the minister's arrival but also in effect the coming of the Messiah. The close of the scene opens up a completely new world both musically and dramatically: "If one seeks musical initiations into the truth of utopia, the first all-containing light is *Fidelio*."[15] This French-inspired German opera poses paradoxes. "When all the inner conditions are fulfilled," quipped Karl Marx, "the German day of resurrection will be announced through the blare of the Gallic rooster."[16] Without the Gallic rooster whose crowing announced the outbreak of the Revolution, Beethoven's opera would not have come into being.

That the 1814 *Fidelio* ends in the light of day heightens the effect of the trumpet calls. The prisoners—and we in the audience—have

emerged from the depths of the prison both psychologically and dramatically. Both calls come at moments when Leonore confronts Pizarro
directly. Though intended to warn him that the carriage of the Minister, his superior, is fast approaching, the calls also serve for those
imprisoned as messages of hope, promises of deliverance, even inti-
mations of happiness to come. Leonore, Florestan, and Rocco, no less
than members of the audience, sense that the trumpet calls announce
a change in their fortunes. Musically, the trumpet solos in *Fidelio* echo
the trumpet passage in the third part of Handel's *Messiah* in which the
bass proclaims the great words in 1 Corinthians 15: "And the trumpet
shall sound . . . and we shall all be changed." In *Fidelio* the trumpet
calls announce that the world will indeed right itself: good will replace
evil; light, darkness; justice, tyranny. By early 1814 Beethoven's desire
for freedom included all of oppressed mankind. In the final scene of the
opera Don Fernando proclaims, "A brother seeks his brothers, / And
if he can help, he helps gladly." His introductory statement explicitly
enunciates the underlying principle of the French Revolution.

Don Fernando's other words in this speech may appear somewhat
ambiguous: "The command and wish of the best of kings leads / Me to
you." Did Beethoven, politically savvy, intend to assuage Franz I with
"the best of kings," and thus possibly increase the opera's chances of
becoming a success? It was not—could not have been—in Bouilly's
original libretto, Beethoven's source, for the French National Assembly had guillotined the last Bourbon monarch in January 1793; and in
1798, when Bouilly's play was first performed, France had no king and
no prospect of a successor. Nor did the phrase appear in Beethoven's
1805 and 1806 texts. It first enters in Treitschke's 1814 version. Praising
"the best of kings" might imply, at first sight, that Beethoven supported
the Austrian emperor Franz I, but that is unlikely. Rather, Beethoven
intended his audiences to realize that Don Fernando is not speaking of
Franz I, who was not inclined to pardon anyone, or even to allow prisoners a few minutes of fresh air and sun outside their cells. In this scene
he means to show what an enlightened and just ruler would do.

Hearing mention of "the best of kings" was intended to suggest to audience members—and Metternich's spies in the audience—that Beethoven intended nothing detrimental to the established order. The reference is tongue-in-cheek. The king may perhaps have noble thoughts, but he is not present. So distant is he that even in imperial Austria we cannot mistake the disdain Beethoven felt for monarchies. It is the people who now reign, and their intervention will make that clear. Beethoven played a cat-and-mouse game with Austrian censorship. In 1814 he did not need the support of the new empress, Franz's fourth wife, to rescue his opera, as a previous empress had rescued the *Leonore* of 1805. Don Fernando's words in 1814, less bellicose than in earlier versions, are firm yet conciliatory. They stress a common humanity. If Franz had a minister of Don Fernando's caliber, wisdom, and benevolence, he remains unknown to posterity.

◆

Napoleon Once More

Ideas about secular messiahs circulated widely at this time. If Leonore serves as Beethoven's Messiah in one sense, Don Fernando surely is one in another. Behind the idea of him there might be lurking still another Messiah. For this role I propose Napoleon. To many contemporaries, not least Beethoven, it was Napoleon who after 1796 gradually, if only intermittently, became the age's Messiah. I intend no exact parallel between Napoleon and Joseph II or Don Fernando. Rather, Napoleon's "presence" in *Fidelio* may lie less in his own being and more in the ideal of civic leadership that, at least until 1804, he embodied. Imperfect he proved to be, yet in the four or five years after he was appointed First Consul in 1799—the years in which Beethoven conceived and wrote *Leonore*, which became *Fidelio*—he still struck many as the closest Europe came to having a savior.

Napoleon, in the early stages of Beethoven's imaginative conception of him, was not only the inheritor of Joseph II's idealistic efforts at reform but the modern Prometheus, the guardian of Europe, even its potential savior. It is hard to gauge Beethoven's thinking about Napoleon at any time, but the possibility of Don Fernando serving as a stand-in for him, or at least as an ideal leader, is one worth exploring, and its implications are worth pondering. In the *Eroica*, a work that in Beethoven's words was "written for or about Bonaparte," he created an idealistic world inspired by the Revolution and Napoleon. Might he not the next year, in the person of Don Fernando, have placed Napoleon *within* the similarly idealistic world he had created in *Leonore?* The two are rarely linked, and the notion that they should be may at first seem far-fetched.

❧

Freedom

Had the composer while revising *Leonore* into *Fidelio* not exclaimed, "Freedom!!!! what more does one want???"[17] Beethoven cherished freedom as an ideal, whether personal, intellectual, or political. "I much prefer the empire of the mind," he affirmed, "and I regard it as the highest of all spiritual and worldly monarchies."[18] Such a belief remained his credo. In the autumn of 1814, after his revised opera had succeeded, in a letter of thanks to his generous supporter, the Czech lawyer, composer, and esteemed amateur cellist Johann Nepomuk Kanka, Beethoven spoke of the duty he had imposed upon himself "to work by means of my art for human beings in distress."[19] He gave willingly of his art to others. He was committed to freedom; his music was meant to be the sound of liberation. Even more than did the earlier versions, the 1814 *Fidelio* reflects his desire for all to live in a republic.

Beethoven had long claimed to be a lover of his fellow man. Sometimes that love manifested itself in acts toward individuals, at other times in the abstract. Though *Fidelio*'s final version hymns humanity more abstractly than those previous, Beethoven often practiced a broad and generous humanity toward individuals. "From my earliest childhood," he wrote Joseph von Varena in 1811 when promising a gift to charity, "my zeal to serve our poor suffering humanity in any way whatsoever by means of my art has made no compromise with any lower motive."[20] He was happy to join with men like Varena who shared his values. "I am thoroughly delighted," he told him, "to have found in you a friend of the oppressed." Even when faced with financial reversals, Beethoven maintained his core beliefs. In 1813, again to Varena, he claimed he never accepted "any money, when it [was] a question of promoting the welfare of humanity." That is, he would not take it if it hurt other people. He professed himself "just as willing to do a good action to the best of my ability for my friends the Reverend Ladies as I was last year and as I shall always be for suffering humanity in general, as long as I live." He will "work as usual," he assured Varena, " for the benefit of all that is good and useful."[21]

╲૭

Fidelio Performed

On May 23, 1814, the final version of *Fidelio* appeared at the Hofburgtheater. "The opera was capitally prepared," wrote Treitschke. Even though increasingly deaf, Beethoven conducted. His ardor tended to put the music out of tune, but behind Beethoven's back the musicians carefully followed the direction of Kapellmeister Michael Umlauf. Ludwig Spohr, a distinguished composer and performer whom we have met already, agreed: the first night's performance was a resounding success. The applause, great on that occasion, increased with every subsequent performance. The mood *Fidelio* expressed appeared to accord well with the widespread rejoicing across Europe over the fall of Napoleon. Beethoven made several additions over the course of its run. One was the return of Rocco's "gold" aria (on July 7), not heard since 1805. A different Rocco also emerges. The somewhat mercenary jailor emerges as a more feeling individual. Three months later *Fidelio* became the first opera that Congress of Vienna attendees would hear.

Beethoven, if unpopular in Hapsburg circles, had a European reputation. During the nine months the Congress met (September 1814 to June 1815) the revised *Fidelio* was staged twenty-one times. It's worth asking why an opera meant to criticize absolute monarchs and represent the oppressed proved so popular. Granted, the rousing music would have thrilled attendees. Most likely, the monarchs and attendant dignitaries viewed Don Pizarro as a stand-in for the now exiled Napoleon. They may have imagined themselves as the Don Fernandos of Europe, rescuing peoples from the Napoleonic yoke. Though no doubt cheered by his opera's success, Beethoven did not intend such an interpretation.

For later listeners, *Fidelio*'s political and humanistic grounding is more evident. Ernst Bloch claimed that the opera was meant to inspire the storming of Bastille-like prisons. After all, its libretto emerged out of experiences undergone and chronicled during the French Revolution. If we integrate Bloch's perspective with the lived experience of Beethoven's day-to-day existence in Vienna, it is clear that *Fidelio*'s score arose out of the music and ideals spawned by the events they chronicle. The opera "does not depict the revolution," asserts Theodor Adorno, "but relives it, so to speak, ritually repeated." Adorno regards it as one of the peaks not just of music but of human culture. He is not the only commentator to recognize *Fidelio*'s pathbreaking nature and continuing relevance. Thomas Mann, living in Los Angeles during World War II, wrote in *Doctor Faustus*, penned late during the war, that "there were years when we children of the dungeon dreamed of a song of joy— *Fidelio*, the Ninth Symphony—with which to celebrate Germany's liberation, its liberation of itself."[22] Listeners, attuned to its message, can find themselves intensely affected. In watching *Fidelio* the art historian Bernard Berenson was so moved that he "began to sob and blubber and choke."[23] This opera, like no other, can move us to tears.

19

The Congress of Vienna and Its Aftermath

The ambition of the House of Hapsburgh
robs me of my sleep!

JAMES FENIMORE COOPER[1]

After Napoleon's surrender in 1814, talk circulated about a European congress to be held in Vienna that autumn to determine the Continent's fate and future. The main powers to be represented were Russia, Prussia, Britain, and Austria. In September over two hundred delegates from states great and small gathered in the Hapsburg capital to chart a future for a Europe without Napoleon. Now in exile on Elba, he was presumed to be no longer a factor. Nearly all of Europe's leaders, along with their huge staffs and thousands of curious onlookers, descended upon the city. Few thought the Congress would last more than several weeks. When it convened, much seemed possible, nothing certain. Deliberations proceeded in a leisurely fashion and, to the amazement of all except Austria's chief minister, Prince Klemens von Metternich, a specialist in organizing distractions and delays, the Congress stretched itself out to nine months. The location of Vienna, the capital of the country that had fought longest, if with least success, against Napoleon, made it an appropriate venue to discuss the future of a Europe without the French emperor. In hindsight, the Congress marked the apogee of Austria's European renown. It became the social highlight of the decade. The city and its dignitaries appeared delighted to serve as hosts. Patriotic Austrian historians look back upon no other event in their history with greater pleasure.

The powers that be at the Congress had no intention of fostering a Europe that valued the ideals of *Fidelio*. Instead, they determined to reinforce or reestablish their respective versions of the ancien régime. In fact, the dignitaries meeting in Vienna would impose upon the peoples of Europe an absolutism even more severe than that which had prevailed before 1789 or at any stage of Napoleonic rule. In addition, the parties involved agreed to hold annual congresses in years to come to support each other and to crush yearnings for freedom wherever and however they might arise. And so it proved.

The official host of this extravaganza was the Austrian emperor Franz I. This individual feared change of any kind. Behind the scenes Metternich pulled the strings, assisted by Friedrich Gentz, the conservative publicist who kept the minutes of the Congress. The foreign dignitaries present included the titled of many lands. Tsar Alexander I, of German extraction, unusually for his time thought in pan-European geopolitical categories. Napoleon had found Alexander mystical and unpredictable, a puzzle he could not solve. His well-liked tsarina would count among Beethoven's most generous supporters at the Congress. Beethoven's former patron, the Russian count Razumovsky, also attended, as did Count Moritz Dietrichstein, an Austrian diplomat well aware of Beethoven. In 1815 the tsar made Razumovsky a prince. To represent French interests Louis XVIII dispatched his enormously intelligent but often duplicitous foreign secretary, Talleyrand. Viscount Castlereagh represented England, and King Frederick William III, Prussia.

While the presence of so many illustrious figures attending the Congress gave the local populace the illusion of civic distinction and European preeminence, the expenses involved in feeding, entertaining, and providing lodging for such a multitude of visitors in effect impoverished the city. Maintaining the varied activities month after month placed a heavy burden upon Vienna's citizens, who in essence paid for the Congress. In order to further Austrian interests and to reestablish Austria as a legitimate Great Power, Metternich included an endless stream of lavish social events—balls, concerts, excursions, and dinners—that deliberately slowed the pace of the proceedings. His policy had the secondary effect of consolidating Vienna's reputation for frivolity.

Among the wittiest of the Congress attendees was the aged Prince de Ligne (he was seventy-nine), a Hapsburg subject and military leader. This veteran (he would die during the course of the Congress) summarized the proceedings in a famous bon mot, "On a dit que j'ai dit que le Congrès danse et ne marche pas" (People say that I have said that the Congress dances and doesn't walk [work]).[2] His pun proved astoundingly accurate. Leisurely and largely social proceedings characterized European diplomacy at this time. What with balls to attend, intrigues to pursue, affairs to savor, and music to hear, resolving the many complex political problems left in the wake of Napoleon's departure did not appear to constitute an overly pressing concern. The delegates intended to redesign a Europe racked by twenty years of war, that is, to divvy up the spoils. The unstated premise of the Congress was to ensure that no country lapsed into revolution in the foreseeable future and that no established monarchy suffered civic disturbance. Most ominous of all, there came into being the so-called Holy Alliance, initially composed of three states—Austria, Prussia, Russia. Later France joined. Protestant Britain refused to participate.

Censorship was harsh during the nine months of the Congress. Metternich ran an efficient spy service. Police spies as well as informers circulated everywhere. The extent of the spying astonished foreign delegates. Not only did Congress spies monitor the activities of diplomats during these months, they kept a close watch on many of Vienna's residents and cultural figures. Though aware of the surveillance exerted over their activities, few congressional delegates or ordinary citizens realized how thorough it was. Women were watched as well as men.

❧

Beethoven Composes for the Congress

Early in the life of the Congress, many delegates came to attend a special performance of *Fidelio* on September 23, 1814—and ended up applauding and expressing pleasure over the opera. Did the delegates respond to the hopes and beliefs Beethoven had expressed in it? Or did they interpret Pizarro as a Napoleon-surrogate, or even (conjectures Berlioz) as a caricature of the defeated and now exiled emperor? Or did they see themselves as the Continent's collective deliverers, the Don Fernandos of Europe? If they truly understood Beethoven's intent in his music, which seems unlikely, most foreign dignitaries would have found anathema the ideals of freedom and liberty in *Fidelio*. The paucity of surviving documentation makes it difficult to draw conclusions.

Beethoven's musical eminence did not place him beyond governmental notice. During the Congress, and possibly earlier, Emperor Franz asked for, and received, police reports on the composer's activities. Officials had long regarded his political thinking—and even his dynamic music—with suspicion. Early on he may have sensed that the major players at the Congress intended to divide up Europe among themselves and for themselves. Such hopes as he had for a new Europe in which governments responded to the needs of the people and promoted respect for basic freedoms must have quickly vanished. Whatever the Congress determined, the result, he sensed, would be a sobering prospect. It even affected the nature of his creativity. By the end of 1813 the musical heroism characteristic of the previous decade had begun to fade. Work on *Fidelio* in the first six months of 1814 marked its close.

Amid the pleasurable activities offered Congress attendees, none attracted more attention than the abundance of music. Delegates attended performances of orchestral and chamber works as well as operas. To these festivities Beethoven made several well-received contributions. The Congress in fact accorded him considerable if temporary public fame. When Beethoven wrote that spring the E-Minor Piano Sonata, Op. 90, deafness had claimed much of his social life and his ability to earn money as a pianist. He dedicated the sonata to Count Moritz von Lichnowsky, younger brother of the late Prince Karl von Lichnowsky, his chief patron until October 1806. The prince, whom Beethoven had long and genuinely liked, had recently died in a fall from a horse. Count Moritz, whom Beethoven also valued, kept up the family's interest in the composer. Another work of this time, the Piano Trio in B-flat Major, WoO 39, Beethoven may have left unfinished. The premiere of the "Archduke" Trio, known by the rank of its dedicatee, had taken place at a charity Akademie on April 11, 1814. Schuppanzigh, again in Vienna, played the violin part, Linke the cello, and Beethoven, in his last public performance as a soloist, the piano. Beethoven's "heroic" style, which had come into being to celebrate the ideals of the Revolution and Napoleon, expired during the Congress in musical vehicles purportedly celebrating the Allied victory over the French emperor.

Performances of the Seventh and Eighth Symphonies earned him approbation, as did performances of *Fidelio*. But it was his compositions designed for special occasions, particularly his "battle symphony," *Wellington's Victory*, which he wrote a year before the Congress, and his cantata *The Glorious Moment*, which he wrote during it, that afforded him his greatest acclaim. Whereas the first celebrated Wellington's victory in Spain against a French army in June 1813, an event regarded by many as a turning point in a seemingly endless conflict, the second celebrated the "moment" when Napoleon's surrender in Paris early in April 1814 ended twenty years of war with Austria and its Allies. Even though both works lack sustained inspiration or deep emotional resonance, when performed during the Congress they drew enthusiastic applause. That the public regarded the glorious Seventh Symphony more as an appendage to *Wellington's Victory* than as a splendid achievement in its own right may shock us, but it would not have disheartened Beethoven. He knew what his symphony was worth. The potboilers that he turned out during the Congress, mostly in praise of the Allied war effort, were designed to entertain Congress dignitaries. Such works include *Tarpeja*, *Germania*, *Leonore Prohaska*, and music for the song "Es ist vollbracht"

(It is accomplished). They earned him both popular acclaim and a considerable measure of financial security. Happily, he was able to convert the funds from his Congress concerts into eight bank shares. Additionally, for his contributions to the Congress, the city of Vienna bestowed upon him the diploma of Honorary Citizen. In response, Beethoven asked privately whether there were also Dishonorary Citizens. That label he thought might fit him better.

The claims made for Beethoven's "patriotism" seem superficial. He had the habit of giving his more important works opus numbers. That he did not give opus numbers to most of his Congress compositions signaled that, for him at least, they were of lesser importance. Written quickly, several of Beethoven's Congress works are indeed mediocre. They reflect his disdain for the Congress and its attendees. The unmemorable compositions that purport to celebrate the Allied cause came about not because of genuine feeling but chiefly for economic reasons. From the concert bookings, he made friends with members of the newly founded Gesellschaft der Musikfreunde (Society of Friends of Music), an organization still active today. He even came to enjoy a modest prosperity. If 1813 had been a hard year for him financially, 1814–15 proved less so. Short as was his time in the congressional sun, Beethoven appreciated, even savored, the recognition he received. In fact, he actively sought it. The assembled dignitaries had ample opportunity to hear his music and to meet him. Some no doubt wondered about his erratic keyboard playing or gawped at his awkward attempts at conducting, but most knew that his deafness, now nearly total, had made both activities precarious. His music impressed some ears, unsettled others. Even those somewhat familiar with it found much that was radically new.

All the same, the Congress marks a decisive moment for Beethoven. It was the one period in his life when the Viennese, in part to please their distinguished guests, fêted him and his music. For the first time he became well known in Vienna. The acclaim he received vastly enhanced his public image abroad. The experience not only shaped his legacy but also affected the subsequent course of classical music. "The myth of 'Beethoven,' perhaps even the whole focus of western art music since," comments Martin Geck, "simply would not have happened without the Congress."[3] Geck's point is valid. As Napoleon's *gloire* faded, Beethoven's rose.

Occasional Music

Military music flourished throughout the revolutionary and Napoleonic eras. It occupies a significant place in Beethoven's oeuvre. Commissions for *Gebrauchsmusik*, "occasional," usually patriotic, music—that is, works meant for a specific event or purpose—had come Beethoven's way before. In 1796 and 1797, as Austrian forces in Italy reeled before Napoleon's advancing army, the Viennese authorities had twice asked the young composer to write a patriotic song or march in support of troops going to the front. Though he complied, both efforts when set against his compositions hymning freedom lack fervor. Other composers wrote compositions for the Congress of even lesser merit. E. T. A. Hoffmann, annoyed by their low quality, declared "war on all shallow musical experiences," not least on "battle symphonies."[4] Alas, too late.

Beethoven's Congress works mark the sacrifice of music to the occasion. In these compositions the heroic style of the past decade and more expires in an inglorious death. Beethoven had taken his time creating his major works. Their composition expressed the grand feelings emanating from his passionate and deeply considered political beliefs about freedom and liberty. These works he had pondered, but his Congress works he dashed off quickly. They detract from, rather than enhance, his reputation. Most have had few performances since and remain largely unknown to concertgoers. Ostensibly these pieces celebrate the end of the Napoleonic era and Austria's survival. That they succeed in doing this is questionable. Only *Wellington's Victory* has enjoyed a slight afterfame, mostly in pop concerts.

᪐

The Glorious Moment

Less than a year after the premiere of *Wellington's Victory*, Beethoven wrote a cantata entitled *The Glorious Moment*. Composed during the summer of 1814 for performance during the Congress, it joined the Seventh Symphony in a concert given in the Grosse Redoutensaal, the large concert hall in the Hofburg, on November 29, 1814. The hall was packed. High-ranking members of the aristocracy joined several monarchs. The work takes as its theme universal love. Yet even after revisions by Beethoven's longtime journalist friend Joseph Karl Bernard, Aloys Weissenbach's libretto seems juvenile in its expressions of unrestrained joy over the new era at hand. The work received several further outings, including being joined with *Wellington's Victory* and the Seventh Symphony on December 2 and 28 of that year.

Like *Wellington's Victory*, *The Glorious Moment* enjoyed tremendous popularity. With the Congress and its delegates in mind, Beethoven expressed hope in it that after more than twenty years of intermittent war an era of peace now loomed on the horizon. The dignitaries assembled in Vienna greeted the work with rabid enthusiasm. Repeat performances during the remaining months of the Congress document its contemporary popularity. Today this work, with its lightweight, somewhat clumsy text, rarely stirs the interest of listeners or stays long in memory. Its abstract figures—"Leader of the People," "Genius," "Prophetess," even "Vienna," along with its idealistic choruses of men, women, and children belting out platitudes—deny it a realistic human dimension. Claiming that it is no worse than other contemporary patriotic compositions offers us one way to evaluate the work. Other ways may hold more promise.

"Did the composer of the *Eroica* ever reflect on the irony implicit" in his celebrating the Congress of Vienna, asks Basil Lam, "that triumph of clericalism and royalism"?[5] Presumably Beethoven did reflect on the irony. Quite possibly, he intended *The Glorious Moment* to parody

Congress reality. Unlike *Fidelio* or his youthful *Cantata on the Death of Joseph II*, *The Glorious Moment* lacks passion and conviction. Beethoven knew well how to adapt his creative gift to circumstances. He could compose masterpieces but also works appropriate for conservative, not particularly musically inclined audiences that would celebrate occasions they deemed significant. In addition, the Allied leaders received as a lagniappe "very beautifully produced copies" of the work. *The Glorious Moment*, Schindler tells us, was extraordinarily well received. That the work did not mean much to Beethoven we may divine from its not being published until 1837, a decade after his death, and only then receiving an opus number.

To those present, delegates aware that the Congress had accomplished virtually nothing positive after several months, *The Glorious Moment* must have sounded like high comedy. In fact, it is best understood as a vocal *tableau vivant*, that is, a staged spectacle, a simulacrum of a politically desirable but unlikely "moment." In truth the "moment" celebrated involved no liberation of any kind. Instead, as Beethoven realized or divined, it commemorated the return of a reinforced and ever more rigid absolutism across Europe.

❧

Napoleon Escapes

Napoleon's diehard supporters in France had not abandoned hope. During the winter of 1814–15, while the Congress met, they thought of Napoleon as *Père la Violette*, "Father Violet." They dreamed that when the violets came up in March he would return to France.[6] And, miraculously for them, while the Congress met and Beethoven produced potboilers, Napoleon did. On February 26, 1815, after eight months of exile on Elba, he slipped away in three ships with twelve hundred men. On March 1 he landed on France's Mediterranean coast between present-day Juan-les-Pins and Cannes. His unexpected return threw European leaders into chaos. Most surprised of all were Louis XVIII in Paris and

Metternich in Vienna, where the news of his escape arrived on March 7. It had taken nine days to reach Vienna. Metternich informed his superior, Emperor Franz, then told the other monarchs in residence in Vienna. The Congress, in the midst of its deliberations, experienced a sudden jolt. The news stunned friend and foe alike. Some Congress conservatives, Prussian nobles among them, even gave Napoleon's escape qualified approval. In their view, the desire for freedom aroused in Germany by the Wars of Liberation against Napoleonic rule needed curbing, and they regarded the exiled emperor as a bulwark against the revolutionary currents of the day.

Upon debarking, Napoleon boldly declared that his eagle, the symbol of Napoleonic glory, would fly northwards from church steeple to steeple and in exactly twenty days would alight upon the steeple of Notre Dame in Paris. No one, he asserted, would lose his life. To oppose him, Louis XVIII had two hundred thousand men under his control. Napoleon, hoping to encounter less resistance along the way, instead of moving northwards up the well-traveled Rhone valley where royalist troops were stationed, shrewdly chose the far less populated but more rugged mountain route through the French Alps up to Grenoble.

When he heard the news of the escape, Louis sent forces to oppose and capture Napoleon. Bonaparte first encountered them in his march northwards before the narrow gorge of Laffrey on March 7. The two sides faced each other. An ominous silence resulted. No one wished to fire the first shot, so Napoleon walked over in front of the opposing troops, many of them veterans of his earlier campaigns. He told them that he, not Louis, was their true monarch. He asked them to abandon the king, who had already made himself unpopular, and join him and support his cause. A long moment's silence ensued. Then one soldier cried out *"Vive l'Empereur!"* Others joined in. Finally the entire force came over and enlisted under his banner. As Napoleon proceeded northwards to Grenoble, then westwards to Lyon, then again north toward Paris, his little army grew by leaps and bounds as he won over the successive forces Louis had sent to arrest him. On March 20, at eight p.m., his car-

riage rolled into the deserted royal palace, the Tuileries, where he rein-
stalled himself. The Bourbons, along with their aristocratic supporters,
had left the city the day before and fled north to Belgium. Napoleon's
"eagle" had indeed arrived on the steeple of Notre Dame on the day he
had said it would. No one had lost his life along the way. Napoleon was
once again master of France.

Thus began his final period of rule, known as the Hundred Days.
Its climax would occur at Waterloo, in Belgium, on June 18, 1815, when
Napoleon would for the first time meet Wellington, in charge of a joint
British-Dutch-Prussian army. The Austrian force was elsewhere. Napoleon lost that epic battle and returned post-haste to Paris. After Waterloo, Britain blocked all escape routes from the French coast. Napoleon
reluctantly surrendered to a British warship, the H.M.S. *Bellerophon*
on July 15. Once again he abdicated. He hoped to be granted refuge
in England, but less than a month later the British transferred him to
the H.M.S. *Northumberland*, which set sail immediately for the isolated
British-owned island of St. Helena in the South Atlantic. A new era for
Europe—and for Beethoven—now began.

ঙ

More Potboilers

Upon hearing the news of Waterloo, Beethoven composed *Die Ehren-
pforte* (*The Gate of Honor*), another potboiler, in collaboration with his
Fidelio librettist Treitschke, for a short dramatic *Singspiel* on the battle.
It had performances on July 15, 16, and 23, 1815. The fourth verse concludes, "God be thanked, and our Emperor, it is accomplished" ("Es ist
vollbracht"). The line, distantly echoing the words uttered by Jesus on
the cross, draws upon both the New Testament and Goethe. Despite
these credentials, it is another trite song. Mephistopheles in the first
part of *Faust* speaks the final three words. The music for "Es ist vollbracht" even quotes the Austrian national anthem! This dismal work
signals the end of Beethoven's heroic period.

Did Beethoven share in the widespread enthusiasm for Napoleon's defeat and exile? That seems unlikely. Otherwise, why had the composer, months earlier, on April 8, 1815, written a friend in Prague, four weeks after Napoleon's dramatic return to Paris, "Tell me, do you want a musical setting of the *soliloquy* of a refugee king [Louis XVIII, who had taken refuge in Belgium] or a song about the perjury of a usurper [Napoleon]?"[7] Beethoven's cryptic comment implies that he regarded the outcome of the decades-long conflict as a version of musical—and political—chairs. Its resolution left him, on the surface at least, indifferent, frustrated, but perhaps even, in some ways, pleased. After all, thanks to the Congress he had acquired a newfound popularity as well as considerable financial gain. In his compositions of this time, probably all four emotions—enthusiasm, indifference, regret, and acceptance—come into play.

Though pleased at the attention Congress attendees had given him and his music, Beethoven remained cynical about its goals. He harbored no illusions about the likely outcome of its deliberations. By late 1814, if not well before, he must have realized that in post-Napoleonic Europe the ideals of freedom in which he believed were at best imperiled, at worst doomed. Not on the table was a Europe of republics, or even a revamped Europe where freedom for the disenfranchised millions would prevail. Beethoven still preferred Napoleon, for all his imperfections, to the restored Bourbons. As his earlier enthusiasm for Emperor Joseph II indicates, he had nothing against monarchs per se. But he did not believe in autocratic government in which the governed had no say. Monarchical rule retained its legitimacy for him only as long as the monarch worked for the benefit of his subjects. Like many Germans of this (and later) eras who valued intellectual endeavor, Beethoven realized that to retain his creative gift he had to distance himself from any active involvement with politics.

❧

After the Congress

The end of the Congress of Vienna marked the beginning of a new era. Europe embarked on a resurgence of absolutism. Another generation of the populace had to live under restored or strengthened rulers. And the decisions they made gave the appearance of having a long life. When the yoke again became too oppressive to bear, that new generation too would revolt.

The Europe that came into being in the wake of Napoleon's exile seemed to many, Beethoven not least, a Europe far worse than the one before. Increased repression and the further loss of political liberties became the norm. During the decade that followed the Congress Beethoven, among others, reassessed Napoleon. Compared to the reigns of monarchs after the Congress of Vienna, Napoleon appeared to the composer and to others almost as a savior. In fact, in Beethoven's native Rhineland, now annexed by Prussia, living conditions had improved under his indirect rule. Absolutist regimes had no intention of bettering the lives of any but the ruling class. If the French emperor had been able to curb his mania for conquest, further advances in civic liberties might have taken place. With Napoleon gone, absolutist regimes could do—and did—as they wished.

Like other progressive-minded Europeans after 1815, Beethoven regarded Napoleon's exile to St. Helena with ambivalence. In the abstract, peace was desirable. The French Revolution had occurred almost twenty-five years before. The anciens régimes had won out after all. Napoleon had come and gone. With the world-shaker, his model and rival, in distant exile, Beethoven sensed that Europe would again undergo major change, that in Hapsburg lands whatever liberties still existed would grow fewer with each passing year.

Restless as always and increasingly dismayed by the political situation in Vienna, Beethoven again briefly thought of relocating to Paris. But in 1815, as in the year previous, the Allies returned the unpopular Louis XVIII to the French throne. Propped up by foreign troops—Prussian, Austrian, and British—who would occupy the country for several years, Louis presided over the reestablishment of an increasingly oppressive absolutism. Such conditions would not suit Beethoven, so he decided to stay on in what would remain the capital of Europe's most unforgiving police state.

Metternich continued to exercise iron control over civic affairs. He maintained an augmented system of surveillance over every aspect of domestic and civic life, including newspapers, journals, literature, the arts, and the universities. Ever insecure, Emperor Franz introduced, in the words of Franz Grillparzer, "a degree of police superstition, which is almost without parallel in recent history."[8] By continuing or reinforcing policies earlier adopted, Franz and Metternich further suppressed the principles of 1789. *Ruhe und Ordnung*—tranquility and order—became Austria's motto. Although most post-Napoleonic European governments enforced repressive measures, Austria became infamous for the ubiquity and omnipresence of its spies. Even the historian C. A. MacCartney, who has attempted to depict Franz more positively, conceded that "it was hopeless to expect anything during the lifetime of Frances [Franz], whose aversion to change of any sort had become almost pathological in advancing years."[9] Hapsburg doubts regarding Beethoven's loyalty remained. During the post-Congress decade the authorities continued to regard him and his friends with suspicion. The emperor still considered him a revolutionary and his music revolutionary in intent. Beethoven knew this. In midlife, his health uncertain, he dealt with his adopted city as best as could.

Censorship of the arts had been ongoing during Franz's reign. By 1815 it had robbed plays of much of their power and wit. Thus the theater gradually became complicit in the repressive Metternich system and further encouraged social paralysis. The "highly touted Austrian system" of benevolent despotism, wrote the talented young Viennese dramatist Eduard von Bauernfeld, in words dripping with sarcasm, was "a pure negative: fear of intellect, negation of intellect, absolute stasis, lethargy, stultification."[10] Though, as his hearing waned, Beethoven frequented the theater less often, he knew that the authorities muzzled the works of playwrights, including those by his young friend Grillparzer. The censorship also imposed tighter regulations upon the press. People retreated increasingly into private life. No less did censorship affect art. Even though Metternich himself did not meddle directly in artistic matters, he insisted that works of art not even hint at criticism of Austrian society. The censor had to approve pictures before artists could exhibit them. Even painting trips by artists into the mountains required government approval.[11]

ঽ

Renewed Creativity

Napoleon's second and final exile beginning in August 1815, along with a resurgent absolutism across Europe, seems to have affected Beethoven at a deep level. The turmoil of the Congress and its aftermath exhausted him. His hopes for change waned. The level of his creativity during the Congress had suffered. Beethoven had led a difficult existence during every stage of his life in Vienna. In the years from mid-1814 to late 1817 he composed fewer major masterpieces than in any other comparable period of his maturity—but compose he did.

Music without words did not usually undergo Viennese censorship. Fortunately, it was largely through music, not words, that Beethoven celebrated freedom. Life in an absolutist state can have positive effects upon the creative energies of its subjects: though it limits options, it tests resources and makes artists more determined to devise new ways for their creations to reach audiences. In the tense post-Napoleonic political scene, after over a decade of heroic striving, Beethoven sought once again a "new path": a path that, at least initially, seemed more tranquil than that with which he had inaugurated his heroic period.

In July and August 1815, after the Congress had broken up, his Fourth and Fifth Cello Sonatas, Op. 102, came into existence. Everything by

way of preparation, all the various portents and new departures apparent in earlier works, hardly mitigated the astonishing impression these
works made. They combine intensity with directness. Cello sonatas were
a relatively new form of music—Beethoven had written his first two in
Berlin as early as 1796, where resided the famed cellist Duport—so we
may assume the instrument was one to his liking. He dedicated them
to King Frederick William II of Prussia, who responded with a generous
gift. Though contemporaries found his two latest cello sonatas wanting,
they are the boldest if most problematic of the five he wrote. They have
established themselves as the gold standard of cello sonatas. Andan-
tes alternate with allegros, and cello and piano carry on a conversation
together. Paul Henry Lang deemed them Beethoven's "first works in this
new style, the beginnings of which are so diverse as to elude definition."
He ranked them "among the wonders of the time."[12] It was Beethoven
who established the cello as an important instrument in the world of
chamber music. The composer also turned to less ambitious subjects,
personal longings as in the song cycle *An die ferne Geliebte* (*To the Distant Beloved*) and the cantata *Meerestille und glückliche Fahrt* (*Calm Sea
and Prosperous Voyage*). Both these compositions seem to foreshadow
his developing evolution, while his "Gesang der Mönche" ("Song of the
Monks") harks back to his enthusiasm for Schiller's *William Tell*.

꒓

To the Distant Beloved

The song cycle *To the Distant Beloved* of 1815–16 ranks among
Beethoven's crowning achievements of these years. In it he set to music
six poems by Alois Jeitteles, a young Viennese medical student. The
work features both nature evoked in all the poems, and—on many
levels—memory. Though a sequence of related poems, it merges into a
single quiet lyric. Adolph Bernhard Marx, a leading nineteenth-century
biographer of Beethoven, compared *To the Distant Beloved* to "a carving
in ivory by Michelangelo."[13] It is that lovely.

Beethoven never totally subdued his longings for a romantic relationship. He had often fallen in love in the past. As the years went
by—with deafness increasing, his general physical state more fragile,
and his personal oddities more apparent—marriage became less likely.
To the Distant Beloved commemorates "the one woman he would never
possess," a bitter renunciation of what he "had regarded as the highest
happiness of his life."[14] Written four years after the fateful summer in
which Beethoven in effect bade farewell to his Immortal Beloved, it
suggests that the relationship continued to preoccupy him. The poems
are about longing, and the music reflects that longing. At this point in
time the identity of the Immortal Beloved matters less than the nature
of Beethoven's emotional involvement, the persistence of his unfulfilled
longings, and how they influenced both his life and his creativity.

To the Distant Beloved is the foundation stone of all song cycles. In
respect to unity, it is still the most perfect of the genre. The art song had
not yet developed a cult and in Austria the market did not exist for it.
Of the host of song cycles by others that followed in its train, including
Schubert's *Winterreise* and Schumann's *Dichterliebe*, none has greater
unity in its structural design than *To the Distant Beloved*.

ᣔ

Calm Sea and Prosperous Voyage

A brief cantata, *Calm Sea and Prosperous Voyage* (1815), lasting in most
performances about nine minutes, melds together two of Goethe's short
poems. The meditative first part anticipates the late string quartets. The
result is magical, one of the most beautiful pieces of music Beethoven
ever wrote. It affects us as powerfully as, in different ways, do the two
late cello sonatas.

It's possible that Beethoven had had actual experience of the sea. In
November 1783 he had gone with his mother to Holland to visit family
and to give a concert on the clavichord in the court residence of Prince
William V in The Hague. It is likely the trip included an excursion to

the nearby seaside resort of Scheveningen, which faces the North Sea, sometimes turbulent, sometimes calm.[15] Never again did he come near so large a body of water. Perhaps when writing the music for *Calm Sea* he recalled this youthful experience. Possibly, too, Beethoven in his cantata had in mind Napoleon's three-month sea voyage (August–October 1815) that took him from England's south coast to exile on St. Helena.

The first of Goethe's poems depicts a ship becalmed. In the age of sail mariners dreaded a tranquil sea because the ship would cease moving, with those on board using up food and resources and with no option to restock. After the excitement and hurly-burly of the Congress, did Beethoven ponder the "quiet deep" of his own soul? Did Goethe's "Calm Sea" resonate in Beethoven's own life? Had his "ship," his muse, become becalmed? How long would it so remain? When could he again sail on?

As an image of both roiling movement and infinity, the sea obsessed the great Romantic poets, among them Byron, Coleridge, and Heine.[16] Heine's cycle *The North Sea* has man brooding upon the mystery of the sea. In Byron's *Childe Harold*'s fourth canto the sea symbolizes immensity, escape, freedom, but also the possibility of return. Coleridge's *Rime of the Ancient Mariner* depicts a ship becalmed that makes a sudden lurch, then races back to port in Britain, an experience that leaves its single surviving crew member forever unbalanced and compelled to tell his tale.

No wonder Goethe's relieved mariners hail their arrival in port. Beethoven's music, in its depiction of quiet calm followed by sudden release, may imply, if interpreted autobiographically, that the future held for its creator the possibility of a "happy voyage." Like the cello sonatas, it promises a respite from the endless turmoil of the preceding decade. One can even imagine *Calm Sea and Prosperous Voyage* prefiguring the closing Adagio of his later Piano Sonata Opus 111, or the solo violin's quiet reflections in the Benedictus of the *Missa solemnis*, or the Adagio of the Ninth Symphony, even the "Heiliger Dankgesang" ("Holy Song of Thanksgiving"), the slow movement of the late String Quartet, Opus 132. Despite these achievements, Beethoven's forward movement in his own "voyage" did not resume with a major work until the autumn of 1817. It happened, with a burst of energy comparable to that in Goethe's poem "Calm Sea," when he began work on his extraordinary *Hammerklavier* Piano Sonata, Op. 106.

ℒ

"Song of the Monks"

Another work of this time, "Song of the Monks," for three male voices a cappella, sets to music the scene ending Act 4 of Schiller's *William Tell*. Beethoven had earlier longed to write an opera based on the work. Even without a commission he wrote this short piece. As recounted earlier, the guileless Tell, tricked by the cruel Austrian viceroy Hermann Gessler, has miraculously escaped from his clutches. He vows revenge. Positioning himself on a cliff overlooking the path that Gessler and his soldiers must take, he witnesses the viceroy's horse trampling a woman petitioner. Immediately he launches a crossbolt at the tyrant. His aim is again unerring, and Gessler falls, mortally wounded. A passing wedding procession converges in horror around the dying man. Then, as the viceroy's soldiers begin to leave, a procession of monks enters and forms a semicircle around the body. Just before they sing their song, Stüssi, one of the Swiss freedom fighters with whom Tell is linked, says sarcastically: "The victim's dead, and so the ravens come!" It is a bitter comment on Church support of tyranny, one that had as much relevance in Beethoven's day as in Tell's. "Song of the Monks" reminds us once again how pervasively Schiller's dramas influenced Beethoven; how, like Schiller himself, he detested tyranny, whether state or religious, and valued freedom.

ℒ

Biedermeier Austria

The era after 1815 in Austria and Germany later became known as the Biedermeier or, jokingly, *Backhendl* ("roast chicken") era. It lasted for over thirty years, from Waterloo to March 1848, when revolution broke out in Austria and in several other European states. The term *Biedermeier* derives from a fictitious humble Swabian schoolmaster and poet who feared change and was himself the creation of two twentieth-century doggerel poets.[17] It suggests quieter times and a focus on simple domestic pursuits. The German literary historian Hermann Glaser wittily defined Biedermeier man as an "introvert" who "escaped inward."[18] In its cultivation of the self, of privacy, of praise for family life, of an unwillingness to deal with a larger world, the Biedermeier era in its reluctance to support art and music and literature all too often thwarted an active rendering of creativity.

What happened all over Europe after 1815 was, to cite James Fenimore Cooper, "that species of desperate resignation which became a habit, if not a virtue, to men long accustomed to be governed despotically."[19] Such turning inward was marked in Austrian domains. Beethoven wrote music for those who he felt could keep alive the human spirit. In this way the work of Schubert, so different in substance from that of Beethoven, forms a close parallel to his. Schubert joined the Viennese men of letters who fled into their own world of poetry. In gatherings of like souls they could express freely bold and revolutionary ideas, filled with secret desires. No less than Schubert, the man who was already pondering his Ninth Symphony did not remain indifferent to the tide of reaction.

Living in Vienna under difficult personal as well as political circumstances did not, Beethoven believed, support the creativity he felt within himself. He not only detested the current regime but blamed it for his malaise. As noted earlier, in 1816, to indicate the misery of his plight, he described himself, half-humorously, as "a poor Austrian musical drudge."[20] Two years later he repeated the complaint in virtually the same words.[21] Only when he wished to accent the agony he felt in being chained to Vienna did this proud Rhinelander present himself, ironically, as "Austrian." Even his efforts to find a worthy housekeeper fueled his dissatisfaction with Viennese ways: "If, despite this utter moral rottenness of the Austrian state," he lamented, "one could feel certain even to some extent of being able to find some honourable person."[22] The years that followed brought no relief. "We poor wretches in Vienna have to pay for almost everything except *the air we breathe*," he complained in 1821.[23] He frequently commented about the grass being greener elsewhere. "It is hard for people living in Leipzig," he wrote the Leipzig publisher Peters in 1822, perhaps with pleasant memories of his stay in the city in 1796, "to realize that people in and near Vienna can never lead an undisturbed life."[24] Located in independent Saxony, Leipzig lay well beyond Hapsburg control.

꙳

Nephew Karl

In 1815 Beethoven's younger brother Kaspar Karl died, leaving behind a nine-year-old boy. He was the only Beethoven brother to have a child. In his will he had initially appointed Beethoven sole guardian of his son. But at the last minute, perhaps nervous about putting his tempestuous older brother in charge of his only child and heir, Karl inserted a coda that declared the boy's mother, his wife Johanna, co-adjudicator with Beethoven. But the composer wanted more, wanted in effect to keep the boy to himself. Sharing the child with Johanna, whom he detested and whom in letters he referred to as the "Queen of the Night" (after the malevolent figure of that name in *The Magic Flute*), did not suffice for Beethoven. He sued for full custody of young Karl. Initially he won the case, then lost it, then—after five long years of back-and-forth legal disputes and changes of custody—succeeded. But the constant legal battles took a toll on him, on the boy's mother, and on the boy. Many had found Beethoven a difficult man to deal with. Now, with his hearing nearly gone and a child to raise, he had to deal with a host of new details and expectations within his social world.

The composer had no experience in raising a child, and Karl caused him great frustration as well as considerable expense. Though Beethoven meant well, he was hopelessly ill-equipped for fatherhood, perhaps even, at this point in time, for any kind of family life. He dutifully concerned himself with Karl's education, insisting, for example, upon Karl's having "*scholarly* instruction in French."[25] Having himself been exposed to hearing French in Bonn, he wished to ensure that Karl had a good knowledge of that language, still the lingua franca among the aristocracy and well-to-do. He believed it would enable Karl to have access to a distinguished career. However, Karl was a rather average boy, and the composer had a hard time grasping his limitations.

Beethoven's letters, Conversation Books (to be discussed in Chapter 20), and the testimony of friends tell his side of the story, but may be lacking in sympathy for the child. Karl had lost his father and now his uncle was banishing his mother from his life. Editha and Richard Sterba, in their pioneering, controversial, but generally convincing study *Beethoven and His Nephew: A Psychoanalytic Study of Their Relationship* (1954), approach the situation from Karl's point of view. They document Beethoven's obsessive behavior toward him and present the boy as decent, thoughtful, and caring of his guardian. The perspective of Karl's mother, Johanna, is even less known. A study of it would complement our knowledge of a complex and evolving situation. In addition, Beethoven during these years often suffered from various maladies, at this late date hard to diagnose. A serious illness during the winter of 1816–17, lasting from October 15 to April 19, kept him from composing.[26] Occupied by legal matters and the guardianship of Karl, he lacked energy to attempt large-scale works.

❧

Meaning in Beethoven's Music

Beethoven claimed he wanted people to think his works had meaning. Partly this was to obscure the meaning, partly to avoid explaining it. Contemporaries close to him recognized how strongly he rooted his compositions in his own life. Certain of Beethoven's works, Schindler implied, contain "extramusical ideas." Beethoven almost invariably had specific meanings in mind for his compositions, and he wished people to learn what those meanings were. Ferdinand Ries, the son of his close Bonn friend, spoke of Beethoven's use of "psychological images." Carl Czerny, his devoted student and lifelong friend, agreed that they were indeed there.[27]

Even as early as 1810 the project of a collected edition, a *Gesamtausgabe*, was dear to his heart. In 1816 and again in 1823 he thought to publish an edition of his sonatas, with accompanying commentaries in which he described the musical ideas and psychological state that had led him to compose each work.[28] If such an edition had materialized—and it remained a hope for him to his dying day—it might well have placed the sonatas in the domain of program music.

The composer's desire to explain his meaning at times extended beyond the sonatas to encompass symphonies, concertos, and other compositions.[29] But Beethoven's bravado, his desire for others to understand his work, had its limits. He had in mind images, ideas, characters, moods, and musical events when he composed, but, fearing they would hinder perception on the part of the hearer, almost invariably wouldn't reveal what they were. Good sense prevailed. He came to recognize that, if he wished to survive in Hapsburg Vienna, he had to make choices. It was not wise for him to name his Third Symphony "Bonaparte"; nor could he, a few years later, dare to give to Napoleon the dedication of his Mass in C.[30] In venturing to think of such dedications he was being impractical, even foolhardy. Beethoven was often the former, almost never the latter.

The composer, let us admit, liked to mystify people. To discuss his works would be to demystify them. If it was unwise to explain his intent directly, might it not be better, after all, to let his contemporaries—and posterity—speculate for themselves about the meaning or meanings of his compositions? Words, Felix Mendelssohn believed, were of limited use in explaining music. For him, the words used to describe a piece "will always express the emotions conveyed by the piece less precisely than the piece itself."[31] Beethoven, I suspect, would have agreed. He left behind few clues; guides to his inner life he kept to himself, most of the time anyway. This meant that later generations, not having their imaginations stymied by any presumably authoritative statements, would continue to discuss his works endlessly. Which is what has happened.

The French Revolution had sought to liberate thought. Beethoven had become, at least to his more attentive listeners, a prophet of this freedom. His music spoke the language of liberty. A number of his works had revolutionary qualities. Talking or writing about them, he gradually realized, especially as repression in Hapsburg domains increased after 1809, and even more after 1815, would benefit few, least of all himself. Had the authorities divined or understood the true meaning of certain of his compositions, they would certainly have forbidden their performance. Beethoven realized his gift was to express meaning not through words, which could be censored, but through the instrumental music he preferred. With his music he hoped to evade censorship. Nietzsche argued for "the importance, for a creative person, of knowing how to wait, of allowing ideas to gestate naturally." That knowledge Beethoven possessed instinctively and to an exceptional degree. But other factors also came into play. The voice of liberty was not to be found in Austrian publications, which had undergone severe censorship.

ક

Beethoven's Journal

We can track Beethoven's development and thoughts before, during, and after the Congress of Vienna through the journal (*Tagebuch*) he kept from 1812 to 1818. It is the only journal he is known to have kept. During its first three years Napoleon's fortunes gradually declined; the second three witnessed the initial period of his final exile. When Beethoven began his journal, Napoleon had suffered his greatest set-back, the loss of most of his Grande Armée in the snows of Russia. It's possible that the Russian debacle prompted Beethoven to begin his journal. In it he pondered his reading, his life, his thoughts, his friends, his purpose and aims as a composer. During the years it covered he wrote less music than at most other times in his maturity. "For six years," comments Maynard Solomon, who has edited and translated the journal, "Beethoven used the Tagebuch to help him take stock of his situation, to regain his equilibrium, to give him insight into his con-flicts, and to externalize his pain and confusion over life's mounting vicissitudes."[32] In short, during this period Beethoven put himself back together again. By 1818, only after completing in the spring of that year one of his most powerful compositions, the magnificent *Hammerklavier* Sonata, to which we shall turn, did he cease making entries. Presum-ably he no longer needed to.

All his life Beethoven pondered the nature of society, of humanity. He often wondered how his music could bring about a better world. Living on the cusp between two eras, the end of the Napoleonic and the arrival of the yet-unnamed Biedermeier, he was too practical, too grounded an individual, to embrace utopian thinking outright. That did not prevent him, however, from attempting to think of ways to amelio-rate through his music the pains of existence.

20

Beethoven Close Up, 1817–20

One evening at Nussdorf in the summer of 1817, when Beethoven and the poet Kuffner were enjoying a fish dinner together at the tavern "Zur Rose," Kuffner made bold to ask the Titan—who happened to be in an amiable mood—which of his symphonies was his favorite (there were then, only eight).

"Eh! eh!" responded Beethoven, in great good humor, "the 'Eroica.'"

"I should have guessed the C minor," remarked his interrogator.

"No," insisted Beethoven: "the 'Eroica.'"

ANTON SCHINDLER[1]

"**D**eafness was to Beethoven what exile had been to others," comments Harvey Sachs. For Joseph Brodsky, who left his native Russia in the twentieth century, exile "accelerates tremendously one's professional flight or drift—into isolation, into an absolute perspective: into the condition in which all one is left with is one's self and one's own language, with nobody or nothing in between."[2] Beethoven's language was music, and he now used it to chart his inner life. As his hearing faded, that music became more unearthly. Living in Vienna was for him a form of exile. Insularity, hitherto largely a state of mind, now became a fact of life. He lived in a world of his own making, one quite detached from attention to everyday details and needs, one in which he strove to maintain his creativity.

When in the summer of 1817 the *Hammerklavier* Piano Sonata, Op. 106, erupted in his consciousness, he sought with it, as he had earlier in the century with the *Eroica* Symphony, a "new path." The *Cantata on the Death of Joseph II* of 1790 had established the foundation for Beethoven's heroic phase. Now, nearly three decades later, frustration with the repressive society in which he found himself propelled him into a new creative surge, also of *Eroica*-like proportions. He completed the *Hammerklavier* the following year, after which he began or sketched numerous major works, including his three final piano sonatas, the "Diabelli" Variations, the *Missa solemnis*, and the Ninth Symphony. In celebrating mankind's liberation, its potential for joy and communion, these works achieve a heroism at once more personal and more universal than that of the *Eroica*. They were followed by the last quartets, searing, unnerving, ineffable.

Europe at this time boasted an impressive array of tyrannies, but in its reactionary policies, in the terror and oppression that they caused, Austria was rivaled only by the somewhat later reign of the Russian tsar Nicholas I (1825–55). Beethoven's railings against the renewed absolutism that followed the Congress of Vienna rise in intensity. He speaks in a letter of 1817 of an Austrian official as "one of the chief asses of the Imperial State (which is saying a good deal)."[3] He continues to criticize Emperor Franz. All the same, through his new compositions Beethoven hoped to improve *"the condition of our country."*

ᘐ

The Lure of London

Searching for a new political model to admire among the "bazaar of nations" represented at the Congress of Vienna, Beethoven gazed across the Channel to England. Ironically, while Byron in Venice excoriated his native land in the years after 1816, Beethoven looked to Britain as an island of freedom. Anglophilia in post-Napoleonic Europe became very much the fashion. "If Germans looked to the West during these years," the German historian Hans Kohn tells us, "they preferred Germanic England, the roots of whose traditional liberty were believed to be firmly implanted in old Saxon soil."⁴ Baron Stein, the distinguished Prussian diplomat, became a determined Anglophile. Many other nineteenth-century Germans did so as well.

Britain's musical traditions had developed in ways different from those in German lands. Jacobean England had been the earliest European society to value instrumental music more highly than vocal. Opera did not gain as solid a footing in Britain as elsewhere in Europe. Popular taste forced Handel, long resident in England, to switch in the late 1730s from operas to oratorios. All the same, England, the wealthiest nation in Europe, had a vibrant musical culture, much of it fueled by foreigners. After Handel, Haydn in two long stays in the 1790s had enchanted London and Oxford society with his new symphonies and his presence. If few foreign musicians settled there, many like Ries, Moscheles, and Weber followed Haydn to earn the success and income they were unlikely to find in their native lands.

Like Haydn, Beethoven came to regard the English as a different order of beings. He had often talked about following in the older composer's footsteps and visiting, even living, in London.

He made several tentative plans to go to there. After 1815 such thoughts, never far away, gained in intensity. During what would be his final decade, few years passed in which he did not express his intention of visiting Europe's largest and richest city, and he often made preliminary preparations to go. As an added incentive, Beethoven became enamored of the British system of rule by Parliament, one in which the monarchy accepted limitations placed upon its power.

As with his earlier longings for Paris, he was fully aware of the hard realities of travel. Furthermore, having to deal with a new language, especially for a man now almost totally deaf, made such a voyage highly problematic. Given his physical handicap, along with the discomforts of travel, he stayed put. In short, for a man past midcareer, particularly one now with a child to raise and educate, starting over would be too hard.

Beethoven had earlier seemed unaware of the extent of censorship in Napoleonic France. After 1815 he seemed unaware of its extent in Britain. His idealistic conception of the English political scene favored the minority Whigs, long in quasipermanent opposition to the dominant Tories. Out of office for decades, the Whigs did not return to power until the early 1830s, well after Beethoven's death. One of Beethoven's great ambitions was to visit the House of Commons. Of Whig statesmen, he responded most to the eloquent Henry Brougham, a lawyer, distinguished orator, and inveterate supporter of liberal causes. Whenever the House of Commons was in session after Waterloo Beethoven would have newspapers delivered to his apartment so that he could follow the parliamentary debates. He read them eagerly, becoming in effect "a man of the English opposition."[5]

English statesmen of the time did not quite grasp the extent of political oppression in post-Waterloo Europe. Nor did they comprehend the extreme fear that European aristocrats felt before liberal thinking. Beethoven, in effect, misjudged the limits on freedom in Britain. Fortunately he never put his notions of going to London to the test. For so committed and fervent an idealist disillusionment would almost certainly have followed.

❧

Post-Congress Vienna

Although Beethoven did not move out of Austria, he moved frequently within Vienna. Its population by 1824 had reached, by one estimate, 289,598, of which only 49,550 lived within what remained of the city walls. By the mid-eighteenth century the nobility, clergy, and court personnel owned seven-eighths of the land within that restricted area. Beethoven's frequent changes of residence were due to the limited availability of housing, as well as to the Viennese custom of tenants being

able to give notice twice yearly on specific dates. But his constant restlessness was more likely a sign of inner unease as well as of societal discomfort and high rents. Although Beethoven liked living in or close to
the city center, it became harder to find affordable lodgings there. Reluc-
tant to put down ties in his adopted city, he never stayed long anywhere
he lived. Sometimes he even held several apartments concurrently, and
occasionally he returned to previous lodgings. Admittedly, Beethoven
did not always make himself welcome as a tenant. He kept his living
quarters in extraordinary disarray, was careless about furniture, played
the piano at night, and while washing himself spilled sufficient water
for it to go through the floor and douse the inhabitants below.

After nearly twenty-five years the Viennese had become more or
less accustomed to Beethoven and his ways. "People in other countries
often said that Beethoven was disregarded and suppressed in Vienna,"
commented Carl Czerny. "The truth is that even as a young man he
was supported, encouraged and esteemed by our aristocracy in a way
that has hardly ever been the lot of a young artist." Beethoven, Czerny
believed, did not deserve too much sympathy. The Viennese allowed
for his temper and hypochondria. "It is doubtful, " he concludes, "that
he would have been treated with such forbearance anywhere else."[6]
Czerny's perspective, sincere and well-intended, holds some truth. But
Beethoven's frequent tales of tribulations amid the Viennese reveal at
least his discomfort there. A "darling of Vienna" Beethoven was not,
and never became. As with Mahler a century later, "the steel in him
reacted against the softness of the Viennese of his day."[7]

The government actively persecuted creative artists only rarely,
but as the fortunes of Grillparzer reveal, persecution existed all the
same. Though Vienna had decreed Beethoven an Honorary Citizen
of the city during the Congress, the honor struck him as hollow, and
he continued to be wary of the authorities. His disdain for Vienna
remained constant after 1815. He complained bitterly and often to intimates about the loss of human rights and the increasing censorship.
Grillparzer once told Beethoven that if the imperial censors under-

stood music the way they understood words, they would throw him into prison.

As the Conversation Books reveal, Beethoven expressed republican sentiments vocally after 1818, but surely he had done so well before. His letters—more of which exist from his final decade than from those preceding (in part because recipients now more frequently kept them)—detail his increasing disillusionment with Viennese life. On February 15, 1817, writing to his Bonn friend Franz Brentano, he attributes his ill-health to the political situation: "As for me, my health has been undermined for a considerable time. *The condition of our country* has been partly responsible for this; and so far no improvement is to be expected, nay rather, every day there is a further deterioration."[8]

Beethoven never truly felt at home in Vienna. He tolerated rather than enjoyed the city. "I may say," he wrote to Karl Amenda in Latvia on April 12, 1815, "that I live almost *entirely* alone in this, the largest city of Germany, since I must live practically cut off from all the people whom I love or could love."[9] Grillparzer felt much the same. He complained "that the conditions which prevailed in Austria were far less favorable to his artistic activity and personal development than those of certain other countries might have been."[10] By 1815 Vienna had already begun a century-long decline. If still a cultural capital of the German-speaking world, the city was no longer its political center or leader.[11] Cultural hegemony gradually passed to the north German cities, Leipzig, Dresden, and, increasingly, Berlin.

و

The Conversation Books

In 1816 his hearing trumpet had still allowed Beethoven to pick up bits of conversations, but by 1818 his deafness was nearly total. Despite claims of loneliness in these later years, he gathered around him a circle of friends and acquaintances, mostly journalists and musicians. Not nearly as well-off as the aristocratic patrons who had favored him in the decades before 1815, and not nearly as well-known as his earlier circle of friends, these individuals yet offered him companionship, even friend-ship. With such mostly like-minded souls he shared his increasingly radical views concerning the nature of Viennese society. The era of the Conversation Books (*Konversationshefte*) had begun.

In early 1818, Beethoven's close friends, aware of his desire to social-ize, began to meet in taverns and coffeehouses, setting down in note-books what they wished to say to him. Beethoven usually answered orally. Sometimes, though rarely, he wrote comments in the notebooks. We thereby catch glimpses of his ideas. Amid this circle, Beethoven could speak his mind. "The foundation of friendship," he told a corre-spondent, "demands the greatest similarity in the souls and hearts of men."[12] He had found at last a group of congenial friends.

According to Theodore Albrecht, Beethoven's Conversation Books once numbered between 250 and 275. After Beethoven's death almost all of them came into the possession of Anton Schindler, his unpaid amanuensis, in 1822 and occasionally at other times. Schindler, conser-vative and a monarchist, clearly felt uncomfortable with the liberal, even radical, political opinions expressed by Beethoven and his friends. After Beethoven's death, Schindler added to the Conversation Books some 240 entries favorable to himself and his activities to suggest that a greater inti-macy existed between himself and Beethoven than in fact did.[13] In 1840 he published the first large-scale biography of the composer, one that included perspectives drawn from the Conversation Books. Schindler then disposed of most of them. One hundred thirty-nine survived, and in 1845 he sold those he still had, some 137, to the Prussian State Library in Berlin. Two others have subsequently turned up. In those that we have, sixty-five entries offer Beethoven's views on current events. If we still had them all, a more radical Beethoven would in all likelihood emerge.[14]

Many of Beethoven's male friends were politically inclined middle-class professionals who relished discussion of affairs in Austria and elsewhere, as did Beethoven. Though Austrian censorship limited domestic coverage, Vienna's newspapers did report goings-on in other

European countries, sometimes in surprising detail. Foreign newspapers were occasionally available. Beethoven was well versed in the progress of the revolutions that broke out in Italy and Spain in 1820 and in Greece three years later. He decried the French invasion of Spain in 1823. And, as noted earlier, he eagerly followed parliamentary proceedings in Britain. Alongside his consistently negative responses to Metternich's policies, the Conversation Books reveal an increasingly positive regard for the exiled Napoleon.

The Conversation Books also introduce us to several of Beethoven's intimates during these years. Whereas before 1815 his circle of friends included a number of aristocrats, his associates in later years were more likely to be working people, journalists, clerks, publishers in the music business, occasionally men of some culture, such as the composer and music critic Friedrich August Kanne. Another was Joseph Karl Bernard, composer of a Faust opera, who met Beethoven in 1816 and became one of his closest friends. A journalist by profession, he seems to have been the most politically savvy of Beethoven's coffeehouse intimates. He helped keep Beethoven informed about political repression in Austria and elsewhere. It was he who in 1817 informed the composer about the extensive student uprisings in Germany. Two years later they discussed the murder, still fresh in the minds of many, of the conservative playwright August von Kotzebue by the German university student Karl Sand.

Almost all exchanges recorded in the Conversation Books occurred in local restaurants and taverns. Any public place Beethoven and his friends chose to meet would likely have government spies present who might overhear them talking. With Beethoven now largely deaf, his friends had to raise their voices. And Beethoven himself, unable to gauge the level of sound his voice produced, often spoke loudly. Tensions among patrons increased correspondingly.

Beethoven's friends constantly warned him against speaking too frankly in public about political issues. It was not just talk. The risks were real. Fear of being overheard limited conversational freedom and no doubt affected the nature of the topics raised. On several occasions one of those present warned the others that a government spy lurked nearby, thus indicating that they should lower their voices or change the subject or remain quiet. An entry in one of Beethoven's Conversation Books (presumably recording a gathering of friends at a café) stops the talk in midflow with the ominous words: "another time—just now the spy is here."[15] Bernard recounted to Beethoven an occasion in March 1820 when Joseph Czerny (no relation to Carl) had told him that the Abbé Gelinek, who had dueled on the piano with Beethoven decades before, had spoken "very angrily" against him at the Camel, a well-known restaurant occasionally frequented by the composer and his friends. Alluding to Kotzebue's assassin, Gelinek "said you were a second Sand, that you abused the Emperor, the Archdukes, the ministers, and would end on the gallows yet."[16] Worse still, Beethoven felt, was the suppression of free speech in public places. "I must add that *everything around* and near us compels us to be *absolutely silent*," he complained.[17]

What has not happened, Nietzsche once remarked, is in the long run more influential than what has happened. Much did not happen in Vienna. Newspapers, books, plays, other kinds of theatrical performances, musical compositions with words: all confronted increased censorship after 1815. Metternich's policy not to disturb the status quo lasted until the Revolution of 1848, the year he had to leave office.

ঙ্গ

Political Ferment

Nationalist enthusiasm in Germany became channeled among the young into the *Burschenschaften*, the often militant student societies. Christian and nationalist, they rejected the oppressive political world imposed upon them and instead looked back longingly to an imagined Middle Ages of liberty. Enter twenty-three-year-old Karl Sand, a theology student at the University of Giessen and a *Burschenschaft* member. On March 13, 1819, he assassinated the popular playwright Kotzebue.

He intended his act as a blow against reactionary forces. He confessed to the crime and was hanged. But his bold deed marked a turning point in public awareness. Originally a supporter of freedom and a democrat, Kotzebue had by 1818 become an obstreperous propagandist for conservative causes. His newly founded *Literarischen Wochenblatt* (*Literary Weekly*) opposed the national uprising of German youth. His risqué comedy *Lovers' Vows* ridiculed the *Burschenshaften*, who resented it bitterly.

The murder of Kotzebue outraged conservatives and launched a period of widening political oppression in the German states. In the wake of his death, Prussia under Frederick William III, guided by Austria's Metternich, put through the notorious Karlsbad decrees, which placed even stricter limitations on personal freedom. The decrees banned the *Burschenschaften* in German universities, subjected them to police surveillance, enforced a rigid censorship on all publications of the press, and made anyone who publicly expressed dissatisfaction with the regime liable to severe punishment. Jews, perennial scapegoats, again could no longer hold office. A conference held in Vienna under Metternich's direction from November 25, 1819, to May 15, 1820, not only adopted the Karlsbad decrees but imposed further restrictions upon the Austrian populace, especially those in universities. Sand's deed had repercussions well beyond the Germanic lands. Radical Russian intellectuals, noted Alexander Herzen, who was himself one, "put on velvet *berets à la* Karl Sand and tied identical tricolour scarves round [their] necks."[18]

These years proved difficult for Beethoven. The political situation in Europe afforded him little cheer. The uncertain course of his nephew Karl's education had become a constant cause of stress, and he continued to suffer from various illnesses that may have included an attack of jaundice and rheumatic fever. Yet he gave no signs of abating his zeal to have basic freedoms established.

❧

Josef Karl Stieler Portrays Beethoven

An indication that Beethoven still wanted to be perceived as politically engaged is his portrait by Josef Karl Stieler. Today it remains the best-known rendering of the composer. A Munich-based artist, Stieler had painted many of that city's worthies. He later did a well-known portrait of Goethe. Earlier he had studied with the leading Viennese artist of the day, Heinrich Friedrich Füger, whom Beethoven had met twenty years before. In the Conversation Books of 1819–20 Stieler occasionally appears among the composer's friends.

In late 1819 Franz von Brentano, an old friend of the composer's then living in Frankfurt, commissioned Stieler to do a portrait of Beethoven. He had painted portraits of Brentano; his wife, Antonie; and their growing family. During the three years they spent in the Austrian capital, 1808–11, Beethoven had virtually adopted them as a surrogate family. It may have been Antonie—long a candidate for Beethoven's "Immortal Beloved"—who wished to have it done. Beethoven granted Stieler three sittings. Being a friend of the Brentano family and of equitable temperament, the artist got along well with his sitter. When Willibrord Mähler had painted Beethoven in 1804–05 he had shrewdly revealed, with Beethoven's assistance, the composer's revolutionary sympathies. Stieler did much the same. His portrait confirmed that Beethoven's revolutionary zeal had not waned, that the hopes he expressed in the *Eroica* and *Fidelio* remained vibrant.

Stieler presents Beethoven even more dramatically than Mähler. As had his predecessor, he drew upon the portrait of Beethoven's grandfather hanging on the wall of the composer's lodging. His pose reverses that of the grandfather. Color also plays a key role in this composition. Though Beethoven owned frock coats in the traditional colors of brown, gray, and bottle-green, he is once again depicted in one dark blue. An unusually large white collar frames the lower part of his face. Artists often painted Byron with such a collar, and Stieler may have seen an engraving of one of Byron's portraits. Much more evident than Mähler's conventional neckcloth, Stieler's exaggerated open collar outdid even those in depictions of the English poet, then much in the news for his active support of the insurgency in Lombardy against the oppressive Austrian regime there.

Stieler used an unusually large bright red scarf to set off both the blue coat and the white collar. Except for military uniforms, red was rare for male attire. The choice must have been Beethoven's. During one of the century's most repressive years, the composer again wished to clothe himself in blue, white, and red. Not only is red the color of revolution, but the artist uses red as an accent in the painting on Beethoven's chin and fingers, even more on his cheeks and lips. The rosy cheeks imply a much younger and healthier man than Beethoven now was. But, though pale and sick in reality, he is portrayed in radiant health and in the full vigor of maturity.

In short, Stieler depicted Beethoven not only in his attire but in his whole being as the embodiment of revolution. Here was someone with a lot of fight left in him. Whereas Mähler portrayed Beethoven sitting within a natural setting rich in symbolic meaning, Stieler portrayed him from the waist up and closer in presence, thus more dominant. Whereas Beethoven in the Mähler reaches out to us, invites us to join him in a revolutionary enterprise, Stieler captures Beethoven in the throes of composition. His facial expression is insistent, determined: his head tilted slightly forward, jaw set, eyes focused, his glance indicative of deep thought. "No day without a line" (*nulla dies sine linea*), the personal motto Beethoven adopted from Pliny, marks him as a man devoted to his art, a man who knows what his role in the world is destined to be.

The composer's uncompromising look indicates that he had not retreated an inch from his earlier beliefs. If anything, his challenging demeanor had intensified over the years. The face depicted in the Stieler, in relation to the body, appears as if magnified. The eyes focus upon a point beyond the viewer toward a world that has not yet come into being. A leonine head of hair, brushed back and lustrous, crowns the visage. Now graying, the hair is longer and thicker than in the Mähler, but still unruly, essentially uncombable. Its wildness indicates the wildness of Beethoven's character and hints at the wildness of his music. The expression conveys the need for societal reform as well as for increased personal freedom. It offers hope that humankind might live in a renewed and more equitable society.

Stieler's verdant landscape, abetted by the composer's determined glance, reinforces the need for a renewal of hope. He presents Beethoven surrounded by the nature in which he reveled. Yet it is a nature Stieler conjured up himself, for he worked on the portrait during the winter months. No Tree of Liberty is in sight, for by 1820 the restored monarchs had uprooted any that had survived. Beethoven is holding the *Missa solemnis* in his left hand. His pen is in the right, poised to compose. In early 1820, the time of the painting's completion, the *Missa* was hardly begun. Work on it would progress slowly. *Leonore/Fidelio* excepted, no other of Beethoven's major compositions would demand so much of his time and cause him so much frustration. Beethoven's intense glance reminds us of the great hopes he placed in his compositions, in particular the *Missa*. It would be a culminating work, one that would embody the ideals he valued most. Beethoven must have liked this portrait. The publisher Artaria had lithographs of it made, and in the last year of his life the composer gave them to friends.

The Stieler portrait presumably went to the Brentano family in Frankfurt, who had commissioned it. As the significance of the Brutus statue in Beethoven's thinking was not fully understood until recently, so only now can the portraits—and what Beethoven, in collusion with Mähler and now Stieler, attempted to achieve by them—be properly assessed. Like the statue, the portraits offer us another way, a separate channel of sorts, to respond to Beethoven's political views as evoked in representations of his being.

21

Napoleon's Death, Rossini's Rise

Always *he*, he everywhere, as people say of Napoleon.

GIOACHINO ROSSINI

W ith the absolutist regimes in Europe seemingly more entrenched in power than ever after 1815, Beethoven had cause to reassess Napoleon. Whatever his deficiencies, the exiled emperor stood head and shoulders above Europe's current rulers. The liberation Beethoven had hoped Napoleon would accomplish two decades before, he through his music was determined to encourage.

Beethoven was not the only creator to set his career against that of Napoleon. Byron had done the same. In April 1814 the poet, furious at learning that Napoleon, instead of choosing death in battle, had abdicated, dashed off in frustration and anger his "Ode to Napoleon Buonaparte." However, his adulation soon returned. In Byron's poems on Napoleon in the years after 1816 the exiled emperor emerges, more often than not, in heroic guise. During these years Byron also became actively involved in revolutionary politics in Italy, then in 1824, in military engagement in Greece.

During the heroic decade that ended in 1814 Beethoven's works had often been dynamic in nature. The post–Congress of Vienna years, a few exceptions aside, provided a lull. In compositions written after 1821, the year Napoleon died, the dynamism returns. Even in exile Napoleon continued to play a significant role in Beethoven's development. The composer boldly drew upon the diverse musical forces active in his creative imagination to produce new works. In his political views, his conception of society, and his music, he remained as much as anyone of his generation a Romantic revolutionary.

٩

Napoleon's Death

On May 5, 1821, Napoleon died in exile on St. Helena. He was fifty-one. The news of his death reached Europe in mid-July. The death capped his martyrdom, making him even more a mythic figure. Sanctified by both his captivity and his departure, the legend achieved a perfection of its own. While Napoleon's death staggered many of his admirers, the great man's example and influence grew exponentially. Certainly after 1821, and perhaps years earlier, Beethoven's reservations about Napoleon continued to fade. Likewise, Byron's. Even Chateaubriand, no liberal but, like Beethoven and Byron, one who gauged his career in relation to Napoleon's, continued to ponder and write about him until his own death nearly three decades later. Napoleon's death profoundly affected countless others across Europe. Both William Hazlitt and Walter Scott embarked on massive biographies of the deceased emperor, one from a liberal, the other from a conservative perspective. To understand him was to understand the era he had dominated—and perhaps even learn something about oneself.

By 1821, with the European alliances that Metternich had so determinedly forged at the Congress of Vienna beginning to fray, revolts major and minor had broken out all over Europe—in Poland, Italy, Sardinia, the Rhineland, Prussia, England, and the Papal States. Napoleon's name was invoked by progressives, liberals, republicans, and, not least, by socialists and revolutionaries. England early withdrew its support for the active suppression of revolts in Europe, and in 1823 France under Louis XVIII invaded Spain alone to restore a fellow monarch, Ferdinand VII, despised by the populace. Many Europeans recalled that Napoleon had once supported not repression but movements of national liberation.

A hero can be perceived as greater in failure than in victory. People often take victories for granted, but defeats can linger longer in memory. Defeat does not destroy the legend; often it creates, amplifies, and sanctifies it. Defeat can become the stuff of epic: Hector killed by Achilles before the walls of Troy in the *Iliad*, Achilles humbled by Priam's entreaties, Leonidas and his three hundred Spartans overwhelmed at Thermopylae, Roland in charge of Charlemagne's rear guard at Roncesvalles crushed by Muslim armies in *The Song of Roland*. And, not least, Napoleon's defeat at Waterloo followed by his exile to St. Helena.

For many, including Beethoven, Napoleon existed in two worlds. One was the world of war and bloodshed, of political reform and progress; the other was the revolutionary world Beethoven dreamed of, a utopian existence he created in his mind and subsequently in his music. That first world was historical reality; the second, an adumbration of things hoped for. The dream, as the French critic Albert Béguin has reminded us, can become the more engaging reality.[1] So it had become for Beethoven.

Well before his death, folklore and legend had enveloped Napoleon. That legend led his admirers to regard him as being as great after his fall from power as during his days of *gloire*. For many Europeans, Napoleon's sufferings on St. Helena only enhanced his messianic aura and became a key aspect of his legend. Admittedly, an opposite tradition existed concurrently, in which Napoleon became not the Messiah but the Anti-Christ, the devil incarnate. This countertradition had its greatest impact in 1814, 1815, and 1821, the year of his death. Beethoven, well aware of both traditions, by and large viewed Napoleon positively.

The Napoleonic legend had emerged as early as the Italian campaign of 1796–97. For about fifteen years Napoleon sought to cultivate the flame of European unity under his aegis. Even after exile to St. Helena, ten thousand miles from the European mainland, Napoleon developed a plan. Having lost at Waterloo, he turned to the pen. With the aid of his chosen associates, he began to issue accounts of his career, by one tally eighteen in all. In these accounts—whether written by those whom he met on board the H.M.S. *Northumberland*, which brought him to St. Helena, or written by visitors to that island, or dictated to the companions who accompanied him into exile—Napoleon defended himself and his policies with his accustomed vigor. He presented himself as the victim of the Holy Alliance and justified his actions as essential for the liberation of Europe. He established an audacious parallel between his fate and that of the peoples oppressed by the victors of 1815. Representing himself as a liberal alternative to the absolutist monarchs of Europe, he rewrote the history of the era. Manuscript after manuscript made its way surreptitiously back to Europe. Quickly published, they mesmerized readers.

Oblivion on St. Helena was thus not Napoleon's fate. Rather, a kind of Romantic halo now settled upon him, self-created but also placed there by his many admirers. On St. Helena Napoleon reclaimed, even increased, his allure as a champion of liberty and as a begetter of change. Isolated from all but the few who shared his exile, he became an object of compassion in Europe. No longer able to fulfill in reality the dreams of many, Napoleon became in legend greater still.

The best-known work by one of Napoleon's companions in exile was the vast *Mémorial de Sainte-Hélène* (1823–24), published after his death. In it Emmanuel de Las Cases argued with great eloquence and in equally great detail for the validity of Napoleon's vision. It presented the emperor as a revolutionary and also as a liberal leader who favored republics. For the Dutch historian Pieter Geyl, "a remarkable ideological feature of the first Waterloo generation," one that included Victor Hugo, Stendhal, Byron, and Beethoven, "is the association of the Napoleonic legend with radicalism." Las Cases's hugely influential reinterpretation of the emperor's career largely determined Napoleon's posthumous fame. For those who were young in the legend's heyday—Berlioz as

well as Hugo among them—Napoleonic Europe constituted a kind of
lost paradise, a might-have-been time, whose disappearance had hurt
them more than they initially realized. Hugo, in a famous poem, "Lui,"
does not mention Napoleon by name. ("Lui" is French for "he.") But all
who read it knew that "Lui" could only be Napoleon and that its author
could only be Hugo.[2]

The young German poet Heinrich Heine, overwhelmed by the
emperor's death in exile, imagined future generations making pilgrim-
ages to his tomb on St. Helena. In Stendhal's *Charterhouse of Parma*
Fabrice del Dongo, the uncertain hero, wonders about a future without
Napoleon. "Now that the revolutionary-imperial adventure has been
snuffed out," he asks, how can I pointedly make something of myself?
Others of his generation who canonized the French emperor posed the
same question. Grillparzer's poem "Napoleon" evinces a more questioning attitude, yet speaks all the same of "the epic breadth and the
heroic lament" inspired by Napoleon. Surprisingly, despite the trauma
of the 1812 invasion and the subsequent burning of Moscow, many Russians also revered Napoleon. Upon learning of his demise, Alexander
Pushkin expressed grief, seeing him "as a figure who has bequeathed
eternal freedom to the world."[3] Other Russian liberals who lamented
Napoleon's death included Mikhail Lermontov, and later Fyodor
Dostoevsky.[4]

ॐ

Beethoven Responds to Napoleon's Death

And Beethoven? The news seems to have affected him greatly. When
Schindler asked him whether he was going to commemorate Napoleon's
death, Beethoven replied that he had "already composed the appropriate
music for that catastrophe." Presumably he was referring to the Marcia
funebre of the *Eroica*.[5] For Beethoven, as for other artists, that death
inspired a new surge of homage. When in 1824 he happened upon a
premature announcement for Walter Scott's multivolume *Life of Napo-*

leon, he exclaimed to Czerny: "Napoleon; earlier I couldn't have tolerated him. Now I think completely differently."[6] Pondering Napoleon's mighty trajectory across Europe, Beethoven realized that at times he had criticized the emperor too severely. When he saw that Napoleon's adversaries had used their victory in 1815 not to bring enlightened leadership to their subjects but to reinforce or reintroduce absolutism, he regarded the exiled emperor with greater indulgence.

The most extended comment on Napoleon in the Conversation Books occurs in an entry in January 1820, more than a year before Napoleon died. In it Franz Janschikh, a customs official, makes a strong case for Napoleon's enduring greatness. Yet as an expression of Beethoven's perspective on the emperor the passage rings true:

> If Napoleon were to come again, he could expect a better reception in Europe. . . . He was acquainted with the spirit of the time, and knew to keep a tight rein on things. . . . Our posterity will value him more highly. . . . As a German, I was his greatest enemy, but with the passage of time, I have become reconciled to it. . . . Promised loyalty and belief are past. . . . His word counted for far more. . . . He had a sense of art and science and hated the darkness. . . . He would have valued the Germans more and ought to have protected their rights. . . . In the final days [of his regime], he was surrounded by traitors, and the spirit had deserted the Generals. The best Field Marshalls had retired. . . . The children of the Revolution and the spirit of the time demanded such an iron will, though he overturned the feudal system in general and was the protector of rights and of law. . . . His marriage to Princess Louise was the highest culmination point. . . . Here the intention was to provide world peace and good laws, and the desire to undertake no more conquests. . . . Greatest good fortune and, through arrogance, greatest misfortune.[7]

Presumably the composer's silence here indicates approval of Jan-schikh's words. The concision and eloquence suggest Janschikh may even have drawn upon Beethoven's own views, for his words clearly reflect the composer's response to Napoleon. Beethoven's friends rarely questioned his opinions. Janschikh urged Beethoven to write a Napoleonic hymn,[8] but Beethoven never did. Instead, he composed such great and humane music as the "Diabelli" Variations, the *Missa solemnis,* and the Ninth Symphony, as well as the last three piano sonatas, all works through which blows the revolutionary breeze.

Three decades of living in the police state that was Austria had convinced Beethoven that whatever Napoleon's flaws of being or deed, he preferred the Europe the emperor had created to the increasingly oppressive regimes the Congress had foisted upon the Continent. "If Napoleon, instead of becoming an insatiable world conqueror, had remained First Consul," commented his sometime Berlin publisher Adolph Martin Schlesinger, to Beethoven, "he would have become one of the greatest men that ever existed."[9] Such a sentiment, one senses, the composer would have endorsed.

Admittedly, Beethoven's responses to Napoleon were never simple or straightforward. As late as 1826, in one of the outbreaks of ill humor that characterized him, he commented: "regarding Napoleon: I was also mistaken regarding that shithead."[10] In his responses to the French emperor he remained a man of extremes. One day he despised him; the next, he revered him. What seems certain is that in contemplating Napoleon, dead or alive, Beethoven was constantly evaluating his character and accomplishments, often against the current social reality.

❧

Chateaubriand and Byron Respond to Napoleon's Death

After Napoleon died, a revised estimate of his achievement gained currency in Europe. "We don't go anywhere in Germany without encountering him," observed Chateaubriand, "for in this country [France] the younger generation that rejected him [that active between 1806 and 1815] has died out." Respect now gained the edge. When Byron learned of Napoleon's death, he expressed the sense of loss many of his generation felt: "*We* live in gigantic and exaggerated times," he wrote. "After having seen Napoleon begin like Tamerlane and end like Bajazet in our time, we have not the same interest in what would otherwise have appeared important history."[11] Tamerlane strode in conquest across Europe; Bajazet, his conquered foe, he placed in a cage hanging from a building. In short, Napoleon's spectacular career dwarfed not only those of his powerful contemporaries but those of the past great.

Like many contemporaries, Byron had long collected Napoleonic memorabilia. He particularly treasured a snuffbox that held a hidden portrait of Napoleon. He had also acquired a number of gold coins with Napoleon's portrait on them. In February 1822, now legally entitled to preface his own name with his wife's family name "Noel," Byron began to sign his letters "Noel Byron" or, more usually, "N.B.," Napoleon's initials. In his great and undervalued poem *The Age of Bronze* (1823), he assessed in pinpoint detail Napoleon's career, before taking up the dismal state of post-Restoration Europe.

No less affected by Napoleon's death was Chateaubriand. Looking back upon his life in his vast autobiography, *Memoirs from Beyond the Tomb*, published after his death in 1849–50, he offered a perspective on the deceased emperor that illuminates Beethoven's. In doing so he interpreted his own life in relation to Napoleon's. He also inserted in it what in effect is a substantial biography of the exiled emperor. Imagining himself twinned with Napoleon, he conceived their destinies as closely linked. Napoleon's omnipresence elucidates Chateaubriand's life; his life story interprets Napoleon's. The result was intended to be, and succeeds in being, a Plutarchian duality of vision that serves to bring each figure into greater clarity.

This duality also holds true for Beethoven. So we may interpret him in the decade after the Congress. Through achievement in his chosen realm of music, he too wished to interpret and undermine the regressive European scene. His final decade in Vienna proved difficult. His health continued to decline. He believed his financial situation was insecure as, after 1817, his position as a composer changed. Tastes in music and audiences for it were no longer the same. Increasingly, the educated middle class became the city's musical connoisseurs. But instead of Mozart and Haydn, and sometimes Beethoven, they now demanded Gioachino Rossini.

~9

The New Star

"Napoleon is dead," we read in Stendhal's gloriously ramshackle biography of Rossini, "but a new conqueror has already shown himself to the world." This new conqueror was Rossini, not yet thirty-two. Beethoven had difficulty grappling with the realization that, as a wave of Italian opera overran Vienna, it challenged his position in the city's musical scene. In its acute form this escapist phase lasted in Vienna for about a decade, but to this day it has never fully disappeared.

Italian influence upon the Viennese musical scene had long been strong. Mozart to his regret discovered this in the 1780s. With Rossini, that influence returned with a vengeance. The opera *Tancredi* (1813) began the Rossini craze. Then, on February 20, 1816, *The Barber of Seville* took Vienna by storm. The popularity of Rossini's operas lasted well into the 1820s. Even Schubert joined the admirers and did not hesitate to appropriate for himself several of Rossini's trademark devices. By this time, Beethoven's fame in Vienna was usually conceded by music lovers, but his works, now out of fashion, were rarely performed.

That Viennese music lovers had fallen hard for the Italian upstart cannot have been a happy experience for Beethoven. Rossini could write an opera in three weeks, have it performed soon thereafter, and the populace would rave about it. His operas enjoyed greater success in Vienna than the single opera that Beethoven, after ten years of struggle, had managed to bring to final form. The seemingly uncomplicated but often glorious music of Rossini's operas embodied for many cultured Viennese the essence of wit and beauty. In *The Barber of Seville* the composer displayed a comic genius that remains unparalleled in the history of Italian opera. *The Barber* turned out to be the very first opera by an Italian composer to earn a place in what was developing into a "permanent" repertory.

Rossini wanted to please and entertain people, not provoke or shake them up. Still, his operas appealed to thinking listeners. He was Schopenhauer's favorite composer. The philosopher's preference for Rossini testifies to the powerful impact his witty dialogue and lively music had upon him. If Beethoven resented Rossini's operas overtaking the playing of his works in Vienna, he genuinely admired Rossini's gift for comedy. What Beethoven could hear of the "nervous burst of vitality" in *The Barber of Seville* must have commended itself to him.

In 1822, sometime between March and July, Rossini met Beethoven in Vienna. Although Salieri had warned Rossini of Beethoven's difficult character, the two men got on well—as well as an Italian with little German and a German with little Italian, and deaf to boot—could. Rossini spoke admiringly of Beethoven. Beethoven's greatness, of which he must have heard much during his Viennese stay, overwhelmed Rossini. "Always *he*, he everywhere, as people say of Napoleon," he observed of the composer.[12]

Beethoven told Rossini he thought he should continue with comic operas. "His reported enthusiasm," as Richard Osborne notes, "seems entirely plausible in view of his own achievement in, for example, the Eighth Symphony," a work that "reeks of joy and humor."[13] Rossini's *buffa* operas helped foster in Vienna an even more relaxed attitude toward music. Such works served to appease and occupy the public, to "make them forget," at least temporarily, the often oppressive conditions under which they lived. But *William Tell* (1829), his last opera, reminds us how serious an interpreter of European history Rossini could be.

It was not just the new lighter virtuosic style of the Italian composer.

Complementing it was, as observed earlier, the increasingly prominent fashion of the waltz in Austrian life. With the Restoration of 1815—and what Herzen ironically terms "the revival of old age," with which "youth was utterly incompatible"—life in postwar Vienna became "mature, businesslike, that is, *petit bourgeois*."[14] To which Alexis de Tocqueville adds, "the generation that came to maturity in 1815 was far enough from the Revolution to feel only fleetingly the passions that troubled the view of those who made it."[15]

Beethoven in his final decade, along with illness, also faced problems of an unexpected kind. One evening in 1822, spending the summer in Baden and having embarked upon a long walk in the wooded landscape between Baden and Wiener Neustadt, he lost his way. The police in the latter village, seeing what they assumed was a shabbily attired beggar without a hat peering into shop windows, arrested him—one further indication of how greatly this once well-dressed man had let his outward appearance go. Despite identifying himself and vehemently insisting he was "Beethoven," the authorities expressed disbelief and put him in a jail cell. Naturally Beethoven made a huge fuss. Finally, upon his unwillingness to cease protesting, they agreed to contact the village commissioner, who consulted one Herzog, the village's director of music who lived nearby and was an acquaintance of Beethoven's. Arriving at the prison shortly before midnight, Herzog vouched for Beethoven's identity, took him home, gave him his best bedroom, and lent him decent clothing. The next morning he had Beethoven driven back in his carriage to Baden.[16]

❧

Waldmüller Portrays Beethoven

The tensions in Beethoven's life in these years find reflection in the 1823 portrait of the composer done by the young Ferdinand Georg Waldmüller. Waldmüller ranks high among the portraitists of the era. Only thirty when he painted Beethoven, he had already achieved fame.

German art historians consider him a greater artist than Mähler or Stieler. Very detailed, his paintings render landscapes and individuals precisely, the latter with sometimes brutal honesty.

Stieler's bright primary colors were unusual in early nineteenth-century portraits. For male aristocrats and wealthy civic leaders sartorial restraint and subdued colors were deemed appropriate. Waldmüller for his portrait uses the colors of contemporary Austrian and German Biedermeier portraiture: a white neckcloth, yellow vest, and dark brown or black jacket. Waldmüller's sobriquet, "the Austrian Ingres," suggests that artist's impeccable technique, dazzling virtuosity, and photographic verisimilitude. In this portrait it is Beethoven's expression and tight-lipped mouth that hold our gaze: the artist has captured the searching eyes of the composer at fifty-three.

Unfortunately, Beethoven and Waldmüller did not hit it off. The composer apparently became irritated when the artist asked him to sit by the window in the bright sun. Well before the end of the first sitting, the impatient Beethoven had sent Waldmüller packing. After he left Beethoven became even angrier. There was no question of a second sitting. So Waldmüller, in his way as stubborn and proud as Beethoven, painted the composer largely from his recollection of their first and only encounter. Luckily, he had a gift for quickly memorizing an individual's features and working rapidly. His rendering is a far cry from traditionally idealized portraits. Having experienced the composer in a foul mood, he painted a grim-faced Beethoven. His portrait depicts anger, yes, but no less does it depict a man determined, resolute, unwilling to yield. His *Beethoven* may also recall the unsmiling visages of Goya's portraits. When the young Richard Wagner first encountered Waldmüller's *Beethoven*, he exclaimed, "I find the interpretation just because it is free from all affectation, as only a true portrait can be. It was preferable to all other Beethoven portraits known to me."[17]

22

Beethoven and Grillparzer

I have learned from Beethoven that whenever something
seems to me false, absurd or weak, I should defer entirely
to him and seek the fault in myself.

THEODOR ADORNO[1]

In the decade after the Allied victory at Waterloo and the subsequent
reinstatement of repressive absolutist regimes, conditions for the
majority of Europeans worsened. Taxes increased, the rich became
more prosperous, the poor poorer, and millions of men remained under
arms. Saddened but undiscouraged, Beethoven persevered. Amazingly,
in his final decade his creativity underwent a majestic late flowering.

❧

The "Diabelli" Variations

Once finished with the gigantic *Hammerklavier* Sonata in 1818, other
works welled up in Beethoven's creative imagination. One day in 1819
the Vienna music publisher Anton Diabelli composed a trite little tune.
Seeking to publicize his business, he invited a number of Vienna's
composers to write a variation based on it. Beethoven initially rejected
Diabelli's invitation, then reconsidered. He set down one variation,
found himself caught up by the idea, and produced a further twenty-
nine; then, as if to prove a point, he wrote two more. Then still another.

In all, Beethoven worked on his variations off and on for more than three years. Not so much in their borrowings or allusions, but in the broader sense of their compositional ideas, these short bursts of music enchant us through their individuality, their inventiveness, and the sheer beauty of the variety of sound. The result ranks among the greatest of Beethoven's piano compositions. Theories and countertheories have been proposed regarding their meanings, but the "Diabelli" Variations refuse to yield their secrets. Beethoven himself continued to play the piano occasionally, no longer in public but rather for friends and acquaintances. George Smart, the English music entrepreneur, visiting Vienna in 1825, reported that on one occasion he "played for about twenty minutes in a most extraordinary manner, sometimes very fortissimo, but full of genius."

ঙ

Piano Sonatas

Piano sonatas demand active mental engagement. Over the course of his lifetime Beethoven kept writing one after another, and by the end he had thirty-two. In 1822 he wrote the last three, Opus 109, 110, and 111. Going beyond what he had achieved before, they differ from his earlier sonatas. Each has a distinct personality, yet they share a family resemblance. Schindler compared their distinctive voices to the variety of characters in a Shakespeare play.[2] Financial considerations again played a role. Beethoven lamented he was not composing the music he wished to, but writing "for the sake of money, that which I have to." Whatever the circumstances, the last sonatas represent a new level of achievement, one that went against Vienna's musical currents.

Of these sonatas, I take up here only the last, Opus 111 in C Minor. Beethoven's previous works in this key include the Third Piano Concerto and the Fifth Symphony, as well as an early Piano Trio, Op. 1, no. 3. Unusually, Opus 111 has only two movements. The first, Maestoso—Allegro con brio ed appassionato, is full of energy, but it is the second, the immensely moving Arietta: Adagio molto semplice e cantabile, that, once heard, can never be forgotten. It proceeds by quiet, unobtrusive shadings and purposeful molding of sound. This sonata can be regarded, Irving Kolodin suggests, as the "thirty-fourth" of the "Diabelli" Variations. One of the effects of Beethoven's deafness in later years seems to have been an obsession with trills, especially in high notes. The trills lift you to a higher stage, then another, and in the end deposit you in paradise, what Jeremy Siepmann designates "a transfiguring serenity."[3]

ℜ

Fidelio Revived

Most of his life Beethoven expressed the wish to write another opera. Mythological subjects and fairy tales held little interest for him. More attractive choices, based on what he had already attempted or wished to attempt, were situations involving political injustice (*Fidelio*) or historical relevance (*Egmont*), or combining both (as had Schiller in *William Tell*). Over the years he considered many libretti. Overtly political preferences would have unnerved opera managements in Vienna. Furthermore, the more adventuresome of the proposed works would never have passed the censorship. Still, operas drawing on Goethe's *Faust* or on Odysseus's return, the latter based on Johann Heinrich Voss's magnificent translation of Homer's *Odyssey*, remained abiding hopes.

In the revised *Fidelio* of 1814, as well as in the *Leonore*s of 1805–06, Beethoven took aim at the political prisons of Austria, full of men unjustly incarcerated, many of them for alleged but never proven revolutionary activity. By 1822 the grim situation symbolized by the imprisoned Florestan had if anything worsened. *Fidelio*, despite its success preceding and during the heady days of the Congress of Vienna in 1814–15, did not receive a revival in Vienna for seven years. When performed again on November 4, 1822, it went up against the current craze in

Vienna for Italian opera, Rossini's in particular. Still, it proved a success. Wilhelmine Schröder-Devrient sang the title role, and sang it well. Anton Haitzinger proved a decent Florestan. Next spring *Fidelio* witnessed another successful revival in Dresden. In Vienna both *Egmont* and the *Eroica* also had successful revivals.

In 1812 Beethoven had asked the young poet Theodor Körner to write for him an opera libretto about Brutus. Körner sketched out a text, but shortly afterwards died in action against Napoleon's occupying forces. A decade later, Beethoven discussed an opera about Brutus with another young poet, Eduard von Bauernfeld. That nothing came of either attempt does not necessarily indicate lack of interest on their part—or Beethoven's. It was one thing for him to contemplate the statue of Brutus in the privacy of his rooms, it was another to reveal his thoughts about the heroic Roman in public. Unpredictable as well as rigorous, the censorship offers one reason why Beethoven wrote no more operas after *Fidelio* and composed little further music for the stage. In Hapsburg domains taking on an opera project about Brutus and the founding of republican Rome, with music by Beethoven, entailed in all likelihood serious risk.

Beethoven wished to dedicate the revived *Fidelio* to the Greek freedom fighters in their newly begun war against the Ottomans. Though it was an endeavor that absolutist Austria had no interest at all in supporting, Beethoven did not feel he was alone. Numerous Philhellenes lived in the German states, some even in Goethe's circle. Along with other major creative figures in Europe—among them Byron, Delacroix, the young Hugo—Beethoven wished to support, at least through his art, the Greek struggle for liberation from Ottoman rule.

❧

The Traumas of Grillparzer

As this book has suggested, we often understand Beethoven better when we set his genius against those of his creative contemporaries.

Such individuals need not live in Vienna or even be of the same generation as Beethoven. In this regard we have looked at Byron, Chateaubriand, Kleist, and Goya, among others, and above all, and most frequently, at Napoleon. Another creative genius, two decades younger than Beethoven, who lived in the same city and whom he had long known—and who had often faced struggles comparable to his own—was Franz Grillparzer.

In *On Revolution* (1963), Hannah Arendt exalts an active engagement with the life flowing around us as the highest of human activities. In the political realm, what Arendt calls "the public space," life in Vienna seemed to Beethoven and his creative contemporaries very limited. To deprive human beings of their public, political identity is to deprive them of their humanity, Arendt believes. By this definition both Beethoven and Grillparzer underwent severe deprivation, but it was Grillparzer, in his métier as playwright, who was deprived more and who suffered more.

Grillparzer's uncle, Joseph Sonnleithner, had prepared the German text for Beethoven's 1805 *Leonore*. It was in Sonnleithner's residence that young Grillparzer first met Beethoven in July of that year. Born in 1790, Grillparzer admired Goethe, and as a youngster experienced his tremendous *Sturm und Drang* drama *Götz von Berlichingen*. The Grillparzers were friendly with the Schuberts, and young Grillparzer had met and befriended even younger Franz. He had lost his father during Napoleon's bombardment of Vienna in May 1809; ten years later his mother committed suicide. The early loss of his parents may in part explain his habitual moroseness. He courted the same woman, Katharina (Katty) Fröhlich, most of his life. Only after he had known her fifty years did he ask her to marry him. She laughingly refused. Yet, in his own way, he persevered. William M. Johnson aptly observes that "Beethoven's is a German temperament, Grillparzer's, quintessentially Austrian. Beethoven's indefatigable determination stands in sharp contrast to Grillparzer's timidity."[4] By the early 1820s Grillparzer was well on his way to becoming Austria's greatest dramatist. His intermittent relationship with the composer had become closer. The checkered nature of his career casts light upon Beethoven's. Evolving in counterpoint to his, it illuminates the life and creativity of both figures.[5]

Grillparzer's somewhat autobiographical tale of 1823, *The Poor Musician*, tells of a musician who barely survives in his native Vienna. In his misadventures we sense those of Grillparzer. The title character may also to a degree reflect Beethoven, who at least twice described himself as a "poor Austrian musical *drudge*." "Poor" Beethoven might be (or become), "musical" he certainly was, but he did not think of himself as either Austrian or a drudge. Still, much of his life he had to watch his expenses because many Viennese did not appreciate or respond to his creative work. No matter. Beethoven prided himself on writing music that would last. Of its ultimate success he seems never to have had any doubts.

A severely repressed individual, Grillparzer felt shy and awkward in Beethoven's company. A poem he wrote about the composer, entitled "If You Please," suggests that the friendship may have been more cordial than deep.[6] Still, the relationship was complex. Long obsessed with Napoleon, young Grillparzer in 1809, as noted earlier, had gone out to the parade ground at Schönbrunn every Tuesday morning to watch the emperor reviewing his troops. His presence mesmerized Grillparzer. All his life he suffered from feelings of inferiority, and so impressive a sight gave him a sense of the power of military discipline. Though conservative in his tastes, politically he was not, as has sometimes been claimed, a simple reactionary. He was already an acute observer of the contemporary scene. Ilsa Barea, the Austrian historian, believed that "nobody was more painfully conscious of the conflicting elements in his city and country than was Grillparzer."[7] He was not a bohemian living on the fringes of society, like Schubert and his friends, but a civic official, thus part of the state establishment. As still happens in other countries, notably France today, Austria often chose for its civil servants literary and artistic figures. Keep them occupied on official business, the thinking in government circles went, and they'll be less likely to write or do something that might disparage the state or cause it problems. Ironically, Grillparzer held a position in the branch of the bureaucracy that determined whether the plays he wrote could be performed.

Even after Napoleon left Vienna in October 1809, Grillparzer's overwhelming initial response to him did not diminish. When Napoleon died in 1821, that response became greater still. Ironically, it was the first of Grillparzer's controversial "patriotic" plays, *King Ottokar's Fortune and Fall* (1823, 1825), that caused him problems, for it drew upon a Napoleon figure to explicate Austria's earlier history. Ottokar's career and fate had parallels to that of the French emperor: behind the king's rise and fall clearly stand the rise and fall of Napoleon. As he did many others, Napoleon continued to tantalize Grillparzer to the end of his long life. The play, considered Austria's greatest national drama, has gained recognition as one of the outstanding historical tragedies of the century.

Grillparzer's evolving perspectives on the French emperor oddly counterpoint Beethoven's. "The Viennese," the young dramatist believed, "hold greatness to be dangerous and fame but an empty play."[8] Ottokar, a charismatic adventurer and despot, ruled over Bohemia in the fourteenth century. But on the Marchfeld, the bloodstained plain northeast of Vienna, Rudolph of Hapsburg triumphed over the Bohemian king in a battle that proved to be one of the decisive confrontations in European history.[9] Defeated, Ottokar died shortly afterwards. Contemporaries saw in him Grillparzer's portrait of Napoleon, himself only recently deceased. But the play, as had Beethoven's first *Leonore*, brought Grillparzer into disfavor in court circles. It ran into censorship problems and was initially banned.

When the dramatist (at Beethoven's prompting) finally screwed up the courage to confront the official responsible for the ban, he was told that, while nothing seemed wrong with the piece, "one can never tell."[10] The censor, fearing he had missed something (and presumably worried about his position), preferred to have the play withdrawn than to allow it on the boards at the Hofburgtheater, Vienna's leading theater. Beethoven, when asked by Grillparzer what he should do, told him to appeal the censor's decision, which he did. Eventually the censor relented, and *King Ottokar* had its first performance on February 29, 1825.

The unpredictability of state censorship was even more upsetting to Grillparzer than its severity. Omnipresent censorship hovered over his cherished creations like the sword of Damocles. "Anyone who does not completely lose heart under such conditions," commented Grillparzer in his diary in 1829, "is truly a kind of hero."[11] Although Ottokar is brought low by fate, the play made Emperor Franz nervous. Despite Grillparzer's apparently patriotic motivation, Franz, as usual prey to suspicions, believed the playwright had deeper intentions. On this occasion he may have had reason. The historicism in Grillparzer's plays often serves as a cover for other preoccupations. Though set in the past, they yet reflect current political issues and situations. Only the intervention of the Empress Caroline Augusta, Franz's fourth wife, allowed its performance in 1825. *King Ottokar* turned out to be a huge success with the public. Its triumph, alas, alarmed the emperor even more. He summoned Grillparzer to an interview, during which he offered to purchase the play from him. Grillparzer instinctively knew that the proposal meant that it would never again be staged. He refused.

"One can never tell" indeed! Problems continued for Grillparzer. After the public in 1836 did not respond to his comedy "Woe to Him Who Lies!" Grillparzer withdrew it from the stage. Feeling crushed by officialdom's unfavorable response to his works, now topped by the public's rejection of his latest play, he refused to submit his subsequent plays for performance or to have them published. "Despotism wrecked my life," he concluded in that year of revolution, 1848, "—at least my literary life."[12] But Grillparzer did not let despotism always get the best of him. By his midforties, somewhat like Beethoven at about the same age in regard to his musical career, he determined to write his plays for posterity rather than for contemporary performance. Only after his death in 1872 did Grillparzer's later works appear at the Hofburgtheater.

"In the days of Metternich the most perilous occupation was intellectual exercise."[13] So claims Edward Crankshaw, a leading twentieth-century historian of Vienna and the Hapsburg empire. "Great writers," generalizes Crankshaw, "even when their thinking is confused, do not flourish in an atmosphere of intellectual timidity caused by a rigid and perennial censorship."[14] He is speaking in general terms, but the words apply well to Grillparzer in Vienna.

✎

Beethoven Befriends Grillparzer

Grillparzer responded strongly to the composer. In Grillparzer's second memoir on Beethoven, he states of their friendship: "I truly loved Beethoven. If I cannot recount many of the things he said, it is mainly because what interests me in an artist is not what he says but what he does." He especially admired Beethoven's courage. "If only I had a thousandth part of your power and fortitude," he lamented to the composer.[15] As a musician, Beethoven had an easier time of it than Grillparzer as a writer, as he well knew and readily admitted. In an entry in one of Beethoven's Conversation Books, Grillparzer asked him, perhaps somewhat enviously, "Does the censor know what you think when you are composing?"[16] Because revolutionary motifs in music are harder to discern than the corresponding sentiments in words, the censors who controlled the cultural scene exercised less discipline upon heard music than upon spoken drama. Ironically, while nearly wrecking Grillparzer's career, they may at times have unwittingly fostered Beethoven's. Being largely able to avoid the censorship left him more time to create. Grillparzer even worried that Beethoven might end up taking unnecessary risks. The dramatist had begun a play *Drahomira*, a tale about Bohemian history, that had potential as an opera libretto, possibly with music by Beethoven. But, he tells us, "I did not want to give Beethoven cause, misled by a half-diabolic subject, to step still closer to the extreme limits of music, which were there in any case, like a threatening abyss."[17]

Unlike the iron-willed Beethoven, confrontations with the authorities left the sensitive Grillparzer uncomfortable. He too, like Beethoven,
gradually succumbed to a kind of internal emigration. The composer,
however, was cunningly aware of how much active rebellion in his
music he could get away with. He continually tested the system. No
censor would stop him from expressing through his music what he
thought and felt about the world. But what Beethoven could get away
with in music, Grillparzer could not in words. He recognized the danger and consulted with Beethoven about it. One senses, in ways hard
to explain, why the stronger-willed Beethoven made him uneasy. Grillparzer lacked Beethoven's courage and, unwilling to contemplate leaving Vienna, feared that a display of resistance might have unpleasant
consequences for him.

In music Grillparzer preferred Classicism to Romanticism. Though
he claimed to love Beethoven, he preferred the music of Mozart.[18] A
half-dozen of his poems take up Beethoven, most briefly. Several focus
on his creations, the most extended of which is "To Beethoven's Music
for *Egmont*," written in 1834. It hails that stirring work, especially its
overture. In "Beethoven," written on March 26, 1827, Beethoven's death
day, he includes the composer amid the past great in music and literature. Most revealing, perhaps, is a reference in Grillparzer's journal,
where he speaks of "Chaos—Beethoven."[19] As Beethoven's music had
proved too much for Goethe to take in, so it may at times have also overwhelmed Grillparzer.

In what is perhaps Grillparzer's best-known poem, "Farewell to
Vienna," he compares the enervating effect of the city to that of life on
"Capua" (Capri). The sensuous atmosphere of that fabled isle had long
ago unmanned Hannibal's soldiers. Of Vienna, the city in which he
spent his long life, Grillparzer writes, "Beautiful art thou, but dangerous too." The poem closes with a lament over the intellectual torpor
of Vienna, "Thou Capua of minds."[20] In so saying he echoes Homer's
depiction of the "Phaecians" in the *Odyssey*, the relaxed people who
metamorphosed for Beethoven into the Viennese.

23

The *Missa solemnis* and the Ninth Symphony

Now that I am old and there cannot be much time
reserved for me, I find that such energy and strength
that are left to me must be directed exclusively to
Beethoven. Of all the composers of the past,
he alone remains unfathomable to me.

ROMAIN ROLLAND

Beethoven's Final Akademie

In 1817 Hans-Georg Nägeli acclaimed Bach's B-Minor Mass as "the greatest work of music of all ages and of all peoples." Nägeli's verdict, the Bach biographer Christoph Wolff has pointed out, was essentially an intuitive judgment. But it may have had for Beethoven one significant result: it challenged him to compose a mass of his own, to attempt a work that would emulate the dimensions of Bach's mass. Originally, he intended his *Missa solemnis* to celebrate the consecration of his longtime student Archduke Rudolph as archbishop of Olmütz. During the summer of 1818, living at Mödling, he made good progress, but the date of the consecration the next year came and went, and he still had far to go. Rudolph had studied piano as well as composition with Beethoven for about a dozen years and at this point in time was his only student. Though Beethoven felt genuine fondness for Rudolph—he dedicated to him more works than to any other individual—he occasionally begrudged the time these lessons took away from his own work. Even though he had never held a post in the Austrian musical establishment, Beethoven still yearned for one. With Antonio Salieri, the longtime court Kapellmeister, ill and frail, he may have felt that a dedication to Emperor Franz's youngest brother might improve his chances to replace him. But no, as it turned out, the court did not want him.

A believer in music's power to effect change, Beethoven sought through his major compositions to express a divine spirit, a celestial fire. Music, as one of his gifted contemporaries, E. T. A. Hoffmann, claimed, "is the most romantic of all arts, . . . since its only subject-matter is infinity."[1] In Beethoven's compositions lies a message for all mankind. Like Handel's oratorios and Mozart's Requiem, performances of the *Missa*, he informed several prospective donors, could go beyond religious occasions and take place in concert halls.

Possibly the most complex composition Beethoven ever attempted, the *Missa solemnis* occupied a good part of his time during the next few years. By 1823 he had essentially completed it. While the work looks back to Bach and Handel, it reveals that Beethoven had also learned much from Cherubini's Requiem in C Minor (1816). Without it, the *Missa* would probably have been quite different. Though it emerges as a profoundly spiritual work, it celebrates a faith that is not bound by external dogma but comes from within. In a strange way, the *Missa* also harks back to the Cult of the Supreme Being celebrated in Paris in December 1793. Michelangelo in his Sistine Chapel ceiling fresco had linked Adam to God. Of Goethe it has been said he felt that "his God is everywhere—in the plants, in the landscape, in the remains of antiquity, in Goethe himself."[2] Johann Tischbein had portrayed the poet surveying the Roman campagna, and the portraitist Mähler had placed Beethoven in an idealized landscape full of meaning.

The composer worked hard to make his new work a financial success. He sent out invitations to royal dignitaries and the great of the day, approximately fifty individuals, asking them to subscribe to and pay for a special hand-copied edition of the *Missa*. Ten of those asked came through, including the Russian prince Nicolas Galitzin and the French king Louis XVIII. The latter even honored Beethoven with a gold medal. Others who responded positively included Ferdinand III, archduke of Tuscany, and Friedrich VI, king of Denmark. Several whom Beethoven would have liked to subscribe, however, including Bernadotte, now king of Sweden, and Goethe, did not respond. Since the latter's good friend and music advisor, Carl Zelter, had already ordered a copy for the Berlin Singakademie, Goethe may have deemed that sufficient. Nor did England's former prince regent respond. Perhaps that is fortunate. Given his failure to acknowledge the dedication to him of *Wellington's Victory*, an explicit refusal to pay for a copy of the *Missa* would only have embittered Beethoven further. That many of the high and mighty found a major work by Beethoven of little or no interest was another indication for him, if he needed any such by now, that others did not deem his achievement worthy of the attention he felt it deserved.

In 1818, when asked which was his "favorite" symphony, Beethoven replied, "the *Eroica*." But on February 5, 1823, writing to a prospective publisher, Beethoven claimed the *Missa* as "the *greatest* work I have composed so far."[3] "Favorite" and "greatest" imply different meanings for different kinds of works. Beethoven's comments on his own compositions, cautions William Drabkin, have to be read in the context of his life and motives, especially, as here, in presenting a choral work that required special pleading because of its complexity.

On May 7, 1824, took place Beethoven's final Akademie. It was his first public offering of new works in ten years. The Akademie began with the overture *The Consecration of the House* (*Zur Weihe des Hauses*). His last music for the stage, it had earlier commemorated the opening of a theater in what is now Budapest. The concert continued with three movements from the Mass in D, that is, the *Missa solemnis*. It concluded with the Ninth Symphony. Beethoven intended his 1824 Akademie to achieve a popular success comparable to that of his Akademie ten years before, when he had triumphed with the Seventh Symphony and *Wellington's Victory*.

In Catholic lands performance of the mass could take place only in

a church. In composing his mass Beethoven, after missing the dead-
line for Archduke Rudolph's inauguration, had in mind a secular
venue. However, even a secular concert required the censor's approval.
Beethoven received permission to have the *Missa* performed only on
condition that he leave it incomplete and not use Latin.[4] So he used
German. He chose three of the work's five movements, as he had in the
concert program of his earlier Mass in C, and called them "hymns."[5]
Had Beethoven remembered that French revolutionary patriots often
designated their songs "hymns"? But which movements? The choice
aroused much debate among Beethoven and his friends. In the end, he
decided on the Kyrie, Credo, and Agnus Dei.

In his determination to liberate humankind, Beethoven in the *Missa*
anticipates Thomas Carlyle's epic history *The French Revolution* (1837).
Each creator stretched his powers to the utmost. Whereas Carlyle advocated mankind's redemption through impassioned language, Beethoven
sought its redemption through music of depths hitherto unknown. The
Eroica had been, in itself, an earlier French Revolution. In composing
the *Missa* Beethoven intended a new Bible for humanity, one that would
redeem the world. Experiencing to the full both Carlyle's *French Revolution* and Beethoven's *Missa* makes you relive the Revolution, making
it part of yourself. Whereas the *Eroica* affirmed the need for revolution
in a secular world, the *Missa* frees spiritual aspirations from the theological strictures of Catholicism decreed by Hapsburg authorities. Both
works open up hope for us all.

ᔥ

Listening to the Missa solemnis

Too long and elaborate for liturgical use, the *Missa solemnis* emerged as
a huge vocal piece and instrumental symphony using as its fabric the
text of the mass. The Austrian scholar Hans Gal rightly claims that the
individual who wrote the *Missa* was a "man, firm as a rock in his artistic ideals and deeply rooted beyond any conceivable shadow of a doubt."

With the *Missa* Beethoven achieved a profoundly personal as well as universal confession of faith. Paradoxically, Gal finds Beethoven "the prototype of a modern, illusion-free skeptic, who was in the deepest sense religious."[6]

The impressive Kyrie announces that a major work is at hand. The Credo that follows, believed Romain Rolland, may have been influenced by the three Egyptian sayings on Beethoven's desk. In one of them, "I am that I am," Rolland finds that Beethoven, "in his pantheistic idealism, . . . merged with God,—When Man has to appear in the Credo, it is in full faith that the words be sung, as a hymn of triumph.—The Son of God is not Jesus; it is Man, man whoever he is. God is in each of us; God is in us, and we are God."[7] Here we are not far from Goethe. The Arietta, the second of the two movements of Beethoven's last piano sonata, Opus 111, contained a similar message, presented in an even more spiritual form.

In the "Benedictus," part of the Credo, Beethoven gives expression, to cite words of Aldous Huxley, to "a certain blessedness lying at the heart of things."[8] It is Beethoven's vision of utopia, believed in only as an ideal, but an ideal worth keeping in view. The intensely moving violin solo in this section hints at the Holy Spirit and the blessedness it creates, "the peace that passeth all understanding." Whereas the wrath of God incarnate was heard in the Gloria, in the "Benedictus" celestial serenity prevails. "The flute in 'Et incarnatus' is a musical representation of the Holy Spirit in the form of a dove," for which Beethoven may have drawn inspiration from his "Pastoral" Symphony.[9] After this music dies away we enter harsher terrain.

The work's final movement, the Agnus Dei (Lamb of God), suggests that mankind will find the path to enlightenment long and difficult. Ultimately, its fate can only be hammered out in the world of reality. In the "Dona nobis pacem" (Give us peace) Beethoven differentiates between the world outside and the world within us. The line "a plea for inner and outer peace," which closes the movement, first appears at the point in which we hear the "Dona nobis pacem." "Nor is this a single, isolated try, endeavor, or outcry," asserts the conductor Antal Dorati. Beethoven

> wrote it down only this once, but it can be heard throughout his music and can be read in and between the lines of many of his writings. . . . That paradoxical "fight for peace" is manifest, often clad in the robes of his two worldly ideals, freedom and loyalty, but as often shown in the direct—one could say: naked—force, that was the driving force of his life.

The *Missa*, along with the Ninth Symphony, Dorati argues convincingly, are "the strongest and most immediate outcries for complete human peace ever uttered in musical terms and, for those who understand the language of music, as strong as can be expressed by any human means."[10]

Just before the work's close, two shattering explosions of worldly chaos erupt without warning. The warlike music of trumpets and timpani brutally disturbs the plea for peace. This final flurry of Beethoven's Michelangelesque *terribilità* dissolves into an almost tortured dissonance. Here the composer, building upon the similarly ironic (if less dramatic) effect in Haydn's *Mass in Time of War*, offers his own sardonic comment on man's inability to attain peace. The solo singers react with panic-stricken terror. As Leon Plantinga has observed, the idea of peace for Beethoven invokes the opposite: "war and tribulation and struggle."[11] Does humanity's capacity for destruction, we wonder, ever go away? But Beethoven quickly restores equilibrium: "O please! may there be peace within and among all of us!" he begs. With echoes of the last movement of the "Pastoral" Symphony, the work ends quietly.

"By the end of his not very long but spiritually eventful life," observes Wilfrid Mellers, Beethoven "had become a religious composer of a kind without precedent."[12] Yehudi Menuhin, discussing the conductor Wilhelm Furtwängler, writes of "the mystical tradition he embodied, the age-old concept of music as the link between man and God."[13] Furtwängler himself spoke of the *Missa* as Beethoven's "greatest work."[14] The implication is that God is beyond all religion. He exists, but no faith can contain him. Earlier, the nineteenth-century Viennese critic Eduard Hanslick had claimed, in regard to Beethoven's *Missa*, that for him all his music was religious.[15] The *Missa*, as Beethoven wrote Archduke Rudolph in 1822, was intended to symbolize "the liberty and the power to go still further" in relating mankind to God. No less does the final work in his Akademie, the Ninth Symphony, also concern itself with that same liberty and power.

❧

Socrates and Jesus

In 1820 Beethoven had claimed that his ultimate models were not earlier composers, but *"Socrates and Jesus."*[16] The actions of Socrates and Jesus are related. Their lives, even more the heroic manner in which they faced death, meant much to him. They died—Socrates drinking the hemlock, Jesus on the cross—because they refused to compromise their survival and ethical ideals. Whereas Socrates was a good, endlessly questioning man betrayed and sentenced to death by the malignant authorities of Athens, Jesus was a liberator of mankind, fearlessly compassionate about the outcasts of society, not one to be bound by prescribed religiosity. Each lived a life of the utmost integrity; neither feared death. Beethoven would have deemed both heroes, martyrs, and revolutionaries. Ideal figures, they challenged received authorities and espoused beliefs that a better world for all humanity was possible, indeed imminent.

Such a liberation of mankind, as Beethoven probably realized while he sat for his portrait by Stieler in 1819–20, would take longer than he had hoped. In 1914, nearly a hundred years after he wrote the *Missa*, a Europe about to explode into war consisted of seventeen monarchies and but three republics. The situation would not, however, have reduced Beethoven's faith in inevitable, if slow, progress. Another cen-

tury further on, one full of horrors virtually beyond belief, the possibilities for liberation may have improved, but perhaps not greatly.
Humanity's moral and social development, Beethoven sensed, moved
forward slowly. Normally impatient, he was, in this regard, patient. He
would wait.

꿎

The Ninth Symphony

In 1812 Beethoven had worked on three new symphonies. The Seventh and Eighth he dispatched quickly, but progress on that which
became the Ninth, in D minor, moved slowly. Though the earliest extant
sketches date to that year, its actual origins go back further. A foreshad-
owing of the Ninth appears in the early Wind Octet, Op. 103, of 1792–93.
The symphony's choral Finale, with its borrowings from Schiller's "Ode
to Joy," goes back further still, to Beethoven's Bonn years. Schiller's
"Ode," first published in 1785, had preoccupied Beethoven's imagination since youth. But not until 1815 did he begin to explore seriously
the ideas it stirred within him. He continued to make sketches for the
Ninth in 1816 and 1818 and to ponder its development, but not until
1821 or early 1822 did he return to the work in earnest. "I carry my ideas
with me for a long time," he once said, "rejecting and re-writing until
I am satisfied." Apparently, the idea of adding a choral Finale to his
new symphony was something of an afterthought, prompted perhaps by
the experience of composing the *Missa solemnis*. The form of the symphony, Beethoven tells us, combined music and words. It was a form he
considered "his true element." The Ninth, he states, was "the work of
my life."[17] Its nearly forty-year gestation spans Beethoven's maturity. Its
aural dimensions span the universe.

An ominous, almost Schubertian stillness introduces the Symphony's first movement. This mysterious opening limns the act of creation itself, the emergence of order out of chaos, the crystallization of
thought from the humming void. Beethoven in these years again stud-

ied Bach and Handel. The eight-and-a-half-minute fugal passage looks forward to the String Quartet Opus 131, itself among the most unusual of Beethoven's unusual late works.

The second movement begins quickly, then slows down. The staggered manner in which the instruments enter, as well as the movement's overall rhythmic thrust, suggest an embryonic version. Beethoven repeats the pattern, which has the tarantella rhythm of a bouncy Italian dance tune. This monolithic movement so intrigued Stanley Kubrick that he used it extensively in his film *A Clockwork Orange,* itself based on the novel of Anthony Burgess, a composer as well as a writer.

The third movement, an Adagio that is in part an andante, constitutes for many the most moving of Beethoven's many moving adagios. The fourth movement begins by rejecting the themes of the previous three movements. Suddenly the bass interrupts, "Not these tones." A sprightly march in 6/8 time provides the first contrasting episode. In the tenor solo that follows, a Bacchic strain intertwines with a revolutionary, both filled with youthful heroism. Democratic in its musical subject matter, the movement recalls the *carmagnole,* the popular dance that had emerged in the early weeks of the French Revolution. Schiller had originally intended his "Ode to Joy" as a drinking song, but it became much more. Beethoven chose passages from Schiller's poem that, in their envisioning a united humanity, are joyous and hopeful.

The Ninth's Finale includes Turkish marching music. Beethoven, responsive to all segments of his audience, had no qualms about introducing into his chorale popular Turkish music and musical instruments. Earlier, he had inserted a Turkish march in his 1811 overture *The Ruins of Athens.* Turkish music jarringly, but provocatively, interrupts the Agnus Dei at the close of the *Missa solemnis.* In the Finale of the Ninth Symphony Beethoven conjures up what at times seems like an Oktoberfest atmosphere, one suggestive of a tavern scene, in which the theme is fragmented, on one occasion crushed down to a single note. "Be embraced, ye millions," proclaims the composer. For him the voice of God speaks to all peoples, not just those of German or European descent.

ᢀ

"Ode to Joy"

Beethoven's journey toward the Ninth proceeded in stages. He endowed the music of his new symphony with a poetic glorification of the humanitarian and progressive ideals of the French Revolution. For over three decades they had lain close to his heart. Composing his *Cantata on the Death of Joseph II* had led him to rethink society in fundamental ways. The words "All mankind are brothers" both honor Joseph II and invoke the ideals of the Revolution. The jubilant music of a second cantata written soon afterwards, *On the Accession of Leopold II*, that celebrating the new Austrian emperor, includes Schiller's theme of joy. Both works, written before Beethoven was twenty, uncannily foreshadow crucial elements in the Ninth's Finale. A decade later, the commemoration of death in the *Eroica*'s Marcia funebre—by turns combative, elegiac, and triumphant—mourns the ideal hero. The next year, the closing chorus in *Leonore* that became *Fidelio* celebrates the deeds of a heroic woman who in fighting tyranny saves a man, her husband. The Choral Fantasy, which ended his ill-fated Akademie of 1808, served as a dress rehearsal for the Ninth. *Calm Sea and Prosperous Voyage*, his exquisite miniature cantata of 1814–15, not only looks back to the Choral Fantasy but ahead to the Ninth and, even further, to the late quartets.

Not until 1822 did the moment come when Beethoven was able to take the essence of Schiller's "Ode to Joy" and find the music to set it to. The poet, who had come to dislike his own work and often spoke of it disparagingly, would have been surprised by the honor Beethoven gave it. Although the text does hymn the spirit of brotherhood, it also contains generous praise of the glories of good drink. Beethoven made selective use of this text, ultimately rejecting slightly less than half. Passages cut include all references to drink as well as Schiller's more extreme sentiments. Beethoven selected stanzas that emphasize the unusual union of humanity through joy, and its basis in the love of an eternal heavenly Father. Like the Fifth Symphony, and truly much of Beethoven's orchestral music, it was meant not specifically for the nobility or for the elite, however defined, but for the people, all the people.

Not everyone has responded positively to the "Ode to Joy." Mahler, during a conducting engagement in Finland in 1907, encountered Sibelius, who expressed to him a low opinion of Beethoven's Ninth. The two composers disagreed about what a symphony should attempt. For Mahler, "the symphony must be like the world. It must be all-embracing." In so saying, he seems to have had in mind the Ninth's Finale. This symphony possesses tremendous variety, being an orchestral work, a vocal concerto, an opera, one with recitative parts, duets, trios, and many musical ranges and types. It even has a Turkish march. And it was and is "all-embracing."

᪥

Dedicating the Ninth

After Beethoven left the Rhineland, change occurred there with bewildering rapidity. By 1794 the French occupied much of the area, including Beethoven's Bonn. When Napoleon set up the Confederation of the Rhine in 1806, Bonn became part of the Duchy of Berg with its capital at Düsseldorf, created by Napoleon as a principality for his brother-in-law, Joachim Murat. The new state lasted only as long as did Napoleon's rule. In 1815, by the accords of the Congress of Vienna, the west bank of the Rhineland, though not contiguous to Prussian territory, came under Prussian rule. In 1818 the university in Bonn was refounded and gradually the city again became a vital cultural center.

Beethoven had intended to dedicate the Ninth Symphony to Tsar Alexander of Russia, but the tsar died in 1825, after the work's first performance but before its publication. The composer then decided to inscribe the score to Prussia's King Frederick William III.[18] Although hardly more liberal than Emperor Franz, he and his policies affected Beethoven less. The composer also had wished to have his new symphony first performed in Berlin. Upon learning the news, his admirers and supporters in Vienna made a concerted effort to have it first heard in the city he had made his home. For this to happen they pleaded eloquently, and with genuine affection and admiration, sending him a lengthy epistle in February 1824, signed by many of his old friends. The guiding force behind this effort was Count Moritz Lichnowsky, younger brother of the prince who had first taken young Beethoven into the family palace more than thirty years before. Beethoven, touched by their concern, yielded. Nonetheless, he used the occasion to declare himself a "citizen of Bonn." With his hometown now administratively part of the Prussian empire, Beethoven could view himself as a Prussian, as a Rhinelander, but not as Austrian. The thought must have pleased him. Even after nearly thirty-two years in Vienna, Beethoven considered himself a citizen of the city in which he had grown up and whose surrounding landscape he yearned all his life to see again.

By describing himself as a "citizen" of Bonn he did not imply that he was a *subject* of the Prussian king. He limited his fealty to Frederick William III, especially as that king's always tentative constitutional inclinations had declined markedly after 1816. Beethoven had long seen himself as a "citizen" of Bonn, as his early music for G. C. Pfeffel's poem "The Free Man" indicates. If in so saying he, in effect, dissociated himself from Hapsburg Austria; he never put himself under Prussian rule.

◦

Freedom or Joy?

In 1989 East Germany was dissolved. Perhaps the most politically appropriate and exhilarating performances of Beethoven's Ninth Symphony ever heard were those that celebrated this epoch-making event on Christmas Day 1989, after the wall separating West from East Berlin had fallen. Leonard Bernstein performed the symphony twice, once in the

Western zone, and once in the former Russian sector. In these historic performances, in the line from Schiller's poem beginning "Joy, divine spark" ("Freude, schöner Götterfunken"), Bernstein changed *Freude* to *Freiheit*, "Joy" to "Freedom." What Beethoven living in Vienna could not do, Bernstein in a reunited Berlin could. The occasion demanded it. An absolutist regime had been toppled by a popular uprising, and Bernstein responded to Beethoven's symphony the way we imagine the composer would have wished him to respond.

There may have been a further historic rationale for the substitution. Charles Rosen has referred to "a well-established theory that Beethoven intended the '*Freude'* of the final ode . . . to be understood as an obvious substitute for the overly inflammatory word '*Freiheit.*' "[19] The academic French Beethovenians, Brigitte and Jean Massin, believe this substitution in Schiller's poem often occurred as far back as the 1790s in lands inhabited by Germans sympathetic to the Revolution. Three decades later, Beethoven, a man who gave every indication of sympathizing with that Revolution, may well have responded similarly.

The concept of freedom is for most of the choral Finale far more apt than the concept of joy. The Turkish percussion is written in military style, yet how often has anyone heard of a combat for joy? Besides, without freedom there can be no true joy. In Beethoven's Vienna years the word *Freude* appears as a leitmotiv in his letters and conversations. He could not write *Freiheit*. In Vienna the word was taboo. Beethoven intended his music to be a voice of hope for mankind. "Hope supports me, it is hope which feeds half the world," he wrote on August 11, 1810, "and during my life I have always had it for a companion, or what would have become of me?" His chorus sings not of what is, but of what might be. At one point Schiller himself had considered altering "An die Freude" to "An die Freiheit." Even if Beethoven did not know this, he would hardly have missed the political message in Schiller's poem: "All men will be brothers where your gentle wings beat, / Your magic unites those whom rigid custom divides!"

If in his personal dealings with others Beethoven may sometimes have been elitist, in his music he was not. Rhenish partisans of the Revolution exposed to the "Marseillaise," which swept over France and crossed borders throughout Europe, had taken on the habit of alternating a couplet of the "Marseillaise" with one from Schiller's "Ode to Joy." That the young Beethoven heard the song sung in this way seems likely. Understandably, an authoritarian government like that of Hapsburg Austria, wary of democratic hopes and processes, had rapidly proscribed the "Marseillaise," which Emperor Franz believed—mistakenly—was no more than a "gentle breeze."[20] No doubt the authorities in 1824 would have liked to have prohibited the playing of the Ninth if they had known in advance what the music was about. But ten years had passed since the performances of Beethoven's Seventh and Eighth Symphonies, and officialdom may have forgotten the exhilarating impact a Beethoven symphony could have on people. By creating the Ninth's final movement as a song for all humanity, Beethoven illustrated his fidelity to an ideal for which he had carried the flame since before he turned twenty.

ॐ

Equality

Amalia in Schiller's early play *The Robbers* recalls her amazement at the reversal of society in the following lines: "Why, this, the world is turned upside-down, / Beggars are kings and kings are beggars."[21] Such expressions of belief in equality constitute a chief reason why Hapsburg authorities forbade performances of *The Robbers* in Vienna. But Amalia has a point: the idea of human *in*equality was embedded in society, at least in the court-aristocratic conception of it. But equality as a notion, if not always as a living reality, appealed to Beethoven. The Bonn professor Bartholomaeus Ludwig Fishenich wrote to Schiller's wife, Charlotte, in 1793 that his young friend Beethoven "proposes to compose Schiller's *Freude*, strophe by strophe. I expect something perfect, since he is wholly devoted to the great and sublime."[22] Beethoven took up Schiller's idea and made it still grander. "Be embraced, ye millions," sings Beethoven's chorus. "Here's a kiss for all the world. / Brothers! above the canopy of the stars / There must dwell a loving father!" It's not merely selected specimens of humanity that Beethoven wishes us to embrace, but all of them, all of us.

The "cult of joy" upon which Schiller and Beethoven drew had deep roots in German lands during the eighteenth century. The concept pervaded German philosophy in the nineteenth. Joy in the Ninth Symphony comes about through fraternity, fraternity understood as a right of all human beings—a right, despite the masculine term, open to women as well as to men. And Beethoven conveys the belief in fraternity with joyous music. "No one to whom his music has really been revealed," comments the Beethoven biographer Richard Specht, "could henceforth be completely unhappy."[23]

For believers in republics and political freedom the 1820s proved a difficult time. With the suppression of uprisings in Italy, Greece, and Spain, opposition groups lost ground. For Hegel, with his paradigm of thesis, antithesis, synthesis, in which the ancien régime served as the thesis, the Revolution and the revolutionary governments it spawned as the antithesis, the synthesis appeared to herald the return of absolutism. After the autocratic rulers who had been overthrown (Napoleon) or restored (Louis XVIII), there appeared little hope for future progress. Reaction was almost inevitable. "Unlike Hegel," writes the critic Martin Jay, "Beethoven refused to reconcile himself to the new realities of Restoration Europe; the late work, with the great exception of the still affirmative Ninth Symphony . . . struggled against the collapse of the revolutionary synthesis."[24] (Jay is on target as far as he goes, but others of Beethoven's late works besides the ones cited here express the same positive response.) More than one commentator has puzzled over why everyone did not have access to the "cult of joy." To be excluded from it, comments Mark Evan Bonds, "is not because of any character defect, but rather because the individual in question has not yet attained a sufficient degree of personal self-realization."[25]

Goethe among others at this time believed that singing in choruses served as an appropriate training for citizenship. "Elysium" in Beethoven's symphony "is set against Arcadia, which is a utopian return to the golden age of the past."[26] Beethoven may not always have felt such optimism himself, but he wrote his music, as he said of the *Missa solemnis*, "from the heart—to the heart." Those who dislike having verse in the Ninth's Finale miss Beethoven's point: he used words in a symphony for the first time because he wanted everyone, the common people no less than aristocrats or intellectuals, to understand his message of brotherhood and freedom. He wanted to make clearer the meaning conveyed by much of his earlier instrumental work. Before him the "Marseillaise" stood as a model; its words no less stirring than its music. Late in life Beethoven wished to re-create through his music, with the help of Schiller's words, the revolutionary fervor of the 1790s. What peace was to the *Missa*, joy is to the Ninth Symphony. Without freedom (*Freiheit*), neither is possible.

᭡

The Ninth Symphony: Reception and Afterfame

The first performance on May 7, 1824, of the reduced tripartite *Missa solemnis* and the full Ninth Symphony went well. The initial audience, as Beethoven had hoped, applauded every one of the symphony's movements. At the end, Beethoven himself received five rounds of applause. Since the emperor was only allowed three, the chief of police stood up and cried out, "Quiet!" Only then did the clapping finally stop.[27] Less than three weeks later, on May 23, 1824, the concert was repeated, this time in the Grosse Redoutensaal in the Hofburg. This second performance fared less well, the hall being only half full and the audience less enthusiastic.

For a period of time afterwards, skepticism would greet the Ninth virtually everywhere it was performed. Some found it overtly didactical, others too long. Many denounced the last movement. Ludwig Spohr, a musician and Beethoven's contemporary, termed it "monstrous." For others at the time, Beethoven's symphony revealed that he lacked a sense of beauty. Even Grillparzer thought the Ninth "abstruse and muddled stuff."[28] Both Spohr and Grillparzer admired Beethoven's music after a fashion, but their comments about it rival in obtuseness Emperor Joseph II's critique of Mozart's *Don Giovanni*: "That is not good for the ears of the Viennese people."[29]

The Ninth Symphony has had enormous repercussions. Wagner thought it invoked Goethe's *Faust*, for "this particular Faust is easily the readiest emblem of Western man, always striving, always becoming, and (thus) always redeemable." So great did the critical commentary about it become over the century that Debussy expressed astonishment "that the Symphony has not remained buried under the mass of prose it has called forth."[30] Not everyone responded positively to the "Ode to Joy." Verdi declared the Ninth magnificent in its first three movements, but regarded the last as inferior to those before. Recently, feminist scholars have attacked the Ninth for what they claim is its aggressive masculinity. Adrienne Rich, in her poem "The Ninth Symphony of Beethoven Understood at Last as a Sexual Message," is one. "Music was no less metaphysical after Beethoven," writes Jamie Jones, a contemporary philosopher, "but the search for transcendence turned inward. Divinity was to be found in the spirit of man, not in a remote and theoretical cosmos."[31] The American musicologist Mark Evan Bonds flatly terms the Finale "a mistake."[32]

Thomas Mann, passionate about music all his life, felt that, after the horrors of two world wars and the Holocaust, Beethoven's symphony did not leave humankind with grounds for optimism. He has Adrian Leverkuhn, the fictional hero of his novel *Doctor Faustus* (1947), desire "to take back the Ninth." In *The Story of a Novel*, his book about *Doctor Faustus*, Mann comments: "Never had I more deeply admired the scherzo and adagio—but once again could summon up no affection for the variations of the dispirited last movement." Earlier, Mann had expressed skepticism regarding the symphony's basic premise: "The general progress of mankind is an unproven thesis. It does not exist for any nations of the East."[33]

While some music critics have found fault with the Ninth, the public over time has been resoundingly and passionately positive. The documentary film *Following the Ninth* (2013–14), directed by Kerry Candaele, displays the symphony's connection to people around the world. In this film Candaele links Beethoven with political protest and revolution through archival footage not only of Bernstein conducting the Ninth on both sides of the fallen Berlin Wall, but also of women in Chile, during Augusto Pinochet's dictatorship in the 1970s, giving hope to their incarcerated husbands and brothers by singing the Ninth's "Ode to Joy" outside of prisons. The Ninth was played at high volume through immense loudspeakers as thousands of students in Beijing's Tiananmen Square courageously protested China's harsh regime. The greatness of the Ninth's appeal not just as a force of revolution but as a quotidian, socially unifying, renewing experience comes alive when the film shows the massive choruses who each year assemble in Japan to participate in singing the Ninth on New Year's Eve. Schiller's "Ode to Joy" stresses the positive, the human, the brotherhood (and sisterhood) included in "alle Menschen werden Brüder" (all human beings are brothers). The word *Menschen*, we should keep in mind, means not just "men" but all humanity, female no less than male, and not least the ideals of which that inclusive humanity at its best is capable.

Though by 1824 a series of raised and dashed expectations had tempered hopes for German unification, many still cherished the notion of a pan-German state. The Enlightenment thinker saw genius as the quality characteristic of a prophet. And Beethoven saw himself as a prophet. But democratic ideals in the wake of the post-Napoleonic Restoration were fast fading in the public consciousness. The Ninth aimed to revive awareness of them. As Beethoven grew older and his deafness increased, his music moved more and more into an ideal world of his own creation. In the Ninth, taking upon himself the role of savior, he determined to succeed where his other heroes, mythical or real, had failed—whether Prometheus or Don Fernando, Tell or Egmont, Joseph II or Napoleon. In his new symphony he no longer evoked a mythic or a historical figure. Rather, people sang Schiller's "Ode to Joy," adapted by Beethoven to make his hope for a radiant future clear, with all their energy.

24

Music at the End

Beethoven, way out there in the yonder, was playing
a piano that was the entire universe.

VED MEHTA

In interpreting Beethoven, Romain Rolland imagined his oeuvre as
a mountain. One way to understand the singularity of Beethoven's
achievement might be, as Rolland suggests, to imagine the great classical composers as constituting an interlocking chain of mountains.
Towering above the others, distinct but clearly part of the range, is
the mountain we shall call Beethoven. It is easy enough to see at a
glance, after the lapse of two centuries, in what respect this mountain
is part of the range, but it is necessary also to distinguish the respects
in which it dominates the others, as well as the declivities, the preci-
pices, the escarpments that separate it from its attendant peaks. Off to
one side of this mountain looms a dark outcropping we may term "The
Last Quartets." Wordsworth in his great poem *The Prelude* envisioned
Isaac Newton voyaging "through strange seas of thought alone." So
Beethoven, in his last quartets, ventured where no one had gone before,
or thought to go.

Composers often gain strength as they get older. We can cite Bach's
Art of the Fugue, Messiaen's *Saint Francis of Assisi*, and, not least,
Beethoven's late music. He realized that his recent works, with the

exception of the Ninth Symphony and the *Missa solemnis*, had not overly pleased the public. Even in these years, the last period of his creativity, his compositions often met with incomprehension. From such affirmative triumphs as the above, he now moved to music of another kind: music that ponders the probabilities of life in which hope, at least in the political sphere, had waned, if not quite departed. The last quartets are bursts of affirmation in a world the composer now found dispiritingly sad. But hope never entirely disappeared.

Beethoven did not fade into the sunset after the mighty Ninth. He had other compositions in mind, several of them partially sketched, including a requiem and a tenth symphony in C minor. But except for drafts of two movements for the symphony, he left orchestral music behind. Instead, he devoted himself to string quartets. We may think of Beethoven chiefly as the creator of symphonies, concertos, and sonatas. Yet the sixteen string quartets he wrote over his lifetime give us as full and varied a picture of his genius as do the symphonies and the other works. Beethoven wrote his last quartets in the final three years of his creative life, from 1824 to 1826.

How do we understand, how deal with, the extraordinary achievement that constitutes the final five string quartets? "When confronted with the works of his last period," wrote Thomas Mann of his composer protagonist, Adrian Leverkuhn, in *Doctor Faustus*, the audience "had stood with heavy hearts before a process of disintegration, of alienation, of an ascent into what no longer felt familiar, but eerie."[1] Though referring to the fictional Leverkuhn, Mann's words have a curious relevance to Beethoven's late artistry. Bold, daring music such as his had often shocked the Viennese. Often he had faced unresponsive audiences.

If the Austrian emperor found Beethoven's music terrifying and many of the public no longer could or wished to support his endeavors, admiring representatives of other nations increasingly encouraged his work. In 1822 the Russian prince Nicolas Galitzin requested from Beethoven three string quartets. Beethoven took up the commission. Under the influence of the German Romantics—especially the writings of the Bavarian Catholic mystic Franz von Baader—Galitzin introduced fresh musical ideas into Russia and even into the thinking of Tsar Alexander. The quartets have little in them that is specifically Viennese, or even Austrian, but Russian influences, as in the earlier "Razumovsky" Quartets, appear frequently.

Since he first arrived in Vienna Beethoven had favored the quartet ensemble formed by Ignaz Schuppanzigh, who became a lifelong friend. They met the challenge of playing his works better than any other group. After Count Andreas Razumovsky's palace, where the quartet was based, burned down in 1814, Schuppanzigh left Vienna. As a result, the prince's spirits as well as his fortunes declined rapidly. But in April 1823 Schuppanzigh returned to Vienna and reestablished his quartet. Beethoven enlisted them to play his new works.

The string quartet ranks among the most sophisticated types of chamber music. The euphonious interplay among the four instruments has often been likened to a conversation, one in which the soloists work together to achieve the same goal. With only four instruments in play, we have the possibility of realizing the Classical ideal of a discourse among equals. However, Beethoven's last five quartets pose problems of a special kind. They constitute for some listeners of his oeuvre something of a black hole. In these quartets the phrases have become detached and separated, yet linked by their emotional power they beckon to each other across the intervening spaces. One of the triumphs of these quartets is that they are both introspective and universal. Great music does not have to be "about" the composer's experiences, it has been claimed, though it should in some way relate to them. Listeners who respond to these quartets sense that they seem to relate to what Wordsworth termed "unknown modes of being."

Nietzsche thought the last quartets Beethoven's greatest works. Music connoisseurs today often agree. In them Beethoven discovered a new means of reproducing the sweeping arc of a passion; by selecting individual points along its trajectory, he let his audience intuit from them the entire line. Beethoven used his final period of reflection to achieve a deep and universal expression of the human spirit. No wonder that artists and admirers who came after him concluded that in music suffering and genius were one and the same. The idea that we need to know music well to appreciate the man many consider Germany's greatest composer is, according to the British cultural critic Clive James, as absurd as "the idea that you need to be able to read music in order to appreciate Beethoven's late quartets."[2] In the nature of Beethoven's development we may draw analogies between his late quartets and Rembrandt's late portraits, and, even more relevant, analogies between the probing quartets and the terrifying late works of Goya.

Goya created works embodying the era's turmoil and tragedy. During the years of crisis in Spain he painted, from 1819 to 1823, what are now known as his Black Paintings. *Saturn Devouring His Children*, perhaps the most famous, shows the Titan as a wild-eyed colossus eating one of his own daughters. Other works present corpses, body parts, witches, and vampires. In his art Goya often contrasted light and dark. But darkness inevitably prevails. His probing of the unknown recalls Goethe's prologue to *Faust*, Part 1, a work long pondered by its author but only published in 1808. "Once again you approach, vacillating figures," a terrified Faust cries out. The figures to which he responds haunted Goethe's contemporaries. As Faust encountered frightening forms, so Goya in his Black Paintings and his extraordinary series of etchings *The Disasters of War* (1820) rendered his grotesqueries in detail. *The Disasters of War* demonstrates through words and images of unparalleled realism the devastation that war had done to his country.

As Beethoven's late quartets anticipate much twentieth-century music, so the Black Paintings and the *Disasters* inaugurate contemporary art. In them, comments the art historian Fred Licht, "the dark matrix of modern life is first laid bare."[3] It is easier for us today, he believes, "to recognize the connections between the aging Goya and our own epoch than it is to place Goya in the context of his own times."[4] I see his point, but disagree.

The three final piano sonatas of Beethoven, a quarter of a century younger than the long-lived Spaniard, are contemporaneous with Goya's Black Paintings. Beethoven's later masterpieces, his string quartets, we may also consider kin to the Black Paintings. If we set the paintings against Beethoven's mysterious last quartets, we find both puzzling, often indecipherable, deeply disturbing, even unsettling, possibly beyond comprehension.[5] Like Goya, Beethoven sought to explore unknown realms of experience. Like the Black Paintings, his late works open up new vistas into humanity's dark corners and plummeting abysses. But unlike Goya's late works, Beethoven's final quartets radiate joy and transcendence. In the five quartets written between 1824 and 1826, I shall focus upon one movement in Opus 130 and one in Opus 131.

The original last movement of Opus 130 is the *Grand Fugue* (*Grosse Fuge*), Op. 133. Beethoven had always found fugues fascinating. Trying to break the bonds he had inherited, he goes back to this older form in which a battle goes on between two subjects, as if the elements had warred with each other and suffered an interruption. Symphonic in its proportions, the *Grand Fugue* has inspired several orchestral versions. Stravinsky, who called it "the most perfect miracle in music," once termed it "an absolutely contemporary piece of music that will be contemporary forever—it is pure internal music." He claimed to "love it beyond all other."[6] Listening to it produces the most intense quarter hour in all music. The *Grand Fugue* continues to challenge expectations. One scholar considers it "the last purely heroic finale" Beethoven ever created.[7]

Several of Beethoven's musically aware friends found the *Grand Fugue* too hard and complex to play or understand and asked him to write an alternate ending for Opus 130. Beethoven, who normally did not take kindly to changes recommended by others, however well intentioned, for once agreed and replaced it with a shorter, less strenuous movement. For his labors he received an extra fee, which pleased him. This alternate Finale seems to have been the last work he wrote. Recent decades have seen the *Grand Fugue* again chosen as the conclusion to

Opus 130, sometimes along with the original movement that replaced it, making for an instructive contrast.

Opus 131, composed from December 1825 to July 1826, is one of Beethoven's most sublime creations. Most string quartets consist of four movements, but several of Beethoven's last quartets have more. Additional movements stretch further the possibilities of the medium. Of the seven movements of Opus 131, numbered by Beethoven himself, two, admittedly, are short and serve chiefly as introductions to the movements that follow, as Beethoven wished no break to occur between the movements. As you listen to Opus 131 you sense that it is a cyclic work. Even though it is enormously complex, all seven of its movements work together. One way to approach Opus 131 it is to think of Beethoven speaking, or even singing, from the depths of his being. In Aldous Huxley's novel *Point Counter Point* (1929) a character points to Beethoven's Opus 131 as evidence of the divine. "It's the only proof that exists; the only one, because Beethoven was the only man who could get his knowledge over into expression."[8]

A fugue is a complex musical form designed for a definite number of instruments (or voices) in which one announces the subject and then each of the others develops it in a strict order. Many think the first movement of Opus 131, an Adagio in the form of a fugue, is Beethoven's greatest. Its sound proceeds at a slow, tempered pace, with all four voices playing equally important roles throughout the movement. Beethoven wanted it played *molto espressivo*. Richard Wagner thought this Adagio a "revelation from another world." He also believed it to be the saddest piece of music Beethoven ever wrote.[9] It reminded him of lines near the beginning of Goethe's dramatic poem *Faust*: he designated it, quoting Faust himself, "as the awakening on the morn of a day that throughout its . . . course shall fulfill not a single desire: not one."[10] Nietzsche eloquently describes this unusual state of being: "The thinker feels himself floating above the earth in an astral dome, with the dream of immortality in his heart: all the stars seem to glimmer about him, and the earth seems to sink ever further downward."[11] The whole work grows from this Adagio. Beethoven by starting Opus 131 with a slow movement intends both sadness and otherworldliness. Although he wrote a fair amount of fugal music, particularly in his later years, rarely before had he begun a composition with a slow movement—a major exception being his early piano sonata in C-sharp minor, known today as the "Moonlight" Sonata.

The Andante at the heart of Opus 131 has a traditionally steady, flowing tempo. Lasting close to a quarter of an hour, it is by far the quartet's longest and most soulful movement. It consists of a gentle theme and a series of six variations, each more heartfelt than that previous. As we've seen, variations preoccupied Beethoven in later years, and this Andante is perhaps his most developed and complex work of art, one he labored hard to bring to completion. Scholars have found fifteen versions of the last four variations. To anyone else but Beethoven, almost any one of them would have served his purpose well enough. But Beethoven, tireless in his search for perfection, kept rewriting them until he was satisfied. The result is one of the most beautiful pieces of music he ever wrote. A Presto, another Adagio, then a brief Allegro follow. Separating the slow movements from the lengthy Adagio, these faster movements pulse with energy. They remind us that life offers joy as well as sadness.

The quartet's depth comes in part from its inclusion of humor along with deep sorrow. In both the Adagio and the Presto that follows, the cellist and sometimes one or more of the other performers plays pizzicato, that is, he or she plucks the strings. The effect sounds, to my irreverent ears at least, something like hiccups. Encompassing frequent changes of mood, the music fluctuates between seriousness and high spirits, keeping you off balance. Beethoven was a master of the art of the unexpected. We can smile, even laugh, or have starts of surprise listening to these changes in the second Adagio. But still, the end result is like hearing a great circle closing.

Beethoven in dealing with his publisher Schott in Bonn wrote him on August 1826 that Opus 131 had been "patched together from pieces filched here and there."[12] Understandably, Schott was horrified. After all, he had bargained for and paid good money for a completely new piece. He squawked, so Beethoven reassured him that the work he'd received was indeed new. Actually, not quite all parts of it were, but the completed quartet most certainly was.

Although Beethoven once spoke of Opus 131 as his favorite of the late quartets, to the best of our knowledge he could only have heard it in August 1826, when the Schuppanzigh Quartet tried out the work.[13] Schott published it a month or two after the composer died on March 26, 1827. One person who did hear it played was Franz Schubert, whose own late quartets rival Beethoven's in beauty. As he lay on his deathbed early in November 1828, Schubert, who worshipped Beethoven, asked to hear Opus 131. Four musical friends obliged. It was the last piece of music he heard. He died five days later.[14]

The first public performance of the work was in 1835. In the nineteenth century, Beethoven's late quartets were thought complex, difficult, dissonant, bizarre, maybe even a little crazy. Thus, for several decades, they were rarely played. The twentieth century saw a rise in their fortunes. Now the late quartets are among the most frequently performed of all Beethoven's chamber works, praised for reasons they were formerly criticized. We appreciate dissonances and complexity more. In fact, many regard these quartets as the summit of Beethoven's quartet writing, a chief glory of his creative artistry.

ی

Two String Quartets and Bacchus

Beethoven wished the third movement of Opus 132, the "Heiliger Dankgesang" (Holy Song of Thanksgiving), played "with the greatest feeling." He had apparently once intended to use its Finale as the basis for the last movement of the Ninth Symphony, a somber, tragic conclusion rather than the exultant anthem that crowns the work. But that did not happen. We may sense a connection between Opus 132 and T. S. Eliot's *Four Quartets*. "I have the A minor quartet on the gramophone," Eliot wrote to Stephen Spender in 1931, "and I find it quite inexhaustible to study." Eliot wondered at the "heavenly or at least more than human gaiety" in some of Beethoven's later works, "what one imagines might come to oneself as the fruit of reconciliation and relief after immense suffering." "I should like," he says, "to get something of that into verse once before I die."[15]

While composing his Opus 135 Beethoven may have realized he did not have long to live. He inscribed on the manuscript the words: "Muss es sein? Muss es sein? Es muss sein" (Must it be? Must it be? It must be). Some have taken the words seriously, others sense a mocking tone, still others view them as a play on language. The point, as Milan Kundera observed in his novel *The Unbearable Lightness of Being*, is that it is not an either/or proposition: it has both comic and serious potentiality.[16]

In his last years Beethoven also sketched part of what would have become a tenth symphony. This incomplete work once again celebrates Bacchus. For Nietzsche, Bacchus was "the highest god, truly revealing himself." In Beethoven, surmises Richard Specht, "the bacchantic mysteries of the Tenth were awake."[17] The heroic struggle of cosmos versus chaos, a lifelong challenge for Beethoven, had not yet ceased.

ৠ

Death Comes for the Composer

In September 1826 Beethoven set off with his nephew Karl on a visit to his brother Johann in Gneixendorf, a village upriver on the Danube, now part of the town of Krems. Being near a great stream flowing placidly before him must have reminded Beethoven of the Rhine landscapes of his youth, though the views across the Danube included nothing as fine as the Seven Hills across the Rhine from Bonn. Eventually, as usually happened, the brothers quarreled, and early in December Beethoven left precipitously. With a carriage unavailable, he and Karl took an open milk wagon for the two-day journey back to Vienna, spending the intervening night in an unheated room in a tavern. Arriving in Vienna the next day, Beethoven, chilled to the bone and sick, went to his bed. In the months to come his condition gradually worsened. Several doctors were summoned, but none could alleviate his illness. Many of his close friends came to visit. One was Count Moritz Lichnowsky, the surviving brother of Prince Karl Lichnowsky, from the family who had taken him into their home thirty-five years before. But many others, including several of his wealthy and aristocratic acquaintances, were nowhere to be seen.

"Das ist die Wahre!" (That's the thing!), said Beethoven in 1827, on what turned out to be his deathbed, upon being presented with a forty-volume set of Handel's scores recently published in England. J. A. Stumpff, a German harp manufacturer long resident in London, sent the set to Beethoven upon hearing he had expressed a desire for it.[18] Handel "is the greatest, the ablest composer; I can still learn from him. Bring the books over to me," the bedridden man said of the volumes.[19] Beethoven had long admired Handel's *Messiah*, and now he could delight in all of his works. Dying, but eagerly perusing the pages, he continued to be awed by the vastness of Handel's genius.

Offered morphine to ease his discomfort, Beethoven refused it (or any other opium derivative). He would remain himself, preferring to stay awake and alert, and so to the end he did. Even now, his biographer Schindler tells us, "his imagination, more capricious even than when he was in health, swept through the universe developing plans for travel and for great compositions."[20] Beethoven was not ready to die. He insisted he had just begun to compose.

The close of the Beethovenian epic took place almost six years after the close of the Napoleonic. On May 5, 1821, the former emperor, in exile on his storm-tossed island in the South Atlantic, had died of stomach cancer. Three years later, on April 19, 1824, Byron, suffering under miserable circumstances at Missolonghi in western Greece, succumbed in the midst of a thunderstorm. On March 26, 1827, it was the turn of Beethoven, the contemporary in many ways closest in genius and in imaginative range to Napoleon and Byron.

On that day in Vienna, between four and five o'clock in the afternoon, dense clouds drifting across the horizon from every quarter increasingly obscured the landscape. It began to snow. All of a sudden, a raging storm broke, with driving snow and hail. Beethoven's last minutes on earth were spent during meteorological turmoil, including a Promethean thunderclap and a searing "lightning stroke," or so it was reported. Beethoven had often read in Plutarch of heroic deaths. Now his became another. From its position on his work desk the statue of Lucius Junius Brutus, the Roman consul who gave his life in the service of his people, could be seen by the dying composer. As death came, among Beethoven's last words were "Plaudite, amici! comoedia finita est!" (Applaud, friends! The comedy is over!) from Emperor Augustus. In recalling them, Beethoven, an emperor of music, wished the world to know he had lived his life to the hilt. He roused himself at the last, shook his fist at the heavens, and departed life at 5 p.m. At the end only Anselm von Hüttenbrenner, a friend of Schubert's, and Johanna van Beethoven, Karl's mother, whom Beethoven had often made miserable, were present.[21] "Full of grief he died," lamented a saddened Robert Schumann, "and, like Napoleon, without a child beside him."[22]

The thunder and the lightning, along with the raised fist, serve as symbols for a man who had long advocated freedom, who had sought to be free himself, a man who valued power, a man who in his own world was a conqueror. These characteristics, as well as a seemingly limitless will, he directed not to the military achievement and political control that animated Napoleon, or to the literary success sought by Byron, but to the musical life of his era. Through his compositions he sought to shape a better future for humanity, to conquer, as has been said, "the most distant spheres of the spirit." He aspired to link music to humankind's highest goals: to serve justice and to promote enlightened behavior.

Beethoven was fifty-six when he died. His was not, by the standards of the time, a short life. More people then died young than old, Mozart at thirty-five, Schubert but thirty-one, eighteen months after Beethoven.

Max Franz, who became elector of Cologne at age twenty-eight and had furthered Beethoven's career, died in exile in Vienna at forty-five. Beethoven's teacher in Bonn, Christian Gottlob Neefe, died at fifty. The Emperor Joseph II, ever a distant beacon for the composer, died just short of fifty. The exact causes of Beethoven's death have been debated ever since the results of his autopsy were made known. The autopsy reveals that he died of cirrhosis of the liver, probably caused by a lifetime of excessive alcohol intake and kidney failure.

The funeral was held on March 29. The large crowd, estimated at between ten and twenty thousand, followed Beethoven's funeral cortège from Vienna's Minoriten Church to his resting place in Währing Cemetery.[23] No representatives from the imperial court attended. Franz Grillparzer wrote the funeral oration.[24] The actor Heinrich Schutz spoke the impassioned words. Although Grillparzer had not greatly responded to Beethoven's music after the *Eroica*, finding it virtually incomprehensible as well as bizarre, he remained a good friend, declaring, "I really loved Beethoven."[25] Coupling the composer's name with Goethe's, Germany's greatest writer, he stressed the uniqueness of Beethoven's achievement. "He who comes after him will not continue him,"[26] because his work so far surpasses anyone's ability. The words ring as eloquently today as when first uttered. Grillparzer does not mention God. The only deity recognized was Music per se. Beethoven served as its high priest.

᙭

"Nature created him as a gift to the world." So Giorgio Vasari began his life of Raphael. No less do his words apply to Beethoven. "In the end," Goethe once wrote, "the only way to move is forward!"[27] And move forward Beethoven did, from earliest maturity until his last breath. No less did and does his music move forward.

Napoleon's career had once inspired many, Beethoven not least, to hope for a Europe free of absolutism, free of state oppression, perhaps even, if the gods were favorable, a Europe of republics. Napoleon, with his ceaseless energy and a life of achievement, represented for Beethoven all that Emperor Franz did not. With Beethoven's death, the age of revolutionary heroes ended. The Napoleonic myth and the Beethovenian myth began to fuse, or so this book has argued, a fusion that in retrospect seems inevitable.

Beethoven dominated nineteenth-century music. "It is striking, if not impossible to exaggerate," comments the cultural historian Peter Gay, "his share in fostering the nineteenth-century art of listening. To the divine Michelangelo they joined the towering contemporary fig- ure, the divine Beethoven. He seemed the embodiment of the roman- tic genius."[28] Beethoven's domination has continued into the twentieth and twenty-first centuries. As a symphonist, though now in competition with Brahms and Bruckner, Mahler and Shostakovich, he set a standard to which his successors can only aspire.

This raises, I think, a larger question. Where, in the end, do we place Beethoven? Should we regard him as the successor to Haydn and Mozart? Musicological studies often classify him as the culmination of the Classicist "Viennese school." Yet his contemporary, E. T. A. Hoff- mann, viewed Beethoven as "a purely Romantic composer."[29] Myself, I lean toward Hoffmann, but sometimes I wonder: why try to classify Beethoven at all? Does any classification do justice to his distinction as perhaps the greatest of all composers? Does the Finale of the Fifth Symphony sound like anything you've heard in Mozart or Haydn? Do we assign to a "school" the great creative spirits of Western civilization, among them Shakespeare, Dante, Rabelais, Rembrandt, Michelangelo? Why, then, should we do so with Beethoven? He certainly learned much from Haydn and Mozart, but he adored Bach, and Handel was his god. He dedicated works to the tsar of Russia, the king of Prussia, the prince regent of England, and he would have liked to have dedicated works to Napoleon; but he never dedicated even a bagatelle to the emperor of Austria. At the time of the Ninth Symphony, after having lived in Vienna for thirty-two years, Beethoven publicly declared himself a "citizen of Bonn." As we have seen, he wished to have his new symphony performed first in Berlin, not Vienna, and only buckled after concerned friends exerted pressure upon him. In the end, he dedicated the Ninth to the Prussian king, in whose territory Bonn now lay.

All the great creators, different as they are, manifest the highest level of genius: Dante, by his determined, obstinate nature, the harshness and acuity by which he judged imperfect humankind; Rabelais, by his Bacchic energy, his exhilaration before life and language; Michelangelo, by his grandiose vision, his strength of will, his immense labor on the Sistine ceiling, hobnobbing with sibyls and prophets and godlike young men; Shakespeare, by the range, variety, and depth of his creative gift; Rembrandt, by the depth of his insight into the human soul.

Perhaps the first to express his awe before Beethoven's genius by comparing it to Michelangelo's was the prescient Johann Friedrich Reichardt in 1808: "Often has occurred to me," he wrote, in thinking about the composer, "Michelangelo's proud, daring thought to place the magnificent Pantheon as the dome of his St. Peter's Cathedral."[30] Later commentators "have likened Beethoven's agony as a composer to Michelangelo's as a sculptor, endlessly chipping away the excess from great blocks of stone to reveal the magnificent, seemingly inevitable forms trapped within."[31] Egon Friedell found it virtually impossible to classify the level of Beethoven's genius, while Hans Keller believed Beethoven "possibly humanity's greatest mind altogether."[32]

Nationalism, though certainly existing in mild forms before 1789, was hardly a factor during Beethoven's youth. The French Revolution gave it its first great impetus. After 1806, stimulated by Napoleon's defeat of Prussia, nationalism in Germany quickly exerted its sway over many. But not over Beethoven (or Goethe). As page after page of his music demonstrates, Beethoven looked upon humanity with a large perspective. Though rooted in German musical culture, he was fully cognizant of and receptive to other traditions. He learned from Slavic, Italian, Turkish, Hungarian, Czech, most of all, perhaps, from French music. Cherubini was his favorite contemporary musician, an admired model. For the songs he was asked to write Beethoven drew upon a dozen national traditions, including English, Scottish, and Celtic. He faced a world transformed and attempted through his music to give it voice. He revolutionized music to match his desire for a utopian republic. He was in truth, as he wished to be, a "citizen of the world."

ACKNOWLEDGMENTS

In writing *Beethoven: The Relentless Revolutionary* I have drawn chiefly on primary documents: letters Beethoven wrote, but also those he received; the journal he kept from 1812 to 1818; the conversations recorded by wine and dinner companions after 1818, along with the reminiscences and letters of those who knew him. I draw also on books and essays in French, German, and Italian as well as in English that take up Beethoven within the musical culture of the age; on studies of Austrian and European history; on interpretations of the French Revolution; on Napoleon's rise to power and the tumultuous decades that followed; and on the musical, artistic, literary, political, and social life of Europe during Beethoven's lifetime.

Completing a book of this complexity has taken a great deal of time and energy. Along the way I have received much help. On the home front, which for me in recent decades has been Santa Fe, New Mexico, I have many to thank. I am grateful both to Steven Smith, former conductor of the Santa Fe Symphony, and to Tom O'Connor, conductor of the Santa Fe Pro Musica, for inviting me to give pre-concert lectures on Beethoven and other composers. I thank Dr. Robert Marcus, an accomplished musician, for his careful reading of several chapters of this book. Peter Pesic, a talented pianist and a leading scholar on the history of music's relation to science, has through his performances, books, and good conversation over the years never ceased to offer perceptive insights and assistance. It was in Santa Fe where I met Bill Kinderman when he was playing a series of concerts at the Santa Fe Chamber Music Festival. I am grateful to Bill for his splendid books on Beethoven, for his enthusiastic response to my essays in the *Beethoven Journal* and elsewhere, and for his sustained interest in this book.

Through correspondence and during research trips I have benefited immeasurably from working amid the priceless resources in the superb Beethoven-Haus Archiv in Bonn, Germany. There Stefanie Kuban and Dorothea Geffert made me aware of the extent of the archive's resources and facilitated my use of them. Dr. Bernhard R. Appel, now retired, then editor of the annual *Bonner Beethoven-Studien,* offered many useful suggestions both in person and by post regarding an essay of mine published in that journal. Closer to home, I have benefited from the very different but equally splendid Beethoven Center at San Jose State University, California. Will Meredith, its founder and longtime director (now retired), and Patricia Stroh, its almost equally long-serving archivist, have in diverse ways contributed greatly to my understanding of Beethoven. Will, as editor of the invaluable *Beethoven Journal*, has through conversations and by publishing in it several of my Beethoven essays, generously supported and improved my work. Patricia has cheerfully guided me on numerous occasions when unexpected difficulties arose in my research.

Different national perspectives deepen our understanding of Beethoven and his age. Scholars interpret Beethoven within their own traditions, which may vary widely. American conceptions of the composer differ from British, French from German, German from Italian, and, in the decades after World War II until reunification in 1989, West German from East German. Having endeavored to take cognizance of other national perspectives on Beethoven in my narrative, I have found that the brilliant criticism coming out of Europe has often not been incorporated into works on Beethoven published by American scholars.

Two of the most comprehensive recent biographies of Beethoven are by the Italian scholar Piero Buscaroli and the Dutch scholar Jan Caeyers. The most up-to-date study of the *Eroica* by Fabrizio della Seta appeared in twenty-first-century Italy, a few years before Benedetta Saglietti's detailed study of the context of Beethoven portraiture and the meaning of Beethoven iconography. Whereas Buscaroli's massive biography (2004) explores unusual perspectives concerning Beethoven, Saglietti's study (2010) illumines well Beethoven portraiture. The classic study remains Alessandra Comini, *The Changing Image of Beethoven: A Study in Mythmaking* (1987).

Beginning virtually with Berlioz, French critics, scholars, and enthusiasts have written with insight and passion about Beethoven. They include François-Joseph Fétis, Vincent d'Indy, Romain Rolland, Jean Boyer, Jean Chantavoine, J.-G. Prod'homme, Édouard Herriot, and Jean and Brigitte Masson. Of their works, only the writings of Berlioz, d'Indy, Rolland, and Herriot have, to my knowledge, received English translations, and that mostly decades ago.

In the twenty-first century it is Elisabeth Brisson, a polymath of staggering ability, who has become the leading French interpreter of the composer. Elisabeth has educated me about Beethoven through books of exceptional brilliance and subsequently through conversation and letters. Her seminal study *Le sacre du musicien: La référence à l'antiquité chez Beethoven* appeared in France in 2000, just in time to inaugurate the new century. The most dazzling recent interpretation of Beethoven's intellectual development that I know, it has more than any other work influenced how I look at the composer. Hardly less useful has been her invaluable *Guide de la musique de Beethoven* (2005). In addition, Elisabeth has published an introductory biography of Beethoven, several important studies relating music to democracy, and a full-length account of the theme of Faust in Western art and literature as well as in music (*Faust: Biographie d'un mythe*, 2013). Another probing study, *Les aires mythiques* (2014), includes Beethoven in tracing the power of song in shaping Western culture.

Beethoven believed that his music could help bring about a better world than the one in which he lived. One who has felt its resonance is Kerry Candaele. His splendid film *Following the Ninth: In the Footsteps of Beethoven's Final Symphony* (2013) depicts that symphony's power both to inspire listeners to resist tyranny and to comfort those subject to it. In Pinochet's Chile in 1973, in Ulbrich's East Germany in 1989, and in Beijing's Tiananmen Square that same year, thousands agitated for freedom with Beethoven's Ninth ringing in their ears. In Japan, participating in a performance of the Ninth on New Year's Eve (an experience known as Daiku) becomes virtually a sacred act, one further instance of Beethoven's music giving, and continuing to give, hope to many. Kerry's *Following the Ninth* appeared to considerable acclaim; his films on *Fidelio* and Beethoven's last string quartets are in progress.

In this country and in Europe I have made peregrinations to what has become a seemingly ever-diminishing roster of secondhand bookstores. Travels to professional conferences as well as trips for pleasure were not complete without indulging in the local shops. In Manhattan how can one not mention the Strand and the Argosy, both happily still going strong. Cincinnati, Berkeley, Boston, and Montreal, among many other cities, have also supplied treasured volumes. Abroad, in London, Paris, Grenoble, Lyon, Milan, Vienna, in the major German cities, including Berlin, Leipzig, Dresden, Munich, and Frankfurt, I have found needed books. Helene Trottmann in Munich, along with her husband, Herr Karl, has been of especial help. In moving to Santa Fe I found myself blessed by two excellent bookshops. One is Nicholas Potter, Bookseller, the name of its longtime owner. The other is Big Star, founded by David Schmid and assisted by Kerry Norton and Lillian Schul. In both I have come across tomes useful for my work, as well as CDs of classical music. Helen McCloud, a longtime Santa Fe friend seemingly forever involved in the local book scene, generously passes on to me every Beethoven tome she comes across.

I wish to thank here the Lannan Foundation, long based in Santa Fe. Its mission is to support through grants and public lectures distinguished writers who are advocates for political and cultural freedom, social justice, and environmental responsibility. Underlying this mission is the belief that if enough people strive for a free, progressive society, eventually, if perhaps not in an individual's lifetime, it will come about. Attending these talks has brightened the lives of innumerable citizens of Santa Fe as well as those throughout the world via the foundation's website. Patrick Lannan and his wife, Andy Tuch, who are our near neighbors, have made sure we have had up-front tickets for every event sponsored by the foundation, nearly all of which are sold out.

In many ways the Lannan Foundation's vision recalls that of Ludwig van Beethoven two hundred years earlier. Though often discouraged, he never wavered in his belief in "freedom and progress." Living in Hapsburg Austria, a society hostile to both new ideas and political freedom, he tells us through his music, and no less through his courage and personal integrity, that he never lost hope. He tells us, too, that we also must never lose hope. Better times, his music proclaims, will come about, may even be inevitable, but—a large but—only if enough of us work hard enough to make them happen.

Finally, of the many individuals who have helped me over the years, several deserve special recognition. Don Lamm, a frequent lunch partner, and one of the wisest people I know, encouraged this project from the start. It was he who suggested I add "Relentless" to the subtitle. I am deeply grateful to Don being himself "relentless" in his support. His advice and insights into the world of commercial publishing have proved invaluable. At Norton I have been blessed by having as my editor Amy Cherry. Her good sense, patience, and command of language have been invaluable. One could not ask for better support and sounder advice. Helpful in other ways and of equal good cheer have been her assistants Remy Cawley and Zarina Patwa. I also wish to thank the talented designer Eleen Cheung, who created the superbly appropriate dust jacket for this volume. I am most sincerely grateful as well for

Marilyn Bliss's astonishingly thorough preparation of the index. Last, my partner Joan Blythe has put up with the author of this project far longer than either of us expected. Besides the troublesome task of keeping me going over the years, Joan has served as the first reader of whatever I choose to write. I happily acknowledge her shrewd insights and patience with both me and my prose. Without her guiding presence this book would not be.

NOTES

Overture

1. Hugh Ottaway, "The Enlightenment and the Revolution," in *Classical and Romantic*, ed. Alec Robertson and Denis Stevens (1968; Harmondsworth, Middlesex: Penguin Books, 1986), 86.
2. Cited in Publisher's Note to *Romain Rolland's Essays on Music* (New York: Allen Towne & Heath, 1948), x.

1: Beethoven in Bonn

1. The identity of the creator of this portrait has been much debated. For a cogent summary, see Ernest Closson, *L'élément flamand dans Beethoven*, 2nd ed. (Brussels: Éditions universitaires, 1946), 251 n4.
2. *Beethoven aus der Sicht seiner Zeitgenossen*, ed. Klaus Martin Kopitz and Rainer Cadenach, 2 vols. (Munich: G. Henle Verlag, 2009), 1: 505; Elisabeth Brisson, *Le sacre du musicien: La référence à l'Antiquité chez Beethoven* (Paris: CNRS Editions, 2000), 12, 125.
3. Willy Hess, *Beethovens Bühnenwerke* (Göttingen: Vandenhoeck & Ruprecht, 1959), 11–12.
4. Hajo Holborn, *A History of Modern Germany, 1648–1840* (New York: Alfred A. Knopf, 1969), 299–300.
5. Gerhard von Breuning, *Memories of Beethoven*, ed. Maynard Solomon, trans.

Henry Mins and Maynard Solomon (Cambridge: Cambridge University Press, 1992), 29.

6. Friedrich Heer, *The Holy Roman Empire*, trans. Janet Sondheimer (New York and Washington, D.C.: Frederick A. Praeger, 1968), 279–81.

7. James J. Sheehan, *German History, 1770–1866* (Oxford: Clarendon Press, 1989), 35.

8. Heer, op. cit., 279–80.

9. Sheehan, op. cit., 31.

10. Anton Schindler, *Beethoven as I Knew Him*, trans. Constance S. Jolly (Chapel Hill: University of North Carolina Press, 1966), 45–46.

11. For this trip (as well as for others to come), see Michael Ladenburger's exemplary *Beethoven auf Reisen* (Bonn: Beethoven Haus, 2016), 35–47.

12. Gunter Fleischhauer, "Beethoven und die Antike," in *Bericht über den Internationale Beethoven–Kongress 10–12 Dezember 1970 in Berlin*, ed. Heinz Alfred Brockhaus and Konrad Niemann (Berlin: Verlag neue Musik Berlin, 1971), 467.

13. Robert C. Solomon, *History and Human Nature* (New York and London: Harcourt Brace Jovanovich, 1979), 291.

14. Richard Friedenthal, *Goethe: His Life and Times* (Cleveland and New York: World Publishing Company, 1963), 272.

15. Robert C. Solomon, op. cit., 18, 66, 101.

16. Ibid., 67.

17. Alan Menhennet, *Order and Freedom: Literature and Society in Germany from 1720 to 1805* (New York: Basic Books, 1973), viii.

18. H. C. Robbins Landon, *Mozart and Vienna* (New York: Schirmer Books, 1991), 45–50, especially 47–48; H. C. Robbins Landon and David Wyn Jones, *Haydn: His Life and Music* (Bloomington and Indianapolis: Indiana University Press, 1988), 63, 172.

19. Hugh Ottaway, "The Enlightenment and Revolution," in *Classical and Romantic*, ed. Alec Robertson and Denis Stevens (Harmondsworth, Middlesex: Penguin Books, 1968), 56.

20. E. M. Butler, *The Tyranny of Greece over Germany* (Cambridge: Cambridge University Press, 1935), 93.

21. Romain Goldron, *Beethoven sans légende* (Lausanne: Cahiers de la Renaissance vaudoise, 1972), 237–39. Stephen Rumpf takes an opposing tack in his mistitled *Beethoven after Napoleon: Political Romanticism in the Late Works*. See my review "Beethoven and Napoleon" of his book and several others relating to Napoleon, in *European Romantic Review* 17.3 (2006): 377–90.

22. Friedenthal, op. cit., 340–41.

23. Giorgio Pestelli, *The Age of Mozart and Beethoven* (Cambridge: Cambridge University Press, 1984), 110.

24. Mark Evan Bonds, *Music as Thought: Listening to the Symphony in the Age of Beethoven* (Princeton: Princeton University Press, 2006), 17. Fontenelle's earlier

and often cited witticism "Sonate, que me veux-tu?" (Sonata, what do you wish of me?) mocked instrumental music as opposed to vocal.

25. Kant, *Critique of Practical Reason*, cited from Sheehan, op. cit., 179, 181–82.

26. J. C. Adelung, cited from Sheehan, op. cit., 175.

2: Key Influences

1. Richard Specht, *Beethoven as He Lived* (New York: Harrison Smith and Richard Haas, 1933), 120.

2. "Ich schreibe als Weltbürger, der keinem Fürsten dient": English version cited from Tim Manning, *The Romantic Revolution: A History* (New York: Modern Library, 2011), 40. Beethoven never became a full-fledged democrat.

3. Bernt von Heiseler, *Schiller*, trans. John Bednall (1959; London: Eyre & Spottiswoode, 1961), 32–33. The chief personal tyranny under which Beethoven suffered was the often cruel behavior of his domineering alcoholic father.

4. Paul Bekker, *Beethoven* (London: Dent, 1927), 54–56.

5. E. M. Butler, *The Tyranny of Greece over Germany* (Cambridge: Cambridge University Press, 1935), 159–60.

6. Ibid., 189.

7. Erich Auerbach, *Mimesis: The Representation of Reality in Western Literature*, trans. Willard Trask (1946; Garden City, NY: Doubleday Anchor Books, 1953), 388.

8. Richard Friedenthal, *Goethe: His Life and Times* (Cleveland and New York: World Publishing Company, 1963), 294–95.

9. Egon Friedell, *A Cultural History of the Modern Age*, trans. Charles Francis Atkinson, 3 vols. (1931; New York: Alfred A. Knopf, 1954), 2: 396–97.

10. Hajo Holborn, *A History of Modern Germany, 1648–1840* (New York: Alfred A. Knopf, 1969), 332, 333.

11. Maynard Solomon, "Beethoven and Schiller," in *Beethoven Essays* (Cambridge and London: Harvard University Press, 1988), 208; Kinley J. Brauer and William E. Wright, eds., *Austria in the Age of the French Revolution, 1789–1815* (Minneapolis: Center for Austrian Studies, 1990), 113.

12. Thomas Mann, *Last Essays*, trans. Richard and Clara Winston (New York: Alfred A. Knopf, 1966), 25, 27.

13. Wordsworth, *The Prelude*, Book 11, ll. 108–09.

14. Schiller, *Don Carlos*, Act 2, scene 2, based on a quotation from Julius Caesar. The unempowered young of Europe would echo his cry throughout the nineteenth century: *My Past and Thoughts: The Memoirs of Alexander Herzen* (New York: Alfred A. Knopf, 1973), 230.

15. Cited from Mann, op. cit., 92.

16. Partial German text (three stanzas) in Christoph Friedrich Cotta, *Eulogius Schneiders Schicksale in Frankreich* (Strasbourg, 1797; rpt. Hamburg: Helmut

Buske, 1979), viii–ix. I translate the two stanzas from Gertrud Wegener, *Literarisches Leben in Köln, 1750–1814*, 2 vols. (Cologne: Heimatverein Alt Köln, 2000), 1: 99.

17. Maynard Solomon, in his *Beethoven* (New York: Schirmer Books, 1977), cites the composer's name on the subscription list for Schneider's poems as evidence that Beethoven subscribed to revolutionary ideas. In his 1999 revision Solomon deletes mention of Schneider and his volume, apparently in the belief that Beethoven's subscription does not, after all, indicate adherence to revolutionary ideals. Solomon's revision also omits other instances of Beethoven's revolutionary thinking that are taken up in the first edition.

18. R. R. Palmer, *The Age of the Democratic Revolution*, 2 vols. (Princeton: Princeton University Press, 1959), 2: 438, 439, 441.

19. Andreas Sebastian Stumpf, *Eulogius Schneiders Leben und Schicksale im Vaterland*, ed. Christopf Prignitz (Hamburg: Helmut Buske, 1792), 43–44.

20. Ibid., xiii.

21. The memory of Schneider remained vivid in Beethoven's mind. For an excellent brief survey of Schneider's career, see Jean and Brigitte Massin, "Beethoven et la Révolution Française," *L'Arc* 40 (1970): 8–10.

3: Two Cantatas

1. Thomas Scherman and Louis Biancolli, ed., *The Beethoven Companion* (Garden City: Doubleday, 1972), 53. Letter to Eduard Hanslick, May 1884.

2. Cited from Friedrich Heer, *The Holy Roman Empire*, trans. Janet Sondheimer (New York and Washington, DC: Fredercik A. Praeger, 1968), 258–59. The brothers, despite their shrewd evaluations of each other's weaknesses and strengths, remained close.

3. Ibid., 138.

4. This painting by Pompeo Batoni commemorates their visit to Rome in 1769. Reproduced in Ernst Wangermann, *The Austrian Achievement, 1700–1800* (New York: Harcourt Brace Jovanovich, 1973), 91.

5. Cited from Gordon A. Craig, *The Politics of the Unpolitical: German Writers and the Problem of Power, 1770–1871* (New York: Oxford University Press, 1995), 5.

6. Michael P. Steinberg and Larry Rothe, *For the Love of Music: Invitations to Listening* (New York: Oxford University Press, 2006), 96.

7. Hajo Holborn, *A History of Modern Germany, 1648–1840* (New York: Alfred A. Knopf, 1969), 280.

8. Madame de Staël, *De l'Allemagne*, introduction by Simone Balayé, 2 vols. (Paris: Garnier-Flammarion, 1968), 1: 79. My translation.

9. James J. Sheehan, *German History, 1770–1866* (Oxford: Clarendon Press, 1989), 54.

10. Cited from Fan S. Noli, *Beethoven and the French Revolution* (New York: International Universities Press, 1947), 64.

11. Philip Mansell, *Prince of Europe: The Life of Charles-Joseph de Ligne* (London: Weidenfeld and Nicolson, 2005), 85.

12. Ibid., 152.

13. German from *Beethoven Texte*, collected and edited by Kurt E. Schürmann (Münster: Ashendorff, 1980), 211, 212. The imperfect English translation is mostly mine.

14. Édouard Herriot, *The Life and Times of Beethoven*, trans. Adelheid I. Mitchell and William J. Mitchell (New York: Macmillan, 1935), 33.

15. Schiller, cited from Claudia Pilling, Diana Schilling, and Mirjam Springer, *Schiller*, trans. Angus McGeach (London: Haus Publishing, 2005), 25.

16. Scherman and Biancolli, op. cit., 53.

17. Konrad Küster, *Beethoven* (Stuttgart: Deutsche Verlag-Anstalt, 1993), 248.

18. Jos van der Zanden, in a letter published in the *Beethoven Journal* (21.2 [Winter 2008], 47), makes a good case for a longer sojourn. He speculates that Beethoven based *Calm Sea and Prosperous Voyage* on actual awareness of the sea near Rotterdam.

19. Mansell, op. cit., 154.

20. Paul P. Bernard, *From the Enlightenment to the Police State: The Public Life of Johann Anton Pergen* (Urbana and Chicago: University of Illinois Press, 1991), 171.

21. Pfeffel (1736–1809) was a blind poet who wrote a number of fables and folksongs attacking privilege.

22. "Jacket" and "smock" refer to aristocratic and clerical attire, respectively.

23. Hannah Arendt, *On Revolution* (New York: Viking Press, 1963), 33.

24. The *Stammbuch* of 1791 has some remarkable omissions. Neither Beethoven's father nor his two younger brothers contributed to it.

25. *Letters to Beethoven and Other Correspondence*, 3 vols., trans. and ed. Theodore Albrecht (Lincoln and London: University of Nebraska Press, 1996), 1: 22.

26. The passages are reproduced in ibid., 1: 17–18.

27. *Letters of Beethoven*, ed. Emily Anderson, 3 vols. (New York: St. Martin's Press, 1961), 1: 6. I have cited the passage from Beethoven's letter rather than from Act 2, scene 2 of *Don Carlos*.

28. Ibid. In 1922 Ferruccio Busoni described Beethoven as "the first great democrat of music" (Martin Geck, *Beethoven* [London: Haus Publishing, 2003],13).

4: The French Revolution

1. Eric Hobsbawm, *The Age of Revolution: Europe, 1789–1848* (London: Cardine Books, 1973), 54, 55.

2. Wilfrid Mellers, *Beethoven and the Voice of God* (London: Faber and Faber, 1983), 4.

3. Donald A. Ringe, citing Cooper in his introduction to *The Bravo* (New Haven: College & University Press, 1963), 9.

4. R. R. Palmer, *The Age of the Democratic Revolution*, 2 vols. (Princeton: Princeton University Press, 1970), 2: 180. Usage of this phrase in France dates only from the short-lived Second Republic of 1848.

5. Dorinda Outram, *Panorama of the Enlightenment* (Los Angeles: John Paul Getty Museum, n.d.), 281.

6. Goethe, *From My Life: Poetry and Truth: Campaign in France*, ed. Thomas P. Saine and Jeffrey L. Sammons (New York: Suhrkamp, 1987), 652.

7. Libretto to the Chandos CD of Gossec's oratorio (Chandos 0727), 47.

8. Ibid., 71, 73.

9. Cited from *Ludwig van Beethoven 1770/1970* (Bonn-Bad Godesberg: Inter Nationes, 1970), 27.

10. So asked Golo Mann, the twentieth-century German historian, in his *Secretary of Europe: The Life of Friedrich Gentz, Enemy of Napoleon* (New Haven: Yale University Press, 1946), 20.

11. Paul Henry Lang, *Musicology and Performance*, ed. Alfred Mann and George J. Buelow (New Haven and London: Yale University Press, 1997), 91.

12. Cited from Jean Staroblinski, *1789: The Emblems of Reason* (Charlottesville: University of Virginia Press, 1982), 44.

13. Bernt von Heiseler, *Schiller: Leben und Werke* (Munich: Bertelsmann, 1959), 35.

14. Palmer, op. cit., 2: 444.

15. Richard Friedenthal, *Goethe: His Life and Times* (Cleveland and New York: World Publishing Company, 1963), 293.

16 James J. Sheehan, *German History, 1770–1866* (Oxford: Clarendon Press, 1989), 212–13.

17. *Letters of Beethoven*, ed. Emily Anderson, 3 vols. (New York: St. Martin's Press, 1961), 1:6. This "letter" was written in the album of a friend, whom Maynard Solomon has identified as Theodora Johanna Vocke (*Beethoven Essays* [Cambridge and London: Harvard University Press, 1988], 344n45).

18. Will Meredith, former director of the Beethoven Center in San Jose University, made this point to me in a 2005 conversation.

19. Tony Tanner, *Venice Desired* (Cambridge, MA: Harvard University Press, 1992), 61.

20. W. J. Turner, *Beethoven: The Search for Reality* (New York: George H. Doran, 1927), 261.

21. Cited from *Memoirs of the Life of Monsieur de Voltaire Written by Himself* (1784), trans. Andrew Brown (London: Hesperus Classics, 2007), vii.

22. Martin Cooper, *Ideas and Music* (Philadelphia and New York: Chilton Books, 1965), 46.

23. Published in 1785, the poem was revised in 1803, but by then Schiller had lost

interest in it. For context, see discussion in H. B. Garland, *Schiller* (New York: Medill McBride, 1950), 97–98.

24. Cited from Claudia Pilling, Diana Schilling, and Mirjam Springer, *Schiller*, trans. Angus McGeach (London: Haus Publishing, 2005), 37–39, 52.

25. Uwe Martin, *Deutschland und die Französische Revolution 1789/1989* (Berlin: Cantz, 1989), 201.

26. Michael Burleigh, *Earthly Powers* (New York: HarperCollins, 2005), 271–72.

27. Le roy de Sainte-Croix, *Le chant de guerre pour l'Armée du Rhin ou la Marseillaise* (Strasbourg: Hagemann, 1880), 32.

28. Ibid., 15.

29. Jean Tulard, *Napoléon et Rouget de L'Isle* (Paris: Hermann, 2000), 9.

30. Zweig used it as the title for one of his popular books, *Sternstunden der Menschheit*.

31. Jean et Brigitte Massin, "Beethoven et la Révolution Française," *L'Arc* 40 (1970): 4.

32. Ibid., 3, citing Michel Venedey and Jacob Venedey, *Die deutschen Republikaner unter der Französischen Republik* (Leipzig: Brockhaus, 1870).

33. Martin, op. cit., 201.

34. Venedey and Venedey, op. cit., 3–4.

35. Massin and Massin, op. cit., 5.

5: Brutus and the Egyptian Mysteries

1. *Letters of Beethoven*, ed. Emily Anderson, 3 vols. (New York: St. Martin's Press, 1961), 1:60. To Wegeler, June 29 [1801].

2. Marion Scott, *Beethoven* (1934; London: J. M. Dent, 1947), 50.

3. Anton Schindler, *Beethoven as I Knew Him*, trans. Constance S. Jolly (Chapel Hill: University of North Carolina Press, 1966), 47.

4. Gilbert Highet, *The Classical Tradition: Greek and Roman Influences on Western Literature* (New York and London: Oxford University Press, 1949), 393–95.

5. *Konversationshefte*, 11 vols. (Leipzig: VEB Deutscher Verlag für Musik, 1972–2001), 1: 211 ("*Socrates* u. *Jesus* waren mir Muster").

6. So J. R. Schulz, an English traveler who met Beethoven in 1823, cited in E. Kerr Borthwick, "Beethoven and Plutarch," *Music & Letters* 79, no. 2 (May 1998): 270.

7. *The Robbers*, Act 1, scene 2.

8. *Thayer's Life of Beethoven*, ed. Elliot Forbes, 2 vols. (Princeton: Princeton University Press, 1967), 2: 680.

9. Harold Talbot Parker, *The Cult of Antiquity and the French Revolutionaries* (Chicago: University of Chicago Press, 1937), 38–39.

10. Ibid., 59.

11. Cited from Howard Mumford Jones, *Revolution and Romanticism* (Cambridge, MA: Belknap Press of Harvard University Press, 1974), 136.

12. Irma B. Jaffe, *Trumbull: The Declaration of Independence* (London: Penguin Books, 1976), 35–36.

13. The best reproductions of the statue are be found in my essay on Brutus and Beethoven in the *Beethoven Journal* 25.1 (Summer 2010): 6.

14. Recent biographers of Beethoven, including Maynard Solomon (1998), Barry Cooper (2000), Lewis Lockwood (2003), Jan Caeyers (2009), and Jan Swafford (2014) do not mention Brutus. My understanding of Beethoven and classical culture owes much to Elisabeth Brisson's magisterial *Le sacre du musicien: La référence à l'antiquité chez Beethoven* (Paris: CNRS Editions, 2000). She opts for Marcus Junius Brutus, one of Caesar's assassins, as the model for Beethoven's statuette, but clearly discernible on its base is "Luc. Brutus."

15. Livy (Titus Livius), *The Early History of Rome* (New York: Penguin Classics, 1960), Books I–V, I, 96.

16. Ibid., 97.

17. Accounts of the rape of Lucretia vary, with either the father or the son or even an uncle committing the deed.

18. Livy, op. cit., 99.

19. "Marcus Brutus," in Plutarch, *The Lives of the Noble Grecians and Romans*, trans. John Dryden, rev. Arthur Hugh Clough (London: J. M. Dent, 1957). Plutarch traces Marcus Brutus's descent from Lucius Junius Brutus, but this has been questioned.

20. "Poplicola" (Publicola), in ibid., 120. Brutus's decreeing the execution of his sons is, for Robert L. Herbert, "the central element of his legend" (*David, Voltaire, Brutus and the French Revolution: An Essay in Art and Politics* [New York: Viking Press, 1973], 17).

21. I translate the French text in Philippe Bordes, *La mort de Brutus de Pierre-Narcisse Guérin* (Vizille: Musée de la Révolution Française, 1996), 8.

22. Carl Czerny, "Recollections from My Life," *Musical Quarterly* 42, no. 3 (July 1956): 306.

23. Cited from François Marie de Chateaubriand, *Mémoires d'outre-tombe*, 2 vols. (Paris: Gallimard, 1951), 1: 690.

24. Étienne-Jean Delécluze, *Louis David: Son école et son temps* (Paris: Macula, 1983), 203–04. My translation.

25. Heyne's autobiography, cited from ibid., 137.

26. *History of the Revolt of the Netherlands*, in *The Works of Frederick Schiller*, trans. A. J. W. Morrison (London: George Bell, 1877), 352.

27. Paraphrased from Günter Fleischhauer, "Beethoven und die Antike," *Bericht über der internationale Beethoven-Kongress 10–12 Dezember 1970 in Berlin*, ed. Heinz Alfred Brockhaus and Konrad Niemann (Berlin: Verlag neue Musik Berlin, 1971), 471.

28. *Spaziergang nach Syrakus im Jahre 1802*, edited with commentary by Albert Meier (Munich: Deutsche Taschenbuch Verlag, 1994), 18. Meier based his well-

annotated edition of Seume's classic travel narrative on the revised edition of 1805. The first edition appeared in 1803.

29. *Beethoven Remembered: The Biographical Notes of Franz Wegeler and Ferdinand Ries* (Arlington: Great Ocean Publishers, 1987), 68.

30. Bettina Hagen, in her *Antike in Wien: Die Akademie und die Klassizismus um 1800* (Mainz: Verlag Philipp von Zabern, 2003), reproduces on p. 44 Füger's *Brutus Judging His Sons*, a chalk sketch for the larger oil of Brutus he completed subsequently.

31. I have used George Gregory's translation of Schiller's essay in *Friedrich Schiller: Poet of Freedom* (Washington, DC: Schiller Institute, 1988), 2: 307–29. I cite this essay from p. 989 of *Die Sendung Moses*, in *Schillers Werke*, 2 vols. (Munich and Zurich: Knaur Klassiker, 1962), 2: 982–99.

32. Carl Leonhard Reinhold's *Die hebräischen Mysterien oder die älteste religiöse Frey-mauererey . . .* (The Hebrew Mysteries, or, the Oldest Religious Freemasonry . . .) may have served as a major source for Schiller. See also an instructive recent pamphlet, *Beethovens Glaubensbekenntnis: Drei Denksprüche aus Friedrich Schillers Aufsatz "Die Sendung Moses"* (Beethoven's Creed: Three Sayings from Frederick Schiller's Essay *The Mission of Moses*), edited and explicated by Friederike Grigat (Bonn: Beethoven-Haus, 2008), in which the Masonic and religious implications of the sayings (on long-term loan to the Beethoven Haus, Bonn) are thoroughly studied. W. A. Thomas-San-Galli, in his biography *Ludwig van Beethoven*, had earlier dated the sayings to circa 1809 (Munich: Piper & Co., 1920), opp. 240.

33. On the dangers of Masonic involvement in Vienna during Beethoven's lifetime, consult C. A. MacCartney, *The Habsburg Empire, 1790–1915* (New York: Macmillan, 1969), op. cit., 163–65.

34. *Letters*, ed. Anderson, 2: 528, where it is misdated October 19 instead of September 19, 1815.

35. Schiller, *The Mission of Moses*, from Gregory, op. cit., 320, 321, 323.

36. I draw here upon Ernest Closson's excellent if misleadingly titled *The Fleming in Beethoven*, trans. Muriel Fuller (London: Oxford University Press, 1936), 116–17, which cites an anonymous pamphlet of 1850.

37. Robert C. Solomon, *History and Human Nature* (New York and London: Harcourt Brace Jovanovich, 1979), 297.

6: Hapsburg Vienna

1. Cited from Marc Vignal, *Mozart et Vienne* (Paris: Fayard, 2004), 20.

2. Janine Burke, *The Sphinx on the Table: Sigmund Freud's Art Collection and the Development of Psychoanalysis* (New York: Walker & Co., 2006), 331, citing Freud, writing in London in 1938.

3. *The World of Yesterday: An Autobiography by Stefan Zweig* (Lincoln and London: University of Nebraska Press, 1964), 1.

4. Frederic Morton, *Thunder at Twilight: Vienna, 1913–1914* (New York: Charles Scribner's Sons, 1989), 80.

5. Ibid., 52.

6. Ibid., 4.

7. Cited from Ilsa Barea, *Vienna* (New York: Alfred A. Knopf, 1967), 34–35.

8. *The Odyssey*, Book 7.

9. *Thayer's Life of Beethoven*, ed. Elliot Forbes, 2 vols. (Princeton: Princeton University Press, 1967), 2: 644, 766.

10. "The Life of the Phaecians," Nicholas T. Parsons's illuminating chapter in his excellent *Vienna: A Cultural and Literary History* (Oxford: Signal Books, 2008), 85.

11. Henry Reeve, *Journal of a Residence in Vienna and Berlin in the Eventful Winter 1805–6* (London: Longmans, Green, 1877), 25. Written by a young Edinburgh-trained doctor on the Grand Tour, Reeve's journal is shrewd and observant about the Viennese.

12. Ibid., 196.

13. *Letters of Beethoven*, ed. Emily Anderson, 3 vols. (New York: St. Martin's Press, 1961), 1: 18. Letter to Nikolaus Simrock, August 2, 1794.

14. William M. Johnston, *Vienna: The Golden Age, 1815–1914* (New York: Clarkson N. Potter, 1980), 215.

15. Ibid., 10, 12.

16. Friedrich Heer, *Der Kampf um die österreiche Identität* (1981), cited by Nicholas T. Parsons in *Vienna: A Cultural History* (Oxford: Oxford University Press, 2008), pp. 138–39.

17. H. C. Robbins Landon, *1791: Mozart's Last Year* (New York: Schirmer Books, 1988), 7. This volume translates substantial portions of Pezzl's narrative. Quotations in my text are from it.

18. Ibid., 55.

19. Ibid., 56.

20. Philip Mansel, *Prince of Europe: The Life of Charles-Joseph de Ligne* (London: Weidenfeld and Nicolson, 2005), 177.

21. Ibid.

22. Landon, op. cit., 186.

23. Ibid., 76.

24. Reeve, op. cit., 115.

25. Ibid., 118, 119.

26. Ibid.

27. Madame de Staël, *De l'Allemagne*, 2 vols. (Paris: Garnier-Flammarion, 1968), 1: 77–79.

28. Paul P. Bernard, *From the Enlightenment to the Police State: The Public Life of Johann Anton Pergen* (Urbana and Chicago: University of Illinois Press, 1991), 181.

29. R. R. Palmer, *The Age of the Democratic Revolution*, 2 vols. (Princeton: Princeton University Press, 1964), 2: 122. Ironically, the nervous new rulers of France often showed little or no tolerance for potential revolutionaries from foreign parts.

30. Reeve, op. cit., 26.

31. Ibid., 30, 44.

32. Ibid., 12–13.

33. Charles Rosen, *Romantic Poets, Critics, and Other Madmen* (Cambridge, MA: Harvard University Press, 1998), 31.

34. Ferruccio Busoni, *The Essence of Music,* trans. Rosamond Ley (London: Rockliff, 1957), 130.

35. Richard Wagner, *Beethoven*, trans. Edward Dannreuther (1870; London: Wm. Reeves, 2003), 93.

36. Friedrich Heer, *The Holy Roman Empire*, trans. Janet Sondheimer (New York and Washington, DC: Frederick A. Praeger, 1968), 279.

37. Egon Friedell, *A Cultural History of the Modern Age*, trans. Charles Francis Atkinson, 3 vols. (1931; New York: Alfred A. Knopf, 1954), 3: 30.

38. Mansel, op. cit., 254.

39. Golo Mann, *Secretary of Europe: The Life of Friedrich Gentz, Enemy of Napoleon*, trans. William H. Woglom (New Haven: Yale University Press, 1946), 78.

40. Stefan Zweig, *The World of Yesterday* (Lincoln: University of Nebraska Press, 1964), 20–21.

41. Hugo Leichtentritt, *Music, History, and Ideas* (1938; Cambridge, MA: Harvard University Press, 1966), 184.

7: Beethoven's Vienna

1. "Beethoven's Tagebuch," in Maynard Solomon, *Beethoven Essays* (Cambridge, MA: Harvard University Press, 1988), 256.

2. See Julia Ronge, *Beethovens Lehrzeit: Kompositionsstudien bei Joseph Haydn, Johann Georg Albrechtsberger und Antonio Salieri* (Bonn: Verlag Beethoven-Haus/Carus, 2011).

3. Martin Geck, *Beethoven* (London: Haus Publishing, 2003), 18.

4. Frida Knight, *Beethoven and the Age of Revolution* (Chadwell Heath: Lawrence and Wishart, 1973), 35; Konrad Küster, *Beethoven* (Stuttgart: Deutsche Verlags-Anstalt, 1994), 248–49.

5. Jean and Brigitte Massin, "Beethoven et la Révolution Française," *L'Arc* 40 (1970): 9.

6. *Letters of Beethoven*, ed. Emily Anderson, 3 vols. (New York: St. Martin's Press, 1961), 1: 24 n1; Bernt von Heiseler, *Schiller* (London: Eyre & Spottiswoode, 1962), 86.

7. H. C. Robbins Landon and David Wyn Jones, *Haydn: His Life and Music* (Bloomington and Indianapolis: Indiana University Press, 1988), 14.

8. *Letters*, ed. Anderson, 1: 246.

9. Geck, op. cit., 11.

10. *Letters*, ed. Anderson, 1: 18.

11. Ibid., 1: 58.

12. Ibid., 1: 200.

13. Ibid., 2: 845. To Bernard, September 15, 1819.

8: Beethoven as Traveler and Composer

1. *Letters of Beethoven*, ed. Emily Anderson, 3 vols. (New York: St. Martin's Press, 1961), 1:23.

2. Shortly before he died in 1965, Fritz Wunderlich left behind a splendid recording of "Adelaide."

3. Alfred Einstein, *Essays on Music* (New York: W. W. Norton, 1956), 247.

4. Eric Blom, *Beethoven's Pianoforte Sonatas Discussed* (New York: E. P. Dutton, 1938), 93.

5. Wilhelm von Lenz first told the story in his *Beethoven et ses trois styles* of 1852 (cited from Elisabeth Brisson, *Guide de la musique de Beethoven* [Paris: Fayard, 2005], 236).

9: The Rise of Napoleon

1. *Letters of Beethoven*, ed. Emily Anderson, 3 vols. (New York: St. Martin's Press, 1961), 1: 49. To Franz Anton Hoffmeister, ca. January 15, 1801.

2. Cited from Robert C. Solomon, *History and Human Nature* (New York and London: Harcourt Brace Jovanovich, 1979), 166.

3. Cited from Clubbe, "Napoleon and the Young Byron," in *L'Europa scopre Napoleone 1793–1804*, ed. Vittorio Scotti Douglas, 2 vols. (Alexandria: Edizioni dell'Orso, 1999), 1: 342.

4. Hajo Holborn, *A History of Modern Germany, 1648–1840* (New York: Alfred A. Knopf, 1969), 2: 268.

5. Cited from *The Life of Napoleon Buonaparte*, in *The Complete Works of William Hazlitt*, ed. P. P. Howe, 21 vols. (London and Toronto: J. M. Dent and Sons, 1930–1934), 13: 273.

6. Maynard Solomon, *Beethoven*, 2nd ed. (New York: Schirmer Books, 1998), 116.

7. H. C. Robbins Landon and David Wyn Jones, *Haydn: His Life and Music* (Bloomington and Indianapolis: Indiana University Press, 1988), 264–65.

8. Douglas Johnson, "Music for Prague and Berlin: Beethoven's Concert Tour of 1796," in *Beethoven, Performers, and Critics*, ed. Robert Winter and Bruce Carr (Detroit: Wayne State University Press, 1980), 37.

9. In his *Heroes and Hero-Worship* of 1840. See Clubbe, "Epic Heroes in the *French Revolution*," in Horst W. Drescher, ed., *Thomas Carlyle 1981* (Frankfurt am Main: Peter Lang, 1983), 175, citing Carlyle, *Works* (New York: Charles Scribner's Sons, 1904), 28: 79.

10. Jean Tulard, *Mythe de Napoléon* (Paris: Armand Colin, 1971), 83. My translation.

11. Ibid., 129, citing Faure's *Napoléon* (Paris: G. Crès et Cie, 1921), 98. My translation.

10: Parallel Lives, Beethoven and Napoleon

1. *Childe Harold's Pilgrimage*, Canto 3, stanza 37, ll. 325–27.

2. The official Austrian history of 1866, cited in Egon Friedell, *A Cultural History of the Modern Age*, trans. Charles Francis Atkinson, 3 vols. (1931; New York: Alfred A. Knopf, 1954), 2: 443.

3. Sir Dunbar Plunket Barton, *The Amazing Career of Bernadotte, 1763–1844*, 2 vols. (London: John Murray, 1929), 1: 70, 71, 69.

4. Alan Palmer, *Bernadotte: Napoleon's Marshal, Sweden's King* (London: John Murray, 1990), 65; Barton, op. cit., 1: 78.

5. *Letters of Beethoven*, ed. Emily Anderson, 3 vols. (New York: St. Martin's Press, 1961), 1: 120.

6. Ibid., 1: 73–74.

7. *My Past and Thoughts: The Memoirs of Alexander Herzen* (New York: Alfred A. Knopf, 1973), 449.

8. *Letters*, ed. Anderson, 1: 32.

9. W. J. Turner, *Beethoven: The Search for Reality* (New York: George H. Doran, 1927), 261.

10. *Byron's Letters and Journals*, ed. Leslie A. Marchand, 12 vols. (London: John Murray, 1973–1982), 9: 152. The passage derives from Staël's *De la littérature*, second part, chapter 3.

11. Friedell, op. cit., 2: 443.

11: The Rise of Beethoven

1. "Beethoven's Tagebuch," in Maynard Solomon, *Beethoven Essays* (Cambridge, MA: Harvard University Press, 1988), 254.

2. Wordsworth, *The Prelude* (1850 edition), Book 3, line 63.

3. *Letters of Beethoven*, ed. Emily Anderson, 3 vols. (New York: St. Martin's Press, 1961), 1: 62.

4. Haydn wrote a mass every year for his former employer, whose son was now Prince Esterházy.

5. Martin Geck, *Beethoven* (London: Haus Publishing, 2003), 24

6. I cite the summary in *Thayer's Life of Beethoven*, ed. Elliot Forbes, 2 vols. (Princeton: Princeton University Press, 1964), 1: 255.

7. Jean and Brigitte Massin, "Beethoven et la Révolution Française," *L'Arc*, 40 (1970): 6.

8. *Letters*, ed. Anderson, 1: 247. November 23, 1809 (in French).

9. Carl Czerny, cited from Philip G. Downs, "Beethoven's `New Way,'" in *The Creative World of Beethoven*, ed. Paul Henry Lang (New York: W. W. Norton, 1971), 83. Downs places Beethoven's alleged statement somewhere between the beginning of 1801 and April 1802.

10. *Letters*, ed. Anderson, 1: 65.

11. Ibid., 1: 68.

12. Elisabeth Brisson, *Guide de la musique de Beethoven* (Paris: Fayard, 2005), 443.

13. One exception is Maynard Solomon's essay "Beethoven's 'Magazin der Kunst,'" reprinted in his *Beethoven Essays*. Although Babeuf studies have undergone a tsunami of scholarship during the last half–century, his impact upon Beethoven, Solomon's essay excepted, has stirred little interest in American musicological circles. For a comprehensive selection of Babeuf's writings, see *Babeuf: Ecrits*, ed. Claude Mazauric, 4th ed. (Pantin: Le Temps des Cerises, 2009).

14. For Babeuf's ideas on European intellectual life, see Edmund Wilson, *To the Finland Station: A Study in the Writing and Acting of History*, rev. ed. (New York: Farrar, Straus and Giroux, 1972), especially 83–93, "Origins of Socialism."

15. *Letters*, ed. Anderson, 1: 48.

16. Cited from Wilson, op. cit., 546.

17. Ibid., 88.

18. *Beethoven: Letters, Journals and Conversations*, edited, translated, and introduced by Michael Hamburger (1951; London: Thames and Hudson, 1991), 48–50.

19. Walter Riezler, *Beethoven*, trans. G. O. H. Pidcock (New York: Vienna House, 1972), 33–34.

20. Joseph Kerman, *The Beethoven Quartets* (New York: Alfred A. Knopf, 1971), 91.

21. Hans Gal, *The Golden Age of Vienna* (London and New York: Max Parrish, n.d.), 46.

22. Yehudi Menuhin, *Unfinished Journey* (New York: Alfred A. Knopf, 1977), 150.

23. Marion M. Scott, *Beethoven* (London: J. M. Dent, 1947), 45.

24. *Thayer's Life of Beethoven*, 1: 330.

25. Ibid., 329–30.

12: The *Eroica*: Meaning and Dedication

1. *Mencken on Music*, ed. Louis Cheslock (New York: Alfred A. Knopf, 1961), 33.

2. *Wagner on Music and Drama*, ed. Albert Goldman and Evert Sprinchorn (New York: Dutton, 1964), 160.

3. Hans Gal, *The Golden Age of Vienna* (London and New York: Max Parrish, n.d.), 52.

4. *The New Grove Beethoven*, ed. Joseph Kerman and Alan Tyson (New York and London: W. W. Norton, 1983), 37.

5. Ernest Wangermann, *The Austrian Achievement, 1700–1800* (New York: Harcourt Brace Jovanovich, 1973), 145.

6. "Thunderstruck": cited from Alessandra Comini, *The Changing Image of Beethoven: A Study in Mythmaking* (New York: Rizzoli, 1987), 228, 243.

7. Leo Schrade, *Beethoven in France: The Growth of an Idea* (New Haven: Yale University Press, 1942), 50–51.

8. Ibid., 51.

9. *Letters of Beethoven*, ed. Emily Anderson, 3 vols. (New York: St. Martin's Press, 1961), 2: 689.

10. Ibid., 1: 68; *Beethoven Briefwechsel Gesamtausgabe*, ed. S. Brandenburg, 7 vols. (Munich: Henle, 1996), 1: 89. Letter of November 16, 1801.

11. Thomas Mann, *Essays of Three Decades* (New York: Alfred A. Knopf, 1947), 188.

12. *Erich Leinsdorf on Music* (Portland: Amadeus Press, 1997), 122.

13. Bruno Walter, *Gustav Mahler* (New York: Alfred A. Knopf, 1958), 90.

14. Cited from Beate Angelika Kraus, *Beethoven-Rezeption in Frankreich* (Bonn: Beethoven-Haus Verlag, 2001), 246 ("La symphonie héroique n'est pas encore comprise, mais on y viendra").

15. Wilfrid Mellers, *Beethoven and the Voice of God* (London: Faber & Faber, 1983), viii.

16. Anton Schindler, *Beethoven as I Knew Him*, trans. Constance S. Jolly (Chapel Hill: University of North Carolina Press, 1966), 1.

17. Czerny, cited from Kenneth Drake, *The Beethoven Sonatas and the Creative Experience* (Bloomington and Indianapolis: Indiana University Press, 1994), 2.

18. Elisabeth Brisson, *Le Sacre de musicien: La référence à l'Antiquité chez Beethoven* (Paris: Éditions CNRS, 2000), 170.

19. Cited from Robert C. Solomon, *History and Human Nature* (New York and London: Harcourt Brace Jovanovich, 1979), 293.

20. Heinrich Eduard Jacob, *Felix Mendelsohn and His Times*, trans. Richard and Clara Winston (Englewood Cliffs: Prentice Hall, 1963), 52.

21. *Beethoven Briefwechsel*, ed. Brandenburg, 1: 121–23.

22. Lawrence Gilman, *Orchestral Music: An Armchair Guide* (New York: Oxford University Press, 1951), 49.

23. Romain Rolland, *Beethoven the Creator*, trans. Ernest Newman (New York: Harper, 1929), 88.

24. John Updike, reviewing Benita Eisler's biography *Byron* in *The New Yorker*, August 2, 1999: 82–87.

25. Arthur Schopenhauer, *The World as Will and Idea*, trans. R. B. Haldane and J. Kemp, 3 vols. (London: Routledge and Kegan Paul, 1948), 1: 261.

26. Ibid., 261, 262.

27. So thought an early reviewer for the Berlin *Allgemeine musikalischer Zeitung*, cited in Robin Wallace, *Beethoven's Critics: Aesthetic Dilemmas and Resolutions during the Composer's Lifetime* (Cambridge: Cambridge University Press, 1990), 62.

28. *The Critical Reception of Beethoven's Compositions by His German Contempo-*

raries, ed. and comp. Wayne Senner, William Meredith, and Robin Wallace, 4 vols. to date (Lincoln and London: University of Nebraska Press, 1999–), 1: 15.

29. "C'était un monarque, mais c'était celui de la Révolution; et ils aimaient un souverain parvenu qui les faisait parvenir" (Ségur, cited from Jean Tulard, *Mythe de Napoléon* [Paris: Colin, 1971], 127).

30. Édouard Herriot, *The Life and Times of Beethoven*, trans. Adelheid I. Mitchell and William J. Mitchell (New York: Macmillan, 1935), 106.

31. Ibid., 106, 108, 111.

32. Cited from Scott Burnham, *Beethoven Hero* (Princeton: Princeton University Press, 1995), 26.

33. Ibid., xv, 26. See also *Wagner Writes from Paris . . .* , ed. Robert L. Jacobs and Geoffrey Skelton (London: George Allen & Unwin, 1973), 181, 185–87.

34. *Letters to Beethoven and Other Correspondence*, ed. Theodore Albrecht, 3 vols. (Lincoln: University of Nebraska Press, 1996), 1:119.

35. *Letters of Beethoven*, ed. Emily Anderson, 3 vols. (New York: St. Martin's Press, 1961), 1: 116, 117; *Beethoven Briefwechsel*, ed. Brandenburg, 1: 218, 219. After Beethoven had renamed the *Eroica* innocuously, a Viennese firm, the Verlag für Kunst-und-Industrie, published it in October 1806.

36. Konrad Küster, *Beethoven* (Munich: Deutsche Verlags-Anstadt, 1994), 252.

37. Carl Dahlhaus, *Ludwig van Beethoven: Approaches to His Music*, trans. Mary Whittall (Oxford: Clarendon Press, 1991), 23.

38. Ibid., 19.

39. Though Napoleon's published writings do not mention Byron, popular poems like *Childe Harold's Pilgrimage* soon became known in France.

13: The *Eroica* in its Literary and Artistic Contexts

1. *Spaziergang nach Syrakus im Jahre 1802*, edited and annotated by Albert Meier (1803; Munich: Deutscher Taschenbuch Verlag, 1994), 21. I previously explored Seume's *Spaziergang* within the context of the *Eroica* in the *Beethoven Journal* 29, no. 2 (Winter 2014): 52–65.

2. Romain Rolland, *Beethoven the Creator* (New York: Harper, 1929), 123.

3. *Letters to Beethoven and Other Correspondence*, trans. and ed. Theodore Albrecht, 3 vols. (Lincoln and London: University of Nebraska Press, 1996), 2: 169–70. Grosheim was a composer and subsequently the author of music treatises.

4. Ibid., 2: 170, n. 4.

5. Piero Buscaroli, *Beethoven* (Milan: Rizzoli, 2004). Translations are mine. A distinguished Italian musicologist, Buscaroli regards Seume as a kindred soul (*lo spirito affine*) to Beethoven—and to himself!

6. Beethoven quotes from the *Walk to Syracuse* in a newly identified entry of 1812 in his *Tagebuch* (no. 138), which suggests that he returned to the book subsequent to visiting Seume's tomb. I owe this reference to Seume's *Tagebuch* to

Dr. Bernhard R. Appel, former director of the Beethoven-Haus Archiv, Bonn. The list of books in Beethoven's possession (in the Archiv der Stadt Wien) at his death includes an entry listing the 1803 edition of Seume's *Spaziergang*. Will Meredith, longtime director of the Beethoven Center in San Jose, kindly sent me a photostat of it. Three of the five books in Beethoven's possession that the authorities sequestered after his death were, it turns out, by Seume. Along with the *Spaziergang* and the *Apokryphen*, the third is presumably *Mein Sommer im Jahre 1805* (1806).

7. In his early play *Intrigue and Love*, Schiller scathingly denounced this traffic in soldiers. The Prince's servant tells his mistress that the casket of diamonds he offers her will cost the state nothing, for "yesterday 7000 of our countrymen left for America—they'll pay for everything" (2.2).

8. See the colored engraving *Seume als gefangener Deserteur* (*Seume as Imprisoned Deserter*) in *Deutschland und die französische Revolution 1789/1989* (Stuttgart: Cantz, 1989), 172. It is also reproduced in the *Beethoven Journal* 29, no. 2 (Winter 2014): 55.

9. "Nachwort," in Seume, *Spaziergang*, 301, 310.

10. Ronald Taylor, *Robert Schumann: His Life and Work* (London: Granada, 1982), 27, 292. Schumann also hung above his desk a portrait of Napoleon and worked the "Marseillaise" into several compositions.

11. Emil Ludwig claimed that "Seume's proscribed book was [Beethoven's] favorite reading, and he annotated it himself." *Three Titans* (New York and London: G. P. Putnam's Sons, 1930), 265. Although Ludwig does not document his claim, it appears likely.

12. E.g., *Spaziergang*, xi, 9. The "Du" also included his travel companion and good friend who went with him as far as Vienna, the artist Veit Hanns Friedrich Schnorr von Carolsfeld.

13. "Wir erkennen daran, wie eifrig der republikanisch gesinnte Beethoven die Schriften des Freiheitsschwärmers Seume las" (W. A. Thomas-San-Galli, *Beethoven*, 7th ed. [Munich: R. Piper & Co., 1920], 68). Among twentieth-century biographers of Beethoven writing in German, only Thomas-San-Galli, to my knowledge, draws upon Seume's account of Vienna to illumine Beethoven's own perspective on life in his adopted city.

14. *Letters of Beethoven*, ed. Emily Anderson, 3 vols. (New York: St. Martin's Press, 1961), 1, 212.

15. *Spaziergang*, 22.

16. Ibid., 21–22. Ernst Wangermann, a leading Austrian historian, considers it "unlikely that Seume was exaggerating" (*The Austrian Achievement, 1700–1800* [New York: Harcourt Brace Jovanovich, 1973], 184). The records of Beethoven's conversations with his coffeehouse friends after 1818 frequently note the presence of spies.

17. *Spaziergang*, 22.

18. Ibid.

19. For the profusion of government spies in Vienna that began in the 1780s, see Johann Pezzl's *Sketches of Vienna*, discussed in Chapter 6. Censorship in Vienna worsened during Beethoven's lifetime and remained omnipresent for decades afterwards.

20. *Spaziergang*, 24. The Viennese dialect often amusingly garbles standard German.

21. After leaving Vienna, Seume headed south to Venice, then down through Italy to Naples, and from there by sea to Palermo in Sicily; he accomplished the return to Leipzig via Paris and Frankfurt. All this in nine months! Seume's journey on foot was, for its time, an epic achievement. In recounting their Vienna sojourns, the travel diaries of Henry Reeve (1805), Madame de Staël (1807–08), and John Russell (1822)—a chapter of the last-mentioned is reproduced in the *Beethoven Journal* 29, no. 2 (Winter 2014)—confirm much of the unpleasantness Seume experienced in the Hapsburg capital.

22. Beethoven's *Tagebuch*, cited from Maynard Solomon, *Beethoven Essays* (Cambridge, MA: Harvard University Press, 1988), 258 n43. Although Solomon doubts that Beethoven's study actually had these portraits, Beethoven's interest in them suggests he had seen engravings, liked them, and wanted them around him for inspiration.

23. François René de Chateaubriand, *Mémoires d'outre-tombe*, ed. Maurice Levaillant and George Moulinier, 2 vols. (Paris: Gallimard, 1951), 1: 1008. My translation.

24. Richard Wagner, *My Life*, trans. Andrew Gray (Cambridge: Cambridge University Press, 1983), 30. The portrait Wagner refers to here is that by Waldmüller, discussed in Chapter 21.

25. Max Graf, *Composer and Critic: Two Hundred Years of Music Criticism* (New York: W. W. Norton, 1946), 167.

26. W. J. Turner, *Beethoven: The Search for Reality* (London: J. M. Dent, 1945), 36.

27. Tim Blanning, *The Triumph of Music. The Rise of Composers, Musicians and Their Art* (Cambridge, MA: Harvard University Press, 2008), 39.

28. Napoleon was 1m 68cm in height, Beethoven about the same. The average height for adult men in France between 1800 and 1820 was a little over 1m 64cm (approximately 5 feet 4 inches). Neither Napoleon nor Beethoven was short for his time.

29. *Beethoven aus der Sicht seiner Zeitgenossen*, ed. Klaus Martin Kopitz and Rainer Cadenbach (Munich: G. Henle Verlag, 2009), 2: 969.

30. Cherubini, in Peter Clive, *Beethoven and His World: A Biographical Dictionary* (Oxford: Oxford University Press, 2001), 71; Goethe, in Kopitz and Cadenbach, op. cit., 1: 359.

31. On the evolution of Beethoven's appearance, the hitherto standard if imperfect work by Theodor von Frimmel, *Beethovens äussere Erscheinung* (Munich:

Georg Müller, 1905) has been replaced by Benedetta Saglietti, *Beethoven, ritratti e immagini: Uno studio sull'iconografia* (Turin: De Sono, 2010). It offers a fuller background to the portraits than the parallel work in German by Silke Bettermann, *Beethoven im Bild* (Bonn: Beethoven Haus, 2012), which gives the portraits insufficient context.

32. Hugh Honour, cited from "Neo-classicism" in *The Age of Neo-Classicism*, exhibition catalogue published by the Arts Council of Great Britain in 1972, xxiii.

33. I draw here upon the brief essay by Ellen Spickernagel "Goethe in der römischen Campagna," in *Museum. Städelsches Kunstinstitut. Städtische Galerie. Frankfurt am Main* (Braunschweig: Westermann, 1983), 73–75, and, even more, on the recent and fuller *Goethe und Tischbein in Rom: Bilder und Texte*, ed. Petra Maisak (Frankfurt am Main and Leipzig: Insel Verlag, 2004).

34. *Thayer's Life of Beethoven*, ed. Elliot Forbes, 2 vols. (Princeton: Princeton University Press, 1967), 1: 337.

35. Goethe would return to this concept in the second part of *Faust*.

36. Goethe, *Italian Journey*, ed. Thomas P. Saine and Jeffrey L. Sammons (New York: Suhrkamp, 1989), 114.

37. Ibid., 171. Comini regards the instrument as an "Apollonian reflection" of Beethoven (Alessandra Comini, *The Changing Image of Beethoven* [New York: Rizzoli, 1986], 35).

38. In her famously controversial "letter" to Goethe, Bettina Brentano claims that Beethoven told her "that music is the highest manifestation of all wisdom and philosophy; it is the wine that inspires us to new procreation, and I am the Bacchus who presses this wonderful wine for human beings and makes them spiritually intoxicated." Cited from *Goethes Briefwechsel mit einem Kinde*, ed. Waldemar Oehlke (Frankfurt: Insel Verlag, 1984), 382. Though somewhat fabricated, the letter's contents may well be substantially true. My translation.

39. Peter Schleuning and Martin Geck, *Geschrieben auf Bonaparte: Beethovens "Eroica"—Revolution, Reaktion, Rezeption* (Reinbeck bei Hamburg: Rowohlt, 1989), 96.

40. Thomas Sipe, *Beethoven: Eroica Symphony* (Cambridge: Cambridge University Press, 1998), 95.

41. *Thayer's Life of Beethoven*, 1: 337.

42. *Letters*, ed. Anderson, 1: 22; *Beethoven Briefwechsel Gesamtausgabe*, ed. S. Brandenburg, 7 vols. (Munich: Henle, 1996), 1: 19 (which dates it "circa 1795").

43. Owen Jander, *Beethoven's "Orpheus" Concerto* (Hillsdale: Pendragon, 2009), 176. The shape is right for conifers, though Theodor Frimmel believes them to be *Pappeln*, or poplars (*Beethoven Studien*, 132, n. 3). Jander assumes the "strange light in the distance" is Hades, but it seems to me the glow of the rising (or, less likely, setting) sun.

44. *Benjamin Franklin: Un américain à Paris (1776–1785)* (Paris: Musée Carnavalet, 2007–2008), 223. Exhibition catalogue.

45. This paragraph and the next owe a debt to the first chapter of David Hackett Fischer's superb *Liberty and Freedom* (Oxford and New York: Oxford University Press, 2005), particularly 19–20, 22, 23 (illustration), 24, 32, 33.

46. For the towns and cities involved, see *Deutschland und die französische Revolution, 1789/1989*, 155. This page has an engraving of the tree planted in Mainz, for several years the leading revolutionary outpost in the Rhineland. Pikes, planted alongside, are topped by Phrygian caps. After counterrevolutionaries destroyed the Liberty Tree planted by German Jacobins in Mainz on November 3, 1792, the local Jacobins riposted on January 3 by replacing it with another tree. A plaque on it stated, "Paix aux peuples—Guerre au Tyrans" (ibid.). Engravings of Liberty Trees in Rastatt, Mannheim, Cologne, Bonn, Speyer, Siegen, and Zweibrücken, as well as in Basel, are reproduced on pp. 264 and 266–67.

47. *Beethoven zwischen Revolution und Restauration*, ed. Helga Lühning and Sieghard Brandenburg (Bonn: Beethoven-Haus, 1989), 47; Edith Ennen and Dietrich Höroldt, *Vom Römerkastell zur Bundeshauptstadt: Kleine Geschichte der Stadt Bonn* (Bonn: Stollfuss Verlag, 1976), 164–65. Illustration of Bonn's tree, a spruce (*Fichte*), no. 38a. This tree, or its successors, stood on the Markplatz for some years.

48. C. A. MacCartney, *The Hapsburg Empire, 1790–1918* (London: Macmillan, 1969), 157.

49. Comini, op. cit., 35.

50. Owen Jander, in *Beethoven Forum* 8: 60, 63.

51. Jander, *Beethoven's "Orpheus" Concerto*, 177.

52. E.g., the fallen beech tree in the foreground of Ruysdael's *River Landscape with a Castle on a High Cliff* (Cincinnati Art Museum). Reproduced in several of the museum's publications.

53. Peter Schleuning speaks of it as a *Konsulmantel*, that is, a cloak in the style of Napoleon's formal attire as First Consul (Schleuning and Geck, *Geschrieben auf Bonaparte*, 96). Napoleon wore the blue-and-white uniform of a colonel of the *grenadiers à pied* when reviewing his guard on every tenth day of the still prevailing revolutionary calendar (Philip Mansel, *Dressed to Rule: Royal and Court Costume from Louis XIV to Elizabeth II* [New Haven: Yale University Press, 2005], 80).

54. Comini, op. cit., 35. For Jander, "Beethoven is clearly alluding to those lurking thoughts of suicide that he had confessed two years earlier in the Heiligenstadt Testament" (*Beethoven's "Orpheus" Concerto*, 173). Well, maybe.

14: Toward Beethoven's 1808 Akademie

1. Carson McCullers, *The Heart Is a Lonely Hunter* (Boston: Houghton Mifflin, 1940), 117–18.

2. Cited from Ernest Newman, *Unconscious Beethoven: An Essay in Musical Psychology* (New York: Alfred A. Knopf, 1927), 61.

3. Donald Francis Tovey, *Beethoven* (London: Oxford University Press, 1944), 116.

4. Cited from David Wyn Jones, *The Life of Beethoven* (Cambridge: Cambridge University Press, 1998), 92.

5. Beethoven, *Violin Concerto*, New Philharmonia Orchestra; Joseph Suk, violinist; Sir Adrian Boult, conductor; Vanguard Everyman Classics SRV 353 SD Vinyl LP, program notes.

6. T. S. Eliot, *The Sacred Wood* (1920; London: Methuen, 1948), 32.

7. Cited from R. Murray Schafer, *E. T. A. Hoffmann and Music* (Toronto: University of Toronto Press, 1975), 96.

8. Romain Rolland, *Beethoven the Creator*, trans. Ernest Newman (New York: Harper & Brothers, 1929), 225.

9. Joachim Maass, *Kleist: A Biography*, trans. Ralph Mannheim (New York: Farrar, Straus and Giroux, 1983), op. cit.

10. Ibid., 92.

11. Gordon A. Craig, *Europe, 1815–1914* (Winnipeg: Holt, Rinehart, and Winston, 1966), 62.

12. Ibid., 222.

13. By "borderline" Kleist means the Rhine.

14. *Letters of Beethoven*, ed. Emily Anderson, 3 vols. (New York: St. Martin's Press, 1961), 1: 164–65.

15. Cited from Dietrich Fischer-Dieskau, *"Weil nicht alle Blütenträume reiften": Johann Friedrich Reichardt, Hofkapellmeister dreier Preussenkönige. Porträt und Selbst Porträt* (Stuttgart: Deutsche Verlags-Anstatt, 1992), 368. My translation.

16. John Clubbe, *Cincinnati Observed: Architecture and History* (Columbus: Ohio State University Press, 1992), 9.

17. *Thayer's Life of Beethoven*, 2: 422–24.

18. Fischer-Dieskau, op. cit., 369. My translation.

19. Cited from Ernest Closson, *The Fleming in Beethoven*, trans. Muriel Fuller (London: Oxford University Press, 1936), 117.

15: Napoleon in Vienna in 1809; Beethoven Befriends Baron de Trémont

1. Golo Mann, *The History of Germany since 1789* (New York and Washington, DC: Frederick A. Praeger, 1968), 25.

2. Gunther E. Rothenberg, *Napoleon's Great Adversary: Archduke Charles and the Austrian Army* (Bloomington: Indiana University Press, 1982), 101.

3. *Byron's Letters and Journals*, ed. Leslie A. Marchand (London: John Murray, 1973–1994), 1: 206 (June 22, 1809). The Tyrolese, in rebellion under Andreas Hofer, were harassing French forces.

4. Joseph Wechsberg, *Vienna, My Vienna* (New York: Macmillan, 1968), 65.

5. Ilsa Barea, *Vienna* (New York: Alfred A. Knopf, 1967), 123–24.

6. *Beethoven, Letters, Journals and Conversations*, ed. and trans. Michael Ham-

burger (London: Thames and Hudson, 1951), 77. Unless otherwise noted all the quotations to Trémont's account are sequential from Hamburger's abbreviated version, pp. 77–80. For full texts of Trémont in French and German, see *Beethoven aus der Sicht seiner Zeitgenossen*, ed. Klaus Martin Kopitz and Rainer Cadenach, 2 vols. (Munich: G. Henle Verlag, 2009). 2: 1003–22.

7. Carl Dahlhaus, *Ludwig van Beethoven: Approaches to His Music* (Oxford: Clarendon Press, 1991), 25.

8. Alfred Einstein, *Essays on Music* (New York: W. W. Norton, 1956), 248.

9. Elisabeth Brisson, *Guide de la musique de Beethoven* (Paris: Fayard, 2005), 466.

10. In December 1817 the London piano maker Broadwoods sent Beethoven a six-octave piano, though it did not reach him until the following June. Beethoven was proud of his Broadwood and cherished it until the end of his life.

11. William M. Johnston, *The Austrian Mind: An Intellectual and Social History, 1848–1938* (Berkeley: University of California Press, 1983), 186.

12. *Selected Letters of Beethoven*, ed. Alan Tyson (New York: St. Martin's Press, 1967), 81.

16: Composing *Egmont*

1. *Beethoven aus der Sicht seiner Zeitgenossen*, ed. Klaus Martin Kopitz and Rainer Cadenbach (Munich: G. Henle Verlag), 1: 230. My translation.

2. *Letters of Beethoven*, ed. Emily Anderson, 3 vols. (New York: St. Martin's Press, 1961), 1: 313.

3. Kopitz and Cadenbach, op. cit., 1: 227.

4. Germaine de Staël writes well about Schiller's *William Tell* in her *De l'Allemagne*, part 1, chapter 20. For a less positive evaluation see Chateaubriand, *Essai sur les révolutions* (1797).

5. Goethe, *Italian Journey*, ed. Thomas P. Saine and Jeffrey L. Sammons, trans. Robert R. Heitner (New York: Suhrkamp, 1989), 129; see n. 135. "*Berlichingen*" refers to *Goetz von Berlichingen*, an early play of Goethe's.

6. *Selected Letters of Beethoven* (New York: St. Martin's Press, 1967), ed. Alan Tyson, 101. To Breitkopf & Härtel, August 21, 1810.

7. Ibid., 113–14. April 12, 1811.

8. Ibid., 95. Beethoven may have proposed marriage to Malfatti in this year.

9. *Goethe: Early Verse Drama and Prose Plays*, ed. Cyrus Hamlin and Fran Ryder (Princeton: Princeton University Press, 1988), 7: 107.

10. Ibid., 7: 107–108, 123.

11. Cited from Richard Friedenthal, *Goethe: His Life and Times* (Cleveland and New York: World Publishing Company, 1963), 270–71.

12. *Letters*, ed. Anderson, 1: 270. May 2, 1810.

13. Ibid., 1: 318.

14. Ibid., 1: 246.

15. E.g., ibid., 1: 232; 234, 235.
16. Ibid., 1: 356.
17. Ibid., 1: 360.
18. Ibid., 1: 372. May 24, 1812.
19. Ibid., 1: 376.

17: Bacchus Triumphant

1. Byron, *Don Juan*, canto 3, stanza 85.
2. *Goethes Briefwechsel mit einem Kinde*, ed. Waldemar Oehlke (Frankfurt am Main: Insel Verlag, 1984), 382. My translation. Beethoven also had a life mask done of himself as Bacchus.
3. The inscription in French on the bust begins: "Moi je suis Bacchus qui pressure pour les hommes le nectar divin." Although the full quotation derives from a suspect letter by Bettina Brentano to Goethe, the thought it expresses appears authentically Beethoven's.
4. After Bourdelle's powerful turn-of-the-century bust entered the Metropolitan's collection in 1900, it received the name *Beethoven dit Métropolitain*. Originally placed at the top of the Met's majestic entry staircase, it is now prominently placed in the museum's library. If the library is closed, visitors may view it through the glass door.
5. *Letters of Beethoven*, ed. Emily Anderson, 3 vols. (New York: St. Martin's Press, 1961), 1: 355.
6. Bettina von Arnim to Goethe, May 28, 1810, in *Goethes Briefwechsel mit einem Kinde*, 382.
7. *Letters*, ed. Anderson, 1: 313.
8. Virgil, *The Pastoral Poems*, trans. E. V. Rieu (New York: Penguin Books, 1949), 77.
9. Tolstoy, *The Death of Ivan Ilyich and Other Stories*, trans. Richard Pevear and Larissa Volokhonsky (New York: Alfred A. Knopf, 2009), 149.
10. André Suarès, *Musiciens* (Paris: Éditions du Pavois, 1945), 35.
11. Cited from Philipp Blom, *The Vertigo Years: Change and Culture in the West, 1900–1914* (Toronto: McClelland and Stuart, 2008), 230.
12. Samuel Taylor Coleridge, *Biographia Literaria*, ed. James Engell and W. Jackson Bate (Princeton: Princeton University Press, 1984), 9.
13. Blom, op. cit., 106.
14. Rudolf Bockholdt, "Freiheit und Brüderlichkeit in der Musik Ludwig van Beethovens," in *Beethoven zwischen Revolution and Restauration*, ed. Helga Lühning and Sieghard Brandenburg, 102.
15. Anya Taylor, *Bacchus in Romantic England* (New York: St. Martin's Press, 1999), 9.
16. Peter Watson, *The German Genius* (New York: HarperCollins, 2010), 99.
17. So Robert C. Solomon, *In the Spirit of Hegel* (Oxford: Oxford University Press, 1983), 2.

18. Theodor Adorno, *Beethoven: The Philosophy of Music*, trans. Edmund Jephcott (Stanford: Stanford University Press, 1997), 167.

19. Recent scholarship has questioned the attribution of *The Colossus* to Goya.

20. *The Musical Journeys of Ludwig Spohr*, trans. and ed. Henry Pleasants (Norman: University of Oklahoma Press, 1961), 103–04.

21. Cited from *The Beethoven Companion*, ed. Thomas Scherman and Louis Biancolli (Garden City: Doubleday, 1972), 588.

22. Martin Geck, *Beethoven* (London: Haus Publishing, 2003), 86.

23. Ernst Bloch, *The Utopian Function of Art and Literature: Selected Essays* (Cambridge, MA: MIT Press, 1988), 125.

24. Bernard Fournier, "La modernité de Beethoven," *Bicentenaire de Beethoven* 31, no. 498 (October 1970): 87–98.

25. Jean de Solliers, "Le langage musicale de Beethoven," in ibid., 78.

26. Ibid., 384, 385, 386.

27. Ibid., 387.

28. Paul Henry Lang, *Music in Western Civilization* (New York: W. W. Norton, 1941), 766.

29. Emil Ludwig, *Beethoven*, 231, 301.

30. *The New Grove Beethoven*, ed. Joseph Kerman and Alan Tyson (New York: W. W. Norton, 1997), 110.

31. Lang, op. cit., 754.

32. J. W. N. Sullivan, *Beethoven. A Critical Study* (London: Jonathan Cape, 1927), 197.

33. Jan Caeyers, *Beethoven. Der einsame Revolutionär. Eine Biographie* (Munich: C. H. Beck, 2009), 335.

34. Cited from Nicholas Mathew, *Political Beethoven* (Cambridge: Cambridge University Press, 2012), 27.

35. Ibid., 39.

18: *Fidelio*

1. Galina Vishnevskaya, *Galina, A Russian Story* (San Diego and New York: Harcourt Brace Jovanovich, 1984), 113.

2. Cited from Romain Rolland, *Beethoven the Creator* (New York: Harper & Brothers, 1929), 208.

3. John Eliot Gardner, "The Case for *Leonore*, a Work in Progress," notes for Beethoven, *Leonore* (Archiv Produktion, Deutsche Grammophon, 1997).

4. Theodor W. Adorno, *Beethoven: Essays on the Philosophy of Music* (Cambridge: Cambridge University Press, 1985), 164.

5. Letter to Franz Brunswik in *Letters of Beethoven*, ed. Emily Anderson, 3 vols. (New York: St. Martin's Press, 1961), 2: 421.

6. Byron, "Ode to Napoleon Buonaparte," stanza 11.

7. *Letters of Beethoven*, ed. Emily Anderson, 3 vols. (New York: St. Martin's Press, 1961), 2: 454.

8. Fritz Zobeley, *Ludwig van Beethoven in Selbszeugnissen und Bilddokumenten* (Reinbek bei Hamburg: Rowohlt, 1965), 39; English edition, *Portrait of Beethoven: An Illustrated Biography*, trans. Ann O'Brien (New York: Herder and Herder, 1972), 42. Though Zobeley refers to Beethoven's Third Trio in C Minor, Op. 9, no less do his words encapsulate Florestan's agony.

9. *My Past and Thoughts: The Memoirs of Alexander Herzen* (New York: Alfred A. Knopf, 1973), 656.

10. Simon Schama, Chapter 10, *"Bastille, July 1789,"* sections i–v, in his *Citizens: A Chronicle of the French Revolution* (New York: Alfred A. Knopf, 1989).

11. Jean Staroblinski, *1789: The Emblems of Reason* (Charlottesville: University Press of Virginia, 1982), 215.

12. Rousseau, *Confessions*, trans. J. M. Cohen (Harmondsworth: Penguin Books, 1954), 166–67.

13. Robert C. Solomon, *History and Human Nature* (New York and London: Harcourt Brace Jovanovich, 1979), 58.

14. Ernst Bloch, *The Principle of Hope*, 3 vols. (Cambridge, MA: MIT Press, 1995), 3: 1099–100.

15. Ernst Bloch, *Essays on the Philosophy of Music*, trans. Peter Palmer (Cambridge: Cambridge University Press, 1985), 240.

16. Marx, cited from Ernst Bloch, *Utopian Function of Art and Literature: Selected Essays* (Cambridge, MA: MIT Press, 1988), 125.

17. *Letters of Beethoven*, ed. Anderson, 1: 453. Letter to Nikolaus Zmeskall, April 1814.

18. Ibid., 1: 475.

19. Ibid., 2: 474.

20. Ibid., 1: 345,

21. Ibid., 1: 411, 419. Varena had asked Beethoven to send him recent compositions for charity concerts he was organizing in Graz.

22. Thomas Mann, *Doctor Faustus*, trans. John E. Woods (New York: Alfred A. Knopf, 1997), 509, 511.

23. Cited from H. C. Robbins Landon and John Julius Norwich, *Five Centuries of Music in Venice* (London: Thames and Hudson, 1991), 182.

19: The Congress of Vienna and Its Aftermath

1. James Fenimore Cooper, *The Bravo*, ed. Donald A. Ringe (1831; New Haven: College & University Press, 1963), 164. I have retained Cooper's spelling of "Hapsburgh."

2. *Beethoven zwischen Revolution und Restauration*, ed. Helga Lühning and Sieghard Brandenburg (Bonn: Beethoven Haus Publishing, 2003), 276.

3. Martin Geck, *Beethoven* (London: Haus Publishing, 2003), vii.

4. R. Murray Schafer, *E. T. A. Hoffmann and Music* (Toronto and Buffalo: University of Toronto Press, 1975), 133.

5. Basil Lam, "The Classical Composers—Haydn—Mozart—Beethoven," in *Of German Music: A Symposium*, ed. H.–H. Schönzeler (New York: Barnes and Noble, 1976), 121.

6. Egon Friedell, *A Cultural History of the Modern Age*, 3 vols. (New York: Alfred A. Knopf, 1931), 2: 440.

7. *Letters of Beethoven*, ed. Emily Anderson, 3 vols. (New York: St. Martin's Press, 1961), 2: 508.

8. Franz Grillparzer, cited in Martin Hürlimann, *Vienna* (London: Thames and Hudson, 1970), 55.

9. C. A. MacCartney, *The Habsburg Empire: 1790–1918* (London: Macmillan, 1969), 146.

10. Ernst Hilmar, "Vienna's Schubert," in *Schubert's Vienna*, ed. Raymond Erickson (New Haven and London: Yale University Press, 1997), 247.

11. Gilbert Frodl, "Viennese Biedermeier Painting," in ibid., 175.

12. Paul Henry Lang, *Music in Western Civilization* (New York: W. W. Norton, 1941), 766–67.

13. Adolph Bernhard Marx, cited in Ernest Closson, *The Fleming in Beethoven* (London: Oxford University Press, 1936), 135. See also Closson, *L'élément flamand dans Beethoven*, 2nd ed. (1946).

14. *The Beethoven Companion*, ed. Thomas Scherman and Louis Biancolli (Garden City: Doubleday, 1972), 1074.

15. So a Dutch scholar, Jos van der Zanden, has speculated in a letter in the *Beethoven Journal* 21, no. 2 (Winter 2006): 47.

16. Kenneth Clark, *Civilisation* (New York: Harper and Row, 1969), 293.

17. *Vienna in the Biedermeier Era, 1815–1848*, ed. Robert Waissenberger (New York: Rizzoli, 1986), 163.

18. Ibid. Also Stella Musulin, *Vienna in the Age of Metternich* (Boulder: Westview Press, 1975), 225. For a fuller account of Biedermeier characteristics, see Ilsa Barea, *Vienna* (New York: Alfred A. Knopf, 1967), 3–29.

19. Cooper, op. cit., 173.

20. *Letters*, ed. Anderson, 2: 592. To Zmeskall, August 18, 1816.

21. Ibid., 2: 704.

22. Ibid., 2: 686.

23. Ibid., 2: 932.

24. Ibid., 2: 970.

25. Ibid., 2: 785. To Nannette Streicher, 1818. For a fuller and more positive assessment of Karl in Beethoven's life, see Beata Angelika Kraus's essay in *Beethoven Liest*, ed. Bernhard A. Appel and Julia Ronge (Bonn: Beethoven-Haus, 2016), especially 93–97 and 218–26.

26. *Letters*, ed. Anderson, 2: 680. To Charles Neate, April 19, 1817.

27. Carl Czerny, *On the Proper Performance of All Beethoven's Works for the Piano*, ed. Paul Badura-Skoda (Vienna: Universal Edition, 2017). Czerny gives instances when Beethoven did explain his intent.

28. Anton Schindler, *Beethoven as I Knew Him*, trans. Constance S. Jolly (Chapel Hill: University of North Carolina Press, 1966), 400, 402, 404. On his hopes in 1810, see *Letters*, ed. Anderson, 1: 291.

29. Schindler, op. cit., 400n.

30. On the initial dedication of the *Eroica* to "Bonaparte," see my "Beethoven, Byron, Bonaparte," in *Byron the Traveller: Proceedings of the 28th International Byron Conference, 30 August–4 September 2002*, ed. Reiko Aiura and Itsuyo Higashinaka (Kyoto: Japanese Byron Society, 2003), 95–111; also my "The Creative Rivalry of Beethoven with Napoleon," *European Romantic Review* 5 (December 2006): 543–58. On the possible dedication of the Mass in C to Napoleon, see my "Beethoven *contra* Napoleon? The *Akademie* of December 22, 1808, and Its Aftermath," in *Bonner Beethoven-Studien* 10 (2011): 33–62.

31. Benjamin Zander, citing Mendelssohn in the liner notes to the CD of Zander's 1996 recording of Mahler's Ninth Symphony (Telarc).

32. Maynard Solomon, *Late Beethoven: Music, Thought, Imagination* (Berkeley: University of California Press, 2003), 162.

20: Beethoven Close Up, 1817–20

1. The C Minor is the Fifth Symphony.

2. Joseph Brodsky, cited from Harvey Sachs, *The Ninth: Beethoven and the World in 1824* (New York: Random House, 2011), 55.

3. *Letters of Beethoven*, ed. Emily Anderson, 3 vols. (New York: St. Martin's Press, 1961), 2: 671.

4. Hans Kohn, *The Mind of Germany: The Education of a Nation* (New York: Charles Scribner's Sons, 1960), 99.

5. Gregor Dallas, *The Final Act: The Roads to Waterloo* (New York: Henry Holt, 1997), 231.

6. Carl Czerny, *On the Proper Performance of All Beethoven's Works for the Piano*, ed. Paul Badura-Skoda (Vienna: Universal Edition, 2017), 8.

7. Bruno Walter, *Gustav Mahler*, trans. Lotte Walter Lindt (New York: Alfred A. Knopf, 1968), 72–73, 40.

8. *Letters*, ed. Anderson, 2: 667.

9. Ibid., 2: 509.

10. Anton Schindler, *Beethoven as I Knew Him*, trans. Constance S. Jolly (Chapel Hill: University of North Carolina Press, 1966), 221; Douglas Yates, *Franz Grillparzer: A Critical Biography* (1946; Oxford: Basil Blackwell, 1964), 5.

11. Yates, op. cit., 3.

12. *Letters*, ed. Anderson, 1: 114.

13. On Schindler, see *Letters to Beethoven and Other Correspondence*, ed. Theodore Albrecht, 3 vols. (Lincoln: University of Nebraska Press, 1996), 1: xxx, xxxvi.

14. In 1972, in East Berlin, scholars working in the Prussian State Library, led by Karl-Heinz Köhler and Grita Herre, subsequently with others, meticulously edited the surviving notebooks of Beethoven's conversations with his friends. They expunged all of Schindler's entries that have proven spurious.

15. *Konversationshefte*, ed. Karl-Heinz Köhler and Grita Herre (Leipzig: Deutscher Verlag für Musik, 1972–2011), 1: 333. Although Beethoven railed long and hard against life under Metternich, it was the relatively apolitical Schubert who, because he knew the wrong people, had the closest shaves with the chancellor's police force.

16. Ibid., 1: 339.

17. Ibid.

18. *My Past and Thoughts: The Memoirs of Alexander Herzen* (New York: Alfred A. Knopf, 1973), 106.

21: Napoleon's Death, Rossini's Rise

1. *L'express* (Paris), November 29, 2004: 23, presumably citing Albert Béguin's classic study *L'âme romantique et le rêve* (1939).

2. Jean Tulard, *Mythe de Napoléon* (Paris: Armand Colin, 1971), 44.

3. R. A. Peace, in *The Impact of the French Revolution on European Consciousness*, ed. H. T. Mason and William Doyle (Stroud, Gloucestershire: Alan Sutton, 1989), 51.

4. Ibid., 54, 55. See also Robert Morrissey, "The *Mémorial de Sainte-Hélène* and the Poetics of Fusion," *Modern Language Notes* 120, no. 4 (September 2005): 716–32.

5. Cited from Lewis Lockwood, *Beethoven: The Music and the Life* (New York: W. W. Norton, 2003), 187. Beethoven penned on the title page of the score the now-famous words "Geschrieben auf Bonaparte" (written for Bonaparte).

6. Carl Czerny, *On the Proper Performance of All Beethoven's Works for the Piano*, ed. Paul Badura-Skoda (Vienna: Universal Edition, 2017), 8. The year 1827 would be more likely than 1824. In June of the latter year Scott's life of Napoleon appeared (in nine volumes) in both London and Paris; "1824" was an advance notice.

7. Theodore Albrecht, *Beethoven's Conversation Books*, vol. 1: *Nos. 1 to 8 (February 1818 to March 1820)* (Woodbridge, UK: Boydell Press, 2018), 210.

8. *Konversationshefte*, ed. Karl-Heinz Köhler and Grita Herre (Leipzig: Deutscher Verlag für Musik, 1972–2011), 1: 247.

9. *Thayer's Life of Beethoven*, ed. Elliot Forbes, 2 vols. (Princeton: Princeton University Press, 1967), 2: 959–60.

10. *Beethoven aus der Sicht seiner Zeitgenossen*, ed. Klaus Martin Kopitz and Rainer

Cadenach (Munich: Henle, 2009), 1: 258. From an account set down by Otto Jahn in 1852. My translation.

11. *Byron's Letters and Journals,* ed. Leslie A. Marchand, 12 vols. (London: John Murray, 1972–1994), 9: 155

12. Kopitz and Cadenbach, op. cit., 2: 749.

13. Richard Osborne, *Rossini* (London: J. M. Dent, 1987), 74–76.

14. *My Past and Thoughts: The Memoirs of Alexander Herzen* (New York: Alfred A. Knopf, 1973), 109.

15. Alexis de Toqueville, *L'Ancien Régime et la révolution,* cited from Clive James, *Cultural Amnesia: Necessary Memories from History and the Arts* (New York and London: W. W. Norton, 2007), 586.

16. The original account is reproduced in Friedrich Kerst, *Die Errinerungen an Beethoven,* 2 vols. (Stuttgart: J. Hofmann Verlag, 1925), 1: 278–79; English summary in *Thayer's Life of Beethoven,* 2: 777–78.

17. Wagner in a letter of March 18, 1869, to Hermann Härtel, cited from *Beethoven und der Leipziger Musikverlag Breitkopf & Härtel* (Bonn: Beethoven-Haus, 2007), 178. The portrait was unfortunately destroyed during World War II, though copies survive.

22: Beethoven and Grillparzer

1. Theodor W. Adorno, *Beethoven: The Philosophy of Music* (Stanford: Stanford University Press, 1998), 86.

2. Anton Schindler, *Beethoven as I Knew Him,* trans. Constance S. Jolly (Chapel Hill: University of North Carolina Press, 1966), 405.

3. Jeremy Siepmann, *Beethoven: His Life and Music* (Naperville: Sourcebooks, 2006), 118.

4. William M. Johnston, *The Austrian Mind: An Intellectual and Social History, 1848–1938* (Berkeley: University of California Press, 1983), 22.

5. Alfred Orel, *Grillparzer und Beethoven* (Vienna: Verlag für Wirtschaft und Kultur, 1941), offers a survey of their relationship and reproduces key documents.

6. Ibid., 81.

7. Ilsa Barea, *Vienna* (New York: Alfred A. Knopf, 1967), 18.

8. Nicholas T. Parsons, *Vienna* (Oxford: Signal Books, 2008), 25.

9. Edward Crankshaw, *The Fall of the House of Hapsburg* (New York: Viking Press, 1963), 5.

10. James J. Sheehan, *German History, 1770–1866* (Oxford: Oxford University Press, 1990), 445, drawing upon, *inter alia,* W. E. Yates, *Grillparzer: A Critical Introduction* (Cambridge: Cambridge University Press, 1972), chap. 6, "Politics and Culture."

11. Douglas Yates, *Franz Grillparzer: A Critical Biography* (Oxford: Basil Blackwell, 1946), 221.

12. Ibid., 222.
13. Cited from Parsons, op. cit., 207–08.
14. Ibid., 237.
15. Ibid., 50.
16. Giorgio Pestelli, *The Age of Mozart and Beethoven* (Cambridge: Cambridge University Press, 1984), 253.
17. Cited from Theodor W. Adorno, *Beethoven: The Philosophy of Music* (Stanford: Stanford University Press, 1998), 154.
18. Alfred Orel, *Grillparzer und Beethoven* (Vienna: Verlag für Wirtschaft und Kultur, 1941), 95.
19. Ibid.
20. Cited from Parsons, op. cit., 42, 80.

23: The *Missa solemnis* and the Ninth Symphony

1. *E. T. A. Hoffmann's Musical Writings*, ed. David Charlton, trans. Martyn Clarke (Cambridge: Cambridge University Press, 2004), 96.
2. John Armstrong, *Love, Life, Goethe* (New York: Farrar, Straus and Giroux, 2006), 181.
3. *Letters of Beethoven*, ed. Emily Anderson, 3 vols. (New York: St. Martin's Press, 1961), 2: 948.
4. *Schubert's Vienna*, ed. Raymond Erickson (New Haven: Yale University Press, 1997), 103.
5. The *Missa solemnis* received its first complete performance in St. Petersburg the next year.
6. Hans Gal, cited from his *Johannes Brahms: Work and Personality* (New York: Alfred A. Knopf, 1963), 119–20.
7. "Bicentenaire de Beethoven," *Europe* (October 1970): 2.
8. "Music at Night," in Aldous Huxley, *Collected Essays* (New York: Bantam, 1960), 177.
9. William Drabkin, *Beethoven: Missa Solemnis* (Cambridge: Cambridge University Press, 1991), 102, 103.
10. Antal Dorati, notes to his 1988 recording of the *Missa* (Bis-406/407 Stereo), 2–3.
11. Leon Plantinga, *Romantic Music: A History of Musical Style in Nineteenth-Century Europe* (New York: W. W. Norton, 1984), 62.
12. Wilfrid Mellers, *Beethoven and the Voice of God* (London: Faber and Faber, 1981), 4.
13. *Furtwängler Recalled*, ed. Daniel Gillis (Zurich: Atlantis, 1965), 41.
14. Elisabeth Furtwängler, *About Wilhelm Furtwängler* (Woodside: Furtwängler Society of America, 1993), 58. Unfortunately the conductor left behind no recorded performance of the *Missa*.

15. Eduard Hanslick, *Music Criticisms, 1846–1899*, trans. Henry Pleasants (London: Penguin/ Peregrine, 1963), 73.

16. *"Socrates u. Jesus* waren mir Muster": *Konversationshefte* (Leipzig: Deutscher Verlag für Musik, 1972), 1: 211.

17. "Bicentenaire de Beethoven," 84–85.

18. The king sent him in return a ring that's worth disappointed Beethoven and which he promptly sold.

19. Charles Rosen, *Freedom and the Arts: Essays on Music and Literature* (Cambridge, MA: Harvard University Press, 2012), 13.

20. *Beethoven aus der Sicht seiner Zeitgenossen*, ed. Klaus Martin Kopitz and Rainer Cadenbach (Munich: G. Henle Verlag, 2009), 1: 249.

21. Friedrich Schiller, *The Robbers* (New York: Penguin, 1980), 55.

22. Cited from Tim Blanning, *The Triumph of Music: The Rise of Composers, Musicians, and Their Art* (Cambridge, MA: Harvard University Press, 2008), 99.

23. Richard Specht, *Beethoven as He Lived* (New York: Harrison Smith and Robert Haas, 1933), 252.

24. Martin Jay, *Adorno* (Cambridge, MA: Harvard University Press, 1984), 143.

25. Mark Evan Bonds, *Music as Thought: Listening to the Symphony in the Age of Beethoven* (Princeton: Princeton University Press, 2006), 78.

26. "Bicentenaire de Beethoven," 28.

27. *Konversationshefte*, 6: 160–61.

28. Schoenberg Center, Vienna: pamphlet on Schoenberg and Mozart, 8.

29. Ibid.

30. Debussy, cited from Ernest Newman, *Unconscious Beethoven: An Essay in Musical Psychology* (New York: Alfred A. Knopf, 1927), 9.

31. Jamie James, *Music of the Spheres: Music, Science, and the Natural Order of the Universe* (Boston: Little Brown, 1994), 196.

32. Bonds, op. cit., 60.

33. Thomas Mann, *Three Essays* (New York: Alfred A. Knopf, 1929), 143.

24: Music at the End

1. Thomas Mann, *Doctor Faustus*, trans. John E. Woods (New York: Alfred A. Knopf, 1997), 56.

2. Clive James, *Cultural Amnesia* (New York: W. W. Norton, 2007), 579.

3. Fred Licht, *Goya: The Origins of the Modern Temper in Art* (London: Palgrave Macmillan, 1979), 238.

4. Ibid.

5. Ibid., 204, 249.

6. Stravinsky, cited in André Gauthier, *Beethoven* (Paris: Classiques Hachette, 1969), 84n.

7. Stephen Rumph, *Beethoven after Napoleon: Political Romanticism in the Late Works* (Berkeley: University of California Press, 2004), 131.

8. Aldous Huxley, *Point Counter Point* (New York: HarperCollins, 1965), 215.

9. Joseph Kerman, *The Beethoven Quartets* (New York: Alfred A. Knopf, 1967), 330–38.

10. Richard A. Wagner, *Pilgrimage to Beethoven and Other Essays*, trans. William Ashton Ellis (Lincoln: University of Nebraska Press, 1994), 62. It is unlikely that Wagner ever heard Opus 131 actually performed, so rare were performances of it during his lifetime.

11. Friedrich Nietzsche, *Human, All Too Human: A Book for Free Spirits*, no. 155, trans. R. J. Hollingdale (Cambridge: Cambridge University Press, 1987), 82.

12. *Letters of Beethoven*, ed. Emily Anderson, 3 vols. (New York: St. Martin's Press, 1961), 3: 1295.

13. Georg Kinsky and Hans Halm, *Ludwig van Beethoven: Thematisch-bibliographisches Werkverzeichnis*, 2 vols. (Munich: Henle Verlag, 2014), 1: 864.

14. Karl Holz, who was present, was the second violinist of the Schuppanzigh Quartet and a close friend both of Beethoven and of Schubert, commented, "The King of Harmony has sent the King of Song a friendly bidding to the crossing."

15. *The Letters of T. S. Eliot*, vol. 5: *1930–1931*, ed. Valerie Eliot and John Haffenden (New Haven: Yale University Press, 2015), 529.

16. Milan Kundera, *The Unbearable Lightness of Being*, (New York: Harper & Row, 1984), chapter 7.

17. Richard Specht, *Beethoven as He Lived* (New York: Harrison Smith and Robert Haas, 1933), 298.

18. Stumpff took care that the Handel set be delivered to Beethoven free of expense.

19. Gerhard von Breuning, *Memories of Beethoven*, ed. Maynard Solomon (Cambridge: Cambridge University Press, 1992), 96.

20. Anton Schindler, *Beethoven as I Knew Him*, trans. Constance S. Jolly (Chapel Hill, University of North Carolina Press, 1966), 31.

21. The account of Beethoven's final moments is Hüttenbrenner's.

22. Alessandra Comini, *The Changing Image of Beethoven: A Study in Mythmaking* (New York: Rizzoli, 1966), 151–52.

23. In the 1870s Beethoven's body, along with Schubert's, was moved from Währing Cemetery to Vienna's newly established Zentralfriedhof.

24. At least three versions of Grillparzer's funeral oration are known.

25. Alfred Orel, *Grillparzer und Beethoven* (Vienna: Verlag für Wirtschaft und Kultur, 1941), 13. The funeral speech (in German) is on pp. 97–98.

26. Richard Taruskin, *Oxford History of Western Music*, vol. 2: *The Seventeenth and Eighteenth Centuries* (Oxford: Oxford University Press, 2005), 689. Later, for a memorial stone on Beethoven's tomb in Währing Cemetery (now a city park), Grillparzer eulogized his friend once again. He was also instrumental in hav-

ing a memorial to Beethoven placed in Heiligenstadt, where Beethoven spent several summers.

27. Cited from Thomas Mann, *Last Essays*, trans. Richard and Clara Winston and James and Teresa Stern (New York: Alfred A. Knopf, 1966), 140. Mann cites Goethe.

28. Peter Gay, *The Naked Heart: The Bourgeois Experience from Victoria to Freud* (New York: W. W. Norton, 1995), 28n.

29. "Beethoven's Instrumental Music" (1810), cited from *E. T. A. Hoffmann's Musical Writings*, ed. David Charlton, trans. Martyn Clarke (Cambridge: Cambridge University Press, 2004).

30. Dietrich Fischer-Dieskau, *"Weil nicht alle Blütenträume reiften": Johann Friedrich Reichardt, Hofkapellmeister drei Preussen Könige* (Stuttgart: Deutsche Verlags-Anstalt, 1992), 366–67. My translation.

31. Frank Cooper, program note to Garrick Ohlsson's CD of the *Hammerklavier* Sonata (Bridge 9262).

32. Egon Friedell, *A Cultural History of the Modern Age*, 3 vols. (New York: Alfred A. Knopf, 1931), 2: 435; Hans Keller I cite from George Steiner, *Errata: An Examined Life* (New Haven: Yale University Press, 1998), 70.

INDEX OF BEETHOVEN'S WORKS

GENERAL INDEX